The Great Conspiracy

Steam rail motors were an early attempt to cut branch line costs. Railmotor No.93 of 1908 has been immaculately restored by the Great Western Society. It makes a fine sight at the Didcot Railway Centre in May 2011. PHOTO: Ian Knight

The fall and rise of Britain's railways since the 1950's

By David Henshaw

Moretonhampstead station, 1973

This book would never have happened (and happened again) without help and advice from many, many people. First, my father Patrick Henshaw, who started the ball rolling by giving me his copy of the 'Reshaping Report'. He would have enjoyed the instances where his photographs ended up on the same page as mine, taken a decade later, when track and trains were gone. Next must come Owen Prosser, who was moving house back in 1990, and provided a car-full of raw material for this book, making research much easier.

Stan Abbot of Leading Edge, who published the first and second editions, and has been enormously helpful with the preparation of the third. Bill Lehan's cartoons graced the earlier editions, and some live on in this edition too. Also Tim Pestridge, whose work always makes me laugh, so something by Tim had to go in.

Proof-reading is primarily the work of my brother Peter Henshaw (it's a real family affair this), the transcription of the thousand-line index is down to my lovely wife Jane, artwork and layout to sister-in-law Diana, and thanks also to Alexander & Orlando for keeping quietish for two months in the winter of 2012/13.

Christopher Austin OBE and Tony Smale of Railfuture spent long hours reading the new chapters, and made many helpful comments. Richard Burningham of the Devon & Cornwall Rail Partnership provided the raw numbers that became the Westcountry branch line graph, Andrew Hunter of Henry Ling patiently explained where the colour could go and where it couldn't. Tim Leunig gave economics advice, and Richard Peace gave general encouragement.

Particular thanks are due to those who helped fill in the many photographic holes. Richard Carr of the Paxman Archive Trust, who tracked down several Wickham photos, Peter Burgess of the Cumbrian Railways Association, who turned up some priceless archive material, Ben Phippen of the Australian Railway Historical Society who provided the Waddington photo. Also Phil Sutters for allowing me to use one of the magnificent Westcountry photographs taken by his father, the Reverend John Sutters, and David Spaven for providing his father Frank Spaven's railbus picture. Brian & Margaret Stevens of the St Ives Museum sent the image of the Cornish Riviera squeezing into a very small station, David Edwards of the Heart of Wales Line Forum found a lovely image, and Cyril Crawley of the RCTS tracked down an interesting Great Central photo. Special thanks to Nigel Tout, whose archive illustrating the last death throes of the Great Central makes grim viewing, and Bruce McCartney who similarly recorded the painful end of the Waverley.

Other photographers are too many to mention, but I'll mention everybody anyway: Kenneth Adams, Dr Ian C Allen, B J Astworth, Colin Baglow, David Black of Eastbank MRC, Ben Brooksbank, Peter Delaney, David Edge, Mike Esau, Anna Finch, Pete Hackney, Christian Hewison, David Hey, David P Howard, R G Jarvis, Paul Johnson, S H Keyse, Ian Knight, Kevin Lane, B Mills, John Parkin, Owen Prosser, Pat Salmon, A R Spencer, Neville Stead, Brian Stephenson, Gordon Thomson, John Thorn, Gary Thornton, John Turner, Michael Wadman, Ken Winney, Robin Whitlock, Frank Wooton, Jeffray Wotherspoon and I L Wright.

Finally, apologies and heartfelt thanks to anyone we've missed. If we've credited you correctly, but have failed to ask permission, we really have tried to track you down. Some photographs have proved impossible to trace, but if you think we've missed your credit, please let us know. DAVID HENSHAW

Contents

At its height in the early years of the 20th
Century, the British railway network reached to
almost every town and village in the country.
Some judicious pruning was essential by the
1960s, but the premise of this book is that the
process went too far, too fast. Closed lines are
shown in black, survivors in red, and those that
have subsequently reopened (or are about to
reopen) in blue or green. Blue lines are 'heritage'
operations, few of which provide any sort of
connections or through ticketing with the railway
network, but the lines shown in green are (or
soon will be) fully reopened.

Introduction

This book was never intended to be republished. After the success of the First Edition, the Second Edition hit the shops in 1994 and the publisher promptly went bust (not, one hopes, through production of this particular title), with much of the stock being remaindered. Many years later, in July 2010, I was invited to debate the Beeching Report by the Dorchester branch of the Institution of Civil Engineers - the motion being 'Was Beeching Right?'

Sixteen years after publication of the Second Edition, my recollections of Beeching's *Reshaping Report* were already hazy, and I was too busy to do any research. On the night, everything went wrong. I was unexpectedly put up to speak first, and I was followed by an old railwayman, who weighed in with the simple argument that he had been there, and that on some mornings his ticket office didn't sell five bob's worth of tickets.

The real problem with this debate was the rather vague motion. It's arguable that Dr Beeching, the Department of Transport (which continued to hurry through closures until well into the 1970s), and the politicians nominally overseeing the process, made the right decisions, *given the information available to them at the time*, and that might also apply to those who recall working on lightly-used secondary routes themselves. But surely very few of those same people would attempt to make a case for those closures with the benefit of the knowledge we've gained in the intervening decades.

The Dorchester debate was wound up by Tim Westwood, Dorset County Council's Traffic Manager, who had previously been tasked with reconnecting the privately-run Swanage Railway to the national network. He added, rather gratuitously, that in his opinion the whole process was a waste of time, that railways were expensive and inconvenient, and so forth. The engineers nodded sagely and I lost the debate overwhelmingly, swaying only one graduate engineer my way. Dorset is a rural (some say feudal) county, and I have only myself to blame for this failure, because the evidence that Beeching really was wrong in many of his assumptions is now irrefutable: Of the branch lines that escaped the Beeching axe, or were subsequently reopened, all are now bulging at the seams, carrying many more passengers than they did in the 1960s. Some minor branches are now busier than the trunk lines of that era.

Anyone attempting to paint a picture of today's world at a 1960s railway closure inquiry would have been laughed out of court. Village gridlock? Passengers unable to board packed commuter trains on rural branch lines? Double tracking, hourly services, half-hourly services, calls for widescale reopenings... All these things are happening now, and writing in 2013 the momentum for rural rail seems unstoppable.

So I have Dorset's antediluvian traffic engineers to thank for my decision to rewrite, update and republish *The Great Railway Conspiracy*. With the 50th anniversary of the Beeching Report in 2013, and work already underway on reopening part of the Waverley route in the Scottish Borders - arguably the biggest railway closure of the lot - this seems a good moment to take stock. The new chapters in this book give some information on the fortunes of lines that have reopened, and puts the case for many others which could do so - some of these are already progressing down the legal and financial road to reopening.

The seeds of *The Great Railway Conspiracy* were sown long ago. The decades that followed the Second World War saw far-reaching political and social changes in Britain. Industrial concerns - some of which had seen precious few change in a century or more - were dragged kicking and screaming into the 20th Century overnight, but none were to suffer as much as the railways. And in no other industry would closure and retrenchment cause quite the same heartfelt public concern and heated Parliamentary debate. If Lancashire weavers were being thrown out of work, it was bad news for Lancashire weavers and their immediate communities, but the loss of a third of the railway network meant a loss of jobs just about everywhere, from Cornwall to the Scottish Highlands. And a loss of transport opportunities for rich and poor alike.

Britain had retained a rather *laissez-faire* parliamentary system from a previous more gentlemanly age, when MPs could - hopefully - be trusted not to take advantage of their privileged position for commercial gain. This was bound to fail under the intense commercial pressures of the late 20th Century, and the road transport pressure groups - the car manufacturers, road builders, oil companies and ancillary industries, plus the bus operators (who were later to change sides) - took full advantage, offering jobs, directorships, and no doubt other murkier inducements to MPs and civil servants. In terms of political patronage, the road lobby completely outclassed the large, yet effectively powerless, nationalised railway industry. Aided by an increasingly anti-rail Ministry of Transport, they had succeeded by the late 1960s, in bringing the railway system to its knees.

Eventually, governments of all political shades would have been happier had the entire railway, with its associated staffing and infrastructure problems, been swallowed up overnight. Divine intervention never arrived but, by the early 1970s, there didn't appear to be much need for a railway system in any shape or form. Some had dared to ask, not, "How large a railway system do we need?", but, "Is any sort of railway system really necessary?" It was not until the Arab-inspired oil crisis of 1973 that the mood changed.

That crucial infrastructure on the closed lines was not immediately safeguarded after this rude awakening (bits continued to be lopped off well into the 1990s) does not reflect well on the political class in this country, and might help to explain why politicians are now falling over themselves to be seen as railway funders and expansionists.

It was very different in the late 1960s, when the railways were perceived to be a hangover from a gloomy industrial past. In Harold Wilson's technological revolution their place would be taken by the bus, the short-haul aircraft, and - especially - by the private car.

That this never happened, and the railway network survived and eventually prospered, was due largely to the work of a handful of far-sighted private individuals and a small, but dedicated, group of MPs. This is their story.

Railway records are not, strictly speaking, government documents, but the British railway system has become so intimately entwined with government affairs since the Second World War that railway files are released under the rules relating to political management and mismanagement, defence matters, and other things governments of all shades would rather keep quiet. Those that are considered suitable for eventual public scrutiny are mostly held for 30 years before release to the National Archive.

But what, one might ask, becomes of the documents that are too embarrassing for release even after 30 years? The official line is that they are carefully sifted to preserve a balanced and accurate cross-section of material. "But why," I asked, "were comparatively innocuous records (such as railway track costs, railbus economics, and branch line closure documents) held for 30 years or more?" The Civil Service reply came right out of the comedy series, *Yes Minister*: "Because no-one made a decision that they should not be..."

Whether there really was a conspiracy to withhold information - either at the Ministry of Transport or the Railways Board - is hard to judge. What's clear from the pattern of release is that the records prior to the late 1950s provide a detailed account of railway affairs, while those from the 1960s do not.

That the movement of royal trains should remain secret for 30 years is perhaps understandable, but should railway reports, statistics, and records of committee meetings really be treated like state secrets? And who actually decided which documents relating to those turbulent years should be withheld, released or destroyed? We may never know. When this book was first written in the early 1990s, the only records covering the critical years amounted to such innocuous matters as locomotive head codes, boxes of holiday guides and the welfare of railway horses. A lot more has come to light since, and many railway managers have spoken out, some defending the closures, and others bitter even today that they had been coerced into running down and closing lines that should have survived.

The first chapter of this book, and the later chapters covering subsequent events, are drawn from a wide variety of sources. Chapter 4 leans heavily on available public records, while Chapters 5 and 6 are constructed around what little written evidence exists, plus interviews with railway managers and others. In Chapter 5 in particular, some broad assumptions have been made, although it's interesting that these assumptions have not been challenged in the 21 years since the book was written. Chapter 9 brings the story right up to date, looking briefly at the disastrous railway privatisation of the late 1990s, and the railway reopening story, which was held back to a trickle during privatisation, but is now very much back on track.

Despite the lack of documentation, a picture has emerged that goes some way towards explaining the near collapse of Britain's railways - incompetence, skulduggery, and finally, an all-enveloping official silence.

Needless to say, this book could not have been written without the kind assistance of those within and without the industry who were willing to be interviewed or provide information. Perhaps understandably, many were not, and one or two must remain anonymous, but particular thanks must go to the staff at what was then the Public Records Office, and to Owen Prosser, one of the founders of the Railway Development Association, who provided unlimited access to his extensive archives.

For historians, I regret to say that in the original edition page notes on sources were not provided, but I have been able to add many notes with this edition. There is a full bibliography on page 294, and the many book references will be self-evident. The bulk of the interesting source material from the late 1950s and early 1960s is contained in Owen Prosser's books, photographs, notes and papers, which are now part of the Doncaster Archive of railway related material (contact details in the Bibliography), where they can be viewed by appointment.

David Henshaw
Dorchester
27th February 2013

1
The Railway Revolution
1825-1945

"...in evolutionary law we come to an instinct to tear down and smash up all
the old and put up the new... A savage man obeys his instincts."

Lord Strange, speaking in the House of Lords, May 1965

"There is machinery for preserving ancient monuments, but I doubt whether
it should be applied to the railway service."

Reply from Lord Silkin

*Early wagons were fitted with plain wheels running on flanged track This arrangement was later reversed, putting
the flanges on the wheels. This is the Denby collieries plateway, a remarkable survivor that opened in 1795 to
carry coal to the Derby Canal and closed in 1908. It is thus one of the few to have been photographed.*

Although the origins of the railways are popularly assumed to lie with the Stockton &
Darlington in 1825, the concept of running wagons on a fixed trackway originated much
further back in time. There are well recorded examples from the Middle Ages, and even earlier,
of mineral wagons running on wooden or stone plateways, and no doubt the first railway
passed by without attracting any publicity at all, as some nameless haulier noted with
satisfaction that his wagon ran more easily when guided on a resilient channelled surface.
Certainly many Roman roads, worn over the years by wagons of a standard width, took on the
appearance of railways, necessitating the standardisation of wheel gauge for Imperial traffic.

It was not until the appearance of cheap and plentiful iron towards the end of the 18th
Century that railways (of an industrial nature at least) became commonplace. At a time when
the condition of even the best roads varied with the seasons from poor to downright
atrocious, colliery owners and others were quick to adopt the new technology, and benefit
from a leap in productivity as a result.

Opening of the Stockton & Darlington Railway September 27th 1825. A slightly fanciful depiction by John Dobbin in the 1880s

Even the crudest of wagonways showed considerable benefits over road haulage by keeping the wagon wheels on a hard surface instead of mushy ground, and it was soon realised that an iron wheel running on an iron rail met even less friction. In early examples, the wagon wheels were guided along the rail by raised flanges on the rail itself, but as time passed the flanges moved to the wheels, a cheaper and much more efficient layout. The horse that laboured to pull a single wagon could now handle half a dozen, and even the most simple minded of colliery owners could understand that sort of message.

By 1800, iron rail industrial wagonways were well established, and as the volume of freight increased, so too did the sophistication of the lines. Efficiency had risen dramatically by adopting rails, and was further improved by the use of a relatively level 'permanent' way, avoiding steep gradients. A single horse could now handle tens of wagons, and if a line was built with a gentle down gradient from pit-head to destination, the train would actually run on its own by gravity, the horse taking a ride on the outward journey and pulling the empties back.

Amid these crude beginnings were sown the seeds that would create the most important technological advance of the 19th Century. It was by chance that a new wagonway between Stockton and Darlington achieved the next great advance, for in its meanderings from colliery to shipping wharf, it linked two large towns. The origins of the line were somewhat confused. The intention, as early as 1768, had been to build a canal, but nothing much came of the scheme, and in 1810 a committee was formed to investigate whether a railway might not be of greater benefit.. Eventually, in 1818, a proposal for a combined canal and railway was rushed before Parliament, only to be thrown out. The committee decided to opt for a railway only, and the arrival on the scene of George Stephenson in the early 1820s, gave further impetus. A Bill was passed, and the stage was set for construction to begin.

The Great Railway Conspiracy

Provisions to allow for the carriage of passengers, and for the haulage of trains by steam locomotives, were included in the Bill as no more than a sideline, because the Stockton & Darlington company assumed that it would make money by hauling coal in the traditional manner, with horses.

Stationary steam engines had been in use for some time by the 1820s, and several pioneers were already testing the technology as motive power on railway lines, but these early steam locomotives were expensive and unreliable. And they were heavy, with a tendency to demolish the fragile colliery wagonways. But under the guidance of George Stephenson, the technology began to advance, and by the time the Stockton & Darlington opened on 27th September 1825, steam locomotives were considered more or less financially viable, although not yet superior to horse power.

The official opening was to change the course of history, for a rudimentary steam engine was provided to haul the inaugural train, which it did with ease. Although only 300 tickets were sold, it is estimated that twice as many people actually clambered aboard, indicating that passenger services might well have a future. It also demonstrated that a single steam engine could do the work of a team of horses.

Ten days later, the company was granted a license to carry passengers, and an experimental horse-drawn service was launched between Stockton and Darlington just three days after that. Not surprisingly, the first passenger coaches looked and probably rode rather like a contemporary stage coach, the horse-drawn vehicles taking a leisurely two hours for the 12-mile trip. It can't have been a particularly lucrative operation either, for a few months later the company let the concession to one Richard Pickersgill, who promptly slashed the journey time to 75 minutes, and reduced the outside fare from 12d (5p) to 9d (4p). Subcontracting the running of services seemed logical at the time, for the Stockton & Darlington was simply following the practise of contemporary turnpike companies and opening its iron 'road' to all comers.

There was, however, a gradual realisation that something entirely new had been created with the opening of the Stockton & Darlington railway. Most traffic was horse-drawn at first, and the track was single, with passing places at intervals, but as fights for right of way become more common, the decision was taken to lay a second track. This was a crucial advance – two dedicated railway lines, one for each direction of travel, a rudimentary signalling system to keep trains apart, and eventually, a single operator, the Stockton & Darlington itself.

It soon became apparent that the horse-drawn traffic was holding back the faster steam engines. Steam haulage was expensive, but a steam locomotive could haul many more wagons, and it could haul them faster. In a typical working day, the expensive steam engine moved a lot more coal than the cheap horse, and in the end it was a matter of simple economics – steam power worked out cheaper per ton of coal or coach load of passengers. As steam engines became more reliable, horse traction was gradually abandoned.

In September 1833, traffic levels really began to explode, and the company bought back the passenger rights, and established its own steam-hauled service. It had invented the first railway, and within a few short years, it had arrived by trial and error at the most effective way of operating it. But by increasing the speed and sophistication of its services, the company had learned the first lessons as well, for 7th September 1833 would go down in history as the date of the first railway passenger service closure, when the horse-drawn coach was taken off the Yarm branch. It was easier, from an operating point of view, for Yarm passengers to join trains at Yarm Branch End station on the main line. And so it was, that 130 years before Doctor Beeching, the first railway company rationalised services on a branch line in order to speed traffic on the main line!

The opening of the Liverpool & Manchester Railway, showing the impressive arch at Edge Hill, Liverpool

The Stockton & Darlington proved to be a phenomenal success. In the first nine months the railway carried a modest 42,983 tons of coal, but by 1860 it was carrying more than two million tons a year. Receipts rose accordingly – from £9,194 in the first full year, to almost £500,000 in 1863. Engineers arrived from all over the world to study the new methods, but it was George Stephenson who carried the word with the most vigour, being instrumental in the construction of many railways, notably the Liverpool & Manchester – the first modern railway – completed in 1830.

This line was built on an altogether different scale. The earthworks, the strength and durability of the track, and – thanks to a single technological advance – the size and speed of the locomotives, left the little Stockton & Darlington looking rather quaint. The technique of using a forced draught, where the energy in the exhaust steam was used to draw air through the firebox, seems to have been the idea of George Stephenson, and he certainly demonstrated the technology on the Liverpool & Manchester. This crucial breakthrough was to have a profound effect on the way railways developed. Previous locomotives were gentle hissing, wheezing giants, but the forced draught worked a bit like a chain-reaction in a nuclear reactor: the harder the locomotive worked, the greater the draught and the hotter the fire, allowing more work and so forth. Almost overnight, the power-to-weight ratio of locomotives was limited only by the available technology to keep the machine from running out of control and exploding. Thanks to the vision of the Stephensons and their contemporaries, technology was set to advance at an astonishing pace.

Within a decade of its first conception, the railway had evolved into its final form. Traffic would be handled (in most cases) by a single operator, and both passengers and freight would be carried in trainloads of hitherto undreamed of size, hauled along a dedicated 'road' by a single powerful locomotive. These working practices – at once highly efficient and dangerously inflexible – were to prove both the saviour and near downfall of the railways when more flexible transport modes arrived on the scene a century later.

The early optimism of the Liverpool & Manchester proved well-founded, for traffic exceeded all forecasts. The line carried 460,000 passengers in its first year of operation – four times the total stagecoach traffic on the same route in the previous year. Clearly the new railway had done more than just leach away the existing road traffic, tapping into a previously unsatisfied demand for travel. It was a lesson that was not to be forgotten and, in the years that followed, investors clamoured to climb aboard more and yet more new railways. In 1830 the 136-mile South Carolina Railroad opened in the United States, 1832 saw the first French railway at Lyon, and by 1842 Britain could boast a network of more than 2,000 miles, linking all the major cities, and turning over about £4 million a year, some £90 million at 2013 prices. It might conceivably have stopped there or soon after, but the profits of the pioneer lines proved so tempting (the Stockton & Darlington was paying a handsome 15% dividend) that there followed a renewed outbreak of speculation that culminated in the 'Railway Mania' of 1844-47. In many countries, the railway network was wholly or partially planned by the state, but in Britain entrepreneurs could build railways anywhere they liked, subject to parliamentary approval.

By January 1846, no fewer than 815 schemes had been laid before Parliament, involving an estimated capital outlay of about £350 million (£8.3 billion in 2012), six times the Gross National Product of the day. Perhaps fortunately, only a minority of these schemes were actually authorised, but the result was 8,600 miles of new track, and a link to every major port and city in the United Kingdom.

The problem was knowing where to stop. If a railway could bring prosperity and growth to a city – and the early lines undoubtedly did – then what might it do for a town, or even a village? The railways were on the cutting edge of a rapidly growing economy, and the authorities were generally unable to persuade the citizens of a particular district that their poor and underpopulated region really didn't warrant the construction of a line, particularly if similar areas were enjoying the advantages of a railway.

There was, of course, another reason for Parliamentary reluctance to turn down fresh railway schemes. The railways had almost destroyed coaching and canal transport, creating a near monopoly on inland trade, competing railways were thought by some to be the only means of ensuring competition.

Amid growing nervousness at the power of the railway companies, Parliament sanctioned the construction of many lines for just this

In reality, it was rare for competing lines to follow the same route, but the area north of Nottingham was a glorious exception, with the Great Northern (in green), Great Central (blue) and Midland (pink), fighting for territory. In the Beeching era nearly all of these lines were closed to passengers, the only surviving stations being those marked in red. The Nottingham-Hucknall-Sutton-Mansfield line has since reopened

reason. It's important to note, though, that in only a very small minority of cases did competing lines actually follow the same route. They were usually built well apart, serving quite different regions to a common destination. A century later, the government of the day would try and prove that these 'duplicate' routes were wasteful and unnecessary, but this was rarely the case in reality, although by quirks of geography or corporate history, some towns ended up with two or even three railway stations, where one would have been more efficient. Even in these examples, they generally served different places, and could often be rationalised with a short stretch of track to bring traffic to a common point, although in practice this was seldom done.

State ownership, as a means of avoiding wasteful competition, had been considered as early as 1844, and the idea was raised at regular intervals thereafter. A possible alternative to full state ownership was to transfer responsibility for fixed assets, such as track and signalling, to the Government, and to lease the operating side to private enterprise. Had such a scheme been instigated, there is no doubt the railways would have developed very differently. The rights to operate railway services would presumably have been leased to the highest bidder, while those lines that failed to receive a satisfactory bid would have become the responsibility of the Government. Investment in new construction, or disinvestment by way of closure or retraction, would all have become the Government's responsibility. But despite various grumbles over the years, private enterprise did quite a good job, and although the State became increasingly involved in regulation of the railways, calls for nationalisation never reached fever pitch.

By the 1860s, railway technology had advanced considerably, both figuratively and geographically. The first railway carriages had been constructed along stagecoach principles, first as a single stage on railway wheels, then as two or three units joined as one. Seating arrangements followed the same lines, with covered accommodation for a lucky minority and open coaches for the rest. After the Gladstone Act of 1844, the railways were obliged to provide Parliamentary Trains for the lower orders, allowing the impecunious to travel for no more than a penny a mile, often it should be added in atrocious conditions. But travel they did, nonetheless. The railway companies were far from happy with what they saw as interference, but the Parliamentary Trains proved a blessing in disguise, widening the appeal of travel and producing a whole new class of passenger. Even a rate of a penny per mile was expensive to most working class people, but the new freedom proved so attractive that by 1860, receipts from 3rd Class passengers had exceeded all others.

One of the most innovative companies, the Midland, introduced Third Class carriages on expresses from 1872, and abolished Second Class two years later, thus effectively upgrading the rudimentary Third Class accommodation to Second Class standard. Such moves were popular with the public, but in operating terms they were expensive.. The 1870s saw the arrival of eight-wheeled double-bogie carriages, together with toilets, dining cars and even sleeping cars, which all increased the size and weight of the trains, necessitating bigger and more powerful locomotives. Heavier trains and higher operating speeds brought a need for improved brakes and signalling, and generally higher standards of engineering. Not all the companies complied quickly enough, and after a few well publicised and spectacular accidents, stricter safety legislation soon followed, which increased costs further.

This increasing sophistication didn't come cheaply. In the 1860s, working expenses had absorbed a reasonable 48% of railway income, but by 1900, the figure had risen to 63%. Despite this squeeze on the bottom line, the railway system continued to expand, although the rate of expansion began to fall, because there were few new routes left to exploit. By the 1860s, most cities were linked to the railway network, and some by two or three competing routes, with beneficial results for the customers, who were at liberty to choose the most effective service for their personal needs.

The railway companies, on the other hand, were beginning to realise that growth, in terms of mileage and profit, would not be infinite. Only a small number of lines were authorised in the last years of the 19th Century, and these were mostly small concerns to connect communities missed by the more prestigious schemes of earlier years. Legislation, in the form of the Light Railways Act, did much to assist the construction of such low-technology, low-cost railway lines, by easing the signalling and maintenance requirements, in exchange for certain limitations as to the speed and weight of traffic.

And there were still a few trunk lines to be built. Some made good economic sense, such as the Great Western Railway's cut-offs, allowing traffic for the West Country and Wales to bypass the long and tedious routes via Bristol and Bath, but some other schemes were based on stonier ground. The last great trunk line was destined to be the Great Central London Extension from Nottingham to Aylesbury at the turn of the century. The Great Central would probably never have been built were it not for the optimism and enthusiasm of Sir Edward Watkin, chairman of the Manchester, Sheffield & Lincolnshire Railway. Although the company controlled a sizeable network in the north, Edward dreamed of joining the big league by adding 'Great' to his company's title and heading south to London and beyond. Quite a way beyond, as it transpired, for Watkin became heavily involved in a Channel Tunnel scheme which, had it borne fruit, would have assured the future of the Manchester, Sheffield & Lincolnshire for all time.

In the event, the Channel Tunnel was put on ice after protestations from Britain's military establishment, but Watkin went ahead with the London extension anyway. The MS&L duly renamed itself the Great Central, as most points of the compass had been claimed by this time, and cut a superbly engineered line to the south, to the wider European loading gauge in readiness for those trans-European sleepers. The Great Central – part folly, part breathtaking genius – was effectively HS2, a century early. The tunnel was never built (or at least not in the lifetime of the Great Central) and the trunk route, much of which really did duplicate other perfectly adequate lines, was destined never to pay a dividend.

Still, such misfires were the exception. Taken as a whole, by the turn of the century, Britain's railways were acknowledged to be the best in the world. The expresses were faster, they included more Third Class accommodation (93% against 27% in France, for example), and the enormous network was, by and large, effectively run. But despite the world-beating statistics, the railways were not universally admired. Traders had long complained about freight charges, which contained many strange anomalies and more than a few sharp practices. Passengers – who could easily transfer their patronage to a competing line – were generally better looked after, but the public, and governments of the day, remained suspicious of the railways' monopoly of inland transport.

Monopoly it was, but the sheer economics of sending goods by rail was still compelling, compared to the alternatives:

"...for the general object of developing the country [the engineer] thought railways so far outstripped canals in terms of efficiency that the latter really had no chance. By the side of the Kennet & Avon Canal there were large works belonging to a gentleman who was an enthusiast on the subject of canals; yet he sent more than half his goods by railway, although the station was more than one and a half miles away. Obviously the gentleman wouldn't use the railways unless it suited the conditions of his business better than the canal..."
Colonel J A Saner presenting the thoughts of a GWR engineer in a paper to the Institute of Civil Engineers.

By 1913, after some 80 years of development, the railway system had more or less reached its zenith, extending to more than 20,000 miles. Had conditions remained locked in that long, glorious Edwardian era, the system would no doubt have proved quite satisfactory, but there were worrying trends even then. Twenty thousand miles was quite a network on an island measuring barely 600 miles by 200. And a quarter of the network, including many of the smaller and more vulnerable lines, had been constructed since the early 1880s.

The smallest and most vulnerable of all, including many of the so-called 'light' railways, had never paid a dividend and were never likely to. A few had so exhausted their reserves in the construction phase that they were unable to purchase locomotives and were snapped up by acquisitive neighbours. Generally, this was a beneficial process, for the larger companies were wealthy enough to carry the losses of a few small concerns, and more than willing to provide a local service in exchange for additional revenue to their wider networks, which could be quite substantial.

Just as the Stockton & Darlington had discovered the basic principles of railway operation, the companies in the fully formed network began to grasp the benefits of 'contributory revenue'. Even before they were grouped into larger concerns, it was becoming clear that the whole railway network functioned more in the manner of a single giant organism than a collection of isolated entities. Fast expresses roared between the big cities, connecting with stopping services to towns and wayside stations, and at junctions with branch line trains to remote villages and hamlets.

If a branch line carried 1,000 passengers a week, each paying a fare of a shilling, the contribution of the branch to the railway network would be a modest £50 a week. If this small income was set against operating expenses of £60 a week, the line would make a loss and be unable survive on its own. If, however, those 1,000 passengers continued their journey on a main line connecting with the branch, paying a total fare of two shillings, the branch itself would still make a loss, but the gross revenue to the network would be £100, less operating expenses, giving an annual profit from the branch of £40. The big railway companies were driven by profit, not philanthropy, and they were well aware that the majority of small lines were worth subsidising for the greater good.

If the big company were to close the branch, many passengers would find alternative means of travelling to the main line (not easy at the turn of the century) and then continue their journey by rail. Others would abandon rail travel altogether and reach their destination by other means, and no doubt a few would cease travelling altogether. The saving in terms of operating costs would be £60, but the loss of income would be hard to calculate, and might well be £100, giving a £40 loss.

In short, every mile of track had a role to play, from the insignificant branches to the major trunk routes. Many of the small branch lines would, in isolation, have been unprofitable, but as part of a unified system they played an invaluable role. In many cases the contributory value of a branch line was much higher than the earnings on the branch itself. A good example was the short link between the main line of the North British company and the town of North Berwick, east of Edinburgh. The branch was only four and a half miles long, but most passengers continued their journey for almost 20 miles along the main line to Edinburgh. Earnings on the branch itself were minimal, but the contributory revenue was quite considerable. North Berwick would come up for closure in the Beeching era, but win through.

Taking the theory a little further, five branches each carrying 1,000 passengers a week might disgorge 5,000 passengers onto a secondary line, and five such secondary lines might feed 25,000 passengers, via a trunk route, into a city centre. In reality, the situation was never as

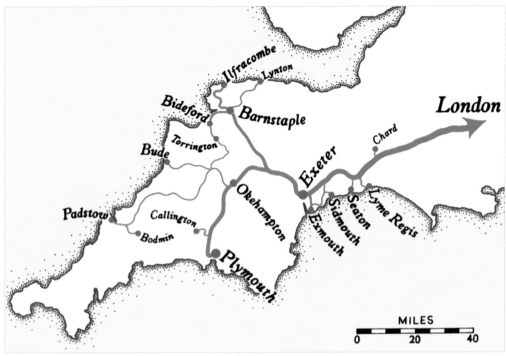

Contributory revenue is the revenue earned by a minor line and contributed to the rest of the network, in terms of through tickets and through freight flows. The former LSWR lines in Devon and Cornwall illustrate this symbiotic relationship very well. The branches were not viable in themselves, but the main line earned much of its revenue from the branches. When these were cut in the 1960s, most of the main line went too.

simple as that, but the theory was perfectly sound. A branch line closure policy might have put the secondary lines at risk, and closure of those could threaten the whole system. The pre-grouping railway companies were well aware of the theory and practise of contributory revenue, and it was this principle that kept many lightly used branch lines alive through some of the rockier financial periods of the 20th Century. The theory could also be applied to a trunk line, by introducing a linear stream of stopping, semi-fast and express services interconnecting at towns and cities along the same route, the stopping services contributing revenue to the semi-fast and express trains.

The innovative Great Western went a stage further and provided buses to contribute traffic from outlying villages without a rail connection. Its neighbour, the Southern, introduced the Atlantic Coast Express that served the West Country by literally dropping off carriages at various junctions down the trunk line from London, thus eliminating the necessity to change trains, and providing a graphic illustration of the benefits of contributory revenue. When the branch lines later closed, the express and its passengers ceased to exist, as did much of the trunk line.

In a near monopoly situation, this all worked very well. There were a few closures in the early days, but by and large – untroubled by road competition – the railways ran a huge transport operation very efficiently.

The onset of the First World War was to change Western civilisation forever. For the British railway system it marked the end of a heady era of growth and development, and from here on the story was to be one of retrenchment and decline. Railway managers were brought together into a Railway Executive Committee for the duration of the war, the railways effectively taken into government control as a single unified system. All war traffic was carried free of charge, but by way of exchange, the Government guaranteed the companies' revenue at 1913 levels. The results of such national organisation were impressive, and in just eight days, 334 trains were run through to Southampton for the military. In total, 69,000 men were whisked to the coast, together with 22,000 horses and 2,500 guns. In the far north, the long and tenuous lines to Kyle of Lochalsh and Thurso carried some 400 trains in six months to assemble the Northern Barrage Minefield between the Orkney Isles and Norway. Notwithstanding these military commitments, most lines continued to operate a reasonable civilian service too, although some of the smaller branches closed, and some were dismantled to aid the war effort. Elsewhere the heavy traffic gradually took its toll, and by 1919, the railway system that had been the envy of the world was run-down and exhausted.

After the Armistice, the railways remained under state control, and there were renewed calls for nationalisation to be be made permanent. Having seen the beneficial effects of state control during the war, even Winston Churchill – still a Liberal at this time – had been won over to the cause:

"Railways in private hands must be used for immediate profit, but it might pay the State to run the railways at a loss to develop industries and agriculture."

The circumstances in peacetime were, however, very different to those of the war. Three years later, after the Government had made a disastrous job of running the railways, the system was handed back into private hands. And Churchill had changed his mind.

There were economic problems aplenty after the war. The promise to guarantee railway income at 1913 levels turned out to be fairly worthless, for inflation had devalued it. Rising prices were behind a series of pay deals that saw the railway wage bill increase three-fold between 1913 and 1920. But politics played a role too. In 1919, the Government placated striking railwaymen with a sizeable pay award – this was just two years after the Russian Revolution, with industrial unrest at home that was itself looking increasingly radical in tone. Further industrial troubles in 1921 led to a coal strike, and the loss of trade that followed caused the railways to plunge £60 million into the red.

Combined with a slow release of government aid and continuing high

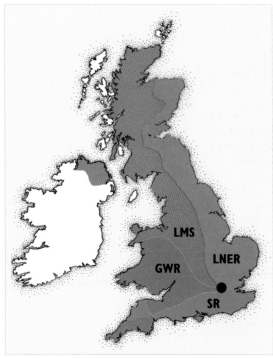

This much simplified map shows the broad geographical areas covered by the 'Big Four' statutory railway companies after 1923. In practise there was a great deal of overlap, with many towns being served by two companies

inflation, these industrial problems precipitated a financial crisis. Fares had risen by 50% in 1917 and by another 25% after the war, but freight charges had remained fixed since 1913, and were soon left far behind. Some of the very minor railways that had closed on the outbreak of war, and had track and trains stripped for the war effort, were never to reopen, for conditions had changed so much in the meantime that rebuilding them was no longer worth the trouble.

The post-war coalition Government, led by Lloyd George, created a Ministry of Transport, and its first Minister, Sir Eric Geddes, decided against nationalisation, choosing instead to amalgamate some 120 railway operators into four regionally-based companies. It was a neat solution and, many would claim, long overdue. By creating four large statutory companies – privately-owned, but obliged by law to carry on their trade in a prescribed manner – the Government had side-stepped the issues that would have arisen under full-blown nationalisation, while successfully tightening its grip on the railways.

Strangely enough, the most vociferous opponents of railway nationalisation had been the road transport pressure groups. Although motoring was in its infancy, the road lobby was already quite well organised. The Automobile Association (AA), and the slightly stuffier Royal Automobile Club (RAC) spoke for motorists. The industry was represented by the all-encompassing Society of Motor Manufacturers & Traders, and special interest groups, such as the London General Omnibus Company. Their chief concern was that the newly-formed Ministry of Transport would inevitably assume a pro-rail bias should the railways be put under state control. But with the railways effectively excluded, the opposite occurred, and from its very beginning, the Ministry of Transport developed a distinct bias towards road matters, because the regulation of roads was its primary function.

They might have been lacking friends at the Ministry, but the new larger railway companies were enormously powerful institutions, and it was felt necessary to prevent them from abusing their monopoly position. This widespread fear was very effectively exploited by the road lobby. The British Road Federation, for example, was established, "to counter the sinister and distorted propaganda of the railways in their efforts to enslave British industry..." No one gave an adequate explanation as to why the railways would want to destroy their own customer base, but the propaganda had an effect, and the 1921 Railways Act contained a variety of provisions aimed at limiting the companies' power and influence. And according to Sir Eric Geddes, amalgamation would help make the railways part of a more efficient and integrated transport network:

"The state must harmonise the operation of the different agencies of transport as between themselves in the interests of the community as a whole. Under a system of competition, not only did one railway or one dock strive to divert traffic from another, but trams sought to wrest traffic from the railways, railways to wrest traffic from canals, coastal traffic to wrest traffic from both, and so on. In future, our effort will be to encourage each agency of transport to undertake that part of the total work which it, owing to its own special qualities, can most efficiently and economically perform." *Eric Geddes, first Minister of Transport*

It was certainly a radical idea, but although the Railways Act was successfully implemented, Geddes' wider vision of a fully integrated transport system met with considerable opposition, and after two years of planning, he resigned in disgust.

The railway companies were not over-enamoured with the new legislation either, but being unable even to voice an opinion, they were effectively powerless. After release from government control in August 1921, the old order was to survive only until the new Railways Act finally came into force on 1st January 1923. Perhaps the most controversial provision of the

Act was to create a Railway Rates Tribunal to standardise freight and other charges, the object being to freeze revenue at the elusive 1913 levels. The railways were now obliged by law to carry any load, however uneconomic, and to publish their rates. To prevent them showing undue preference to one trader at the expense of another, rates for the carriage of particular commodities were fixed, irrespective of the actual costs involved. Employee costs, including hours of work, wages and conditions of service, were all fixed by national wages boards.

The Government's intention was to control the railway companies' hold on inland transport, and maximise the social and commercial benefits that a unified railway system could offer the nation. For example, rates for the carriage of raw materials were set on the low side, while those for finished products were generally higher, a policy that assisted the all important manufacturing industries.

This was all very reasonable as a means of harnessing a monopoly carrier, but within a few years of the Act's implementation, the railways were faced with competition from private road transport that didn't need to publish rates, could pick and choose the most lucrative traffic, and obtain it by undercutting the railways, which were powerless to intervene. Between 1919 and 1921, when ex-army lorries came onto the market and were bought by new haulage operators, the number of goods lorries doubled. By 1926 they had doubled again. The forces of the state had moved painfully slowly to control the railway companies' monopoly, and by the time they did, circumstances had changed sufficiently to make the legislation an unnecessary burden.

Inevitably there were problems amalgamating the companies, some of which were already very large, and some of which were purely local operations. There had been little or no consultation, and the legal tangle created by the various companies over the preceding century or so created all sorts of complications. The reorganisation would also create some strange geographical and strategic anomalies, some of which would continue to reverberate for decades, and even have an influence on closure decisions made in the 1960s. Some railway companies, such as the Great Western, had built up a comparatively compact and unified territory, by construction and acquisition of smaller concerns. This fiercely independent company subsequently emerged almost unscathed from the amalgamation, even retaining its full title.

Creating the other three of the big four companies wasn't to be so straightforward. For strategic reasons of its own, the Midland had driven tentacles (mostly under joint operating agreements with

With tracks and running rights from Northern Ireland to Stranraer, Lowestoft, Southend and Bournemouth, the Midland caused a few headaches

other operators) into almost every corner of the land. The Great Central, which had arrived too late to carve out a clear-cut territory of its own, crossed several regions, and duplicated more than a few lines. It was absorbed into the London & North Eastern Railway, a massive (though relatively unsatisfactory) combine, formed of the old Great Northern, the Great Eastern and others, controlling the whole east side of the country north of London.

The west coast saw an even less happy amalgamation, for the new London Midland & Scottish had absorbed two sworn enemies – the London & North Western Railway, and the Midland. The various Scottish companies were divided up between these two massive English concerns, those on the west coast coming under the jurisdiction of the LMS, and those to the east falling to the LNER. The most successful alliance was probably that of the new Southern Railway,

SOUTHERN ELECTRIC

NEW EXTENSIONS

July 1937	**LONDON** TO **PORTSMOUTH** via **GUILDFORD** and Woking to Aldershot and Alton
July 1938	**LONDON** TO **PORTSMOUTH** via **HORSHAM** including the Lines from Three Bridges to Horsham – from Worthing to Fratton and branches to Bognor Regis and Littlehampton
Jan. 1939	**STAINES** TO **READING** – **ASCOT** TO **ALDERSHOT** AND **GUILDFORD**
July 1939	**SEVENOAKS** TO **HASTINGS** AND **BEXHILL**
1940	**GRAVESEND** AND **SWANLEY** TO **CHATHAM** AND **GILLINGHAM–STROOD** **MAIDSTONE**

RIGHT: Under Sir Herbert Walker, electrification of the Southern Railway continued right up to the war

BELOW: A key milestone was electrification to Brighton, completed in 1933. The flagship electric service was the 'Brighton Belle', which survived until the 1970s. Five of the original carriages have been restored and are expected to run heritage services from 2014

composed of three former companies (dominated by the London & South Western) whose territories were generally complementary.

Despite all this upheaval, the amalgamation was to have beneficial results, as Geddes had predicted. Once the new organisations had settled down, many economies were realised by way of standardisation and centralised control, yet the companies were not so large as to lose their regional identities and specialist knowledge of local traffic. And although the four companies adopted very different styles of management, they remained on friendly enough terms to co-operate and learn from each other, even sharing research and development costs on a few occasions.

Because of continuing economic difficulties, investment remained no more than piecemeal in the 1920s, and was largely confined to the Southern Railway. Under Sir Herbert Walker of the London & South Western, the Southern continued the process of electrification that Sir Herbert's company had pioneered, utilising the 'third-rail' current collection system well suited to the strategic conditions and compact geography of the south-east.

The North Eastern Railway had also adopted the third-rail system on the Tyneside suburban network, which had been electrified as early as 1904, and continued to give good service until the 1960s, when this isolated electric network was torn up and replaced by diesel traction. Within a few years, the network had been re-energised with overhead wires, as the core of the Tyne & Wear Metro system.

By 1926, electrification on the Southern had been completed outwards from London to Guildford, Sutton, Coulsdon, Orpington and Dartford, and in 1930 conversion work began on the Southern's most important line, the trunk route down to Brighton, the electrification of which was completed in 1932. Despite the untimely arrival of the Depression, electrification continued,

Between the wars, the GWR was enthusiastic about lightweight diesel railcar technology, but very few of these machines were introduced, and most branch lines remained steam hauled to the end. The broad gauge track in the foreground suggests this is a modern museum photograph! Didcot Railway Centre, May 2011. PHOTO: Ian Knight

Like the GWR, the LMS experimented with railcars in the 1930s: first with steam-powered Sentinel machines, but later with diesel-electric cars of its own (LEFT), which were quite advanced for their day. In 1938, working with the Derby Carriage & Wagonworks, it introduced a prototype diesel multiple unit of very modern appearance (BELOW). The prototype gave good service on the Oxford to Cambridge 'Varsity' line, and had they been introduced in any number, the fate of such secondary lines might have been very different. PHOTO: R G Jarvis

and by 1937 almost a quarter of the company's network had been converted. By 1939, most of the major lines east of Portsmouth were using electric traction, and electric trains accounted for more than half of the passenger services on the Southern Railway.

The impact of these swiftly executed and cost-effective investments by the Southern were of real importance, for they turned out to be the principle modernisation achievement of the railways in the first half of the 20th Century. The newly electrified lines offered fast and frequent services to and from London and, besides improving the operational efficiency of the railways, they encouraged the creation of whole new communities around suburban railway stations. As a direct result, passenger traffic on the Southern Railway increased by a quarter between 1923 and 1939.

Investment that made a lot of sense on the south-east did not, however, necessarily point the way forward for the rest of the country. The LNER received government aid to electrify the line from its Liverpool Street terminus out to the northern suburbs of London, and the company also began work on a major project to convert the former Great Central trans-Pennine route from Manchester to Sheffield to overhead electric traction. But both schemes seem to have been undertaken rather grudgingly, and it was to be many years before either came to fruition.

There were several reasons for this lack of enthusiasm for modern technology. Cash was painfully short between the wars (and some investment plans appeared to show little in the way of returns), and the lack of an effective national electricity grid ruled out widespread electrification. As for diesel, the railway companies saw no reason to invest in locomotives burning expensive imported oil, when steam engines operated very well on home-produced coal.

Steam technology was, by this time, very well understood, and remained relatively efficient for long-distance passenger and freight services, but for stopping and branch line trains it had always been costly. Despite this, new technology arrived very slowly on the minor services. In the early years of the century, several companies had experimented with the 'railmotor', a carriage grafted onto a small steam locomotive that promised to cut costs on lightly used services. The railmotors could be driven from either end, eliminating run-round manoeuvres, and they were demonstrably cheaper to operate, but for the passengers, they were the cause of considerable distress:

'Its power and flexibility, its acceleration and de-acceleration [sic] were all that could be desired. It fulfilled its duty efficiently... and very uncomfortably. Vibration on the locomotive footplate has come to be recognised as part of the day's work for the driver and fireman. Its transference to the seats of the passengers was not accepted by them as a part of their daily journey, and the experiment was not a success.'
E Kitson Clark

Although the railmotor turned out to be an evolutionary dead end, experiments continued with more sophisticated machines. In 1923, the Sentinel company introduced a steam railcar – broadly speaking, a passenger carriage powered by a small steam motor – that seemed to point the way to the future. The LNER bought 22 of these between 1927 and 1928, and by 1931 it had introduced another 50, of a more advanced design.

But steam wasn't entirely suitable for powering railcars, and it was only in 1933 when the GWR began tentatively to introduce diesel-powered machines, that railcars truly came of age. Although the company had introduced only a handful of railcars by the outbreak of the Second World War, they proved outstandingly successful, and would remain in use for several decades.

The LMS went a step further in 1938, introducing a prototype three-car streamlined

While the British railway companies were making a few tentative experiments to replace steam-hauled trains, the French were introducing small railcars for branch line services and some very powerful ones for the main lines. Ettore Bugatti tested his first railcar near Alsace in 1933, and had produced more than a hundred within five years. They were produced as single, double or triple units, powered by two or four centrally-mounted 12.7 litre petrol engines. The two-car, four-engined 'Presidential' achieved a world record speed of 122mph in 1934. The French later put resources into main line electrification.

diesel multiple unit that was effectively a 21st Century machine. This attractive and practical machine was expected to go into series production, but the war intervened and the project was never relaunched. The company also discovered the merits of diesel-powered shunting locomotives, introducing about 50 before the war. Again, these would almost certainly have become the norm quite rapidly had peace and stability continued.

These were very minor advances in a generally bleak investment picture. The railway companies had emerged from the First World War in an impoverished and run-down state, only to be subject to the turmoil of reorganisation. No sooner had they drawn breath after amalgamation than they were hit by the General Strike in 1926, followed by the Depression of 1929. It was a series of blows from which they would never fully recover. And the companies did little to help themselves by spending what little money was available by attempting to diversify, buying into road haulage firms, bus companies, even fledgling airlines. To a limited extent these were useful, feeding traffic to the core railway businesses, but generally these acquisitions were ill-timed and inappropriate.

With little cash available for investment, the railway system largely stagnated during the 1930s. Productivity rose by a meagre 1.2% per annum during this period, and the tight fiscal controls of the 1921 Railways Act proved a major burden. The intention had been to fix revenue at around £51 million from 1928 onwards, but in 1929 earnings barely reached £41 million, falling remorselessly thereafter, to a mere £28 million in 1938.

Despite various measures aimed at tightening control over road transport in the early 1930s, the railways experienced a slow haemorrhage of traffic to the roads. By the end of the decade, car production had reached levels undreamed of 20 years before, and most of the growth was in smaller, cheaper vehicles, bringing personal transport within reach of the middle classes. As the new industry began to find its feet, so did the increasingly powerful alliance that formed the road lobby. Pressure from these groups brought an abolition of the 20mph speed limit in 1930, causing a dramatic increase in the number of road accidents, casualties reaching an horrendous peak in 1934, when 7,343 people were killed. With the exception of the wartime black-out years, that figure wouldn't be exceeded until 1964, when there were more than three times as many cars on the road.

The imposition of compulsory driving tests and a 30mph speed limit in urban areas went some way to reducing the death toll, but did nothing to calm the spectacular growth of the motor industry. With the rapid increase in both cars and lorries, the road lobby began to press for wider, faster roads, and finding few Government supporters in Britain, they looked abroad and discovered an unlikely ally in the form of Adolf Hitler.

In Europe, the mighty forces of fascism were working miracles on the transport front. While Mussolini struggled to make the trains run on time in Italy, Hitler announced the Volks Wagen or 'people's car', and a network of new autobahns, or motorways, for people to drive them on. To the British Road Federation it was all too good to be true, and in 1934 it invited Ministry of Transport officials on a fact-finding tour of the Fatherland. Sadly, the men from the Ministry declined, and they missed the opportunity to see Herr Hitler's road programme forging ahead – the first autobahn opened in 1935, with almost 2,000 kilometers following the year after, before the Fuhrer began to divert resources into more dangerous things.

In 1937, as the clouds of war gathered, the British road lobby sent a sizeable delegation to Germany. It was a major propaganda coup for Hitler (the delegation included 58 British MPs), and an opportunity for the roads groups to press for motorway construction at home, although the Ministry remained unconvinced, preferring instead a measured policy of road widening.

The following year, there were signs that Minister of Transport Leslie Burgin was weakening, although his suggestion of an experimental motorway was firmly quashed by Treasury which was, by this time, overwhelmed by demands on the defence budget. Amazingly, the road lobby suggested that some of the defence budget be reallocated towards road construction. Had common sense not prevailed, Hitler might have found little opposition from the RAF in 1940, and a convenient network of motorways to aid the progress of his motorised divisions across southern England...

The primary aim of the road lobbyists had been frustrated, but they had succeeded in severely denting the profitability of the railway companies, for railway dividends never came anywhere near the levels of 1913. Even the Southern paid only 0.5% in 1938, and the LNER failed to pay a single ordinary dividend between 1925 and 1938. The GWR dividend fell from a healthy 7.5% in 1929, to 3% in 1931, then artificially subsidising it by drawing on capital reserves. But by 1938 even the GWR bowed to the inevitable, cutting the rate to 0.5%, but not before it had poached £8 million from its reserves and modernisation fund. This affair provided wonderful ammunition for Labour MPs in later years, when a Conservative government blocked railway investment proposals, for among the GWR directors was none other than Harold Macmillan, a future Conservative Prime Minister.

Artificial dividends aside, the big four private companies had survived all manner of upheavals between 1923 and 1939 without once returning a loss. It was quite an achievement, and as a lobby group, the railways were still a force to be reckoned with, for in 1938, no fewer than 24 railway directors sat in the House of Lords, and 11 in the Commons.

Throughout the inter-war years, there were few attempts to close loss-making services, with just 240 miles of unprofitable or duplicate routes being closed outright, and a further 1,000 miles being closed to passenger trains.

The brief flowering of high speed services in the 1930s was eventually to give Britain the steam-powered world record

The Great Railway Conspiracy

This was partly due to the railway companies' healthy regard for the contributory value of branches, but was also because they had no clear idea of where profits were actually being made – or money lost. Without a doubt, many minor lines could have been closed and replaced by bus services, something that would have seemed a natural progression, given that the railways had bought substantial shareholdings in many of the bus companies by this time. Railway involvement in bus operators should also have brought about a degree of bus/rail co-ordination, such as the running of buses from stations to outlying suburbs, or through ticketing, but very little was achieved. This lack of co-ordination has never been adequately explained, although one suspects the railways simply had a blind faith in the future of rail, and considered themselves far too grand to become involved with mere omnibus timetables.

This faith in their own enterprise emerged briefly and gloriously towards the end of the 1930s when – despite financial pressures – the two largest companies introduced competing high-speed express trains that put Britain back at the forefront of railway technology. In 1935, the hard-pressed LNER introduced the Silver Jubilee, running between London and Newcastle in four hours. In 1937, the express services were extended to Edinburgh and, in the same year, the LMS responded by slashing the headline journey times on its own route to Scotland, from seven and a half to six and a half hours. Finally, in 1938, the LNER took the world speed record for a steam locomotive at 126mph. It was a sign of things to come that this record was never beaten – the Americans, the French and, most notably, the Germans, were pouring investment into high-speed diesel and electric traction.

The impressive point-to-point express schedules and record speeds of the 1930s were to remain unconquered in the UK for many years too, for by this time, war in Europe had become inevitable, and the Second World War was due to deal the railways a far more serious blow than had the First.

In an effort to put their financial affairs back in order, the big four railway companies belatedly launched a 'square deal' campaign aimed at rectifying the imbalance between road and rail legislation. The intention was to persuade the Government to relax financial controls and give the railways a bit more commercial freedom, to tender for suitable traffic at a price that reflected the ability of the market to pay.

The issue of 'preferential charges' legislation had already been deliberately brought to a head, after one of the companies offered a trader a flat-rate contract that ignored the Railway Rates Tribunal fee structure. After the affair had been brought to court, the Government agreed to loosen the rates structure to allow similar schemes, but such 'agreed charges' still needed to be settled in open court, and other traders had the right to object and demand equal treatment. It was a long way from the free market that the road hauliers enjoyed, and the square deal campaign was launched to remove, or relax, the remaining controls.

Just as the campaign was reaching a successful conclusion Britain declared war in September 1939. The railways were rapidly put back under state control, leaving the long-standing question of rates and charges unsettled. Once again, a Railway Executive Committee took control, and compensatory income was set to pre-war levels. Fortunately, not to those of 1938, which had been a particularly gloomy year, but to an average of the revenues between 1935 and 1937.

As before, the railways gave sterling service, although this time the demands on the network were much more severe. Almost immediately, 1.3 million parents and children were evacuated (mostly from London and the south-east) aboard 4,000 trains. And as in 1914-18, an expeditionary force was carried to the south coast, although this time the troops were rapidly brought home again after the evacuation from Dunkirk, an operation involving 620 train movements, carrying 319,000 men.

The Blitz caused terrible devastation. The carriage shed at Clapham Junction took a direct hit in September 1940. The railways became very skilled at patching things up in record time, but a backlog of maintenance was building up, that would eventually absorb a great deal of time and money.

Throughout the darkest days of the war, when Britain stood alone and the might of the German army waited across the Channel in preparation for an invasion that never came, the railways received a merciless pounding. Nine hundred staff and passengers were killed and 4,000 carriages and wagons destroyed in no fewer than 9,000 'incidents'. Yet, strangely enough, only eight locomotives were put out of action. It was, perhaps, fortunate that the railway companies had had neither the capital nor the imagination to invest heavily in fragile and temperamental electric and diesel locomotives, the latter reliant on imported oil, now very much at a premium. And this was just the beginning. The real pressure came during the build-up to the D-Day landings in 1944, an operation of unprecedented size and complexity in which the role of the railways was paramount.

Altogether, some half a million trains are thought to have been run on behalf of the State during the war; railway factories produced tanks, aircraft and munitions, and many locomotives were sent abroad to assist the war effort elsewhere. But after five and a half years of war, the railways were in a sorry state. With the exception of a few improvements to speed the flow of military traffic, investment had almost ceased, leaving track and equipment close to collapse. A system that had once provided the finest trains on the densest railway network in the world, was almost in ruins.

The railways were primarily a heavy industry, and heavy equipment could survive without maintenance for quite a period. Track renewals had been suspended, bridges patched up, and steam locomotives run – as steam locomotives will – without proper servicing or repair. By 1945, the backlog was immense, and the Government owed the railways a vast sum – would the General Election, the first for ten years, bring a change in policy?

2
State Control
1947-1951

"I am not unmindful of the fact that nationalisation does not give the workers control of the industry. But each and every locoman sincerely hopes that the first is the biggest stepping-stone to the second... Was I wrong to look for an indication that we would not be 'supervised' by incompetent position-seekers? Was it wrong to believe that with nationalisation would come a clear-out of the old school tie and the 'wizard show' clique?"

Railwayman E J Doody in a letter to the Locomotive Journal (ASLEF magazine)

There were rail buses all over the world by the late 1940s... except Britain. This is a 1937-vintage Waddington rail bus in New South Wales, Australia. With seats for 18 passengers, it could exceed 50mph. Six were made, and some stayed in service until the 1960s. This example was converted into a 'pay bus', for carrying wages to outlying farms. It was destroyed in an explosion during an attempted robbery in 1941! PHOTO: Australian Railway Historical Society NSW Division, image 113160: Ken Winney, 16/12/1938

Within months of VE Day, Britain had returned a radical socialist government. The election was held on 5th July 1945, but with many servicemen still overseas, it was several weeks before all the proxy votes had been counted and a result declared.

Labour achieved an overwhelming victory, and the new Prime Minister Clement Atlee found himself holding 393 seats in the House of Commons against the Tories' 213 and the Liberal's 12. No fewer than 13 cabinet rank Tories had been defeated, leaving Churchill with just a handful of suitable Shadow Cabinet appointees. The upset surprised almost everyone, for Churchill had been a popular wartime leader and during the election campaign he had been welcomed as a hero throughout the land. One interesting theory was that the people had lived for so long under a 'national' administration that they fully believed it would be possible to vote Labour, yet keep Churchill as Prime Minister. Whatever the reason, it was, according to Mrs Churchill, a blessing in disguise. "It seems quite effectively disguised," was her husband's laconic reply.

The new Government rapidly implemented a policy of nationalisation, and on 1st January 1948, the railways were absorbed into a vast national undertaking, the British Transport Commission, charged with integrating and rationalising inland transport in all its forms, including canals and road haulage as *well as railways. Under state ownership, a policy of branch line closures was implemented, as the British Transport Commission had investments in competing bus services, and was generally in favour of cheaper road transport for minor services. There was to be no more than a trickle of successfully implemented closures though, for the Commission found the process to be fraught with legal, social and technical difficulties. Meanwhile, the Railway Executive had begun to introduce a range of standardised steam locomotives for main line services, completely ignoring well proven diesel railcar technology that might have improved the viability of the branch lines. Meanwhile, the introduction of new equipment was painfully slow, the financial compensation paid to former railway shareholders proved to be more of a burden than had been expected, and road hauliers fought long and hard to frustrate the policy of integration.*

The House of Commons reopened in August 1945 amid some extraordinary scenes. The Tories rallied around Churchill, singing 'For he's a jolly good fellow!,' while the Labour ranks replied with a massed rendition of 'The Red Flag.' The Speaker, Colonel Clifton Brown, later remarked: "I wondered whether I was going to be Speaker or director of a musical show!" The 1945 Labour Government was certainly radical, but it had been a very British revolution.

The new administration was determined to do more than voice socialist rhetoric in the House of Commons. After sitting largely on the political sidelines for almost half a century, the Labour Party had at last been given an overwhelming mandate to press ahead with socialist policies, and it wasted little time in preparing legislation for wide-scale public ownership (or nationalisation), of heavy industries, including coal-mining and steel-making, health, transport, and even the Bank of England, which was the first to be nationalised, in 1946. The Government also announced a programme of prestigious public works to rebuild the economy after years of neglect.

Germany had already established a world lead in the design and construction of motorways, and in 1945, the British Road Federation (BRF) and the Society of Motor Manufacturers & Traders (SMMT) sent another delegation to Germany to investigate. Predictably, their report to the Ministry of Transport and Civil Aviation was strongly in favour of motorway construction:

"The results of this enquiry show that the construction of motorways is more than justified solely on economic grounds, apart from any considerations of safety, convenience and amenity."

In fact, the BRF had already decided to press for 1,000 miles of motorway, and all that remained was to persuade the Government to do something about it. In May 1946, the Minister of War Transport, Alfred Barnes, announced a motorway programme extending to around 800 miles, to be completed within ten years. These initial proposals included what was to become the core of the British motorway network, some 30 years later:

- **London-Cardiff (later to become the M4)**
- **London-Carlisle via Birmingham (the M6)**
- **Bristol-Leeds (partly M5 and M1)**
- **Warrington-Hull (the M62)**

The various motorway construction plans culminated in the Special Roads Act 1949, which legalised the construction and use of motorways. Legislation was easy, but a massive investment programme of this kind was little short of make-believe in the late 1940s, for Britain was on the verge of financial collapse. A loan from America of almost $4 billion had served to stave off bankruptcy after the war, but by September 1947 it was almost exhausted, and being depleted at the rate of almost $500 million a month.

The Great Railway Conspiracy

Britain was unable to pay for even the most essential imports, and faced with a mounting financial crisis, the Government introduced a round of austerity measures. With no prospect of a relaxation in fuel rationing, motorway construction plans were put on ice. Indeed, the total spending on roads was destined to run to no more than £35 million in the following six years, and it was not until 1955 that a rather more modest programme of 147 miles of motorway was once again under active consideration. This delay should have given the railways an opportunity to start constructing a modern cost-effective network, but events were to prove otherwise.

While money remained tight, nationalisation was rather more easily achieved than grand capital-intensive projects, and in the early post-war years, it was pushed forward with great zeal. State control of health resulted in the formation of the National Health Service, which was generally welcomed, though the Bank of England's new ownership was accepted with less enthusiasm in some quarters, as was that of the civil aviation industry. But on 18th December 1946, Parliament voted in favour of a much larger and more controversial proposal – the nationalisation of the entire transport industry.

Amid wild scenes, and renewed outbreaks of revolutionary refrains from the crowded Labour benches, the House of Commons voted to bring the railways, road haulage industry, waterways and ports under state control. A fortnight later, on 1st January 1947, the coal industry was nationalised – almost unnoticed among the mountain of colliery assets was a small passenger railway in South Shields that passed into history as the first nationalised passenger line in Great Britain.

In the months since the arrival of the Labour Government, the four big railway companies had been more or less biding their time, for rail nationalisation had been on the agenda from the beginning, and with compulsory purchase just around the corner, the companies were content to assume a caretaker role. But just a few years before, the situation had been very different.

During the war, the four companies had studied every private, public and quasi-public railway network in the world, and concluded (perhaps inevitably) that private ownership worked best. They had been weighed down by restrictive legislation before the war, particularly where rates and charges were concerned, but with every prospect of Churchill leading a peacetime Tory government, it was hoped that this would be eased. Providing the railways were granted a reasonable sum by way of war reparations, the financial position – if not healthy – would be enough for them to carry on. The companies had even given some thought to the question of uneconomic branch lines, and reasoned that a future government would probably be prepared to grant cash assistance to maintain services where they were deemed to have a social function.

The Labour Party wasn't the slightest bit interested in these ideas, and the proposals of the big four were ignored. In retaliation, the railway boards declined to offer any assistance with the long-winded and complex process of nationalisation. A few good men stayed, notably Sir Eustace Missenden of the Southern Railway, but many of the best managers and administrators left the service, including a few with unique knowledge, such as the GWR's Sir James Milne, who had assumed the role of Deputy Chairman of the Railway Executive during the war. Lord Portal, also of the Great Western, declined to stay, and refused an offer of financial compensation, but he did force a remarkable concession from the railway's new masters, insisting that former Great Western directors should retain their travel passes! Generally speaking, the railway company directors began to lose interest in day-to-day operations and put their energies into fighting for favourable compensation instead.

Whoever owned Britain's railways, they faced a formidable task, as the network had emerged from the war in a terrible state. Traffic had been exceptionally heavy for six years, yet the system had been given minimal maintenance. It was estimated that 1,400 miles of track needed immediate replacement, and a much greater mileage was in need of urgent repair. Speed restrictions, which had stood at 90mph in the late 1930s, had been reduced to 60mph or even lower, while coal was of such inferior quality that few locomotives could exceed the new limits anyway.

The railways needed five years of sustained investment, but as a direct result of the impending upheaval of nationalisation, the management lost interest, and the system stagnated instead. The immediate post-war years, that should have seen frantic reconstruction and forward planning, were largely wasted.

To add to the confusion, the small body of Conservatives under Winston Churchill did everything in their power to fight the Bill's long passage through the Commons. In all, some 800 amendments were tabled by the opposition, some serious, others implemented as blocking manoeuvres to delay the legislation, though most fell by the wayside.

Amid mounting controversy, Labour introduced a guillotine, so that if discussion of an amendment ran beyond a prescribed time limit, it was simply abandoned. Despite this, some of the more radical proposals were lost at the Committee stage, including a provision to restrict all lorries, even those carrying a trader's own goods, to within 40 miles of their depot. No western country had yet attempted to place all transport undertakings under state control, and public interest proved so intense that the 1947 Transport Act document became an overnight best-seller, running to more than 30,000 copies. At midnight on 31st December 1947, the railway system came under state control. A month later, as a financial crisis gripped the nation, the recently nationalised coal industry announced losses of more than £5 million for the last quarter of 1947. It was not a very encouraging omen.

The Government had chosen to put all the transport undertakings under the control of a comparatively small organisation to be known as the British Transport Commission (BTC). According to the Transport Act, the role of the Commission would be:

"...mainly concerned with questions of policy, including general financial control, the preparation of schemes relating to fares, rates and charges, supervision of research and development, and arrangement for the co-ordination of inland transport."

The powers of the British Transport Commission were wide-ranging. At the start, it had an almost total monopoly in the carriage of passengers and goods by rail and inland waterways, and provisions to create a similar monopoly for road transport, shipping services, port and inland waterway facilities, hotels, hostels, and even places of refreshment. In the light of subsequent events, there were two provisions that were to have a particular significance. The first outlined the duties of the Commission:

"It shall be the general duty of the Commission so to exercise their [sic] powers... as to provide, or secure, or promote the provision of, an efficient, adequate, economical and properly integrated system of public inland transport... for passengers and goods... in such manner as to provide most efficiently and conveniently for the needs of the public, agriculture, commerce and industry."

Another gave guidance on the disposal of surplus equipment:

"The Commission may dispose... of any part of their undertaking or any property which in their opinion is not required by them for the discharge of their duties under this Act."
Transport Act 1947, Part 1, Subsection 2, Provision 4

The Commission had been empowered to co-ordinate and integrate public transport so as to produce an 'efficient' and 'adequate' system, a very commendable aim. Unfortunately, many of the road, rail and shipping interests which had fallen into its hands had previously been run in competition with each other, not least the rural railway lines and country bus services. Competition, of course, had little to with integration, leaving the Commission with the difficult task of deciding which services should be earmarked for development, and which might have to go.

In theory, the BTC was to assume central control of the entire transport industry, so by juggling fares and charges for different modes, it would have the power to fine-tune the balance of transport economics. Traffic would be guided to the most efficient carrier, not through force or legislation, but by a subtle adjustment to the charging structure. As the Commission was bound by law to produce neither a profit or loss overall, it would also be possible to cross-subsidise loss-making but useful services with profits from more lucrative areas. So it appeared logical that the BTC would concentrate resources on the most efficient and effective carriers, withdraw the least competitive services, and balance the books at the end of the day.

There were, however, some fundamental flaws to the legislation, for the 1947 Act had upheld the freedom of traders to move between carriers, implying that the BTC would be expected to provide a choice of services. And the Commission had only two weapons with which to alter the balance between the various modes of transport – price and quality. Price wasn't really an effective option, because rates and charges would be tightly controlled by a Transport Tribunal, the equivalent of the old Railway Rates Tribunal. Ultimately, the only means by which the all-powerful Commission could effect the removal of traffic from one carrier to another was to reduce the quality of the service it intended to run down. As a policy it would become ingrained in the thinking of the BTC and its heirs, and was later used to devastating effect.

The BTC was also constrained by some rather vague social obligations. The Labour Party had been determined to beat the capitalists at their own game, but it sometimes had difficulty reconciling socialist doctrine with the demands of the market. The resulting policy directives were carefully worded so as to say very little, leaving the Commission to make its own judgement as to whether to provide a social service or succumb to commercial pressures. Typical was the following Labour Party policy statement issued during the war: "In the case of real conflict between public desires and sound commercial practise, it does not necessarily follow that the latter should prevail."

To keep the vast transport monolith in touch with consumer and business demands, the

LEFT: The original 1948 British Railways logo was applied by transfer to a great variety of locomotives and other equipment in a vain attempt to make it all look reasonably unified

RIGHT: From 1956 it was replaced by this less stylized emblem on coaching stock and some diesels, including early multiple units, with a slightly different design for other locomotives

BRITISH RAILWAYS

Transport Act made allowance for the establishment of Transport Users' Consultative Committees (TUCC) to liaise between the Commission and the public. It was a difficult solution to a tricky problem – there was little point in state ownership if the people had no opportunity to communicate their desires and grievances back to the transport concern over which they held nominal ownership.

Nine regional English Committees were established, together with a single body covering Wales and Monmouthshire, and a similar body overseeing the whole of Scotland. Each local committee comprised a chairman and a wide selection of members representing various sections of the community, such as agriculture, industry, labour and local authorities. All were chosen at the discretion of the Minister of Transport. Less reasonable was the provision that other members would be appointed by the Transport Commission itself. And rather ominously, the regional TUCCs (with the exception, after 1953, of the Scottish and Welsh bodies) were bound only to report the views of the public to a Central Transport Consultative Committee (CTCC) funded by, and partially staffed by, the BTC. The CTCC would report, in turn, to the Minister of Transport.

Timetables, quality of service, even complete loss of service: any matters relating to BTC operations would be discussed at local TUCC level, and the recommendations passed up to the BTC via the CTCC. Where services were to be withdrawn, the views of the local population (usually overwhelmingly against) would be discussed locally, and condensed into a report forwarded to the CTCC. This process later became synonymous with railway closures, although the Consultative Committees performed many less notorious tasks as well.

Whatever the feeling might be locally, the Transport User's Consultative Committees had no real teeth, for rates and charges were in the hands of the Transport Tribunals, and the BTC had no obligation to act on a TUCC report. But they did at least provide a forum for limited discussion on transport affairs, and a means by which ordinary people could get their views across, although as the reports were never published, it was impossible to say whether a grievance had even reached the CTCC, let alone landing on a BTC desk. In any event, the British Transport Commission was by no means the end of the chain of communication, because day-to-day operations were carried out by Executive Committees.

Initially there were four Executive Committees: Docks & Inland Waterways, London Transport, Road Transport and Railways. The shipping and hotel interests of the former private railway companies remained for the time being under the control of the Railway Executive, which made sense.

At first, it was unclear who was actually in charge – the BTC or the Executives. According to the Transport Act, the Executives were merely agents, to 'assist the Commission in the discharge of their duties'. The British Transport Commission, under the Chairmanship of Sir Cyril (later Lord) Hurcomb, had initially empowered the Railway Executive to function broadly as the former statutory companies had done, with the proviso that it was bound to obey any directives that might be passed down from the Commission. This was where conflicts later arose, for to enable a policy of transport integration to be developed, the BTC would sometimes pass down directives that ran contrary to the wishes of the Executives, who often had their own agendas. On the other hand, the Executives had no powers to borrow money, and they were obliged to carry all of the rights, powers, obligations and liabilities of the BTC. No doubt, the Executives learned to delay or frustrate unpopular directives by dragging their feet.

As far as many at the Commission were concerned, the Executives were merely employers of staff with control over day-to-day operations. As employers, the Executives initially undertook to negotiate with the trade unions over wages and conditions, but even this limited role was later subsumed by the BTC.

Some Executive Committee appointees considered themselves mere agents of the Transport Commission, while others interpreted their role as being similar to that of the former railway company directors. Sir Eustace Missenden, the first Railway Executive Chairman, subscribed to the latter view, and rather looked down on the BTC from his imposing headquarters at 222 Marylebone Road. To make matters worse, company and regional loyalties meant that regional managers often adopted a similar attitude to Sir Eustace and his Railway Executive. The result was a long-running and sometimes bitter war of attrition between the regions, the Executive Committee and the Transport Commission.

Sir Cyril Hurcomb, as a former Permanent Secretary at the Ministry of Transport and a career civil servant, had interpreted the rules along civil service lines and decided that the Commission should assume a loose policy-making role, between the Government (which wanted rapid transport integration) and the Executives (which, by and large, did not). And so it was that the British art for compromise and fair play more or less neutralised the radical socialist legislation, transforming it (in the best traditions of the civil service) into an extra tier of bureaucracy. The relative independence of the Executives made progress on integration difficult, because there was little dialogue, and not much goodwill between the Executives. For example, the bus and road haulage firms owned by the pre-war railway companies had achieved a measure of integration with the railways in the 1930s, but they were handed to the 'competing' Road Transport Executive after nationalisation.

When the dust had settled, the BTC found itself in nominal control of a vast empire. The Railway Executive alone had inherited between 632,000 and 649,000 staff (no-one seemed quite

The Government found very few examples of modern traction in the 'poor bag of assets' it had inherited. Apart from a few shunters and ten year-old railcars, there were very diesels. The LMS prototype D10000 was an imposing (if underpowered) machine, but it didn't start trials until two weeks after nationalisation.

sure of the exact figure), together with 20,000 steam locomotives, 1,223,000 wagons (half of which had been inherited from private owners), 56,000 coaches, 19,414 miles of track... and 7,000 horses. Surprisingly, horse traction outlived many of the steam locomotives, the last animals not being retired until March 1964.

According to the Labour Chancellor, Dr Hugh Dalton, a man renowned for his outspoken and indiscreet manner, the nation had got hold of a "poor bag of assets." This off-the-cuff remark caused widespread resentment within the industry, although there was a certain amount of truth in it. Besides the Southern electrics, a small collection of state-of-the-art express steam locomotives and a handful of diesel railcars, the nation had acquired very little in the way of new technology.

The LNER had produced an electric locomotive for the still-born Manchester to Sheffield electrification project as early as 1939. It gathered dust throughout the war until, in 1947, it was lent to the Dutch railways, presumably to keep it out of the hands of the Railway Executive. The LMS, on the other hand, had put its money on the express diesel locomotive, although it was not until two weeks after nationalisation, on 14th January 1948, that Britain's first main line diesel-electric locomotive began operational trials. D10000 proved underpowered for fast main line duties, but in September 1948 it was joined by a sister locomotive, and the two went on to perform very well as a pair, providing useful feedback that could have been used to good effect, but wasn't.

The BTC had been obliged to acquire a vast assortment of good, bad and indifferent private railway wagons, as private owners would henceforth be banned from the network. Some of these were ancient, as illustrated by the sliding scale of compensation for the private owners, starting at £16 10 shillings for eight-ton wagons built before 1902 – almost half the private wagons qualified! At the other end of the scale, a large modern wagon was valued at £430. Unfortunately, these were few and far between, while the antiquated Victorian variety emerged to be counted from overgrown sidings the length and breadth of the railway system.

Nationalisation also created some extraordinarily difficult legal and financial complications, for it emerged that several ancient railway companies had remained technically independent, thanks to the rather untidy corporate affairs of the railways over the preceding century or so. In total it was found necessary to absorb no fewer than 60 railway companies and 17 canal companies, some of which were inextricably linked with railway concerns.

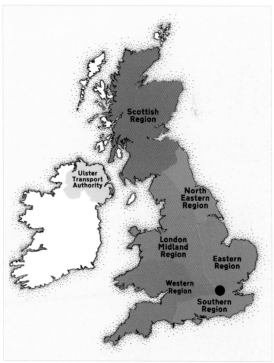

Except for the Scottish Region, the new Regions were based broadly on the territories of the former statutory companies, but where possible 'infiltrating' competing lines were handed to the 'opposition' to tidy up geographical boundaries. Inevitably, this resulted in disinvestment, and for some lines, eventual closure

The Great Railway Conspiracy

A further 28 railways, mostly pitifully unremunerative narrow-gauge lines, were deemed worthless and allowed to escape the net.. However, a few delightfully ramshackle, but equally worthless, Light Railways, such as the Kent & East Sussex, the East Kent, and the Shropshire & Montgomeryshire, were absorbed into the nationalised railway system, together with a handful of little known independents, such as the Easton & Church Hope Railway Company in Dorset, which had been jointly operated by the Southern and Great Western since 1923.

Initially, the railway system was divided into six regions that more or less mirrored the territories of the former private companies:

- **London Midland Region - *largely LMS***
- **Western Region - *largely GWR***
- **Southern Region - *largely SR***
- **Eastern Region - *southern area of the LNER (London to Doncaster)***
- **North Eastern Region - *northern area of the LNER (Doncaster to Berwick)***
- **Scottish Region - *LMS and LNER territory in Scotland***

This rigid adherence to a simple geographical structure looked tidy, but it was to effectively seal the fate of a handful of 'cross border' lines, such as the Somerset & Dorset, and Oxford to Cambridge. Old rivalries die hard, and having fallen into the hands of the 'enemy' after nationalisation, these were largely ignored, receiving little investment or sensible rationalisation, and most were subsequently put up for early closure.

How the Government, in the midst of a desperate financial crisis, paid for all this was another anomaly. Outright purchase of every piece of railway infrastructure from its private owner was out of the question. Instead, it was decided to compensate former railway and canal shareholders by exchanging their shares for a holding in the Transport Commission in the form of British Transport Stock, of which £1,150 million was issued.

Rather than yielding an annual dividend based on trading performance, the Transport Stock would pay a fixed rate of interest for a set period, thus compensating former shareholders from railway income. The nation would, in effect, purchase the assets over a period by paying a small surcharge on transport costs. The value of individual shares was set with regard to the Stock Exchange standing of the various companies on set days in November 1946. Interestingly, the financial state of the Southern, Great Western and London Passenger Transport Board were quite healthy at the time of the take-over, although the others were less buoyant.

The scheme looked like a masterstroke, but it pleased no-one. Former railway share-holders argued, understandably enough, that the railways had been driven into the ground during the war, and with nationalisation a done deal, share prices were depressed, making the market valuation of around £1 billion (for the entire portfolio of railways and canals) artificially low. Others argued that the market value of the companies was relatively high in 1946, because demand for transport was increasing, and there were still restrictions on road transport, making the railway financial position look much rosier than it was. And although the railway shares were valued in relation to a low 2.5% gilt-edged interest rate, the return on Transport Stock was not fixed until later, when rates had risen. As a result, the value of railway assets was fixed far too high, and the burden of interest payable to former shareholders came out at 3%, on stock that was to be redeemed over 40 years.

Fair or not, the valuation was to saddle the railways with a crippling debt in future years, because in lean times – when a private company would have paid little or no dividend – the return on British Transport Stock was guaranteed at a healthy 3%. The Commission was later to claim that a payment of 2% would have been nearer the mark, even in the best trading years, yet the railway was obliged to find around £40 million a year to pay its previous owners, even when it was making substantial losses. The relative value of that £40 million would fall gradually with inflation, but in the first year it equated to a very substantial £4.8 billion in modern terms.

Nationalisation, formulated to take the railway out of capitalist hands, and put it in the ownership of its passengers and employees, had the unfortunate effect of enslaving the network to former shareholders who now received a guaranteed income and were insulated from the vagaries of the stock market, but no longer needed to lift a finger. It would have been much fairer if the interest rate had been allowed to float with the fortunes of the Commission, but no-one seems to have expected the BTC to fail.

Road transport presented more of a problem, being something of a moving target. It would have been impractical to nationalise every delivery van or owner-operated haulage firm, so it was decided to nationalise only those lorries undertaking journeys in excess of 40 miles, which extended more than 25 miles from the vehicle's 'operating centre'. Traders' own vehicles were excluded.

Nearly 3,800 road haulage firms eventually became involved, and the BTC found itself holding all manner of dubious operations. Sometimes the fly-by-night operator flew, leaving the Commission empty-handed. A process that had been accomplished with remarkable speed on the railways dragged on interminably for road transport, and two years later, many companies remained in private hands. This was partly due to the rearguard action by the British Road Federation, and other lobby groups, who fought a long and bitter campaign against nationalisation.

Once the commercial vehicle industry had settled down after the disruption of war, the manufacturers began to produce and market an impressive range of lorries and coaches, most of which would end up competing with the railways one way or another. This is the 1954 Commercial Motor Transport Exhibition. PHOTO: Coventry Transport Museum

The Great Railway Conspiracy

It was not until 1951 that road haulage was finally dragged kicking and screaming into the public domain, and by then the opportunities for integration had largely passed. A unified system of road charges, that would have treated road transport in the same manner as the railways, was never established.

As compensation was fixed at the value of the assets at the time of transfer, implementing the legislation proved an administrative nightmare, and there were plenty of loopholes that enabled shady operators to make a bob or two at the Government's expense. If he wanted to keep his vehicles, he had only to prove that they were used for local deliveries. If he wanted to dispose of a clapped-out lorry, he only needed to send it on a few long-distance jobs in the days before the Ministry inspector arrived to fix the level of compensation.

The winter of 1948 provided the first opportunity for the BTC to manipulate the transport system on a large scale. The previous winter had thrown up the worst blizzards and frosts for several generations, so it was decided to mobilise the forces of the state to guard against a repeat performance. The Commission formed a Winter Executive Committee, which came to the somewhat quixotic conclusion that certain freight flows should be transferred from the railways to the roads for the duration of the winter. In the event, this winter was no worse than average, and when the Commission came to wind up the scheme in March, it proved much harder steering the traffic back to the railways. It was a rather unsatisfactory start to state control as far as the Railway Executive was concerned.

All in all, the railways were in a sorry condition. In March 1948, the Railway Executive completed an appraisal of the system and informed the BTC that arrears of maintenance totalled around £179 million (about £22.9 billion today [1]), taking into account the size of the economy, but finance was short, and nothing was done to alleviate the situation.

The Executive was, however, looking for ways to make worthwhile capital investments, taking advantage of the economies of scale offered by the nationally-owned railway. After holding a number of inter-regional locomotive trials in 1948, it was decided to design and build a range of standard steam engines using the best available technology, to replace the bewildering array that had fallen into public ownership from the old companies.

In April 1948, Sir Cyril Hurcomb of the Transport Commission suggested that the Railway Executive should also investigate other forms of motive power, principally diesel and electric, but such was the inertia engendered by the complex BTC/Railway Executive relationship, that it wasn't until the end of the year that a Railway Motive Power Committee was formed.

Even before the Committee had begun its deliberations, the Executive's Chief Mechanical Engineer R A Riddles was already pressing ahead with the construction of a range of new steam locomotives, and the Executive was busy cancelling experimental diesel designs ordered by the former private railway companies. It was not until 1951 that the Committee reported in favour of the tentative investigation of diesel traction, by which time the Executive was fully committed to steam. It was the wrong decision - the American railroads already had considerable experience with diesels, and the European railways – rebuilding from scratch in many places – were generally going down the electric route.

Much has been written about the failure of the Railway Executive to invest in the right technology at this critical time. The problem stemmed partly from lack of funds: steam engines were well understood, comparatively cheap (diesels costing two to three times as much), and although they were expensive in manpower terms, labour was still relatively cheap in the 1940s. Another dampener on investment came from the restrictive charging structure imposed on the railways. The Executive could see little point in investing in, say, a major electrification project when it would be unable to capitalise on the improved service by raising fares.

Riddles's Standard Class locomotives were elegant and relatively efficient machines, but they were introduced when the Railway Executive should have been investing in diesel and electric traction. This Class 4 2-6-4 was the last steam locomotive to be outshopped from Brighton works in March 1957, after the last 15 of the class had been cancelled. By that time stopping steam-hauled trains were already looking anachronistic... and losing a lot of money. PHOTO: Pat Salmon Collection

In the event, Riddle's standard class steam engines were mostly excellent machines, but their late introduction did nothing to reduce branch line operating costs, and most of them were to be scrapped prematurely following another disastrous policy lurch, little more than a decade later.

New investment was not the only divisive issue in the late 1940s, for it was already clear that a considerable number of lines would need to close as part of the Commission's transport integration policy. Some commentators put the mileage as high as 30%, and within weeks of nationalisation, the first lines were earmarked for closure. In the firing line were the quaint and by this time, semi-derelict Light Railways. Many of these should really have closed a decade earlier, but war and endless reorganisation had kept the railways busy with more pressing affairs. Now, their time had come.

A handful of dedicated enthusiasts set off to explore these remote corners of the network before the Transport Commission could implement a closure programme. Late in 1947, Owen Humberstone Prosser, a young ex-serviceman, discovered a run-down Kent & East Sussex Light Railway:

"We didn't stop at Salehurst, the first halt, the platform at which seemed as much overgrown as is the track along most of the route. We stopped at Junction Road Halt at 11.50 and ten minutes later reached Bodiam, where No.4 shunted for some time with passenger coaches attached. This all had to be done over the level crossing, at which pedestrians and vehicles impatiently waited. I found that the other five people who had come from Robertsbridge had alighted, and for the rest of the journey to Rolvenden I was the only passenger..."

The Great Railway Conspiracy

This sort of thing was pure anachronism to a Transport Commission empowered to integrate and streamline transport. Five passengers could be carried much more cheaply by bus, and without the mixed-traffic shunting, they could be carried more quickly too. It was a situation that couldn't continue for very long, and on 1st May 1949, closure of the equally bucolic East Kent Light Railway was announced, and subsequently implemented under the TUCC procedure, although the Kent & East Sussex survived a little longer. Writing some years later, when closures had become commonplace and much more controversial, the Committee Chairman, Sir Egbert Cadbury, looked back rather wistfully on the process he had unwittingly set in motion:

"I am in favour of closing really derelict lines, but not some of the lines which I think could add to the railways being a little more efficient, and where – by improving the lines rather than, to my mind, using every possible device to make the service uncomfortable and inconvenient to passengers – the public could be encouraged to use them."

The closure of a handful of unremunerative lines did little to satisfy the Transport Commission, which could see its goal of efficient transport integration receding into the next century or beyond. To accelerate the programme, a shadowy Branchline Committee (later the Unremunerative Railway Committee) was established at the behest of Sir Cyril Hurcomb in March 1949. Composed of representatives from the regions, as well as the Railway Executive, the Committee was charged with the unsavoury task of seeking out and destroying uneconomic branch lines, and a team of full-time officers set to work, putting forward a steady stream of closure proposals for loss-making lines, which were generally unopposed.

It was hardly surprising that these early closures met with little opposition, for although some 86 lines had been partially or wholly eradicated by October 1950, many had lost their

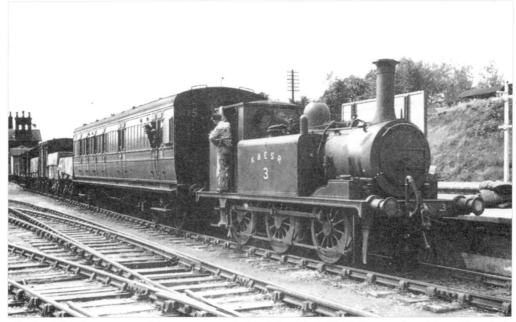

The Kent & East Sussex was one of the more remunerative branch lines inherited by the Transport Commission and it survived until 1954, attracting many enthusiasts in its latter years. The southern section of the line is now gradually being brought back into use as a heritage railway. PHOTO: I L Wright

regular passenger services years earlier, and some had been derelict since before the war. But under the stewardship of the Branchline Committee, the programme began to gather pace, and 152 proposals were put forward for consideration during 1951. In the event, by June of that year the hit list had been revised downwards to 146, and nothing like that number actually closed. Fewer than 100 proposals were formally investigated that year, and the remainder were put aside for consideration at a later date.

The problem with these early closures stemmed not so much from public opposition, but with legal issues, for all manner of legal obligations remained in force from the previous century to hinder the closure process. When, for example, the Branchline Committee investigated the Yealmpton branch in Devon, it discovered that the railway was obliged under a Statute of 1899 to maintain Billacombe station in perpetuity for the convenience of the Duke of Bedford and his heirs. The Committee noted, however, that regular passenger services had been withdrawn some years previously, and the Duke's heirs had failed to object! A similar situation arose at Plodder Lane station in Lancashire, where the BTC discovered that an Act of 1871 empowered the then railway company to maintain the station for the Earl of Bradford. As the Earl had long since expired, the Committee was left with the choice of closing the line and hoping for the best, or instigating an expensive and time-consuming search for his heirs...

In west Wales, a closure proposal brought an objection from a Captain Lewes, who claimed that his grandmother had sold land to the railway company at £25 below the market

The Transport Commission found the Welsh border country overrun with dubious branch lines. Lonely Titley Junction was very typical. The branch to Eardisley had closed in 1940, but services to Presteigne, and the 'main line' to Kington and New Radnor lasted long enough to be nationalised. The Branchline Committee dealt with these lines quite swiftly: New Radnor and Presteigne losing passenger services in 1951, and Kington in 1955. A daily freight rambled on until 1964. PHOTO: B J Ashworth

value, on the provision that she was given a station. Lengthy research proved the claim to be perfectly legitimate, leaving the Railway Executive liable to the tune of £25.

Occasionally, railway passengers took advantage of legal tangles to force the Executive to reinstate a service. A few years later, the authorities innocently withdrew passenger trains between East Grinstead and Lewes, including the stretch that was later to achieve fame as the first standard gauge preserved passenger railway – the Bluebell line. According to one railwayman, it had never been a particularly lucrative operation:

"What they call the Bluebell line? We never done nothing much. Well, we used to take the goods up there and that. It must have made some money or they'd have closed it down, wouldn't they?"

Sensing that even the staff were aware that profitability wasn't what it might have been, they did exactly that, but a wily passenger invoked an Act of 1878 requiring the former London, Brighton & South Coast Railway to run at least four trains per day in perpetuity[2]. The authorities had no choice but to comply, and it took another 18 months, and an Act of Parliament, before the service could be finally laid to rest.

Despite the legal complications, these minor closure proposals were mostly unopposed by the travelling public, for even the most significant affected only a handful of regular passengers. But as the net tightened, and the Branchline Committee looked further afield for candidates, public concern began to mount. As a result, several rather scatter-gun proposals relating to busy branch lines, such as those to Swanage and Hayling Island, met with considerable opposition, and were rapidly shelved. But it was clearly just a matter of time before the Railway Executive found itself in open conflict with rail users.

Elsewhere on the system, a very limited amount of modernisation was talking place. In November 1949 the Minister of Transport, the Rt Hon Alfred Barnes, officially opened the electrification scheme between Liverpool Street and Shenfield, instigated by the LNER before the war. The project

The Yealmpton branch had succumbed to bus competition in the 1930s. It reopening again during the war to carry night-shelterers away from the bombing of Plymouth, but passenger services ceased for good in 1947 just prior to nationalisation, leaving the BTC to tidy up the legal niceties. Freight survived until the 1960s.

proved an immediate success, boosting passenger figures by almost 50%, a figure than one hopes was made known to the Motive Power Committee, still considering the ins and outs of modern traction at 222 Marylebone Road.

Far away, in the corridors of power, the winds of political change were beginning to blow. In November 1949 it was revealed that the Labour Party, unnerved by public criticism of the nationalisation schemes, was busy diluting socialism for the forthcoming election campaign. The results of the BTC's first trading year did nothing to assist the embattled administration, the Commission returning a trading loss of some £4.7 million. And in January 1950 it was announced in the House of Commons that the railways were to return a loss of around £20 million. Sure enough, despite increasing its share of the vote, Labour's majority of 166 seats was demolished at the general election the following month, leaving the party hanging onto power by a thread, with a majority of just six seats. It was really the end of the socialist experiment, for the reduced majority had left the Government effectively powerless.

Meanwhile, the Transport Commission was still engaged in the unequal task of implementing the 1947 Transport Act and, as late as 1950, it still believed the elusive goal of full integration might be realisable:

"The Road Haulage Executive will employ the Railway Executive's rail services for direct trunk haulage of long-distance 'smalls' and wagon-load traffic where the Railway Executive can make available suitable terminal accommodation, containers and train services. The Railway Executive will employ the Road Haulage Executive's road services for trunk haulage of cross-country traffic and wherever use of road transport will reduce staging and transit time, and facilitate rail movement of direct train loads between main centres... Where branch lines are wholly or partially closed to freight traffic, the Road Haulage Executive will provide an alternative service where this can be justified."

It was now clear that the BTC had decided to withdraw many railway services. Steam-hauled branch line trains were horrendously expensive to work, and to a Commission which also controlled a network of fast, modern and economical road buses, the answer seemed clear-cut. Thus, while the Motive Power Committee continued its long deliberations on the subject of cost-effective haulage, the Branchline Committee was spurred on to renewed efforts in weeding out and disposing of the uneconomic services. The process generated little enthusiasm at the Railway Executive, where most staff were understandably loath to see even the smallest traffic flows handed to the opposition. There was, of course, an answer to their dilemma, and it had been operating on the Great Western, and then the Western Region for almost 20 years by this time.

As we have seen, the GWR had begun to introduce railcars from the mid-1930s. It was not a unique idea. Many railways abroad had discovered railcars were cheaper to run than steam-hauled trains, and the County Donegal Railways (Joint Committee) in Ireland was about to bestow honorary retirement on its first lightweight diesel railcar, or 'railbus', introduced back in 1931.

The County Donegal had been a world pioneer in the railbus field. Like many other Irish narrow gauge lines, this one served a sparsely-populated area, but when the economics of steam traction began to look impractical, it had decided against transferring traffic onto the roads, and bring the bus to the rails instead. As early as 1926, the County Donegal's Traffic Superintendent had outlined ideas that were to prove revolutionary:

"My idea would be to get an engine of the Ford lorry type, easily driven, and have it built into a chassis at Stranorlar by our own men, with a very light body, preferably aluminium, and fitted with comfortably upholstered seats, as in a bus, attractively painted in artistic colours inside and out, one class only.

One man only to be employed: the driver would also issue tickets at halts and collect them from passengers alighting, and would also be required to assist in handling mail, papers and parcels at stations.

I have figured out that we could almost pay for the car (the cost alone not exceeding £300) in one year by the saving effected in fuel alone, apart altogether from the reduction in wages."

In the event, the railway adapted a couple of secondhand petrol road buses, and it was soon in a position to implement its railbus policy. Where steam had cost as much as 11³/4d (nearly 5p) per mile, it was found that the railbus could operate for just 3³/4d (about 1¹/2p) per mile, and the saving was sufficient to produce a small profit from previously uneconomic services. The little railbuses were soon running 2,400 miles a month, but on 19th November 1926, disaster struck, as perhaps it could strike only in Ireland:

"As the 12.10pm bus from Stranorlar was running from Ballinamore to Fintown, and on a level part of the road, about a quarter-mile from the former station, while travelling at a moderate speed, the driver heard a loud crack, applied his brake, and immediately after, the right-hand front wheel flew off and ran down the slight embankment at the place into the bog below..."

A month later, the other vehicle was similarly struck, when "both wheels flew off", but repairs were soon made, and the policy of substituting railbuses for steam-hauled trains carried on. In 1931, the company introduced one of the first diesel railbuses, and three years later, introduced an updated type that could seat about 40 passengers in comfort, and was fast, reliable and economical to operate. By 1941, this small Irish company was running half as many railbuses as the entire British railway system. County Donegal had proved that railbuses were suitable for the least remunerative lines, and developments elsewhere were indicating that bigger, multi-car machines, known as diesel multiple units, were capable of handling heavier traffic, and even relatively fast services, with great economy.

By 1950, diesel multiple units were appearing all over the world, except of course, in Britain. The machines were usually powered by one or more road bus engines mounted under the floor, and the individual cars could be coupled together

The County Donegal may not have been the first railway to introduce diesel (initially petrol) railbuses, but it was an early pioneer. This is No.2, converted at Stranorlar in 1926 from a petrol bus. Despite teething troubles, the vehicles proved very cost-effective

to produce 'units' of two, three, six or more vehicles. In most cases, every car was powered, but there were many variations of powered and trailer cars. With a driving cab at each end, the multiple units were particularly well suited to branch line operation, where they could arrive, disgorge passengers, and accelerate away in search of fresh revenue in just a few minutes. For the operator, they were flexible, and cheaper to run and maintain than steam, while for the passenger they were more comfortable and cleaner than steam-hauled trains, and faster than buses. By 1950, several British manufacturers were producing multiple units, but only for export, as they had yet to make an appearance on British railways.

In June 1950, a number of three-car multiple units had been introduced on the Great Northern Railway in Ireland, to operate the main line services between Belfast and Dublin. So successful was this experiment that by October, multiple units and single railcars were operating a quarter of all the services in Northern Ireland. In Britain, the Railway Executive found itself in the unusual position of condemning steam traction while continuing to invest in it, and according to Sir Eustace Missenden, there was no future at all for the branch lines:

"In the next 30 years many unremunerative lines and the smaller intermediate stations will be closed; time interval services will operate where possible; and a cleaner more up-to-date service must be provided if the railways are to survive...

The steam locomotive has served the world faithfully, but with the march of progress it has been dethroned from its pedestal of public esteem... except in the eyes of enthusiasts. Smoke, steam, dirt and smells... once the symbol of power... are now hurled at us as evidence of a failure to modernise and of the approaching end of the railway era."

By the 1950s the County Donegal was operating a whole fleet of relatively modern machines. In 1958, No. 19, travelling from Killibegs with a mixed traffic train, passes No. 14 at Inver. After the line closed, Nos. 19 and 20 were sold to the Isle of Man Railway where they found various uses until withdrawn in the 1990s. They will now, hopefully, be restored. PHOTO: Owen Prosser

The Great Railway Conspiracy

Meanwhile, the railway press was viewing the situation with mounting concern, as summed up by the *Railway Magazine* in March 1950:

"[Comparison of] the recovery of several Continental railways from the effect of the war has often been made with that made in this country... It is a constant source of dissatisfaction that countries like France and Greece, whose railways suffered terrible devastation, should have made such a success of their rehabilitation schemes, whereas the future of Britain's railways is obscure...

The praiseworthy experiment now being carried out on the Hetton-Sunderland branch line of competing with the buses in fares and service, could surely be extended by the conversion of many such branches to light railway working..."

Of course, the Transport Commission, as both a railway and bus operator, had mixed feelings about such experiments and was understandably lacking in enthusiasm. In that same month the Western Region took delivery of one of the first of the new standard steam locomotives, an 0-6-0 tank engine which would replace similar models dating from 1875-1905. It was a delight to steam enthusiasts, being outwardly much the same as its predecessors, and far from the cutting edge of technology. It was presumably just the sort of dirty, smelly machine that the Railway Executive Chairman wanted to see eradicated. By the end of 1951, his Executive had introduced six out of 12 standard steam locomotives, although some minor services were suspended that year for a lack of suitable coal.

A handful of independent observers were aware of the gravity of the situation, and notable among them was a gentleman of Dutch extraction, a certain Professor E R Hondelink, M.Sc, M.I.C.E., M.Inst.T. Born in The Netherlands in 1890, the Professor later adopted British citizenship and established a formidable reputation in transport circles. Before the Second World War he worked in an advisory capacity for railways across the globe, gaining vital experience in China, Japan, New Zealand, The Netherlands, Britain and many other countries. As the Allied armies advanced across Europe in 1944-45, Professor Hondelink's job was to restore railway services in their wake, a difficult and exacting task that progressed remarkably smoothly under the circumstances, giving a major boost to the war effort.

After the cessation of hostilities, Hondelink became a senior transport and communications consultant to the United Nations and the World Bank, a position he was to hold for many years. Despite this return to his pre-war globe-trotting existence, the Professor kept a close eye on railway matters in his adopted country, noting with alarm the increasing bureaucracy of the BTC.

Hondelink was not particularly enthralled by the nationalisation process – not for political reasons, for he had worked under most systems of government in his long career – but because of the overwhelmingly top-heavy administration it had created. He was also very critical of the strange BTC/Railway Executive relationship, which appeared to have generated no fewer than 13 tiers of management (some pulling in opposite directions), when according to the Professor, five would have been more than adequate. On the 1947 Transport Act, he was forthright in his opinions, claiming with some justification, that the legislation was "...conceived and passed in the greatest hurry; no time at all was taken to study and digest lessons which other world systems could have taught us."

In short, bureaucracy was strangling the BTC, and the push towards centralisation and standardisation was achieving nothing and wasting a great deal. The BTC had inherited 400-odd classes of steam locomotive and dealt with the problem by introducing another 12 standard classes. The result, for a while at least, was 412 classes, and as the Professor pointed out with unerring foresight, the whole lot would soon be scrapped and replaced by a multiplicity of hastily introduced diesels.

There was plenty of evidence to back up Hondelink's views at the time. The number of administrative staff employed by the BTC – although commendably low in the early days – had almost doubled by 1950, and headquarters expenses had risen to £14.5 million, increasing to £18.5 million the following year, which doesn't sound much, but equates to about £1.32 billion in labour costs today... a massive bureaucracy. As the Professor attempted to explain, in a sentence almost as long as the railway chain of command, the administration of the railways was in a hopeless tangle:

"The Railway Executive can be abolished completely. An executive board of members who individually exercise executive functions, yet must submit to collective responsibilities and permanent consultations, plus regional officers whose authority and responsibility are seriously reduced, plus dual responsibility of the region's chief officers (to their regional chief and executive member); this is a system which, wherever tried, has always proved inefficient."

Such pronouncements did nothing to endear Hondelink to the Government, although by 1950 it was becoming clear that Churchill might well return to power, and the professor cannily switched his lobbying efforts to the Conservatives.

In the summer of 1951, the Branchline Committee discovered the Isle of Wight. The real problem for the island's railways was not so much a lack of traffic, but a marked imbalance between the summer and winter trade. The Isle of Wight was a popular holiday destination, and

For the Railway Executive, the Isle of Wight was a particular problem - the loading gauge was limited, so trains were unusually small, and the railway had to deal with a huge influx of business for just a few weeks in the summer, and very little at other times. The busiest stretch of all was Ryde Pier, from whence the railway carried visitors to every corner of the Island. In the early 1960s, one of the Island's delightful little tank engines 'Merstone' hauls a train from the pierhead. PHOTO: Christian Hewison

being relatively small, with excellent rail and bus links, many visitors came by train. In the summer of 1945 for example, some 982,000 tickets were issued on the island, but no fewer than 1,830,000 were collected, suggesting that a large proportion of visitors had begun their journey on the mainland. Despite this influx, the island railway network was losing money on a year-round basis, and the Branchline Committee, flexing its muscles for the first time, concluded that the whole lot could be closed with relative ease. But in choosing to fight on this particular landing ground, the Committee had made a serious strategic error.

The busy holiday line from Ryde Pier Head to Sandown was carrying almost 4,000 passengers *an hour* on summer Saturdays, as ferries disgorged passengers onto a continuous stream of trains onward to holiday destinations. The protesters had soon calculated that without the railway, no fewer than 62 buses an hour would be needed from the pier head to Shanklin and Sandown. Theoretically possible on near empty roads, but a practical and strategic nightmare in reality. According to a prophetic letter from a Mr R F Hathaway, published in *Railways* magazine, the island closure scheme was the precursor to something far more sinister than simple rationalisation:

"... the island closure schemes are but the thin end of the wedge for even bigger things; there are those who stand to gain financially in countries which have 'passed out of the railway age'."

In the event, the Railway Executive backed down, and the Branchline Committee was sent in search of easier candidates. Whether sinister forces really were at work is hard to tell. There was certainly nothing sinister about the behaviour of the Executive, which didn't seem able to develop a coherent policy, let alone make back-room deals with other operators to share out the proceeds from railway closures. The Transport Commission certainly had interests in buses and lorries, but it was bound by the sometimes contradictory requirements of the 1947 Transport Act, and trying to do the right thing by way of transport integration. The Labour Government was almost moribund by this time, and more or less viewing developments from the sidelines. There were many who stood to make fortunes on the fall of the railways, but they were not, for the time being, in positions of any real power.

In 1951, the railway's biggest problem was the awesome size and complexity of its own bureaucracy, including the plethora of committees, some duplicating each other's work, while others pulled in opposite directions. In October 1951, after considering the matter for more than three years, the Motive Power Committee finally produced a report: diesels were very suitable for shunting duties, express diesel locomotives should be tentatively explored, and diesel multiple units were worthy of further study for the branches! After a gestation of three years, the Committee had simply reiterated what everyone had known five years earlier, but the decision to explore multiple units was welcome, although predictably it resulted in the establishment of a Lightweight Trains Committee to consider the matter further.

After four years of nationalisation, the Holy Grail of road/rail integration remained as elusive as ever. The high hopes of the 1947 Act were never to be realised, in part because the individual Executives were increasingly concerning themselves with their own schemes and ideas, but also as a direct result of the BTC's failure to take control of long-distance road haulage, the acquisition of which was not full realised until 1951, by which time the opportunity was lost.

On 26th October 1951, an elderly Winston Churchill returned to power, vowing to free his country from the shackles of socialism. He was not exactly in a position to do much about it at first, because the Conservatives had won with a wafer-thin majority of only 17. As the last ballot papers were counted, and the Tories slipped into power, Churchill announced: "We've won... I have the reins of the country in my hands again. But we're in a bloody mess."

3
The Net Closes
1951-1954

"Almost from the beginning of the working of these nationalised industries, we have heard profound dissatisfaction expressed at the way they render their accounts. We hear from commercial industries that if they
rendered their accounts in the same manner as the nationalised industries, they would find themselves in gaol."

Sir Peter Macdonald, MP for the Isle of Wight

"No-one could claim that the closing of one small branch line was a matter of public interest in the wider
sense of the word, but the closure of a whole group of branch lines is at once a matter of public interest."

Hon. John Maclay, National Liberal & Conservative MP for Renfrewshire West. Hansard, February 1954

*By the 1950s and '60s, most British railway branch lines were in desperate need of modernisation. An
Edwardian-vintage Class M7 tank engine arrives at Wareham with a Swanage branch train in October 1963.
A magnificent machine, of which tragically only two were preserved (one, incidentally, at Swanage), but a
costly anachronistic relic in the swinging sixties. PHOTO: Patrick Henshaw*

With the return of Winston Churchill and a Conservative administration, most integration plans were
halted and steps taken to amend the 1947 Transport Act. But it was thought that the transfer of
heavy industries back into private ownership was impractical, and work began on a compromise that
could be enshrined in a new Transport Act. The Conservatives were clear on three points: the integrated
transport system was dead; the BTC was unlikely to survive in its present form; and the road haulage
companies would be denationalised as soon as possible.

Overnight, the BTC's development schemes were put on hold, but such was the inertia within
the Commission that little actually changed on the ground, and integration policies continued to be
implemented: minor railways would be closed and handed to road transport, and trunk haulage of
passengers and freight steered towards the railways, although it was clear that the two modes would

soon be operating in competition. Adding fuel to the conflict, the Railway Executive began tentative experiments with the diesel multiple units on the branch lines, in competition with BTC road buses.

Meanwhile, the Branchline Committee was widening the closure net, and introducing underhand methods to achieve its targets, putting it in conflict with a fledgling protest movement. As we have seen on the Isle of Wight the pro-rail movement successfully questioned the railway authority's financial assumptions. It was a decisive moral victory, but the Isle of Wight did nothing to reverse the attitude of the CTCC, which continued to recommend closure in almost every case it considered.

In October 1953, the Conservatives introduced their long-awaited transport legislation. Only road haulage was to be denationalised (the term 'privatisation' was known, but not in general use), while other transport operations would remain in public ownership. The Railway Executive was abolished, and steps taken to delegate power down to the regions, but the BTC was effectively still in control of the the railways and was to grow into a vast and bureaucratic organisation. Disturbingly, relatively few railwaymen ended up in the higher echelons, with only two at Board level, out of 15 members.

The branch line closure policy was pushed forward with some determination, but the pro-rail movement began to fight back, using increasingly sophisticated techniques, and the diesel multiple unit experiments did cause a slight drop in the rate of closures. In 1954, the BTC announced a massive modernisation programme that promised at last, to fund branch line modernisation.

The change in government illustrated a problem that would plague the railways in the coming decades. They would no doubt have thrived under a planned socialist economy, and they might have gone on to thrive – albeit in a different form – under a stable Conservative administration. But they would have neither in the postwar period, as the political pendulum swung back and forth. What they really needed in the 1950s and '60s was a period of stability, of whatever political colour.

The Labour Government had run out of time on the policy of transport integration, and with no concrete results, the whole experiment becoming seen as pointless ideological meddling, and a waste of precious time, when the railways needed investment in modern equipment. There were even grumbles that Labour had a vested interest *against* modernisation, as an early end to steam traction would have reduced the demand for coal, at a time when the nationalised coal industry was in financial difficulties. Modernisation was bound to mean a reduction in manpower too, which was hardly in the best interests of a party whose grass roots lay in the trade union movement.

The railway had become a political pawn, its affairs increasingly being debated in the House of Commons. This was no part of the Labour or Conservative game plans, but inevitably, each side blamed the other for interfering. According to Alan Lennox-Boyd, the incoming Conservative Minister of Transport, managers should be free to manage: "I do not think anybody would think it was a good idea for the Minister to assume day-to-day responsibility for the running of the railways." Clearly, it was not a good idea, but the railway's dirty linen continued to be aired in public, to the commercial advantage of the soon-to-be-privatised road haulage operators.

To those seeking to prevent railway closures, it didn't look as though much would change. As early as December 1950, Owen Prosser (who we left exploring the Kent & East Sussex railway) had reached the conclusion that a national lobby group should be formed to fight key railway closures. The only militant pro-rail body at that time was The Light Railway Transport League, and its journal *The Modern Tramway* was more than willing to publish a manifesto in December 1950.

A German railbus at Niendorf in 1958, typical of those investigated by the Lightweight Trains Committee. PHOTO: A R Spencer

Following Mr Prosser's article, affirmations of support were received from various quarters, most notably from Robert Aickman, founder of the Inland Waterways Association, who had been performing much the same rearguard action on the canals and waterways. The following year the two men were ready to hold a public meeting, and this was duly arranged for 16th November 1951, at the Fred Tallant Hall in central London.

Prosser and Aickman addressed the audience on the seriousness of the situation, and from those present was born the Railway Development Association, later the Railway Development Society, rebranded in the modern era as Railfuture. The raison d'etre of the group was to fight the BTC's policy of closing lines which might have proved viable with the application of diesel railbuses or multiple units, and other sensible operating economies. Even as late as 1951, the BTC was designing and building steam push-pull units that were slow, dirty and expensive to operate. Equipment of this kind was being delivered to the lightly-loaded branch lines that were most in need of economical modern equipment, and most at threat from comfortable, modern road buses.

Progress on modernisation had been slow, but the wheels were gradually turning. After publication of the Motive Power Committee's report in October 1951, the bureaucratic Commission had established a Lightweight Trains Committee. Its first stop was in the West Country, as the former Great Western Railway had by far the greatest operating experience with railcars in the UK, having introduced 30 single-car units between 1933 and 1941, plus a handful of bigger multiple units. As there had been no significant advance in Britain since, the Committee decided to extend its investigations to the near Continent as well.

Experiments in Germany and France had proved conclusively that modern railcars were able to fight off road competition. By 1939, the Germans had introduced 850 diesel units, and with characteristic precision, the German managers gave a simple reply to the BTC representatives: "The units have enabled unremunerative services on branch lines to be operated at a profit."

In terms of traffic density, Germany was similar to the UK, but in France – a big country with widely dispersed rural population – the branch line problem was much more acute. Nevertheless, the French had taken to diesel railcars with some enthusiasm, and been impressed with the results. The Annemasse to Geneva was a largely urban line on the French/Swiss border, plagued, like many branch lines, by road competition. After conversion to diesel multiple unit operation in 1949, the line experiencing an impressive increase in passenger income, with receipts at Annemasse increasing from a paltry 19,000F to 126,000F in a single year. Thanks to this turnaround, the line survived and thrived, to such an extent that by 2017 it will have been completely reconstructed and extended to create a through route.

In more rural areas, branch line income was never going to amount to much, but the French had been introducing railcars since 1933, and had a body of data to prove that the vehicles were 30% to 75% cheaper to operate than steam trains on a seat-for-seat basis, and much more popular with the travelling public. By 1952, SNCF had introduced 720 railcars, from tiny single-car units to powerful multiple units intended for long-distance express services. All were considerably more economical than their steam equivalents. Using a steam-hauled French express train as a yardstick, the Lightweight Train Committee's inquiries yielded the following figures:

Relative cost per mile

French steam-hauled express train	100
French steam-hauled stopping train	76
GWR steam-hauled stopping train	66-87
GWR 420hp DMU (four-car)	42
GWR 420hp DMU (three-car)	41
French 600hp express DMU (two-car)	35
GWR 210hp DMU (two-car)	24-28
French 150hp railbus (single car)	16

Thanks in part to the overwhelmingly positive evidence from France and elsewhere, the Committee finally came down enthusiastically in favour of modern traction, producing a glowing report in March 1952. Here, at long last, was official confirmation that steam railcars and push-pull units were officially off the agenda.

AEC (trading at the time as ACV), had used its pre-war railcar experience to build the PUP multiple unit in 1948. This was a clever design featuring two types of vehicle: a single powered railcar with a cab at either end, and an unpowered trailer unit. They could thus be operated alone, or as a two- or three-car unit. Both types were lightweight two-axle machines along the lines of the German and French railbuses, and the three-car set had an impressive 129 seating capacity.

Presumably the concept was gently sold to the Railway Executive, because with the gradual move away from previous 'bustitution' policies, the PUP came to be regarded as a joint venture project. The prototype must have been reasonably successful, because the Railway Executive bought several more in the mid-1950s for "marginal or uneconomic services".

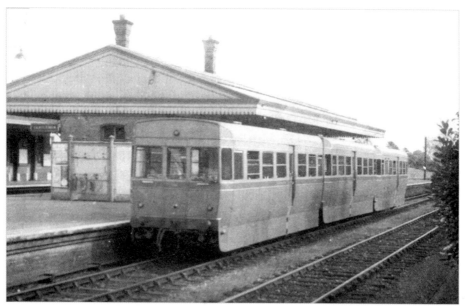

Having built the GWR's railcars in the 1930s, AEC was a suitable partner to produce the experimental ACV PUP lightweight railcar, pictured here at Henley-in-Arden. PHOTO: S H Keyse

In many ways, this machine proved to be the 'missing link' between pre-war designs and the classic diesel multiple units that later emerged. The Lightweight Trains Committee commented that, "there might be scope for the use of lightweight railcars, possibly of the four-wheel type", but the diesel multiple units were bigger, heavier, more conventional twin-bogie machines. Sadly, the ACV units were all scrapped in the early 1960s.

The change of policy had come very late in the day because even busy urban lines were losing traffic to the roads at a frightening rate. The Birmingham to Walsall line, for instance, had experienced a 78% loss of traffic between 1939 and 1950, and there were many similar examples. Through modern eyes, this haemorrhage of passengers to buses seems unaccount-able, but we have to look back to an era when trains were slow and irregular, and traffic congestion had yet to become a serious issue on the roads. Today, the train from Walsall to central Birmingham takes about 23 minutes, and the 'express' bus takes 41 minutes. In the 1950s, both would have taken about an hour.

For the BTC, the priority was to choose suitable areas to test the new diesel units, and the Lightweight Trains Committee came up with three schemes. The first would be in Lincolnshire, taking in Grimsby, Skegness, Boston and Retford. Most of these lines were very busy in the summer, but it was a huge, sparsely populated area, and winter traffic was losing a lot of money. Thirteen two-car units would be allocated to Lincolnshire at a cost of £325,000, displacing 11 steam locomotives and 38 coaches, giving a potential saving of £121,000 a year.

The second multiple unit trial would take place in urban Yorkshire, between Halifax, Bradford and Leeds. The requirement here was for eight two-car units at a cost of £200,000, with estimated savings of £25,000 a year, and – perhaps more importantly – new traffic worth an estimated £31,000. Clearly, there was suppressed demand for rail services in big urban conurbations, but no-one yet knew how much.

The biggest trial of all, and – with respect to the prospects for lightly used branch lines,

The London Midland region made good use of their new rail cars, running 'land cruises' into the Lakes. On 31st July 1955, the inaugural John Peel Land Cruise made up of 3 x two-car Derby Lightweight units takes the tablet at Bare Lane. These popular trains started in Blackpool and ran via Morcombe to give three hours in Keswick. PHOTO: Cumbrian Railways Association Collection

the most interesting – was to be in the Lake District, where 13 two-car units, two three-car units and ten four-car units would be allocated. The cost was £915,000 (some £91 million today), but the savings were estimated at £99,000 a year, with the more conceptual figure for increased income put at £34,000. If this was achieved, the return on the investment would be very good.

As more diesels became available, other trials were proposed for Bristol, West Hampshire and the Waverley route between Edinburgh and Carlisle. The first two were quite compact urban areas, but the Waverley was almost exactly 100 miles long, and like Lincolnshire it had a large but thinly spread population. The projections suggested a 25% traffic increase on the Waverley route, plus the usual substantial reduction in operating costs, and in Hampshire, 13 diesels would replace eight steam locomotives and more than 100 coaches. In most of the trials, the aim seems to have been to operate a more intensive service in the places where more revenue could be extracted.

All was not to proceed smoothly. After protracted negotiations with the trade unions, it was finally agreed that the new machines could operate without a 'fireman' in the cab, provided no shunting was involved. The trade unions were, of course, fighting to keep men employed, but they seem not to have taken on board that the very future of many rail services depended on the cost savings that could be identified by these experiments. There were organisational difficulties too. The Lightweight Trains Committee had failed to give much thought to the fact that rival road services (especially in Lincolnshire) were operated by its parent company the British Transport Commission. According to the Committee, now openly enthusiastic about the prospects of what we might now call regional rail services, "Road services in [the Lincolnshire trial] do not show any great advantages over the railway in either speed or frequency, and on some routes are decidedly inferior." This was the sort of fighting talk the railways needed, but their masters at the BTC had still failed to absorb the implications of the change of government, and ruled that the trial would be a threat to the policy of transport integration. The Lincolnshire scheme was consequently vetoed, on the premise that it would damage the profitability of Lincolnshire Road Car, the local bus operator. The Lightweight Trains Committee wasted no time in organising an East Anglian trial instead, but the affair serves to illustrate how vulnerable rural railways were at this time. The Railway Executive was only charged with the task of operating railways, and not of attracting new traffic to rail – certainly not where the BTC operated rival buses, and considered them more appropriate.

By this stage, with transport integration dead in the water, and a degree of commercial freedom just around the corner, a war of attrition seems to have developed. The Executive was dragging its feet on railway closures, and the BTC was unwilling to release investment to make the rural railways more profitable. There must also have been conflicts within the Railway Executive itself, because the work of the Lightweight Trains Committee was often contradictory to that of the Branchline Committee, whose primary role was to seek out and close unremunerative services.

Whatever the political tensions, the report on diesel multiple unit experiments could not be ignored forever, and after a painfully drawn out eight-month delay, the Commission agreed to the amended trials, and manufacture of the diesels began in November 1952. They were not the first diesel multiple units, of course, as the Western Region had inherited a handful of GWR machines, and an experimental lightweight unit of three four-wheeled carriages, known as the ACV set, had been introduced into revenue-earning service around Birmingham early in 1952. But it had taken seven years since the end of the war for even limited manufacture to commence.

As the newly-formed Railway Development Association suspected, the BTC had been putting pressure on the Railway Executive to prepare a programme of cuts. What the Association didn't know was that the cuts were to run far beyond the branch lines, as the Commission was already pressing for closure of less remunerative secondary lines, once the first round of branch lines was out of the way. The hapless Executive seems to have dealt with the problem by paying lip-service to its masters, and processing the Branchline Committees closure proposals as slowly and clumsily as it could. In December 1950, the Commission had sent a stiffly worded letter to the Railway Executive in an effort to speed up the closure process:

"It is hoped that the remaining investigations will be pressed forward as quickly as possible... The Commission wish to receive a report setting out shortly the reasons in each case which have led the Executive to decide that certain branches, which have been considered for closing, should be kept open. The Commission will also be grateful if you will now furnish the report on the Scottish lines...

...it is felt that the total effect of the closings already achieved or in prospect... will not amount to the 'streamlining' of the railway system which has been described as the main objective."

The Executive was playing for time. The new Conservative Government was making it clear that transport would see some major upheavals, and the Executive – while prepared to lop off a few branch lines – was understandably loath to hand serious traffic to BTC-owned bus companies that could be back in private hands in a matter of months. Incredibly, it was not until 24th September the following year that the Transport Commission got a reply:

"...many schemes are now delayed owing to their having to go to the Area TUCCs... in some cases such delay is up to six months... the Commission will realise that there are likely to be great difficulties in closing down many of the more important secondary lines. Some of them (such as the Dingwall to Kyle of Lochalsh and Fort William to Mallaig lines) are the only railways in large geographical areas. Such secondary lines represent national, social and economic obligations which the Executive can see no means of escaping...

There is a further important point to be borne in mind in considering the closing of these lines. Since 1948, decisions to close branch lines have had regard to the fact that the Commission own or have a financial interest in many of the road passenger and freight services of the country. This not only means that much of the traffic diverted from rail is automatically picked up by existing road services of the Commission, but that the comparative ease with which alternative facilities can be provided is a powerful factor in counteracting opposition... Much, if not all, of this co-operation with road services might disappear if the Transport Bill goes through... in its present form."
A J Pearson of the Railway Executive

By this time the Government had published a White Paper outlining the proposals that would soon be enshrined in the 1953 Transport Act. The shock news was that it was the Executive that would probably be eradicated, and not the Commission. Once again, the whole pyramid of command was thrown into confusion. The BTC began finally to wind-down transport integration, and consider itself primarily as a train operator, while at the Executive, plans for both modernisation and rationalisation were suspended.

Meanwhile, the Government was showing itself to be closely aligned with the private road haulage lobby groups. According to *The Times*, a newspaper that could hardly be accused of harbouring left-wing sympathies, the road hauliers were attempting, "to secure political favour at the expense of all serious consideration of transport economics and organisation." The road lobby had suffered grievously under the socialist administration and it had fought hard to bring the Conservatives to power. This finally, was pay-back time, and the organisations were demanding such things as higher lorry speed limits, motorways and the denationalisation of road haulage.

Backed up by an increasingly road-friendly Ministry of Transport, the Government agreed to every demand. This should have set alarm bells ringing at the BTC, but the Commission remained stubbornly complacent, thanks in part to better trading figures from the Railway Executive, which had made a £26 million profit in 1950, rising to a healthy £40 million in 1952.

Masked by the figures was the inescapable fact that the railway system was decades behind with investment, services being broadly the same as they had been 30 years before. By June 1952, the situation had become so serious in the Midlands that the Birmingham Junior Chamber of Commerce set up an inquiry. The report, published in February 1953, made sobering reading, and resulted in the West Midlands Railway Passenger Transport Scheme, an ambitious project to reopen railways and stations throughout the Birmingham area. No fewer than 56 new or reopened stations were envisaged, based around an intensive diesel multiple unit operation:

"Experience in other areas shows that track electrification where introduced has resulted in a considerable increase in traffic and there is every reason to suppose that the introduction of diesel traction within a network of comprehensive local services would have similar beneficial results... The mind of the public is so firmly made up in favour of road transport for local travel, that mere palliatives would not result in any substantial change-over to railway travel... a complete change of outlook by the railway authorities can produce the desired results..."

The Chamber of Commerce had certainly done its homework, for the report noted that the Railway Executive's three-car ACV PUP was undergoing trials between Marylebone and Princes Risborough. It was exactly the sort of thing they wanted for Birmingham, but the Executive, although interested in the report, was hamstrung by its own impending doom, its fractured relationship with the BTC and severe capital constraints. Nor did it have the authority to act, or come to that any desire to get involved.

Far from taking the initiative on railway investment schemes, the hapless Executive was about to be vilified for implementing the closure policies passed down by the BTC. Early in 1953, a year that saw introduction of the Elizabethan, a steam-hauled crack express that achieved a post-war record speed between London and Edinburgh (but failed to outpace the pre-war Coronation Scot), the branch line closure policy finally came to a head.

The Branchline Committee had been back to the Isle of Wight, and reached the same conclusion as two years earlier: the entire network was unremunerative and should be disposed of. The trains were hauled by steam, primarily delightful little tank locomotives dating back to the 1890s. Because of unusually constricted tunnels, these little engines were hard to replace, and there were no plans for diesel multiple units on the island, which would have required a special non-standard class. So the railways were expensive to run, and there was no immediate prospect of economical, passenger-friendly diesel units making an appearance. On the other hand, they did have an enthusiastic and vociferous following.

By this time, the railway authorities had learnt to be economical with the *actualité*. The initial closure proposal would cover only the weakest lines, leaving the rest to be picked off at a later stage as they began to wilt with a loss of contributory revenue. The anachronistic branch from Merstone Junction to Ventnor West had slipped quietly away the previous year, but in May 1953, the Executive put forward a proposal to close another 24 miles out of a total of over 50.

The public announcement generated an uproar, in part because the island had an immaculate and delightful railway network, but primarily because some parts of it were very busy, and the Railway Executive was claiming losses of no less than £271,000 a year – a little over £24 million today. The Brading to Bembridge branch, and the major lines from Newport to Sandown and Newport to Freshwater would be closed, saving an estimated £90,000 a year, or £8 million at 2012 prices. The stated loss sounded unlikely, and in fact could only make sense if the trains were running empty for most of the year, which patently wasn't the case.

The Railway Development Association soon became involved, in what was to become its first high-profile campaign. It was convinced that the Executive had started 'cooking the books', to provide false figures to TUCC inquiries so as to smooth the flow of closures, and was determined to force a public debate on the issue. The result was a headlong confrontation between the Executive and the protesters which culminated in the most celebrated closure inquiry of the 1950s that came to be known as The Great Isle of Wight Train Robbery, spawning a book of the same name by R E Burroughs.

Edward Kenworthy, treasurer of the Association's Midland Area, set to work in consultation with F W Bright of the Newport Chamber of Commerce to analyse the claimed losses, while the Isle of Wight County Council engaged a distinguished barrister, Melford Stevenson QC, to fight its corner. (Mr Stevenson was later to become known for defending Ruth Ellis, the last woman to hang in Great Britain.) It was an unlikely alliance – a rail advocacy group from the Midlands, a top barrister and a County Council – but it worked.

At the TUCC hearing, Melford Stevenson argued that the objectors would be unable to present a proper case without access to all the facts. How could they debate the issue if they did not have before them an analysis of the losses as claimed by the Executive? Perhaps naively, the South Eastern Area TUCC agreed, and the inquiry was adjourned until June 1953 to give the Executive time to produce the relevant figures.

No-one was more surprised than the protesters at this turn of events, but when the inquiry reconvened in London on 20th June, the revelations would put in question the integrity of the whole BTC organisation. Back on the Isle of Wight, the Council engaged an expert witness, one Stanley Hill, an accountant involved in railway nationalisation. His investigation was to yield some interesting results, for it appeared that the Railway Executive's figures were indeed, false, or according to Melford Stevenson:

"The issue is now clearer than it has ever been since the inquiry began. You have been presented by the Railway Executive with a set of figures that are false, possibly by carelessness or inadvertence. It is no part of my function to assign motives, but the figures have now been demonstrated beyond any doubt as quite wrong. If the same form of accountancy as has been applied to the Island were used for the whole of British Railways, their 1951 profit of £34 million would be turned into a loss of £40 million."

If the figures really were false, how exactly had the Executive falsified them? Firstly, it had quietly omitted the effects of contributory revenue generated by the threatened lines – in other words, the value of traffic passing to and from the rest of the island and mainland rail network. A traveller from, say, Bembridge, would very likely change at Brading and travel on to Ryde, and possibly beyond by ferry to Portsmouth, and perhaps – for the sake of argument – on to Manchester. If the Brading branch closed, the railway would lose a few inconsequential shillings for the branch journey, but if the traveller either stayed at home, or made the whole trip by car, the railway might also lose the whole fare to Manchester. Adding estimated contributory revenue increased the claimed income from £37,400 to £45,900. By this single step, the protesters were able to prove that the branch lines were actually covering their direct

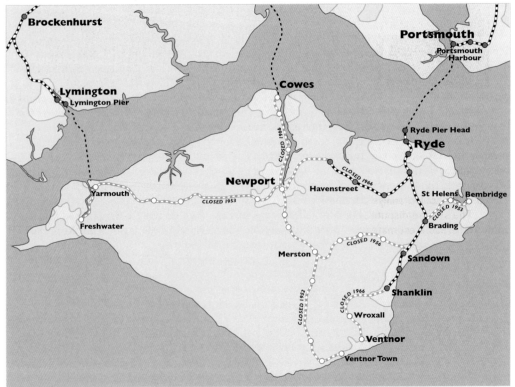

Railways on the Isle of Wight were decimated in the 1950s and '60s. Stations in red are still open, and those in green have reopened since, but these are mainly for 'heritage' services. Shanklin to Ventnor and Ryde-Newport-Cowes should not have closed.

A Bembridge to Brading train at St Helens, the only intermediate station on the three-mile branch, which closed in September 1953. Interestingly, in the light of what transpired, there appear to be some new sleepers in the foreground. PHOTO: S H Keyse

movement costs of wages, train workings and maintenance.

It could be argued that the Executive was quite within its rights to omit contributory revenue from the accounts, but by doing so it had given a very false idea of the financial savings that would accrue after closure. The suggestion that the Executive was unsure of the contributory value of the lines can be excluded, for the Branchline Committee always made a point of providing a detailed analysis of the figures.

The second dispute arose over operating expenses, where the Executive had claimed some remarkable estimates for stock maintenance, particularly on the little Bembridge branch:

"In the case of the Bembridge line there was one engine in steam, three push-pull coaches (one used in the winter, two in summer and three on Saturdays), and half a dozen coal wagons a week. For the maintenance of these, the Executive included a figure of £4,245. This was £80 a week for one engine, three coaches, and six wagons...

The Bembridge contingent, though it represented 3.5% of the total, was claimed to cost 7.5% of the total maintenance bill. This [Mr Bright] had found generally to be the case with the figures in the maintenance and renewal section. The engines, for example, were shown to be replaced at a rate which could only mean brand new stock, yet the youngest locomotive in the island was dated 1896."
Isle of Wight County Press report

In fact, far from being replaced new, the island's rolling stock had traditionally been replaced with equipment surplus to requirements from the mainland, making a fiction of the Executive's figures. The same was true of the track. The Executive had suggested a figure of £500 per mile per year for track maintenance. This was almost equal to the average national cost, but the threatened railways were single track, subject to speed restrictions, and largely maintained with secondhand materials.

The only figures which the County Council was able to verify from its own records were those for season ticket holders. The Executive had claimed revenue of just £5 a year between Newport and Freshwater, but according to the *Isle of Wight County Press*, Mr Bright knew of revenue from three sources, which totalled £98, including £53 from the County Council itself for school children:

"A table compiled by the County Treasurer, analysing the total payments by the County Council to the Railway Executive in respect of scholars... shows the total as £1,721 and, on the Freshwater line, £53 12s 4d. None of this is included in income. Mr Bright added that season ticket income on the Brading-Bembridge line was given by the railways as £42, whereas the County Council alone paid £72. There must be other season ticket holders."
Isle of Wight County Press report

The whole affair smacked of sharp practise, particularly after C P Hopkins, the representative of the Railway Executive, agreed to answer questions, but refused cross-examination. "What's the difference?" inquired the wily Melford Stevenson, who knew very well what the difference was. If the Railway Executive was wrong, what exactly was the financial position for the threatened railways on the Isle of Wight? Mr Hill, the expert witness, refused to be drawn, but Melford Stevenson claimed that the annual loss was around £20,000, rather than £90,000, and the entire loss could be attributed to the Freshwater line on the sparsely-populated west side of the island, as the others were more or less paying their way. Many years later, the BTC inadvertently confirmed this by announcing that the annual savings for all the railway mileage closed in 1953 (more than 160 miles) had amounted to an estimated £146,000, suggesting that the savings on the Isle of Wight would indeed have been about £22,000.

This might have looked like a local skirmish, but the repercussions were to be very serious, as revealed by Mr Hopkins of the Railway Executive:

"...the analysis of the position in the island was based on a system devised by the BTC in 1949 to permit the rapid examination of the position of any branch line. It had not been devised for any special line. Its basis was change... as between the position of the railways with the line open, and with it closed."

This was supposed to reassure the protesters that their lines had been treated fairly, but as the Isle of Wight figures were false, it left a strong suspicion that all the figures put forward by the BTC since 1949, and all those put forward in the future, were suspect. This first public admission that the Branchline Committee might be using underhand methods to achieve closure targets, was a crucial turning point. With Melford Stevenson sniffing at his heels, poor Hopkins was finally driven into a corner on the unlikely subject of railway sleepers:

STEVENSON: "You said, 'In the Island we always use new sleepers'. Can you explain the most recent replacements then, where [secondhand] sleepers were used from North Kent and Faversham?"

HOPKINS: "You will recall that I wanted to close the Brading-Bembridge branch a few days ago. I thought it would help towards amity if we forewent economies."

STEVENSON: "That statement is only useful as a general measure of how much reliability one can place on a railway statement."

The barrister concluded with some justification that, "if a case with such a degree of prevarication and inaccurate figures had been presented in a court of law, it would have been thrown out with contempt".

The 1953 Isle of Wight inquiry was a small victory for free speech, but it did nothing to change the TUCC inquiry procedure, or indeed to amend the policies of the Branchline Committee, the Railway Executive or the BTC. The protesters had proved that the Railway Executive's figures were largely false and that the island's railways (and presumably many others) were losing far less than had been claimed, even without the proven economies of diesel operation. The false figures stiffened the resolve of protest groups up and down the country to fight almost everything, because there was no longer any confidence in the figures. For its part, the Executive (and later the BTC) simply took more care to avoid being tripped up by learned counsel.

The problem was that some railways really did need to close during this era. There was very little social or commercial justification for keeping some lines open, and the country really would have been better off if they had been allowed to close, preferably with a degree of consensus over alternative arrangements. But the false figures had led to an atmosphere of suspicion and a general hardening of attitudes on both sides, and closures became so controversial,

After the 1953 Inquiry, the Isle of Wight lost its minor branches very quickly, but the lines from Ryde to Ventnor and Newport/Cowes were to survive almost unchanged until the late 1960s. No. 18 'Ningwood' pauses at Ryde St Johns with a Ventnor train. Ventnor, Newport and Cowes would all close in 1966, leaving a stub to Shanklin.

that in the end the rules were changed to prevent discussion altogether.

Following the inquiry, the local area TUCC recommended closure of the Newport-Freshwater line immediately, and gave the Sandown-Newport line a two-year stay of execution. As for the little Bembridge line, with its single antiquarian

After the 1953 TUCC Inquiry, the Freshwater line was put quietly to sleep. This is Yarmouth station in 1973, 20 years after closure. It has changed little today. PHOTO: David Henshaw

locomotive and three carriages, the Committee was divided and unable to make a recommendation. The Central TUCC made a decision on its behalf, and the branch line was put up for immediate closure. In its annual report, the central committee felt it necessary to say that it accepted the Railway Executive's figures in full, and repudiate any suggestion that the accountancy had been questionable. Such pronouncements seemed to make a mockery of the consultation procedure and led many to believe that the central body was merely an organ of the BTC, and not impartial, as was claimed.

In October 1953, the Minister of Transport presided at a joint BTC/County Council meeting on the Isle of Wight and succeeded in convincing the Council that money would be available for road improvements. Thus, when the Sandown to Newport line came up for closure again in 1956, there was little protest. And the Minister had another trick up his sleeve, leaving the track in position. The logic of this move soon became clear, for according to the Minister, the aim was to enable a private concern to purchase and operate the line if it wished:

"...[the BTC] want it to be open to private enterprise to take over and run the line, if private enterprise believes that it will make a good thing of it when British Railways were unable to do so. Provided that we have adequate safeguards about the price paid to British Railways, I see no objection to that at all in principle. I can only mention that the rails have been left in the Isle of Wight right to the present time... that is for two years... waiting for some enterprising speculator to start running a service, and so far, no-one has been willing to do so..."

It was a skillful sleight of hand, and evidence that the British establishment was doing what it did best in times of revolution – closing ranks. During the Isle of Wight inquiry, Melford Stevenson had quoted from the minutes of a Southern Region/National Union of Railwaymen meeting where, according to the union, "the management admitted quite frankly that it was their intention at a later stage to close the railways altogether as far as the Isle of Wight was concerned."

A single small concession was ultimately obtained, for the Executive agreed to give five years notice of closure in the case of the Ryde-Newport-Cowes line, and seven years for Shanklin to Ventnor. Otherwise the Isle of Wight inquiry achieved very little, apart from, "exposing painfully undemocratic aspects of a country that calls itself democratic," in the words of cricket commentator and railway enthusiast John Arlott, writing in the *Hampshire Magazine*.

It was the beginning of the end for the railways on the Isle of Wight, but a gateway to much bigger things for Melford Stevenson QC, who became a High Court judge in 1957, and later dispatched the Kray Twins, the Angry Brigade and a clutch of IRA terrorists with the same vigour he had applied to poor Mr Hopkins of the Railway Executive.

Late in 1953, Parliament passed the long-awaited Transport Act, abolishing the Executives. Deep among the clauses and sub-clauses, there lay a subtle but important phrase. The 1947 Act had empowered the Commission to provide 'adequate transport services' but under the 1953 Act, the word 'adequate' had been dropped, leaving the BTC free to provide whatever services it deemed suitable: adequate, inadequate or non-existent. Paradoxically, the BTC board was increased in size to deal with its new enhanced role, its membership growing from nine to 15. An unfortunate side-effect of the new legislation was that, whereas the nine-member Railway Executive had included five railwaymen, the new-look Transport Commission included only two members with railway knowledge.

For a variety of reasons, it had been decided that privatisation of the railways would be impractical, so the intention was to devolve power down to the individual railway regions, which would be controlled by Area Boards, rather in the manner of the former statutory private companies. The BTC would be encouraged to allow more local decision-making, creating a new commercial freedom, which sounded much the sort of thing Professor Hondelink was advocating. The BTC's new chairman, General Sir Brian Robertson, was keen to strip away bureaucracy, dismantle the unwieldy management system and see a return to regional loyalties, and a certain *esprit de corps*. But the details of reorganisation were in the hands of the very bureaucracy the General was hoping to sweep away, and Hondelink was dubious that any changes would be more than superficial.

The 1953 Act marked the end of the road for the long, and ultimately fruitless, experiment in transport integration. The road services, which had proved so difficult to nationalise, would be sold off as quickly as possible, and from the end of 1954, the 25-mile lorry limit was repealed. This new freedom for road transport would in theory be matched by a new freedom for the railways, for at long last, the restrictive rates and charges legislation was to be liberalised.

The railways would now be empowered to operate at a profit, with greater freedom to set passenger fares, and commercial rates that more closely mirrored the costs. It was not complete freedom though. The railway no longer had to charge a set price for each commodity, or publish this list of charges, but it had to publish maximum rates, which continued to be set by the Transport Tribunal, which could veto increases, as could the Minister of Transport.

In the event, the process of liberalisation was frustratingly slow, and the railways continued to charge some 14% less than the road hauliers for uneconomic short-haul business, and 5% more for the middle-distance business they wanted to attract.

It took four years for a modified version of the proposals to be published by the Transport Tribunal. It was a gift to the road transport operators, who were free to carry whatever they wanted at a commercially confidential price, while the railways remained shackled to outmoded rules and regulations. It was not until July 1957 that the railways were finally given the freedom to adjust rates to suit the market, to reduce charges to attract traffic they were well suited to carrying, and increase rates for less profitable traffic. But it had come much too late. The cost was already driving the railways into a vicious spiral of decline.

The Great Railway Conspiracy

Meanwhile, the 1953 Act had resulted in the sale of 24,000 lorries to small road hauliers, who proceeded to undermine the railways wherever they could.

Professor Hondelink was profoundly disappointed with the 1953 reorganisation, for the Commission decided to oversee railway operations itself, taking up residence at the former Railway Executive headquarters at 222 Marylebone Road, and employing many of the staff. The combined operation grew to such a size that it was soon necessary to build additional offices next door.

The Area Boards were supposed to function like loosely-regulated regional companies, but it didn't work out that way. They took on extra staff, but little in the way of extra responsibility, while the BTC cheerfully carried on micro-managing from the centre. The design and manufacture of locomotives, track and signalling equipment remained under central control, as did negotiations over major wage claims and changes to the charging structure.

It took more than a year to complete the reorganisation, and once the complex new administrative machine was up and running, the regions found themselves even more tightly restrained than they had been before, with rates and fixed costs imposed by the bloated bureaucracy in London. As Professor Hondelink saw it, the chain of command had increased to no fewer than ten levels. By 1958, the number of administrative personnel per mile of railway line had almost doubled from the pre-nationalisation days. And the gradual closure of railways on the ground only made matters worse, reducing the number of rank-and-file railwaymen and women, while the number of clerks, secretaries, superintendents, committee members and middle managers increased. By this time, the railway's income was steadily increasing, but costs were starting to run out of control, and 1953 saw the operating profit fall to £34.6 million, a figure that was more than swallowed up in central charges to the Transport Commission.

According to Hondelink, the rapidly deteriorating financial situation stemmed primarily from poor management, and the branch line closure policy was little more than a red herring to disguise the inadequacy of the administration. He calculated that a reduction in the number of BTC clerical staff, cessation of the standardisation programme, and a few other sensible economies, would improve railway finances to the tune of some £10 million a year – considerably more than the closure programme was realising:

"I do maintain with all my vigour that such economies would far outstrip in value any that may be made by closure of stations and branch lines...

If a complete railway administration, in the shape of a combined Commission and Executive, remains superimposed on the systems, with another level of boards and delegated executives interposed, then all the faults of the existing cumbersome, inanimate, rigid and slow-working machine will be made even worse than they are now."

Nothing was to change. Indeed, the number of administrative personnel continued to rise. Professor Hondelink was a world authority on transport affairs, but he had now drawn the fire of politicians of all shades in his home country. His continued exhortations to save the industry began to fall on deaf ears, as his views were quietly and comprehensively suppressed.

The innovative decentralisation policy ("make believe" said Hondelink) ultimately proved quite worthless. It was, after all, a completely artificial situation. The Tories had assumed that the railways would simply shake off the administrative yoke of socialism and return overnight to fighting their corner in a commercial world. But the railways had been discouraged from behaving in a commercial manner for nearly 40 years, and they now had to compete with much nimbler, more efficiently managed forms of transport as well.

In the regions, long-suppressed rivalries began to resurface, and the more positive aspects of nationalisation, such as inter-regional trials and a general cross-fertilisation of ideas, were largely put aside. For lines that had been assigned to the 'wrong' region at the stroke of a pen in 1947 – such as the former LSWR network in the West Country, the Somerset & Dorset, and the Oxford to Cambridge – the new commercial freedom proved disastrous. These 'foreign' lines were perceived by regional managers as abstracting revenue from historic regional trunk routes, and were either deliberately run down, or simply left short of sensible investment and modern economies. For the time being this didn't matter, but it left the lines in a very weak position when the financial situation got worse later on. Most would ultimately close.

Even seemingly innocuous ideas, such as allowing the regions their own colour schemes, fell flat, for some long-distance passenger trains began to take on a distressingly piebald appearance. It was a fine idea, but it had come at the wrong time, and when the railways needed to be pooling resources to fight a much bigger foe on the national stage, regional identity was something of a retrograde step.

Yet, in some ways, this was a glorious Indian summer for the railways. Economies had as yet failed to bite, and for a few years there was something of a return to pre-war conditions. In the former Great Western territories in particular, where the drab uniformity of nationalisation had been kept at bay, the early 1950s were wonderful years. Once again, resplendent Kings and Castles hauled rakes of coffee and cream carriages west to the Cornish Riviera, and the old guard of the GWR held their heads high once again. No-one really cared that traffic was steadily increasing on the A30 trunk road, or that the French and Germans were pressing ahead with rail modernisation. It was a chance to relive the golden years, and they took it.

But according to Owen Prosser of the Railway Development Association, the lack of judgement shown by the BTC at this time amounted to an almost criminal irresponsibility:

"The original BTC executive member for engineering went right ahead and designed steam engines and had the authority to build them. They built dozens and dozens and dozens of small lightweight 2-6-2 tanks for branch line services in the 1950s, after I'd made the plea for more railbuses..."

Despite the major investment in steam, the Commission was about to take a few decisive steps towards modernisation. In 1953 it decided to look into the economics of individual lines and services, some of which had changed little in 50 years or more. This research made it clear that *something* had to be done to the branch lines, and quickly. Of the BTC's passenger services, express trains were earning a healthy surplus over movement costs of £33 million, while suburban services were earning £7 million, but stopping and branch line trains were *losing* £14 million. As we have seen, the contributory value of these lines tended to muddy the financial waters, but on the basis of this survey, conducted in October 1952, it appeared that almost *all* of the branch lines were losing money.

Late in 1953 the Commission appointed a Modernisation Committee to investigate suitable areas for investment, and of course disinvestment. When the first draft of its report surfaced early in 1954, it included a recommendation that at least half the stopping trains should be withdrawn, and 30% of the network closed to passenger services altogether. Clearly, if diesel multiple units were to save the branch lines, they would have to be introduced very rapidly.

The indecisive management, lack of communication and inexplicable delays had created a deficit time-bomb, and a few arbitrary rail closures were doing nothing to ease the situation. Five years after formation of the Motive Power Committee, the railway workshops were still churning out steam locomotives, and beyond Greater London, stopping passenger services were almost exclusively steam-hauled. The 1953 locomotive renewal programme had made allowance for construction of 300 steam locomotives and only 68 diesels – all the diesels were destined for shunting duties. The following year, construction of another 330 steam locomotives was authorised, together with 125 diesel shunters, but the Western Region (presumably using its new regional freedom) ordered 20 *steam* shunting locomotives.

There was mounting frustration among pro-rail MPs and others that branch lines were being prepared for closure that had never even seen a modern diesel railcar or multiple unit, lines that might have been turned around with modern technology. But introduction of the new vehicles had been painfully slow, as witnessed by Rupert Spier MP in October 1953:

"I believe that if nationalised transport had really made an effort to convert some of these branch lines to light railways, and to employ... railcars, they could have effected considerable economies... All I have found out so far is that British Railways, after a great deal of effort, have instigated one diesel car service between Bangor and some place which is unpronounceable to me but which is spelled A M L W Y C H."

This was the very same ACV railcar spotted at Princes Risborough by the Birmingham Junior Chamber of Commerce, and it was still the only post-war railcar on British Railways.

By June 1954 however, the first diesel multiple units were going into service between Bradford and Leeds. And in October the same year, the Lightweight Trains Committee had completed preliminary trials of the new vehicles in the Lake District, in the build-up to the much larger Cumbrian scheme:

Arrangement/No. of vehicles	Weight	Power	Fuel Consumption
Power-car plus trailer (2-car)	47½ tons	300hp	4.7mpg
Two power cars back to back (2-car)	54 tons	600hp	3.2mpg
Power-car, trailer and coach (3-car)	83½ tons	300hp	4.2mpg

If these machines sound uneconomic, it should be borne in mind that they had a seated passenger capacity of about 70 per car, giving a fuel consumption *per passenger* of up to 450 to 880mpg. To put this into context, it would be similar to a single-decker bus from the 1950s, and at least four times as fuel-efficient as one of the new standard class steam locomotives. Modern express steam was (and remains), relatively efficient, at least where coal was cheap and plentiful, but stopping services were another matter. Local steam services pottered lethargically from station to station and bubbled gently at sleepy termini when they weren't earning any revenue. Unlike a diesel, they couldn't be turned off between duties, and even when stationary, they consumed a lot of coal. They also needed a two-man crew all day. And fuel efficiency was only half the story, because the comfortable new diesel trains were generating far more in terms of extra income than they ever saved in fuel.

The Lake District trials were generally satisfactory, with most vehicle combinations reaching 60mph without too much difficulty, and returning adequate fuel consumption. The exception was the 300hp three-car combination, which had been reduced to an embarrassing crawl on even very slight gradients, and was considered too lethargic for general traffic.

While the diesel units plodded around the Fells, branch lines continued to close, and in October 1954, the attention of the Branchline Committee became focussed on Northeast Wales. Faced with the complete loss of rail services, Denbigh County Council held a joint meeting of all interested parties, including representatives from the Railway Development Association.

The Transport Commission had already closed the sparsely populated stretch from Ruthin to Corwen, leaving the long tenuous branch from Ruthin through Denbigh to Rhyl, and an even less remunerative line from Denbigh via nowhere in particular to Mold (a fair sized town, then as now) and on to civilisation in Chester. One councillor asked how far the closure process would go:

"Now they are starting to drive the wedge home. Will it be the Denbigh-Mold line next, and then the Mold to Chester line? Are we not to have any train services at all?"

In this respect he was quite correct, for within a few years all these lines would be closed to passengers. Feelings were running high that night in Denbigh, and a Churchillian fighting spirit began to pervade the council chamber:

"Marshal your forces in the fight against a dictatorship of a new and impersonal kind which is becoming too rampant in this country... Let us realise that the battle will not be an easy one, for it is impossible to apportion blame when we condemn a national undertaking. There is not a soul to be damned nor a body to be kicked."

It was a good point. The citizens of Denbigh had found Hitler an unsavoury opponent, but nothing to the faceless bureaucrats of the Transport Commission, something not lost on the County Council Clerk, W E Bufton:

"It is exactly the policy that Hitler adopted. After each nibble he said that no more territorial claims would be made. I wrote to the traffic superintendent after the proposals had been received and asked him whether he would give an undertaking that in the next ten to 15 years the Chester-Mold-Denbigh line would not be closed. He could not give that undertaking!"

The mood of the meeting was further inflamed when it was revealed that the local traffic superintendent, a Mr Fisher, had made the following extraordinary remark regarding the future of the line:

"The reason why railway fares could not be brought down was that it would deflect railway passengers from the roads!"

It would not have escaped the attention of Denbighshire County Council that trials were going on elsewhere with lightweight, cost-effective diesel multiple units that could have transformed their own lines and services. But to be brutally frank, the Lake District had a lot more tourist potential than Mold. The London Midland region seems to have worked harder than most to publicise the new diesel trains

DIESEL TRAINS-quick, clean and comfortable, are now well established and extremely popular. Holiday makers, shoppers and commuters, all find them a great attraction. Their observation windows are excellent for sightseeing.

Among the lovely holiday areas served by London Midland diesel trains are English Lakeland and North Wales, where reasonably priced Day Trips and Runabout Tickets (in the season) help you to "get around and about".

The Great Railway Conspiracy

Momentarily off his guard, the hapless official had revealed the true situation. There was the usual bandying about of figures, with the usual claims and counter-claims as to the true worth of the line, but it all came to nothing. The BTC was closing the line to passengers, not because it made large losses (goods traffic would continue in any case), but because it intended to transfer traffic to its own road buses. The wishes of the local people, the anger of their councillors, and the RDA's railbus evidence did nothing to alter the situation. The line, like many others, was doomed before the inquiry had even commenced. The Rhyl line closed in 1955, and Denbigh's sole remaining railway to Mold and Chester followed seven years later, in 1962.

After the usual prolonged gestation period, the final months of 1954 saw completion of the Modernisation Committee's report. Generally optimistic, the report recommended a programme of wide-scale capital investments, but ended on a cautious note:

"Railways are a national necessity. The need to modernise them is urgent and immediate. With the implementation of this plan, a long period of stability, good leadership and goodwill within the industry, British Railways can be made financially self-supporting. During the years of fructification of the plan, however, it will be extremely difficult, if not impossible, to meet the additional interest burden."

In other words, unless some major capital restructuring was on the cards, the modernisation plan was almost bound to drive the industry into debt. Such gloomy forecasts were ignored at the BTC and in January 1955 the substance of the report was published, under the title *British Railways Plan for Modernisation & Re-equipment – a 15-year investment programme aimed at restoring the network to health.* Publication of the plan provided little comfort for the county councillors of Denbighshire, because local railways were to see little in the way of modernisation, something spelt out starkly in the report, which made it clear there would be, "a marked reduction in the stopping and branch line services which are little used by the public and which... should be largely handed over to road transport."

Neither was there to be a huge investment bonanza for the trunk lines, as half of the £1,240 million cost of modernisation would be swallowed up covering arrears of maintenance. The greater proportion of the remainder would be spent on pensioning off the recently introduced steam engines and replacing them with new diesel and electric locomotives. After falling far behind the rest of the industrialised world in such matters, the BTC had made the dramatic decision to scrap thousands of steam locomotives, although given that they were still being built (and would be for some years). It was envisaged that the change-over would be phased in over several decades, with steam still accounting for more than half of the estimated 12,800 locomotives in service in 1970.

All freight wagons were to be equipped with continuous brakes, and many antiquated marshalling yards swept away and replaced with a handful of modern facilities. Electrification on the Southern Region was to continue where it had left off before the war, making electric traction universal east of Portsmouth and Reading. Similarly, the East Coast Main Line, from King's Cross to Doncaster, Leeds and York would be electrified, as would the West Coast line from Euston to Manchester and Liverpool. The Liverpool Street suburban scheme would be extended to Ipswich, Felixstowe, Harwich and Clacton.

The electrification plans were long overdue, and freight was crying out for investment too. The inefficiency of operating loose-coupled wagons had become all too apparent by the 1950s, with research suggesting that freight locomotives were spending half their working lives shunting. It was estimated that eradication of the loose-coupled wagons would take 2,000 locomotives off the books, a huge cost saving.

One of the first results of the plan was a rush to diesel traction by the regions. Each produced its own designs, some of which were quite successful (and a few are still working today), while others failed miserably. But after such a late and over-enthusiastic start, it's not surprising that the scheme ran into problems. The extraordinary speed of dieselisation meant that some designs entered service before prototypes had even completed proper trials. This proved costly, not just it terms of cash, but in public confidence too, for some of the early diesels were chronically unreliable.

By the time the modernisation plan had been approved, the BTC deficit had reached a record £70 million. The railways managed to make a £16.4 million working profit in 1955, but after paying central charges to the Commission (largely dividends to the former railway share-holders), the profit had become a £21.6 million loss. Freight traffic was in steady decline and passenger traffic – although apparently holding its own – was really losing out in a growing market. To make matters worse, the rather vague financial assumptions in the modernisation plan were out of date before they had even been approved. During 1954-55, prices had risen by 10%, leaving the modernisation costings way behind, and threatening to engulf the modest 6.9% return predicted by the Committee.

As the plan was hastily implemented, road traffic continued to increase. The Government already had a pretty shrewd idea that the future lay with the roads and in the corridors of power plans began to take shape. In February 1955, two weeks after publication of the railway modernisation plan, the Ministry of Transport announced a four-year scheme to modernise the road system: £212 million would be spent on motorways, which the British Road Federation said was not nearly enough.

In April, with an election on the horizon, an ageing Winston Churchill handed the reins of power to Anthony Eden, who went on to tighten his grip the following month by winning the election with an increased majority of 58. The Conservatives now had 344 seats in the House of Commons and a clear mandate.

Meanwhile, the Branchline Committee was sweeping the country in its search for unremunerative railways, closely followed by the Railway Development Association, which was fighting every proposal that didn't appear to be in the public interest. The RDA was well aware that a forthright condemnation of every closure proposal would get nowhere, and argued that resources should be concentrated on lines that could either be turned around with investment, or that performed some special social or environmental service. John Betjeman (later Sir John, and Poet Laureate), now Vice-President of the RDA, reluctantly concluded that a selective policy was the only option:

"I love the branch lines because they are little quiet worlds of peace and seclusion. But in order to try and preserve them, we have got to be what is called practical!"

One of the great milestones in the story of the railway closures came with the South Western TUCC inquiry into the Princetown branch in Devon. It was, by all accounts, an unusual and interesting branch line: 10¹/2 miles long, winding steadily up onto Dartmoor from Yelverton to Princetown, a small community adjacent to HM Prison Dartmoor, and one of the few inhabited corners of this bleak and lonely moor. With an almost continuous climb to 1,400 feet above sea level, and little indigenous traffic, the line was difficult and expensive to operate, making it an ideal candidate for closure, but there were some special circumstances to confuse the TUCC. The prison generated quite a lot of traffic, and in winter, when snow could make the moorland roads treacherous for weeks at a time, the railway was often the only route onto the moor. Finally (though vaguely worded at the time) there was the prospect of tourism.

As usual, the Commission, and before it the Railway Executive, had done nothing to attract tourists to the line, but there was every indication that the Princetown branch, winding through some of the most rugged and beautiful scenery in Britain, would have proved an outstanding attraction. There were also practical environmental reasons for keeping a rail link onto the moor, because the roads then, as now, were quite unsuitable for heavy tourist traffic.

The Branchline Committee produced figures suggesting an £11,000 annual loss (about £860,000 today), much of which, as it transpired at the inquiry, was being wasted through over-manning. The little branch supported no fewer than 19 staff, including four signalmen and seven permanent way men. As usual, the objectors had no access to vital statistics, but they could count on some formidable names. Besides Major G B Harvey, the Governor of the prison, there appeared among the protesters a retired Lord Justice of Appeal, Sir Henry Herman Slesser, one-time Solicitor General in Ramsay MacDonald's Labour Government of 1924, and a Dartmoor resident. According to Owen Prosser of the RDA, he had retired there, "possibly with a sentimental interest to be breathing the same air as some of his old clients." Whatever the reason, he had also developed a more than sentimental interest in preserving his local branch line.

The South West TUCC, under the chairmanship of a ship-owner, Colonel Mark Whitwill, initially refused to allow the press access to the inquiry, but the story aroused so much interest that the national press followed every word of the debate. The TUCC, perhaps unnerved by the calibre of the opposition, was clearly split over whether to approve the closure or not. So heated did the debate become, that one member, in a moment of rare pique for such an

Princetown station was a gloomy place at the best of times, but on a snowy morning in December 1955, the line's future was very much hanging in the balance. It finally closed just over a year later. PHOTO: B Mills Collection

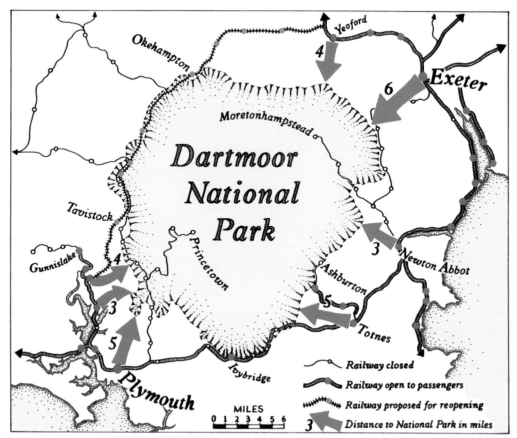

There were once nearly 30 railway stations in, or close to, the Dartmoor National Park. After the closures, there was only the 'heritage' station at Buckfastleigh. In 2013, the situation is improving: Ivybridge reopened in 1994, Okehampton sees summer Sunday services, and Tavistock is expected to reopen soon. The missing link from Okehampton to Tavistock cannot be far behind.

appointee, shouted at a railway official: "If you pursue your policy of self-extermination to its logical conclusion, you will be out of a job as soon as you have closed all the lines that don't pay." Wisely, the Committee decided that it needed more time to arrive at a suitable verdict, and the unsavoury moment was put off for two months. When the decision was finally passed down in September 1955, it decided in favour of the protesters. The line should stay open, partly due to the 'special circumstances' of the prison.

Much to the chagrin of those who had fought so long to save the line, the CTCC once again summarily dismissed the local verdict, and came down in favour of closure. It was an odd decision, echoing a verdict some months previously, when protesters at the Horncastle branch line inquiry had found to their surprise that the East Midlands TUCC agreed with them, only to hear subsequently that the central body had over-ruled the area committee.

The Princetown closure procedure ran its fateful course, and the last train departed in March 1956 after the winter snows had cleared. All appeared to be lost, but the BTC had reckoned without the tenacity of Sir Henry Slesser. The former Solicitor General was appalled at the CTCC decision and wrote in forthright terms to Viscount Garnock, then President of the RDA:

The Great Railway Conspiracy

"My principal grievance is that I was not offered an opportunity to put our case before the Central Transport Consultative Committee; I should have thought that at any rate if they were inclined to reverse [the decision of] the local body, who knew the conditions as they did not, they would at least have had the courtesy to offer us a chance of advocacy. As an old member of the Court of Appeal, I am rather horrified by this denial of natural justice, and had I been able to come would have spoken on this very serious matter."

The RDA hoped to use this eloquent condemnation of the Consultative Committee system as a lever to force change on the authorities, but it is rather more likely that opposition from witnesses of the calibre of Sir Henry Slesser was instrumental in the Government's subsequent decision to reduce the powers of the TUCCs still further in the 1962 Transport Act.

Despite several attempts to preserve the line, the track was soon lifted and the land sold off, but this was not quite the end of the story, for the Dartmoor weather was to wreak wicked revenge on the authorities. In the winter of 1963, Princetown was completely cut off for three days, receiving food drops by helicopter. By 1971, seasonal road congestion was so appalling that the National Park Committee (chaired until 1964 by Sir Henry Slesser, incidentally) was considering banning cars from parts of the moor altogether. The following year two coaches met on a narrow lane and enforced a temporary ban of their own, traffic grinding to a halt for three hours. Today, Dartmoor has around 2.4 million visitors a year, many of whom would gladly have used the Princetown branch to access this wild and lonely countryside, had it been available.

The Branchline Committee had made 130 outright closures since 1947, and about another 70 lines had been partially closed (usually remaining open for freight), a total of 1,546 route miles. The BTC tried hard to reassure its staff that this measured retrenchment was in everyone's best interests or, in the words of the Western Region railway staff magazine:

"The closing of branch lines and stations *does not mean* that the railways are dying on their feet. It means they are moving with the times... and 'streamlining' their services... remember that pruning is done to promote vigorous growth!"

There was still a ring of truth to this statement in 1954, for the trunk routes and secondary lines were still intact. Many of the branch lines lopped off in the early 1950s would have failed to survive whatever the BTC had done in the way of efficient operating practices and service enhancements. And as the moral boosting article in the staff magazine pointed out, branch line closures were nothing new. Many infamous examples had failed to survive even until the Second World War. Among the worst offenders was the Fort Augustus branch in Scotland, which had been built in 1903 as part of a proposed Great Glen trunk route to Inverness, at a cost of £322,000. In the event, the line never went any further than Fort Augustus, and earned just £907 in the normally euphoric first six months of operation. In 1933, the final year before this extravagantly engineered branch line was laid mercifully to rest, it carried only 1,911 passengers, who paid a total of £179 for their tickets, an income of little more than £3 a week.

In all, the big four railway companies had disposed of some 240 miles of branch line between 1923 and 1947, with a further 1,000 miles closing to passengers, but kept open for other purposes. After nationalisation, with the emphasis on 'bustitution', the process had accelerated, and a far higher mileage had closed in the six years since 1947 than in the previous 24 years of private ownership. The protesters argued, with good reason, that branch lines were being closed with no serious investigation into reducing costs and increasing patronage, and the closure techniques were being 'run in' on the branches in preparation for a much larger round of closures.

Not surprisingly, considering the limited traffic and wasteful operating methods, many of the early closures really did yield savings. According to the CTCC (hardly, of course, an unbiased source), the annual saving from the branch line closure programme had topped almost £1.5 million. That estimate would amount to around £140 million today, although for an industry with income and expenditure in billions at modern prices, it was small change.

There were plenty of contenders for the title of 'least remunerative branch line'. Perhaps typical was the line from Monmouth to Pontypool Road which, according to the Branchline Committee, earned just over £1,000 a year from passenger traffic prior to closure. Even less lucrative was the Tenterden to Headcorn section of the Kent & East Sussex, the last vestige of Colonel Stephen's light railway empire, which had been put up for closure after earning just £405 in passenger income.

Many communities had prospered with the arrival of the railways, but some had singularly failed to do so. A good example was the remote village of Llangynog in the Welsh borders, that had grown in less than meteoric fashion, reaching a population of 292 potential travellers by the early 1950s. Considering the sparsity of the population, the annual income of £252 was quite respectable, but it didn't sway the Branchline Committee, which recommended closure forthwith. Many other remote branch lines had survived as long, but the figures from Llangynog were probably a record of sorts.

In order to justify the closure programme, the CTCC tended to adopt a rather defeatist stance with regard to road competition, although this line seems to have softened slightly by the time the 1954 annual report was released:

"Both we and the area committees are reluctant to withdraw their transport services unless there is no reasonable prospect of maintaining them on a more or less economic basis. Later in this report we refer to our suggestions for making rail services more attractive, though we realise that these could not always be successfully applied, owing to the substantial advantages provided by the modern road facilities."

In fact, the results of the diesel multiple unit experiments were coming in thick and fast, and the new units were proving a great success with the operators and travelling public alike. In the first three and a half months of the Yorkshire experiment, takings were up by £10,500 (a little over £900,000 today), yet the CTCC prognosis remained gloomy: "Despite this substantial improvement in financial results, the point has not yet been reached at which the receipts cover the full cost of providing the service."

The vehicles might not have been covering their full costs, but they were certainly running close. The final figures from the West Cumberland experiment told a similar story, with the lines now on the verge of full profitability. The former steam-hauled trains had cost £150,000 a year to run, against income of £40,000, while the new diesels were costing £80,000, and earning £70,000. In other words, an operating deficit of £105,000 had been slashed to £10,000 on the sort of rural lines that were being prepared for closure.

A comprehensive series of experiments on the Western Region in June 1955 gave further evidence of the efficiency of the diesel multiple units, one four-car set operating a stopping train over the 193-mile route from Paddington to Newton Abbot on £2 2 shillings-worth of fuel. Consumption was better than five miles per gallon.

Further proof of the efficacy of the new units came with the internal publication of an Eastern Region traffic census for March and September 1955. The new traffic costing service, introduced by Sir Reginald Wilson, was exactly the sort of innovation that the railways needed, although other regions were slow to adopt the techniques, and it was not until the arrival of

THE CONWAY VALLEY

Enjoy the lovely North Wales scenery
from one of the new Diesel Trains

Faster – Cleaner – More Comfortable – BRITISH RAILWAYS

Frank Wooton's glorious Conwy Valley poster for the London Midland Region was an attempt to capitalise on the tourist potential of the new diesel multiple units. In just a few years, this line would be condemned by Beeching, but against all the odds, it survived

Dr Beeching some years later that accurate traffic surveys were produced on a national basis.

The census, covering 40% of Eastern Region stopping trains, was conducted among the branches and secondary lines of rural Lincolnshire and East Anglia, where the BTC had opposed diesel experiments and, consequently, there were few of the new units in evidence.

Generally, the situation was pretty bleak, for apart from the well-patronised services to the coastal resorts of Hunstanton, Mablethorpe and Skegness, the picture was one of mounting losses. Overall, annual receipts were £880,000, against movement costs of more than £2 million. Some steam-hauled trains were costing five to nine times as much as they were earning, carrying an average of 37 passengers per train, a 20% load factor. Half the trains surveyed were earning less than four shillings per mile (£16.50 today), and quite a few were carrying less than ten passengers at a time.

In contrast, the modern diesel-operated services, apparently introduced on a few routes at random, had earned a total of £2,100, against movement costs of £1,600. Only one service was failing to cover its costs, and a few were very profitable indeed. The report summed up by tentatively suggesting that, had all services been diesel operated:

"...the direct cost of operations would have been covered by revenue, but there would have been no significant contribution to the cost of terminals, or of track, signalling and general administration."

Again, these were mostly very rural routes, many of which were already earmarked for closure. Results of this kind were beginning to cause heated debates within the BTC between those who thought a big round of closures was just a matter of time, for which poor financial figures would just make life easier, and those who believed that the branch lines really could be turned around. As the results rolled in, the latter group were starting to win the argument.

The BTC was beginning to realise that the railways needed to make a quantum leap of modernisation in the 1950s, to deal with competition from road transport, and private cars in particular. The good news was that the fast, comfortable diesel units really were able to draw passengers back, but where they had not been tried, people were deserting the railways in droves.

In general terms, the British railway system of the 1950s was a drab and demoralised version of the same system in the 1930s. The motor car, on the other hand, had improved immeasurably in 20 years, and it was about to change out of all recognition with the release of compact, economical and efficient vehicles, such as the Austin Mini and 1100. In a consumer society, success or failure turned on such qualities as value, convenience, reliability, not to mention status, and this was as true for a rail service as it was for a new television or a vacuum cleaner.

As more than one commentator was astute enough to observe, the railways had become victims of their own heritage. If the flanged steel wheel had been invented in the middle of the 20th Century, the railways might have been greeted as the saviours of the age. As it was, the Victorian infrastructure was regarded as anachronistic and outmoded. Post-war fuel and raw material rationing had provided a breathing space by keeping the brakes on car construction and use, but after 1955, road transport took off, and railway operating costs overtook income for the first time, resulting in a spiral of decline.

Hasty implementation of the railway modernisation plan did little to help, and the waste associated with the new regime served merely to accelerate the impending financial collapse. In cost/benefit terms to the nation, the railway closures were terribly wasteful. Costly assets were liquidated for scrap value, and the cuttings, tunnels and viaducts of the railway formation itself – hewn at such cost a century before (and still being paid for in British Transport Stock) – were returned to nature. It certainly didn't *look* like progress.

4
You've Never had it so Good
1955-1959

"Last Saturday night, for example, I was on Gloucester Station, and I asked the guard of a train what was the object standing at the platform and where it was going. He told me, "That train has been running to Cinderford since 1907". Whether he meant the timing of the train or the actual engine and coach set I do not know, but it might well have been the latter, since it appeared to be contemporaneous with George Hudson if not George Stephenson... It appeared to me... to be carrying something less than an ordinary small bus load..."

A J Champion, MP for Derbyshire East, House of Commons, Transport (Rural Areas) debate, 24th April 1956

Old meets new at Mellis Junction, Suffolk in June 1956. The more efficient, passenger-friendly diesel trains began to enter service from the mid-1950s, but in small numbers and much too late to arrest the decline. PHOTO: Dr Ian C Allen

In 1955 the Society of Motor Manufacturers & Traders set up a Roads Campaign Council to co-ordinate the various road lobby pressure groups and fight a 'roads crusade' for motorway construction. With little effective opposition from the Transport Commission and the vociferous but small pro-rail groups, the road faction won almost all of its demands, and continued to tighten its stranglehold on the Government and the Ministry of Transport. By 1957 the Roads Campaign Council had spawned an all-party Roads Study Group within Parliament, further strengthening the road lobby's tangled patronage and funding relationship with the Government, and weakening the waning influence of the BTC.

By the end of 1955 the railways were in a worrying financial plight. A pay strike had brought the network almost to a standstill in June, and modernisation had caused further expense and turmoil. There were also problems in the remote corners of the system - the rural branches and secondary lines that were still largely steam operated and grossly overstaffed. Nationwide, passenger figures remained more or less static, but money was being lost somewhere, and as far as the BTC was concerned, the scape-goat was to be the unmodernised and over-manned rural branch lines.

It was, however, a confusing period for the British Transport Commission. With pro-rail pressure groups briefing friendly MPs on the successful diesel multiple unit trials, railway management began to waver, and suddenly the mood changed. At the 11th hour, the closure programme was scaled back and the Commission decided to save the branch lines by applying a large and expensive dose of modern technology in the form of diesel multiple units for the major services and economical diesel railbuses for the less remunerative lines.

Meanwhile, the financial state of the Commission itself continued to deteriorate, until a mild economic recession in the late 1950s precipitated a complete collapse. To both the Ministry of Transport and the road lobby, which had felt considerable anxiety over railway modernisation, this turn of events could hardly have been more satisfactory.

In 1955, mounting disquiet in the rural shires about the future of rail transport had drawn the attention of MPs and prompted the Rural Transport Improvement Bill, introduced by Archer Baldwin, MP for Leominster, in consultation with Robert Aickman of the Railway Development Association. By this time, the RDA had grown from a small body of enthusiasts into an influential pressure group, and the introduction of the Bill to Parliament was the culmination of a sustained and successful campaign by the Association. Superficially, the Bill was drafted to improve rural transport, but the real intention was to save railway branch lines by a combination of measures.

The main bone of contention was the unsatisfactory performance of the various Transport Users' Consultative Committees. The TUCCs, overseen by a central body, had been created as part of the nationalisation process in 1948, to liaise between the Transport Commission and transport users, one of their major roles being to judge the merits of closure proposals put forward by the Commission, taking account of local conditions and local feeling. There was, however, mounting concern that the committees were not always acting in the best interests of the public. According to Archer Baldwin MP, of 118 closure proposals submitted to the TUCCs between 1948 and June 1955, they had acquiesced in all but two cases[3]. There was now a widespread and quite justified belief that the committees, funded and staffed by the Commission, was not in the slightest degree independent.

The matter was repeatedly raised in Parliament to little effect, and as closure followed closure, and the local consultative committees continued to agree to the BTC proposals, MPs became increasingly frustrated:

"I am beginning to wonder whether, in the light of experience, the role of these consultative committees should not be changed from one of acting as an advisory body to the Minister and the Commission to one of acting as watch-dog on behalf of the users... There seems to be a widespread view that these area committees are somewhat ineffectual and very remote."
Julian Snow MP for Lichfield and Tamworth
Transport (Consultative Committees) debate, 10th December 1957

But according to the Government, the consultative procedure was perfectly adequate. Some years later, reeling from a barrage of criticism, the Parliamentary Secretary to the Minister of Transport gave a reply:

"I want to make it clear that these committees are not 'stooges' of the BTC, as some people are inclined sometimes to think or say... all I can say here is that the form in which the data are given to the committees is now generally agreed by the area committees and the Central Transport Consultative Committee and by the Commission itself."

The Great Railway Conspiracy

Outside the Commission and the Government front benches, however, it was generally agreed that the Central Transport Consultative Committee was hardly ideal. Few observers felt that the area committees were similarly biased, but they were composed of lay people with little knowledge of transport and railway operations, easily intimidated by the central body. The problem for the area committees was in reconciling local interests, where the populace was generally - and sometimes violently - opposed to railway closures, with the greater good, particularly after the railways began to lose money in 1955. Without any real understanding of the frightening losses thrust in front of them at inquiries, they were unable to suggest economies, and so they usually advocated closure in the national interest.

The Rural Transport Improvement Bill set out to rectify the situation:

Clause 1 would require the BTC to announce closure proposals in advance through advertisements in the local press and to furnish the relevant local authorities and the TUCC with all the statistics.

Clause 2 would require the BTC to give reasons for closure proposals, should any interested party wish to know. This would expose the dubious practice of forcibly transferring traffic away from a particular line.

Clause 3 was a retrospective version of Clause 2 that would have widespread implications were it to become law, for it aimed to force the Commission to explain the reasoning behind every closure that had taken place in the previous five years.

Clause 4 specified that if there were objections to a closure proposal, the whole matter should be handed to the Transport Tribunal, which would be empowered to hold a local inquiry.

Clause 5 dealt with updating the Light Railway Act of 1896.

Clause 6 sought to exclude the TUCCs from the entire closure procedure.

The Transport Tribunal had been created under the 1947 Transport Act and was mainly concerned with rates and charges. But it was an independent quasi-judicial body and would be well suited to adopt the role of adjudicator at railway closure inquiries.

The most interesting section of the Bill was deep in Clause 4, subsection 2: should the Transport Tribunal reach the conclusion that a line was hopelessly uneconomic, it would give directions to the BTC to offer the line to another body as a Light Railway, and the BTC would be empowered to offer the line to the highest bidder. This might be a locally constituted group of individuals, one or more local authorities, or even a workers co-operative.

The general aim of Archer Baldwin and the Railway Development Association was to force the BTC to downgrade the branch lines, both in terms of manpower and operating expenses, until they could pay their way. If a line was subsequently put up for closure, the Commission would be forced to give evidence in public detailing the operational economy measures that had been tried. And the entire consultation procedure would be held before the Transport Tribunal, a truly independent body, rather than the TUCCs.

The Bill put forward some imaginative solutions to the rural transport problem, and to the delight of all concerned, actually went before Parliament in 1955. The prospective legislation had arrived not a moment too soon, for branch lines were typically carrying as many staff, wagons, coaches, locomotives and manpower as they had in Victorian times, when rolling stock and labour was relatively cheap. By the 1950s, manpower was accounting for no less than 62% of total railway operating expenses. So reduced manning levels were key to making branch lines viable, and for the busier lines, a suitable recipe might include diesel multiple units and

Wickham railcars were exported all over the world in the early 1950s, long before Britain's railways started experimenting with the technology. No.3, exported to Bolivia in 1953, is pictured at Vischa near La Paz in 1981. It certainly remained in service longer than that, and is known to have survived until at least 2008.
PHOTO: Paul Johnson

economies such as unmanned stations. For the quieter lines, there were more radical solutions, such as running under a Light Railway Order.

There has always been some confusion as to what actually constituted a light railway or tramway. Under the provisions of the original Act of 1868, and further legislation of 1896, a 'light' railway could forego certain signalling, communications and maintenance standards in exchange for lower speed limits and other measures. Certain railway companies had experimented with light railway standards prior to nationalisation, but these had never achieved widespread popularity in Britain.

Some very insignificant lines with light traffic had been run under Light Railway Orders, but most of these had now closed, and the aim was to apply the principles to busier branch lines, on the basis that a 'light railway' was immeasurably better than none at all. The risk was that a light railway service would prove even weaker against the growing competition from buses and private cars and rapidly lose what little traffic remained. This remains a problem today, but as we shall see, a few lines were eventually kept open by using cheaper, simpler operating methods.

These could deliver substantial savings, and smaller, lighter versions of the new diesel multiple units (smaller even than the AEC experimental vehicle) would reduce costs further still. Such a vehicle would use less fuel, need fewer staff and be more gentle on the track, leading to savings in maintenance. A typical British steam engine weighed about 70 tons, with coaches of 25 to 30 tons each - say 150 tons for a three-coach stopping train. It was a lot of hardware to carry ten to 15 passengers, as was all too often the case.

By contrast, the three-unit AEC experimental railcar weighed in at just 42 tons overall, and there was plenty of experience both at home and abroad to suggest that a single unit

In September 1957, Standard Class 2-6-0 78054 makes a fine sight leaving Boat of Garten in the Scottish Highlands, but although only two years old, it was already considered out of date, and would be withdrawn and scrapped eight years later. Hauling a two-carriage stopping train with a locomotive like this made economic nonsense.

weighing as little as 15 tons might prove even more cost-effective. British manufacturers had been producing such diesel railcars for years, most of them going for export. The Hertfordshire firm of Wickham built its first railbus in 1937, and by the end of the war was exporting machines to Jamaica, Peru, Kenya and Uganda, building up a lot of expertise in the process.

Most Wickham railcars were rated at less than 200hp, yet they generally carried around 50 seated passengers and proved more than a match for the torturous gradients and switch-backs of the developing world.

In theoretical terms, all other factors being equal, a railbus was bound to have an advantage over its road equivalent either in terms of speed, fuel economy or both, thanks to easier gradients and reduced rolling friction. A steel tyre running on a steel rail was (and remains) fundamentally more efficient than a rubber tyre on tarmac. In the 1920s, several of the light railways built rudimentary multiple units by placing two road buses on the rails back to back, and operating the combination with just the forward facing engine in operation!

There were many other practical economy measures that could cut branch line costs. British practice favoured staffed level crossings, even the lowliest crossing being equipped with a signal-cabin and keeper, who on a minor branch might only be required to open the gates half a dozen times a day. Once again, Continental European railways had made economies years before by installing fully automatic crossings. In Britain, this was painfully slow: the first experiments with lifting barriers took place at York in 1953, and legislation followed in 1957, but the first trial crossing (at Uttoxeter) didn't arrive until February 1961.

On 9th December 1955, the Rural Transport Improvement Bill arrived in the House of Commons for its Second Reading, the debate stage of the legislative process, and Archer Baldwin set about persuading his colleagues that branch lines could be saved through cheaper operation.

County Donegal was cited as an example: the rail network here had nearly closed, but after the introduction of modern diesel railbuses, the passenger service in this sparsely populated corner of Ireland had survived, albeit on a shoestring. In fact, the entire County Donegal rail network would be closed by 16th February 1960, but the railbuses had worked well, and the principle could help to turn around more lucrative enterprises. The USA provided another interesting test case: a group of citizens had purchased an 18½-mile branch line and operated it themselves, even reaping a 4% return on their investment. A ten-mile branch, claimed Mr Baldwin, could be maintained for about £60 a mile if operated by light railway methods, and a single diesel railbus could be bought for £9,000 – less than £6,000 if mass produced.

There was general agreement with the provisions in the Bill, especially from MPs with rural seats who knew only too well the political damage that railway closures were causing. Typical of the support was that from John Hill, MP for Norfolk South:

"If the Bill can produce one such diesel railcar service and if one branch line can find a new life on a lesser scale, then in my opinion the Bill will have amply justified its existence."

Inevitably, the Isle of Wight inquiry was raised, amid mutterings that the BTC, with a monopoly of road, rail and ferry undertakings on the island, intended to push traffic onto the roads until the remaining railways proved uneconomic and could be withdrawn.

The debate was wound up by Hugh Molson, Parliamentary Secretary to the Minister of Transport. Railway branch lines, he said, were worthless speculative ventures that would never pay their way, and the AEC experimental railcar, busy on the network since 1953, had cost £22,000, which sounds a high figure given that the small pre-production run of railbuses built a few years later cost only £12,500 each, but of course it was a one-off, and composed of three carriages. Interestingly, Mr Molson – who had clearly been well briefed – added that the simple four-wheel design had resulted in rapid flange wear, which may well have been true, although it would certainly not have been an insoluble problem. He went on to claim that the BTC was underestimating the losses on rural branch lines by excluding the cost of track maintenance, which *wasn't* true, but this insinuation made it clear that the Department was out to kill the legislation at all costs.

The only light relief came when Hugh Molson was pressed on his Ministry's failure to initiate promised road improvements on the Isle of Wight: "The question whether there should be trunk roads in the Isle of Wight is one which I have previously argued with my Hon. Friend, and I have pointed out that the roads in the Isle of Wight are of only very limited value to through traffic."

The Rural Transport Improvement Bill failed to attract enough support. From a near empty House of Commons, 31 members voted for the proposals, 27 against, but according to the rules of the House, the majority was too small for the Bill to survive. In the words of Owen Prosser of the RDA:

"The Bill failed, not through Labour opposition, although there was Labour opposition. In fact the big names of the day were there, including the immediate ex-Prime Minister, Clement Attlee, and that stormy petrel from the Welsh valleys, Aneurin Bevan. The Bill failed its Second Reading... through Tory apathy, because Mr Baldwin didn't have enough Tories to support him in the Division Lobby."

At this time, closures were largely confined to villages in the rural shires, leaving urban MPs somewhat apathetic, for the time being at least. Yet, with hindsight, it's unlikely that apathy alone was to blame. Why did such high ranking politicians put their weight behind defeating a minor Parliamentary Bill? Labour was in opposition at the time, and a Bill which threatened to disrupt Government transport policy – as well as seeking to improve the amenities for poorer people in rural areas – might have been expected to appeal to Labour politicians.

The Great Railway Conspiracy

But Labour could hardly advocate the reopening of railways in private hands when it had gone to a great deal of trouble to nationalise the industry. Under the spirit, if not the *actualité*, of integration, traffic was to have been steered to the transport undertaking best suited to carrying it. And following the rules (if not the spirit) of capitalism, the socialists had allowed uneconomic nationalised branch lines to close, cheerfully transferring traffic to nationalised bus companies.

To be fair, Labour was also faced with intransigent union problems in relation to privately-owned railways. Volunteer staff would be beyond the reach of the NUR, and they would be taking bread from the mouths of the bus drivers, some of whom were themselves NUR members.

For the Conservatives, the forces of capitalism naturally carried more weight. In a free market, the travelling public and freight customers were free to choose their own transport, and if this meant that a railway ceased to make a profit (Hugh Molson had pointed out that the BTC now had a statutory duty to make the railways pay) it would have to make way for something else. Individual Conservative MPs were bound by loyalty to the Government, and it was a government whose victories were funded in part by road transport and road construction interests.

Another possible explanation has even more sinister overtones. For politicians of all shades, the Bill came dangerously close to undermining central government by handing decision making to the regions, an unpalatable suggestion for most Westminster politicians at the time. Given sufficient funding and enthusiasm, a local authority really would be able to buy and run its own railway – just as many were running local buses, but this could be a slippery slope. What if the Scots got a taste for running their own affairs? Railway closures were set to cause a lingering resentment against the the Union, because in Scotland – where some remote branch lines really did hold communities together – it was perceived that local politicians and TUCC members were calling for restraint, while English politicians were signing the death warrants of communities they knew little or nothing about. This was all to come to a head later on.

During 1956, the BTC's financial situation continued to deteriorate. In February the Commission applied for a 10% increase in freight charges, together with increases in passenger fares to cover rising costs. The Ministry of Transport granted a 5% increase for freight, but refused to allow any change in passenger fares for six months. At a time of relatively high inflation, the hapless Transport Commission had become an instrument of government economic policy.

Even the Ministry of Transport was later to accept that the loss to the railways was about £8.4 million, while the BTC put the true figure nearer to £17 million, about £1.3 billion today. Against a background of rising prices and falling receipts, it was a crippling blow that led to borrowing, interest charges and further losses.

However dubious the economic situation, the BTC was nonetheless beginning to reap the rewards of modernisation, and paradoxically, the greatest success story at this time was the branch lines, where diesel multiple units were proving more popular than anyone had dared to imagine. In Birmingham to Lichfield traffic was up 210%; Leeds to Bradford and Harrogate, 144%, and even the little Silloth branch in Cumberland had achieved a 66% rise. DMUs were popular with the public, and they were cheap to run, the BTC now having firm evidence that they cost about 3s 4d per mile, against 10 shillings for steam-hauled trains.

At last, the Commission gave the green light in favour of diesel operation on local and rural services. Orders were placed for 2,400 DMUs to enter service by the end of 1958, with a prediction of 4,600 being required by 1961. Such was the demand from the regions, however,

The battery-electric multiple unit was unique in Britain, although battery power was tried elsewhere, notably on the Dublin suburban services. The experimental unit seems to have worked quite well on the Ballater branch, but without additional economies, it could never have saved the line from closure. PHOTO: *Owen Prosser*

that the initial order had increased to 2,741 by early 1957, then to more than 3,000, with a prediction that 5,144 cars would be in service within 18 months. The BTC was finally taking small diesel railbuses seriously, announcing that a new unit would undergo trials in 1957. Intriguingly, there was even talk of an experimental two-car battery-electric unit, to be tested on the Ballater branch in Aberdeenshire, to take advantage of cheap hydro-electric power. Battery power had the advantage of very cheap and quiet operation, but the disadvantage of considerable weight – 10 tons of batteries in a 25-ton railcar, said the Minister of Transport dismissively. This unique machine went into service in 1958, and worked to Ballater on and off until the branch was closed in 1966. Against all the odds, it survived, and is now undergoing restoration back in Aberdeenshire, where part of the Ballater line is being reopened.

In the late 1950s it became clear that the BTC was becoming increasingly enthusiastic about the prospects for some rural branch lines. By this time, it was broadly in favour of modernising the secondary lines, but there remained little doubt that a proportion of the branch lines – perhaps a substantial proportion – would have to close, and as late as 1956, the BTC had warned the CTCC that widescale closures were in the pipeline. Generally though, as the positive results from DMU experiments began to percolate through the industry, the Commission's resolve to eradicate branch lines began to weaken.

It was a confusing period. Some officials were openly speaking in favour of railbuses for lightly trafficked lines, and even light rail methods, while others held the view that the rural branch lines should be closed *en masse*. Sir Reginald Wilson, Chairman of the Eastern Area Board, had long spoken in favour of closure, recommending that as many as 4,000-5,000 small stations should be eradicated. Others were not so sure – if modern technology could turn around the secondary lines, surely it would make sense on many of the branch lines too?

Eventually, even Sir Reginald seemed undecided. The Government, on the other hand, was starting to make its views perfectly clear, and doing everything in its power to resist cost-saving measures on the rural lines. As a result, the policy objectives of the BTC began to slide further and further away from those of the Conservative administration.

Meanwhile, someone at the BTC seems to have leaked confidential documents on branch line economics to officials at the Ministry of Transport. The documents – prepared during an early pro-closure phase – appeared to make an overwhelming case for wholesale railway closure. The result was a flurry of memos on the timing and scale of an accelerated closure programme:

"If we want [the TUCCs] to perform this task more quickly and more ruthlessly, then I think we and the Commission must give them more positive help. There seems to me to be a necessity for some really startling and comprehensive statement of Commission policy which could... be timed to coincide [with] or follow the announcement of the 1955 deficit."
Alison Munro, Assistant Secretary at the Ministry of Transport, in an internal memo, February 1956

There are shades here of the Government trying to 'bury bad news'. By April 1956, the Ministry had drawn up a broad plan, although the details were to remain shrouded in secrecy for obvious reasons:

"It should be possible to impress on the public the size of the amputation contemplated without listing actual services. Secondly, any such list will lead to the organisation of opposition – possibly on a national scale – which might otherwise have remained dormant."
Alison Munro, April 1956

In a vain attempt to limit the damage, Sir Reginald Wilson – now generally in favour of branch line retention – wrote in these terms to Hugh Molson, the Joint Parliamentary Secretary:

"...quite often these services were ancillary to other services and should not have been charged, even theoretically, with a full share of the costs... The charges were, therefore, too heavy; on the other hand, credits were probably too light because they failed to take into account the contributory value of the traffic which these ancillary services brought to the main services.

Unfortunately, the figures have, in fact, become known outside the narrow circle for which they were intended, but I am glad that they have not gone further than the Ministry. But if the confusion they have caused in your office is any indication of the upset which would ensue if the calculations reached a wider public, then I feel amply confirmed in my view that the sooner the figures themselves are forgotten, the better it will be..."

Of course, the figures were not forgotten, and as Sir Reginald seems to have belatedly realised, they were now in the hands of the enemy. This fascinating exchange raises all sorts of questions. Why were such unflattering figures floating around at the BTC in the first place? Presumably they had been manipulated to give a deliberately negative view of the prospects for rural rail. Clearly, the BTC's own management now believed that they presented a distorted picture of minor railway economics, but with the benefit of hindsight, they would have been safer almost anywhere than on the files at the Department of Transport.

That the mood was hardening in the Department can be gauged from a parliamentary exchange on 24th April 1956, when Archer Baldwin attempted again to bring up the subject of Irish railbuses during a debate on rural transport:

"I have had sent to me by the Railway Development Association particulars of a rail bus which is operated on the Sligo railway in Ireland. It is operated on a steel-rubber wheel. In fact, it is a bus which is being converted at the cost of £100... If they can do that in Ireland, I should hope that something similar might be done in this country. It has been said that this is not operated on the

Continent, but only last week I had a letter from a man serving in Germany who says that out there the railways seem to be flourishing. Branch lines abound and on most are rail cars which are run very efficiently."

Mr Baldwin rose to speak at 4.48pm. What he could not have known was that the Minister would be waiting in ambush, having made enquiries to Ireland that morning in anticipation of such a confrontation.

Exactly who the representative of Her Majesty's Government chatted to, and exactly what was said, will sadly never be known. The phone call might have been answered by some lowly minion in the railway yard who knew little or nothing about the railbus. Then again, the whole affair might have been a ministerial bluff. Or perhaps, as the RDA concluded, the Minister's representative had actually rung the rabidly anti-rail Ulster Transport Authority. But the result was to silence further Parliamentary debate on the matter. At 6.34pm, the Minister rose and settled the railbus affair once and for all:

"I asked one of my officers to telephone to Ireland this morning to find out about its present state of health. I learned that it was very bad indeed, and that steam trains are having to replace it for many operations. So I am afraid that the attempt to put a bus on the railway... has not worked."

Whatever the truth of the matter, the official from the Ministry had certainly not spoken to the General Manager of the railway concerned, who later confirmed to the RDA that the railbus had achieved a considerable mileage and was in a good state of health. The Minister went on to claim that the BTC had disputed Mr Baldwin's figures for the maintenance of a ten-mile branch line, stating that the true cost would be nearer £300 per mile annually than £60, and that maintenance would require a full-time gang of four. And the Government figures kept coming:

The Sligo, Leitrim & Northern Counties Railway railbus which achieved Parliamentary notoriety in 1956. Its apparent failure was to silence parliamentary debate on railbuses for good. PHOTO: Owen Prosser

allegedly, of 80 million train-miles operated the previous year, only five million had been moderately loaded (carrying in excess of 125 passengers); 45 million had been poorly loaded, and 30 million very poorly loaded, carrying fewer than 20 passengers.

Meticulously (if one-sidedly) briefed by Ministry officials, Mr Watkinson continued to spew forth statistics. The Netherlands, he claimed, had closed 691 stations out of 1,000, and a third of British passenger trains were covering no more than a third of their costs. Of course, any of these figures could just as easily have been used by the pro-rail lobby to justify provision of light-weight railbuses, but Archer Baldwin and his conspirators were by now thoroughly demoralised. Despite the evidence of fixed figures, and the potential for cheaper operational costs, Parliamentary discussion about railbuses and light rail techniques was effectively at an end.

Paradoxically, the pro-rail lobby was also standing down because Britain's railways appeared to have turned the corner. Modernisation was well under way, and traffic was starting to grow, hitting some 21 billion passenger/miles in 1956, one of the highest figures yet recorded if we ignore the 'demob' year of 1947, when passenger-miles peaked briefly at 29 billion. By the end of the year, more than 400 diesel multiple units were at work, drawing in new business the length and breadth of the system. Fares and charges, however, continued to lag well behind inflation. In the summer of 1956, the Chancellor, Harold Macmillan, instructed the nationalised industries to freeze their prices to fight a rising tide of inflation. But the TUC refused to take part, so wages continued to rise, the and the effect was further to weaken the financial position of the railways and shorten the fuse on the deficit time-bomb. Overall losses for 1956 hit £57.5 million, and for the first time since 1921, the railways experienced a working deficit, sliding £16.5 million into the red.

The BTC explained it all away as a side-effect of modernisation, and it was partially correct, because the hasty implementation of the schemes had been shockingly wasteful. The sudden demand for DMUs had resulted in orders for 53 distinct types, as the regions made their own choices and negotiated with different manufacturers. To be fair, nearly all of these designs were successful, but it wasn't the cheapest way to do things. The mainline diesel programme had resulted in orders for 230 machines, but only 43 of those were built in the railway's own workshops, such was the haste to bring diesels in. No fewer than 14 designs were involved, from seven different manufacturers. Privately, the Commission had estimated that at least 10% of the new designs were likely to prove expensive failures, and even that gloomy prognosis proved rather optimistic.

With no fire to clean or boiler to wash, the main line diesel locomotives should have been available for almost 24 hours a day, with the official estimate being 85% availability. But so unreliable were the new machines that many failed to exceed 60%, and a few managed no more than 50% availability, or rather less than the labour-intensive steam engines they were replacing. One particular rogue averaged no more than 8,000 miles between breakdowns. Interestingly, the DMUs appear to have been relatively reliable, although they were just as innovative.

Electrification plans were continuing apace too. In March 1956, amid a fanfare of publicity, the BTC Chairman Sir Brian Robertson announced (rather prematurely as it transpired) that Britain's railways were about to witness 'the end of steam'. The first new overhead electrification project would be from Euston to Liverpool and Manchester, and it would be completed by 1959. The line was to become a test-bed for one of the most prestigious and exciting modernisation schemes in Europe, and whatever else happened, the BTC wanted to make a success of it.

Generally, the Commission was confident with progress, and optimistic about the future, although costs were running ahead of predictions, and in October 1956 a reappraisal suggested that external finance would be required, in part to cover the mounting deficits. Grudgingly, the

Once the BTC had decided on a railbus trial, orders were placed for 22 prototypes. ABOVE: One of five Waggon und
Maschinenbau railbuses, newly commissioned at Stratford, Eastern Region. PHOTO: John Turner, 53A Models Collection
BELOW: One of five built by Park Royal, shown here at Craigellachie in 1960.

Government gave the green light to advance money to cover the deficit and defray the cost of modernisation.

The BTC was well aware that the Government had control of the purse strings, and now that modernisation had ceased to be self-funding, it could pull the plug at any time. And to complete the programme, more time was needed, as was more cash and less interference. From the safety of its ninth Annual Report the Commission launched an ill-timed broadside at the Government, demanding among other things:

"...reasonable freedom and a period of stability to press on with recon-struction, and that the whole fabric of public transport will no longer be subject to periodic seismic upheaval on political account."

Wickham produced five railbuses fitted with Meadows six-cylinder 105hp engines and pneumatic doors. This one is bound for Craigendoran on the West Highland line

The new somewhat belligerent attitude was partly a result of changed circumstances. The BTC had entered the 1950s as a vast body with a near monopoly on inland transport, but by 1956 it was mostly concerned with railways. Almost half its lorry fleet was handed to the private sector when British Road Services was sold, while the road freight industry continued to expand at a rapid pace, with more than a million lorries on British roads by 1957. The Government helped, with measures like an easing of licensing restrictions in 1953. Slowly, the message sunk in with the BTC, that it was now defending the railway corner against the Government, the road haulage industry and anyone else who tried to interfere.

Attitudes were changing at the Central Transport Users Consultative Committee too, which finally agreed that lightweight railbuses should be given a fair trial. Its favourable report on the matter led the BTC to authorise the construction of 22 vehicles during 1957 and '58.

ABOVE: One of two Bristol railbus chassis, prior to being fitted with Eastern Coach Works body. Note the simple two axle layout.
BELOW: The completed railbus. Although political changes would make the working lives of the railbus fleet very short, six would survive long enough to be enthusiastically grabbed by heritage lines, but sadly neither of the Bristol machines

The Great Railway Conspiracy

The railbuses came from four British manufacturers: two from Bristol/Eastern Coach Works, five each from Wickhams, Park Royal Vehicles, AC Cars, and – in view of the European lead in the field – another five from the German company, Waggon und Maschinenbau, of Donauwörth.

It had taken the Commission eight years to adopt diesel multiple units, and another two to accept the principles of railbus operation, but by late 1956, the Commission was firmly in favour of exploring new technology, advocating closure only as a last resort:

"Any plans for refashioning the railway system to suit modern transport conditions must first explore alternative methods of operation. Thereafter, those services which cannot possibly be made economic by modern rail methods but can be better catered for by road transport must be eliminated."

The railbuses were immediately put into service on lightly used lines around the country, and it was perhaps fitting that one of the bravest and most innovative experiments was attempted on former Great Western territory, the GWR having pioneered railcar and multiple unit operation almost 30 years before. This was wonderful news for the Railway Development Association, for the experiment was to embody almost every cost-saving measure it had advocated.

Kemble, on the main line between Swindon and Gloucester, was the junction for two rural branch lines, a shorter one running north to Cirencester, and a long rambling one south to the little town of Tetbury. Both lines had operated at a substantial loss for years, the more tenuous Tetbury branch reportedly carrying no more than 100 passengers a week. They were, however, ideal candidates for railbus experiments. Tetbury, with a population of only 3,000, was typical of the smaller communities with a branch line under threat, while the market town of Cirencester (population of 13,000) represented larger towns at the upper end of railbus economics. A great deal depended on these trials, because the Western Region was poised to launch similar railbus services on other West Country branches if the trial proved its worth.

A few 'heavy rail' single-car diesels were introduced as well as the railbuses. Notable survivors were those made by Pressed Steel from 1960. Number 121034 still works some Aylesbury to Princes Risborough services, as well as special excursions, such as this one to the Didcot Railway Centre in May 2011. PHOTO: Ian Knight

On 2nd February 1959, the steam locomotives were retired and three AC Cars railbuses started work. Several new simple halts had been constructed, and the diminutive four-wheel railbuses made up for their lack of seating capacity by operating an intensive service over the branch lines: eight trains a day to Tetbury, and 14 over the shorter Cirencester branch.

Within a few weeks, the preliminary results revealed that the Tetbury railbus was still failing to cover movement costs, despite increasing patronage by 250%, but the Cirencester line was proving very successful, carrying 2,500 passengers a week – an average of almost 30 per train. As the railbuses seated only 46, the most popular Saturday services were often severely overcrowded, and on one notable occasion no fewer than 110 passengers squeezed aboard!

Ironically, when Dr Beeching's notorious 'station viability' maps were published four years later, the receipts from Cirencester were high enough to put it into the mid-range '£5,000 to £25,000' annual income category, an outstanding result that was quietly suppressed.

Railbuses had proved themselves to be excellent low-cost tools for getting the best value from lightly used lines that might never be profitable, but would be required to stay open for other environmental or social reasons.

Even Sir Reginald Wilson appears to have been swayed by the new technology. According to David Blee, General Manager of the London Midland region, Sir Reginald was, "...more in favour of keeping such lines open, operated with what he described as 'the lowest form of life', i.e. an ultra-cheap railbus." It was not unusual for career railwaymen to be condescending about railbuses! But they were beginning

In this February 1962 view, the AC Cars railbus is dwarfed by Cirencester Town station. Two years later, despite realising some impressive operating economies, the railbuses and the branch line would all be swept away. In an era of widespread closures, the railbus experiments made life difficult for British Railways at closure inquiries. PHOTO: Ben Brooksbank

to realise that a minimalist service would enable the Commission to keep track on the ground, leaving the door open to reinstatement of 'heavy rail' multiple unit and/or freight services, should the industrial, economic or population circumstances change. In a fast-changing world, this policy made

A brand new diesel multiple unit at Birmingham New Street in May 1955. The units were used to shuttle passengers to the British Industries Fair at Castle Bromwich. PHOTO: Owen Prosser

a lot more sense than outright closure and permanent eradication of a railway corridor.

The London Midland Region had experimented with a slightly heavier solution between Buckingham and Banbury, using a single-car diesel unit rather than a railbus. "All the indications," said the General Manager, early in 1958, "were that it would continue to be a dead loss-maker, but I will be happy to try it." Even this limited experiment generated a four-fold increase in traffic and a 28% reduction in costs, and a railbus would have reduced costs a lot further. The predictions of the RDA had, at last, been vindicated, and it looked as though many rural branches could be saved.

Elsewhere, the larger DMUs were continuing to break records. By February 1958, earnings between Birmingham and Lichfield had increased almost three-fold, while the Bradford-Leeds-Harrogate service (extended to Knaresborough in 1957), had earned £114,700, against £29,000 in the last days of steam. The following year, a new service between Leeds and Barnsley increased traffic by 416%. Such figures resulted in a new confidence in the industry that modernisation would be a success. With modern diesel and electric trains on the trunk lines, multiple units on secondary services, and railbuses on the branches, how could it fail? Perhaps the BTC was getting a little too confident. In March 1957, the original modernisation plans were swept aside and replaced with new ideas that went a good deal further.

The Report on Diesel & Electric Traction, and the Passenger Services of the Future, was probably the most expansionist document ever considered by British Railways. Very much overshadowed today by Beeching's *Reshaping* report, which reached rather different conclusions, it was a blueprint for a step-change in the way Britain's railways were operated. And perhaps ominously – at a time when the Government was rapidly losing confidence in the railway industry – it represented the biggest single investment in rail since Victoria was on the throne.

The scale of the electrification proposals was quite staggering: 2,213 miles of overhead catenaries for the East Coast (including quite a few minor branches), 809 miles on the West Coast, 632 miles elsewhere on the London Midland region, 741 miles in Scotland and 346 miles on the DC third-rail system in the Southern region, together with 338 miles of AC overhead electrification to Weymouth and Exeter. The prediction was for construction work to reach a peak of 800 miles a year in the mid-1960s, the whole programme to be completed by about 1980. This didn't happen of course, but writing in 2012, it's interesting to note that most of the uncompleted plans are back on the agenda and expected to come to fruition within the next 20 years or so. We can only speculate as to how the network might have developed if these schemes had been realised in the 1960s/70s.

These 1957 proposals made the 1955 Modernisation Plan look half-hearted, with its modest provision of 1,200 miles of overhead electrification and 250 miles on the DC third-rail system, for the BTC was now intending to convert 2,800 miles immediately, with the aim of putting 5,100 miles under the catenaries within 20 years. Massive though it was, the programme would only electrify 29% of the network, the bare minimum to chase the lead of other European countries, which were already far ahead with electrification. By 2008, Germany had electrified 60% of its rail network, and the European average stood at 52%, pulled down somewhat by the UK figure of 33%[4].

The cost was put at £250 million (£18 billion today), against which branch line losses paled into insignificance. But there was money for secondary and branch lines as well. In addition to the small railbus fleet, the BTC had placed firm orders for 5,144 DMUs, with another 300 under consideration. In the summer of 1956, the BTC actually put pressure on a bemused Metro-Cammell to speed up deliveries.

After years of tight financial control, the Modernisation Plan resulted in an orgy of spending. By the end of 1957, the total cost was re-appraised at £1,660 million, a staggering £120 billion in 2012 terms. Ministry of Transport and Treasury officials had previously allowed the Commission considerable freedom, but now it was proposing a huge increase in spending of public money, they began to look more closely into railway affairs.

From the Treasury point of view, the problem lay with the state of the economy. In September 1957, the Government introduced a credit squeeze, cut public investment and raised the bank base rate from five to seven per cent to stave off a run on the pound. Superficially, the situation looked quite healthy (the bank rate fell back within a few months), but it was hardly a suitable time to announce massive increases in public spending. What the Treasury didn't know was that the BTC's Modernisation Committee – the architects of modernisation – had warned that it might prove difficult or impossible to cover the interest payments on the modernisation schemes. In other words, financial collapse could be imminent.

Perhaps the Commission had been influenced by the mood of the times. In January 1958, Harold Macmillan was handed the premiership by an ailing Anthony Eden and in July the new Prime Minister uttered what would become his most famous words:

"Let's be frank about. Most of our people have never had it so good."

For the railways, the good times were to prove very short-lived. Money was being poured into a handful of prestigious schemes, leaving the greater part of the network starved of investment, and in the case of the many remaining local steam services and other outmoded practices, losing cash. At the same time, no-one seems to have properly considered the long-term financial implications of piecemeal modernisation.

Few commentators were sufficiently well informed to understand what was happening. A marked exception was our friend Professor Hondelink, who returned from his work at the United Nations to find the situation at home sliding from bad to worse. In April 1958, he wrote to the Permanent Secretary at the Ministry of Transport, Sir Gilmore Jenkins, in a last rather desperate attempt to influence events:

"A combination of modernisation and retrenchment can only have a disastrous effect, namely a few spectacular services here and there, but the railway system as a whole becoming a perpetual burden on the taxpayer."

His advice was quietly ignored. In any event, road transport, and motorways in particular, were in the news. Work was well underway on the Preston Bypass, the first section of the M6. Of much greater importance was the mileage then going through the planning stage – another 73 miles to be completed in 1959, 45 in 1960 and a gradual increase thereafter.

Motorway construction was enormously expensive, and such an outpouring of Government funds was bound to cost someone dear – the BTC would foot the bill. On 5th December 1958, Harold Macmillan opened the Preston Bypass, describing the new motorway as, "...the symbol of the opening of a new era in motor travel in the UK." It was to prove a major headache for the railways, partly because modernisation was still barely out of the planning stage (electric trains didn't reach Preston until 1974), but because the Government was now openly saying what it had felt for some time: that roads were the primary transport of the future.

Events began to move at lightning speed. In February 1959 the Government published a White Paper, *Proposals for Inland Waterways*. Like the railways, the canals had remained under state control (the BTC) when the Conservatives came to power. By the late 1950s, their finances were in an even more parlous state than those of the railways, but the way the Government dealt with the problem was very different, and it's worth looking at in some detail.

In June 1958, the Bowes Committee had reported to the Government with various proposals. It had recommended that the canals and navigable rivers should be divided into three groups: class 'A' (such as the Severn and Aire & Calder) that carried plenty of commercial traffic and were mostly profitable; class 'B', that carried a little commercial traffic but lost money; and class 'C' – 770 miles of canal thought to be of no commercial value, and mostly derelict or semi-derelict.

The Committee judged that class A waterways should have profits ploughed back for investment and that class B should be reinstated to a prescribed standard and maintained thus for a period of 25 years to allow future trade to develop. The burden would be met largely from the public purse. In the meantime, steps would be taken to find non-commercial uses for these waterways.

Generally, the A and B class canals would be treated in a similar manner to the trunk and secondary railway lines, but the class C canals – which corresponded roughly to the railway branch lines – were to be dealt with very differently. The future of each canal would be determined on its merits, some being developed and others allowed to die. The real breakthrough was that any interested body, such as a preservation group or local authority, would be encouraged to share in the redevelopment of such canals, provided that it bore a proportion of the costs.

The Bowes Committee had produced an admirable report. It was honest and it gave plenty of answers, and by and large, the Government agreed with its findings. There would be a two-year experiment to test the proposals, and an Inland Waterways Redevelopment Committee to assist in the promotion of redevelopment schemes. The Bowes proposal that the Government (perhaps inevitably) felt unable to commit to was maintaining 900 miles of class B waterway at public expense for 25 years. But it was impressed with the idea of 'privatising' the lesser waterways, and it agreed with Bowes that abandonment was a 'negative' option, and redevelopment a 'new and positive approach':

"The Government would be prepared to bridge a small gap by a special *ad hoc* grant towards the capital cost of the redevelopment... it is also important that voluntary organisations... which have shown so much interest in seeing canals preserved and restored, should take the opportunities for joint effort and contribution which the preparation of schemes should offer."

At the risk of jumping some years ahead of our story, the White Paper of 1959 led to the establishment of the British Waterways Board, whose enlightened and flexible attitude brought immediate results. Discussions began with canal users, local authorities and others to formulate a policy for the restoration of the non-commercial waterways.

One successful scheme involved the lower section of the Stratford-upon-Avon canal, proposed for closure by the BTC in 1955. This less than strategically placed backwater had lain abandoned for many years, but under the provisions of the White Paper, and the 1962 Transport Act which followed it, was restored to health in 1964, in a partnership between the British Waterways Board and the National Trust, using a mixture of state and volunteer capital and labour. As a result, many miles of canal were saved, and in time became leisure assets in their own right.

If such schemes were suitable for the minor canals, then why not for the railways? After all, the provisions of the Bowes Report were not so very different from those of the Rural Transport Improvement Bill that the Government had gone to such great lengths to destroy. If uneconomic canals were to be offered to groups of private individuals or local authorities, then why not the uneconomic branch lines, for which abandonment was just as negative an option?

One reason was the high cost of abandoning canals. It had been estimated that to close all the uneconomic canals would cost £600 million, but that only another £340 million would be needed to keep them open to toll-paying pleasure craft. In the case of the Kennet & Avon, it

The Lower Stratford-upon-Avon Canal was restored with a mixture of volunteer labour and state funding. PHOTO: Wikipedia Creative Commons

had been judged that the cost of closure was more or less the same as restoration.

The canals had also become essential for drainage, water supply and irrigation, so even if they were closed to traffic, some sort of water channel often had to be kept in place anyway, and it could cost more to rebuild the canal into a narrower channel or pipe than to restore it to health as a useful thoroughfare.

There were hidden costs involved in closing the railways too, which by this time must have become self-evident. The value of the realisable capital assets, such as station buildings, track and equipment, was more than offset by the cost of demolishing or maintaining redundant bridges, tunnels and viaducts. Fences, hedges, culverts and ditches still had to be maintained by someone after the railway was gone, and it was generally the Commission which picked up the bill.[5] In addition, the replacement bus services were failing to fulfil their early promise and some routes were losing both customers and money at an alarming rate. Once again, the Commission was generally liable, and the cost was growing steadily. But the Government continued to treat the railways very differently to the canals.

One possible explanation was that the Government (and more particularly the Ministry of Transport) saw canals as useful amenities, even if they had no commercial value. But a privately operated, locally controlled railway was another matter entirely. It might become a serious transport undertaking and, as such, might create all sorts of problems, particularly with the road lobby and the unions. More importantly, it would encourage others to fight for their local railways, and the Government had already decided to eradicate local services as quickly and ruthlessly as possible. On 11th June 1958, Viscount Hinchingbrooke, MP for Dorset South, asked the Minister of Transport Harold Watkinson whether he might foster a similar scheme to the canals for the railways:

Viscount Hinchingbrooke: "Will my Right Honourable Friend set up a Departmental committee jointly with the British Transport Commission to examine the way in which... branch lines might be sold or leased to private firms or agencies... Is he aware that there is something rather disagreeable, as well as uneconomic, in the policy now being pursued by the Commission in ripping up the metals, removing the girders of the bridges, and allowing the embankments and the cuttings to grow weeds..."

Mr Watkinson: "I will gladly look at any suggestions my Noble Friend makes, but I hope what he is saying does not mean that he opposes the closing of uneconomic branch lines, because I must warn the House that this closure must go on. Perhaps I might take this opportunity of warning the House that it will be greatly expedited in the very near future."
Parliamentary Questions, House of Commons, 11th June 1958

It's hard to understand why the Government was so determined to eradicate branch lines when there was ample evidence that some could justifiably be kept open, while others could be operated for leisure purposes, or at the very least the trackbed could be mothballed pending future transport use. Certainly, many of those in positions of authority saw the roads as the transport of the future, and the railways as the last vestige of a grimy, labour-intensive heavy industry. The Commission's extended reliance on steam traction hadn't helped.

In Government eyes, road buses could carry passengers more efficiently on the new motorways, and private road haulage contractors most of the freight. And it was these same haulage contractors that were to influence Government behaviour, for in the 1950s the Government owed a great deal to the road haulage industry.

According to *The Railwaymen*, the official history of the NUR:

"The Transport Act in 1947 created something of a vacuum which was filled by the emergence of the Road Haulage Association, the principle agency for advancing the interests of the road-construction firms, the road-hauliers and motorists in Parliament."

When the Labour administration finally succeeded in bringing road haulage interests under state control in 1950-51, there was an upsurge in anger from private hauliers. Consequently, they did their utmost to secure a Conservative administration and to keep it in power. Such patronage was expensive. The Conservative Government had handed back the lorries at knock down prices, but sensing a political advantage, the road lobby demanded more. It wanted new roads, and the Government was glad to oblige, but the prize was to humble the railways, leaving a near-monopoly for road transport. The BTC modernisation plan threatened to make railways more successful at attracting passengers and freight, and with a limited financial pot, money spent on railways was money taken out of the motorway programme. Meanwhile, the BTC was bedevilled by mounting losses, and this proved to be the road lobby's strongest card.

Exactly when the Government began to plan its assault on the railways is hard to judge. The Ministry of Transport had been critical of the BTC's performance for some years, and it was admitted in April 1963 that plans to close a large proportion of the network had been under active consideration for, "more than three years." No doubt Government attitudes had begun to harden after the ASLEF strike in the summer of 1955, which effectively held the economy to ransom for most of June. Plans must have been firmly in place from the time of the October 1959 election. In the sort of terms even the dippiest Tory MP could understand, the railways were over-unionised, over-manned and outdated, while road transport was modern, efficient and responsive to the jungle drums of the free market. Self-employed lorry drivers and the hordes of small, responsive road haulage companies were the very stuff of right-wing transport ideology, and these people were natural Tory voters and patrons too. The involvement of the road haulage interests reached untold heights during the 1959 general election campaign, and according to *The Commercial Motor*, the journal of the Road Haulage Association:

"The Conservative Party promise the answer to the haulier's prayers. Any financial contribution he makes towards this success may be partly selfish, but wholly natural."

The financial contributions were most welcome and the Conservatives spent almost £500,000 (£33 million today) on advertising during the campaign. As there was no compulsion to reveal political donations in the 1950s, it is hard to judge exactly what proportion of this came from companies with road interests. By combining the available evidence with the picture revealed by the pattern of donations since disclosure became mandatory, it seems reasonable to conclude that as much as a quarter of this budget came from these firms, who also provided finance for the various pressure groups

Transport Minister Ernest Marples at the opening of the M1 motorway in November 1959. PHOTO: Press Association

that made up the road lobby. Harold Macmillan easily fought off the inexperienced Labour leader Hugh Gaitskell, to return to power with an increased majority of 100 seats, and a clear mandate to push through the policies demanded by his supporters.

The road groups were handsomely repaid, for the new administration offered them a Minister of Transport who was not only road-biased, but Managing Director of a successful firm of road engineering contractors into the bargain. His name was Ernest Marples.

In an era when Conservative big-wigs still tended to be drawn from the ranks of the Eton-educated classes, Marples was a self-made man – a former Labour supporter who had made a bit of brass and jumped ship. To the decidedly upper crust Harold Macmillan, the brash little Mancunian was just the fellow he needed for the rather distasteful task of cutting the once proud railway industry down to size.

As it transpired, the opportunity to humble the railways fell straight into Marple's lap. In 1958, a substantial decline in the output of coal and steel had resulted in an 8% loss of freight traffic for the railways. Day-to-day expenditure remained well under control, and passenger figures were rising, but a mild recession allied to the after-effects of the rise in interest rates the previous year caused income to fall, triggering the deficit time-bomb.

The financial house of cards collapsed, and the railways returned a working deficit of £48.1 million, an overall loss of £90.1 million, and earnings well below the level anticipated in the 1956 modernisation proposals. The Commission had no reserves of capital and was unable to cover the loss.

The Government demanded an urgent reappraisal of the financial implications of modernisation, and the Commission complied, publishing a report as a White Paper in July 1959, just before the election. The ambition of the modernisation plan had been to achieve a working surplus of £55-100 million on passenger services by 1963 and £5-35 million on freight. These targets were clearly drifting out of reach, and the Government hoped the White Paper would give a few answers. It particularly wanted to see a few examples of good housekeeping – perhaps a degree of retrenchment to consider the worsening financial crisis, or at least some plausible explanations as to what had gone wrong.

Despite the gravity of the situation, the BTC saw no reason to scale back its plans. On the contrary, it proposed bringing forward expenditure into 1959-63, so as to deliver the financial benefits earlier. There would be a modest programme of rail closures amounting to about 1,800 miles, or rather less than 10% of the existing network. These would exclude many threatened branches, and a few main lines that had previously looked weak, such as the Great Central and Settle & Carlisle. The Commission also suggested that its financial structure should be reformed to remove the burden of high fixed rates of interest.

But it was already much too late for such changes. The problem was that most of the modernisation plans involved very long-term investment. Only a paltry 24 miles of overhead electrification had been completed, but there would be no return until the services were at least partially operational; 1,500 miles of concrete sleepers had been laid, but the return on that investment would be decades away. To a lesser extent the same was true for resignalling schemes, marshalling yards and modern locomotives – there would be financial returns, but they might not be fully apparent for 40 years.

If the BTC had prepared accurate and detailed plans of where the money was going and the sort of return that could eventually be expected on each investment, all might have been well, but officials at the Treasury and Ministry of Transport had concluded that many of its figures were flawed. A good example was the set-piece electrification from Euston to Liverpool and Manchester, the jewel in the modernisation crown that should have been one of the most easily justifiable schemes. The BTC had originally estimated that this would cost £75 million, convincing the Government that any borrowings would be repaid through increased returns. However, after a change of policy on the technical details of the scheme in 1956, an increase in scale during the 'never had it so good' era, and a later, more realistic, appraisal of costs, the projected expenditure had doubled to £161 million.

A closer look at the proposed benefits indicated that income might rise by £3 million a year, and operating expenses would be cut by £5 million – a gross benefit of £8 million, or a net return of about 5% on the investment. Unfortunately, interest rates were running at about 5-6% at the time, which made it unlikely that the scheme would cover interest, let alone repay any capital.

The Commission replied that it had probably miscalculated and that income would probably increase by more than £3 million following electrification. In other words, when its own figures indicated that its most prestigious scheme was unlikely to make much of a return, the Commission swept them aside. The affair was an unmitigated disaster for the BTC, as unfriendly civil servants proceeded to tear apart the estimates and assumptions. and gave the Government the ammunition it needed.

If the figures for Euston to Liverpool and Manchester didn't add up, what were the returns likely to be on the less favourable routes? It emerged that the Commission had given the matter little thought, and it could give no clear indication as to which schemes were likely to show a return at the end of the day, and which were not.

In reality, the benefits of the electrification 'sparks effect' had been grossly underestimated, and had the costs and benefits been calculated in a different way, the figures would have looked very different. For instance, the Ministry of Transport was already developing a technique to justify new motorway construction, a notoriously difficult cost/benefit calculation. It was solved by attributing a value to the time drivers saved by switching to the new road. Had the Ministry allowed the Commission to cost its schemes on the same basis, most would have proved overwhelmingly cost-effective.

The Ministry could also have taken account of the fact that major railway investment projects were bound to save money in other areas, such as reduced hospitalisation costs through a reduction in road casualties, or perhaps by tipping the balance against an expensive motorway scheme. But it was too late to open a debate on the unfairness of the methodology – most of the modernisation schemes were already doomed.

Immediately after the October 1959 election, the Government asked the Parliamentary Select Committee on Nationalised Industries to examine the railways as a matter of urgency. The Committee responded with great speed, publishing a report by July 1960[6]. Ominously, it had not had time to seek the views of outside experts, but had talked to Ministry of Transport and Treasury officials, who were by now totally opposed to the modernisation process, and to the BTC, which was equally determined to press ahead.

Generally, the Select Committee was satisfied with the way the Commission was handling its affairs. True, the losses were continuing to mount, but the 1959 figures had suggested that improved efficiency was starting to have an impact on the bottom line. Track costs were down, movement costs were down, manpower was steadily being reduced, railway workshops would be halved by 1964, and the number of locomotives had been cut from 18,500 in 1955 to 14,000, with a reduction to 10,700 in the pipeline for 1961. The diesel multiple units – still accounting for only a small proportion of passenger trains – had, on average, increased revenue by more than a third where they had been introduced, and the Commission was committed to closing any lines that failed to show a decent return after modernisation.

According to the BTC the losses still stemmed mainly from stopping and local services, but the Select Committee disagreed. The financial crisis had been precipitated by a number of factors. Firstly there was the awesome burden of British Transport Stock, issued to finance the nationalisation of the railways in 1947 and still providing the railways' former masters with a guaranteed income of around £40 million a year. Further stock had been issued to cover losses and keep the system afloat.

The 1947 Transport Act had empowered the BTC to establish a reserve fund to guard against contingencies, but for various reasons this had never been done. Such a fund might have helped the railways from sliding into debt, and might have prevented the organisation from becoming enslaved to interest payments. It's true that the Government had advanced funds to cover modernisation, but this all had to be repaid, with interest. The money had come from a special account that had accrued a deficit of more than £360 million by 1959.

This was how the financial situation had so rapidly reached crisis proportions. The BTC had been formed as a transport monopoly with a statutory duty to break even, and its financial structure had been created according to those rules. After the disposal of road haulage interests from 1953 onwards, the situation changed dramatically. The Commission found itself with a run-down railway system, no capital, and trading in a competitive environment, but without the freedom to fix rates and charges. By 1955 the railways were long overdue for investment, but with no reserves and no opportunities for cross-subsidy from other businesses, it was obliged to borrow from the Government at commercial rates. When the turmoil of modernisation and the disastrous 17-day ASLEF strike of 1955 conspired to push the operating figures into the red from 1956 onwards, it was also obliged to pay interest on its short-term deficits.

According to the Select Committee, tight Government control of railway fares and charges was largely to blame. Since 1938, prices across the economy had risen by 171%, but railway fares by only 145%, and freight charges by 144%.

Government interference had caused all manner of problems over the years, as in 1952 and 1956, when the Minister had intervened after the Transport Tribunal agreed to grant fare increases. The financial implications of were hard to quantify, but the BTC put the cost at about £50 million for 1949-55, and at least another £17 million in 1956. Some commentators put the 1956 cost alone at more than £50 million. Then in September 1957 the Government announced without warning that capital expenditure in 1958/59 would be restricted. The result – with schemes already well underway – was an expensive fiasco, with planning work wasted and financial penalties paid to contractors.

Not that the BTC itself was totally blameless. It had failed to respond to private coach operators, who were taking considerable traffic on some routes by adopting an aggressive pricing strategy. In November 1959, shortly after the opening of the M1 motorway, the coach operators had introduced a fare of £1 1s 3d (£1.06p) between London and Birmingham, while the railways had stuck rigidly to a fair of £2 2s (£2.10p). It all sounds charmingly unworldly in today's more competitive environment, but it demonstrated just how out of touch the Transport Commission was. Even after Government controls were relaxed in 1957, the Commission had stuck with an inflexible charging system based on mileage, and taking no account of local competition, disposable income and traffic potential. The same was true with freight charges, allowing the small private road haulage operators to run rings around the unwieldy railways.

As we have seen, branch line policy had also been woefully mishandled. The Commission had deliberately run down most of the branch lines with the intention of closing them, then more or less cancelled the policy, pouring millions of pounds into DMUs in an effort to make the branches pay. But a railway line is a bit like a super-tanker when it comes to changing direction. The threatened lines needed track upgrades, signalling economies, and above all, active promotion. After decades of miserable decline, the BTC needed to get across to local travellers, local authorities and commercial organisations that the railway was there for the long haul. New rolling stock was a great start, but it wasn't enough, and many of the branch lines were still unable to meet interest payments on the capital outlay, let alone make a profit. Had the Commission made it clear to the Government and the public at large that certain lines were unlikely ever to make a paper profit, but there were good commercial, social and even environmental reasons for keeping them open, all might have been well.

The real problem was that the BTC had failed to distinguish between the commercially viable services and the socially desirable ones. Tentative internal studies were already suggesting that it might make more commercial sense to subsidise certain lines than to close them down, even ignoring wider questions of social desirability in keeping a railway open. An investigation in 1959 looked in some detail at passenger services on some 1,400 miles of lightly used railway in central Wales, Devon, Cornwall and Scotland. The total annual income was £5.2 million, against expenses of £8.7 million, giving a paper loss of £3.5 million. However, the lines generated contributory revenue of more than £6 million, of which it was estimated that nearly £5 million would be lost after closure. On that basis, the subsidy of £3.5 million could just as easily have been promoted to the Ministry of Transport as an investment generating a healthy return. The Commission could have made a case that such lines were not only worthy of retention but of renewed investment.

Had such arguments been given a proper airing at the time, the mood might have swung the railway's way, but the Commission did nothing, and appears to have had little idea where profits and losses were being made. Under Select Committee scrutiny, it emerged that the BTC was unsure of the financial performance of individual regions, and the Area Boards didn't seem to have much idea either. It was also claimed that the Commission had failed to study the performance of local lines and services, though as we have seen, there had been numerous studies (on a local level at least) since the early 1950s.

Had the BTC kept a clearer eye on the performance of the regions, losses might have been kept in check, but the only records were of *originating* receipts, which tended to favour industrial areas, such as the North East, and work against holiday areas such as the West Country.

All the same, the figures for 1959 make interesting reading. Ignoring central charges, three regions – North Eastern, Eastern and Southern – made a small profit. The Scottish region fared less well, but the majority of the £42 million loss that year could be attributed to the London Midland and Western regions. Perhaps rather more relevant was the fact that all the regions, with the exception of London Midland, had improved their financial performance against the previous year.

In truth, the situation wasn't nearly as bleak as the Government was about to make out. Passenger figures were close to 23 billion passenger/miles, one of the highest figures ever recorded, and passenger receipts were up by about £2 million on the previous year, while operating costs had been substantially reduced. Parcels traffic too, had grown by 15% since nationalisation. The real decline was in heavy freight, particularly coal, where £13 million-worth of traffic had been lost in 1959. Despite this fall, the figures remained quite buoyant. After carefully considering all the evidence, the Select Committee concluded: "There is no doubt that a large-scale British railway system can be profitable." It also tentatively concluded that a few loss-making services might be worth subsidising for 'social' reasons, the first time such a suggestion had been made. But it was not what Mr Marples wanted to hear. Railway finances were in a disastrous tangle and he had already decided to sort out the ailing industry once and for all. For the branch lines – many of which were busier than they had been at any time in their existence – the end was in sight.

5
The Marples-Beeching Axis
1960-63

"It is a difficulty which we all face, including the Commission, of trying to trace exactly where the money is being lost... the Commission itself admits that it cannot say with any precision where the money has been lost. All we know for a fact is that large sums of money are being lost...
...to talk as some do of the plan we have for the railways as being one for closures, and for closures alone, is claptrap and drivel. It has a positive and constructive side to it and that is what I want to emphasise.."

John Hay MP, Joint Parliamentary Secretary to the Ministry of Transport
Speaking during a debate on the British Transport Commission, 29th November 1962

MARPLES GENERAL HOSPITAL
ORTHOPEDIC WARD

DR B.

" The Doctor says you will be much more efficient now"

With acknowledgements to the Railway & Public Transport Users Association

*I*mposing draconian cuts on a large nationalised industry is liable to lead to the sort of nightmare of which politicians live in constant fear. As Minister of Transport, Ernest Marple's first move was to tighten control over the BTC management and rein in the modernisation programme. Early in 1960, the Commission was informed that any investment project over £250,000 would have to be cleared with the Ministry, the ultimate decision resting with Marples himself.

The effect of these new controls was to virtually wind up modernisation, for a scheme instigated at Area Board level now had to be cleared by the Commission's Works & Equipment Committee, the Commission itself, the Ministry, and finally, the Minister of Transport. As had been intended, the new system proved more or less unworkable. The flagship London to Liverpool and Manchester electrification was by this time well advanced, and was allowed to continue, although financial controls remained tight, and the completion date was set back several years. On the branches and secondary lines, investment ceased almost immediately, and the authorities began to prepare the ground for widespread closures.

Many voices would have to be silenced to bring about a bloodless road transport revolution: politicians, the rail lobby, the railway management, the unions... and the public at large, few of whom had any idea that their Conservative vote had effectively endorsed a railway cull. The Government launched a systematic and well-organised campaign.

In Government circles, the railways were considered a near worthless Victorian encumbrance in the age of mass motoring. What was the point of paying for railway modernisation in 1960 when roads were already under construction to carry ex-railway traffic?

There was a genuine and rather naive belief that lorries would handle the nation's freight, the private car would cater for personal transport, and buses would more than suffice for those who could not afford (or chose not to own) a car. If the railways were to remain for the time being (and it was politically expedient that they should, in some form) the network would be cut to a size where profitability could be assured.

There had been an ongoing debate for many years as to whether certain railway maintenance and investment costs should be borne by the State. After all, the Government was pouring large sums into a new road network that would effectively be free at point of use. Why should it not pay for enhancements to the railway network too? The railways were just as much a state network as the roads – why should they alone be required to operate profitably on a route-by-route basis? The official reply was that roads were effectively self-financing, through income from vehicle licenses and fuel taxes. But this was (and remains) a contentious issue. It was impossible even to prove whether the income covered the true cost of building and maintaining the road network, let alone other consequential costs. Clearly, the balance sheet for many roads didn't begin to add up against the cost of maintenance, bridge repairs, snow clearance, and other less obvious costs, but nobody was talking about axing the worst loss-makers.

According to the road lobby, road 'income' exceeded direct expenditure on construction and maintenance by a healthy margin. But that income appeared to fall well short of the true cost, including environmental and health costs from pollution, accidents, policing, congestion, hospitalisation costs and deaths. The National Council for Inland Transport, a generally pro-rail pressure group formed in 1962, attempted to estimate the real cost of the road network, and concluded that the annual roads income of £610 million covered less than half of the true expenditure of about £1,486 million. The shortfall of £800 million exceeded the railway deficit many times over, but such arguments were lost on a Government that now openly favoured the road lobby.

Had the Government paused for a moment in 1960, weighed up the relative worth of various forms of transport with an open mind, and concluded that individual roads should be placed under the same financial constraints as individual railways, the majority of minor roads would have been deemed uneconomic. The density of road traffic was spread just as unevenly as rail traffic, leaving much of the system 'uneconomic' in straight financial terms. But the railway was considered a secondary, duplicate means of transport and to Mr Marples, a Minister with a substantial interest in road construction, the answer was obvious.

Public Opinion

The first, and probably the most difficult, task was to win the public relations battle. A head-on attempt to close a large proportion of the railway network would be bound to cause trouble, if not a degree of civil unrest, without careful PR. The message would be a simple one: that sacrifices would be needed by the few in the interests of the nation as a whole. The emphasis was always put on the rural nature of the closures, and the handful of country folk who would be affected. In fact, some of the closures were to affect huge populations. Closure of all stations in Mansfield, Kirkby-in-Ashfield and Sutton-in-Ashfield, would leave more than 115,000 people without rail services by 1964, and this Nottinghamshire conurbation was by no means exceptional.

It all had to be handled very carefully, and the Government decided to bring out the big guns right at the beginning. The Prime Minister launched the campaign on 10th March 1960, delivering a suitable speech while introducing a debate on the Guillebaud Committee report on railwaymens' wages:

"The carriage of minerals, including coal, an important traffic for the railways, has gone down. At the same time, there has been an increased use of road transport in all its forms...

First, the industry must be of a size and pattern suited to modern conditions and prospects. In particular, the railway system must be remodelled to meet current needs, and the modernisation plan must be adapted to this new shape.

Secondly, the public must accept the need for changes in the size and pattern of the industry. This will involve certain sacrifices of convenience, for example, in the reduction of uneconomic services...

The public has to accept that it cannot ask the industry to take on some of the old functions such as fell upon a common carrier, and some of the old restrictions which were quite reasonable when the railways were a monopoly, of which there are signs still, and it must also accept the inconvenience of certain lines being closed and other means of transport being made available."

It was a masterpiece of spin. Railways would be 'remodelled' and 'adapted' rather than closed, and the process would merely involve sacrifices of 'convenience', which made it sound as though trains might be disrupted for a few weeks while new faster services were introduced. But behind the silky words there was serious resolve: the public would have to accept it. There was an authority behind the words of the Prime Minister that made the thing seem inevitable, and with a few carefully crafted slogans for the press, the campaign was under way. Again, the emphasis, without any actual promises, was on the replacement of an outmoded railway network with something better and more modern: "The railways are supposed to meet 20th century demands with 19th century equipment."

John Hay, Mr Marple's Parliamentary Secretary, similarly put emphasis on the age and inadequacy of the railways, remarking that, "The existing system was laid down for horse-and-cart delivery and collection." Again, the emphasis was on the age of the system, keeping well clear of a more general debate about whether any sort of railway was fit for purpose in the brave new world of the 1960s.

Other claims could be more defensive, such as Marple's own Parliamentary reply of 4th July 1962 that, "traffic is going onto the roads because the people wish it to go onto the roads; I am not forcing it!"

Another slogan that caught the attention of the press was an implication that the proposed railway closures would increase road congestion by no more than 1%, equivalent to two months' normal growth. This back-of-an-envelope claim was quite false, and based on a rather dubious accounting procedure, but it simultaneously implied that railway closures were of little consequence, and road traffic their natural replacement. It was widely quoted and widely believed.

Plenty more figures were brought into play, and the Government made good use of them. The BTC was £353 million in the red by 1960; the Government had loaned £600 million; the overall railway deficit for 1961 would top £150 million, £160 million in 1962 and so on.

Most spectacular of all was the near £2 billion overall capital liabilities of the BTC, a mind-boggling £95 billion today. As most of this was in the form of British Transport Stock, issued to buy the railways in 1948, it was a meaningless figure unless weighed against the railways' old but extensive asset base. It was quite unreasonable to claim this figure as debt, but the gloves were clearly off. To put these huge figures into perspective, the actual working deficit of the railways was about £60 million a year – a lot of money at the time, but against Gross National Expenditure of around £7 billion, not an outrageous amount. These figures were given little emphasis.

Gradually, the Government began to lay the blame for these overwhelming losses on the size and unwieldiness of the railway network, implying that all would be well once the loss-making lines had been eradicated. There was no direct reference to the size of the proposed cuts however, and the newspapers and opinion makers began to produce answers of their own. Typical was the view of Gilbert Walker, Professor of Economics at Birmingham University, writing in *Westminster Bank Review*: "Railway route mileage to be closed cannot be less than 60%. The proposition may be as high as 80%." Even *The Times* fell victim to the misinformation campaign, arguing that, "half the track mileage and a very much larger proportion in Scotland, Wales, South-West England and East Anglia," would close. These sort of pronouncements were a gift to the Government, because when the actual proposals were released, they looked mild and well-reasoned by comparison with these inflated expectations.

Even when it became clear that substantial chunks of the network *would* be eradicated, the Government continued to emphasise their rural nature, and the very small number of travellers who would be affected. This had been largely true during the 1950s, as the Transport Commission lopped off a few remote branches, but the plans of the Marples regime were on an altogether different scale. There was suddenly a very real threat to the entire network, but the emphasis on minor rural hardship and small-scale inconvenience was so successful that although the general need for cutbacks was sinking in, few people thought it would affect their local services until it was too late.

The public, media and even the specialist press began to accept the view that the BTC was making overwhelming losses, which were predominantly caused by rural railways, and that the only reasonable answer was to cut out this dead wood.

The Road Haulage Association was only too glad to assist in the campaign, and in April 1960, its journal *The World's Carriers*, went for the railway jugular:

"It is understood that the Government have already settled the principles of reorganisation, and it will be for the Board to work out the detailed application...

We should build more roads, and we should have fewer railways. This would merely be following the lesson of history which shows a continued and continuing expansion of road transport and a corresponding contraction in the volume of business handled by the railways...

A streamlined railway system could surely be had for half the money that is now being made available... We must exchange the 'permanent way' of life for the 'motorway' of life... road transport is the future, the railways are the past..."

Inevitably a lunatic fringe took the whole thing even further. According to Colonel John Pye, Master of the Worshipful Company of Carmen:

"...a look should be taken at the widths of pavements and, where possible, steps taken to cut them down to widen the road space... there should be more control of pedestrians."

Oddly, no-one objected, but that was very much the mood of the times, because in the early

"...there should be more control of pedestrians."

1960s, the motorcar really was king. Many of the claims of the Railway Conversion League – a dubious amalgam of thinly disguised road interests which campaigned for railways to be converted into roads – were equally ludicrous. The railways had few friends at the time, while the road lobby was becoming ever more powerful. And that, really, was the problem – the railways had already lost the public relations battle.

General Sir Brian Robertson, the BTC Chairman, desperately mustered his troops in a last-ditch manoeuvre to turn the tide: "Our aim must be to counterattack and not merely defend!" But it was too late – the old soldier was buried beneath a welter of invective from the heavy artillery of the road lobby, the Ministry of Transport and Government. The BTC, never very adept at the art of PR, effectively disappeared from the public gaze, although it remained in existence for some time.

In a few short years, the road interests had become sufficiently powerful to influence political events, making it difficult for any government to hold out against them. From this viewpoint, the question of whether there was, or was not, a conspiracy to crush the railways – and who might or might not have been involved – becomes irrelevant. The road transport machine, once it had gathered momentum, was to destroy every obstacle in its path. Whether it began to move of its own accord – or was pushed – was no longer important.

Popular mythology has it that people were so used to national governments in 1945, they thought they could vote for Labour yet keep Churchill at the helm. Many now believed they could have motorways, and keep their local branch line. The Government did nothing to dispel the illusion.

Parliament

It might have been winning the public debate on railways, but the Government faced a tougher job in Parliament. Opposition members had a tendency to ask awkward questions and rake up unpleasant facts, and if the Government lost the support of its own backbenches, the Marples plan would be doomed to failure. Railways were an emotive subject, and some of them cut through several marginal political constituencies. It was essential to push the negative aspects of the BTC – the mounting losses, the misman-agement, and the charmingly vague cost/benefit analysis of the modernisation plans – while holding back on the very real successes, such as the DMU programme. Unfortunately for the Government, the Select Committee on Nationalised Industries was about to release a fair and well-balanced report that would give ammunition to pro-rail MPs. Something stronger would be needed to counter it.

The Minister of Transport invited a select team of industrialists to investigate the 'railway problem' and find a solution. The trouble-shooting committee would be led by Sir Ivan Stedeford, Managing Director of Tube Investments, with Frank Kearton (later Lord Kearton), joint Managing Director of Courtaulds, Henry Benson (later Lord Benson) of Cooper Brothers, a firm of Chartered Accountants... and Doctor Richard Beeching (later Lord Beeching), Technical Director of ICI. Marples had

Dr Richard Beeching, Technical Director of ICI, was invited to join the Stedeford Committee and later became the BRB Chairman

initially asked the distinguished scientist Frank Ewart Smith[7], Beeching's predecessor at ICI, but he seems to have concluded that sorting out the railways was a retirement project too far.

Inevitably, the Committee had no railway input at all, but it contained two senior civil servants representing the Treasury and Ministry of Transport. Mr Stevenson from the Treasury appears to have done nothing controversial, but David Serpell – a former Treasury mandarin, newly seconded to the Ministry of Transport – would infamously suggest widespread railway closures several decades later...

Why did the Government appoint the Stedeford Committee? As early as 1956 the BTC had made it clear that modernisation would take at least ten years to bear fruit, but even in 1960, decentralisation and more efficient working practices were beginning to show a return. The Commission had already started slimming its organisation down to size, predicting an alarming but bearable 1,000 station closures by 1963, and a loss of 10% of route mileage. In February 1959, it had actually closed its first (and many assumed last) trunk line – the old Midland & Great Northern that meandered for 170 miles across mostly rural Lincolnshire and Norfolk and was allegedly losing £640,000 a year in the process. It was a measure of the serious financial situation, and weakness of the M&GN, that it was closed in record time, with less than ten weeks between the announcement to final implementation, which was unopposed by the Railway Development Association. A Parliamentary Select Committee had just produced a helpful report on the railways, and if the Government was unhappy about the quality of management at the BTC it had unlimited powers to do something about it.

The Stedeford Committee appears to have been set up for the sole purpose of facili-tating railway closures. According to the Select Committee for the Nationalised Industries, "a non-parliamentary planning board was later set up to cover much the same ground, *for the Government's own purposes*" [8] [author's italics].

The Great Railway Conspiracy

There seems little doubt that the Stedeford Committee (originally described as a planning board, but later as an advisory group) was set up to provide a smoke screen. The Government intended to cut the railways to size, but such a radical move would have been unacceptable without the backing and 'evidence' of an expert committee.

Mr Marples would ensure that the committee reached suitable conclusions by doctoring its terms of reference. The precise wording of the Stedeford Committee's terms of reference were the subject of considerable parliamentary interest at the time: Marples claimed they were both flexible and wide, although he went on to add that the Government had already, "laid down the broad plan," which implied that the committee would be concerned with no more than detail.

On 6th April 1960, in the face of repeated questions in the House of Commons, Mr Marples revealed what he claimed were the Stedeford Committee's terms of reference:

"To examine the structure, finance and working of the organisations at present controlled by the Commission and to advise the Minister of Transport and the British Transport Commission, as a matter of urgency, how effect can best be given to the Government's intentions as indicated in the Prime Minister's statement."

As the Prime Minister had clearly indicated that many railways would close, we must assume that the Stedeford Committee received a similar brief: to advise the Government on how to close railway lines.

It was to be no ordinary Parliamentary Committee however, for the Government needed a group that would produce an exclusive report for the Minister that echoed the Minister's own views. Superficially, the Stedeford Committee would be an independent body reaching independent conclusions, but in reality its task appears to be simply to rubber stamp various conclusions that the Government had already reached. Perhaps understandably, the resulting report was not made public, and was only finally released under the 30-year rule in the early 1990s.

No member of the Stedeford Committee had railway experience, there was no BTC presence, no input from the unions or from pro-rail groups, and no consultation as such. According to Marples, "the advice of the Commission and the unions can best be put forward without inhibitions and in all freeness if they are not on the body itself." It was claimed that the Committee 'hoped' to take note of the views of various parties before producing its report, but only if it had time, which of course, it didn't. Strangely enough, the Stedeford Committee *did* find time to consult the Central Transport Consultative Committee, the Road Haulage Association and the Railway Conversion League!

The RHA saw a Darwinistic inevitability in the eclipse of the railways:

"... no permanent subsidy should be granted to the railways before it is established exactly what services, passengers and freight are conducted at a loss... the railway's subsidisation would retard the natural evolutionary process in transport by which road transport services are replacing rail...

The railway system has a fairly long history of failure, and the decline in the importance of rail can no longer be concealed."

According to the available evidence, the Stedeford Committee had little or no contact with groups that might have helped balance such views, besides accepting representations from the Locomotive and Allied Manufacturers Association, and the Wagon Repairing Association, whose main concern was obviously with the carriage of freight.

Politically, the whole affair was skillfully orchestrated. Labour objections were silenced when the Minister revealed that the socialists had set a precedent for secret committees some years previously by commissioning a report on efficiency in Royal Ordnance factories. That was hardly comparable, for the ins and outs of munitions manufacture were hardly a subject for widespread debate, whereas the future of public transport certainly was. Labour MP Francis Noel-Baker, whose Swindon constituency was bound to be affected, was in no doubt as to the purpose of the Stedeford Committee:

"The conclusion that many of us have reached about the Stedeford Group is that what happened was that the civil servants in the Minister's Department and in the Treasury got cold feet.

When they saw the railway deficits mounting and they saw the Guillebaud Report, they lost their heads. They then realised that things were in a mess and that if there was a row they might not get proper backing from the Minister of Transport because he had always wanted to sell out on the railways anyway and that therefore to shift responsibility and to protect the Government and protect Ministers, who had not the courage of their own convictions, the Stedeford Group would provide an amenable and respectable-looking front, and incidentally make it easier to ignore a good deal of the serious and factual reporting of the Select Committee."

The truth seems to have been even more sinister, and many Labour MPs knew why. Back in May 1960, as the Government/road haulage public relations assault reached its climax, John Hay MP had spoken at the Road Haulage Association annual dinner. Relaxing in the company of friends, the Minister's Parliamentary Secretary made a speech which included the following tantalising items:

"I know that our idea of getting advice on the detailed application of Government policy towards the railways from a group of businessmen... is a sensible approach which will commend itself to those present at this dinner.

We were very glad to know what you thought... and the views of your Association have been brought to the attention of Sir Ivan Stedeford's group.

...in the search for transport efficiency, the Government is prepared in a most practical way to do what it can to help. I refer of course to the road programme. It would be too optimistic to expect you to say that what we are doing is enough. No Ministry of Transport spokesman will ever expect that from his friends in the industry.

You and we worked together against the threat of nationalisation of road haulage. We won that battle. Now we must show that we were right to win it...

We in the Government will back you all we can... we shall try to make sure that the roads we have and the new roads we build give the best possible dividend... sometimes in this we shall be forced to requite some sacrifices by individuals or by groups in the interests of the many. Road haulage will enjoy many of the benefits..."

It was hardly coded language. The Parliamentary Secretary had implied that the hauliers could safely assume the Stedeford Committee would produce a report in favour of the road lobby, and that railway passengers and employees would have to endure the inevitable sacrifices. That the Parliamentary representative of the Ministry of Transport should stand at a private function and openly toast the past and future patronage of a lobby group, leaves one wondering exactly where power lay at the time. Were Harold Macmillan and Ernest Marples really in control of events, or had they simply become caught up in a private battle between the Ministry and the road haulage industry on the one hand, and the embattled British Transport Commission on the other?

Harold Macmillan had been a director of the Great Western Railway before the war and was known to have retained a degree of sympathy for the industry. Ernest Marples, on the other hand, had a personal stake in road transport that amounted to some 80% of the shares in his own road construction firm. Although the Minister claimed to have divested himself of the shares by this time, he had in reality put the shareholding in the hands of Mrs Marples.

Politicians are, of course, little more than front men where power is concerned. It was the anonymous civil service mandarins at the Ministry of Transport and the Treasury who wielded the real influence, and they had a great deal to gain by supporting road interests to the detriment of the railways.

It was really just a matter of power. After the dissolution of the 'big four' railway companies in the 1940s, the railways effectively ceased to function as a lobby group, leaving a vacuum that was rapidly filled by the road interests. Road affairs necessitated a vast administrative machine, commanding a substantial budget, while the railways were partially self-governing. By 1966, no fewer than 80% of the Ministry staff were concerned with road matters while just 1% handled railway affairs, the majority dealing solely with occasional accident inquiries. In the upper echelons of the service, 11 Under Secretaries dealt with road matters and only one with the railways. Whatever your personal views, if you wanted to gain promotion, you needed to adopt a pro-road stance. After retirement, high-flyers might be recruited take up lucrative part-time posts in industry through what became known as the 'revolving door'. If civil servants left after a decent interval, and used their experience in a neutral and balanced way, this sort of relationship could be quite positive, but there are plenty of examples of public servants leaving indecently early and using their contacts to further the interests of pressure groups.

The Select Committee for the Nationalised Industries had cross-examined several key civil servants, including Sir James Dunnett, the Permanent Secretary at the Ministry of Transport, in an attempt to unravel Ministry policy, and it had received some masterful civil service replies:

Mr Albu (MP for Edmonton): "I want to know whose business it is within this estimate of the country's general economy to make estimates of the return on capital invested in the railways... to put it crudely, whether the return on building more roads or modernising certain lines of the railway is likely to show the better return?"

Sir James Dunnett: "That is a very difficult thing. The problem does not, in my experience, arise in quite that form."

Mr Albu: "You are saying that it is not the business of the Treasury or the Ministry to have a transport plan? I do not mean forcing everybody to travel a certain way, but a structure based on the consideration of giving the best economic returns?"

Sir James Dunnett: "What kind of thing would you have in mind?..."

Sir James later left the service to chair the International Maritime Industries Forum, a think tank on shipping.

The Stedeford Committee's main source of information had been the Ministry of Transport, and the Committee had been carefully briefed by Ministry officials on the weakness of the BTC's book-keeping and the general inadequacy of the railways as a means of transport. Stedeford was already firmly opposed to the modernisation plans, even the completion of the electrification from Euston to Crewe, the Crewe to Manchester section having (fortunately) already been commissioned in 1959. According to internal Ministry records on a top-level meeting between the Minister and Sir Ivan Stedeford on 10th May 1960:

"The Stedeford Advisory Group has sought, but completely failed to find, any evidence that the BTC's modernisation proposals had any adequate commercial basis. His view was that there was no prospect of railway finances moving from the 'red' into the 'black' during the first half of the 1960s, as claimed by the modernisation plans; it would be the late 1970s, if ever, before the railway system paid."

All the same, Stedeford seemed to be getting cold feet, and perhaps sensing that his committee was being asked to rubber stamp a policy that really needed more careful study. He asked for reassurance that the Government really was planning and implementing an adequate road network to replace the railways, because the committee might otherwise be forced to recommend that certain traffic be encouraged back to the railways. Naturally, Mr Marples was only too willing to reassure him on that score:

"[The Minister] pointed out that [road] congestion occurred primarily in towns, and that in the future there would be still less congestion on the routes between towns. There were in any case objections to directing traffic to rail because of the economic burden this would place on industry...

In the light of the future road schemes, Sir Ivan agreed with the Minister's view and said that, in the circumstances, it was all the more important to prevent new railway modernisation projects being started."
Excerpts from Ministry notes relating to a meeting between Sir Ivan Stedeford and Ernest Marples, May 1960

By October 1960, after six months of intensive work (and three months after publication of the Select Committee report), the Stedeford 'Special Advisory Group' had completed its report. Mr Marples prevaricated over whether the report would be published, finally announcing that it would not, to cries of anger from the Labour benches:

"We have been told that we may not debate the report, to which, apparently, they attach real significance and on which they propose to base their legislation...

[The railwaymen] take a very gloomy view of the present Minister of Transport. They see in him a Minister who is entirely disaffected, who has apparently no understanding of the railways, who hates them and the BTC and wants to write the whole system off, and whose whole attitude towards the railways is one of utter frivolity and irresponsibility....

If one looks at the relation between the Conservative Party and the road haulage interests, one cannot come to any other conclusion than that they have had a dominating influence on the policy of the Government and their attitude towards the railways."
Francis Noel-Baker, MP for Swindon
Excerpt from a speech during a debate on British Railways, 26th October 1960

At least Marples had admitted there was a report. John Hay was later to deny that the Committee had produced a report at all, merely that, "advice has been tendered to my Right Honourable Friend and a number of recommendations have been made." Weasel words, but more or less true, because it seems the Stedeford Committee's deliberations really were released as a series of recommendations, and never actually compiled into a report. This was a most useful ruse, which was used to good effect in later years, enabling officials to declare, hand on heart, that the Stedeford Report did not exist. In a reply to a question by Robert Adley, the pro-rail Tory MP, in the late 1980s, Margaret Thatcher was to state that the report could not be found, which was hardly surprising.

The findings of the Stedeford Committee remained such a well kept secret that even Barbara Castle was unable to see them on becoming Minister of Transport in 1966, just a few years after they were delivered to Ernest Marples.

Mr Marples made only one, rather ominous, remark on the Stedeford Committee's deliberations. It had, he said, answered the questions that the Select Committee had asked.

The Great Railway Conspiracy

According to Henry Benson, the only member of the Stedeford Committee to make any sort of public pronouncement on the Committee's conclusions, the group had failed to reach unanimous agreement. Beeching and Benson had recommended the course of action that the Government favoured, while Stedeford and Kearton had taken a different and unspecified line. In the event, there was a damaging and divisive split, and Beeching was left to write the majority of the recommendations.

Whatever the political situation inside the Stedeford Committee, its final recommendations were pretty innocuous according to the available records, and broadly in line with the conclusions of the Parliamentary Select Committee. Initially it had adopted a hard line with regard to modernisation, recommending in June 1960 that all schemes that had yet to pass, "the point of no return," including the majority of the Euston to Liverpool and Manchester project, should be set aside for review. But, interestingly enough, the Committee did not feel qualified to conduct the review itself, suggesting that another body be set up with very much broader terms of reference:

"...to consider the size and pattern of the railway system required to meet current and foreseeable needs, in the light of developments and trends in other forms of transport, changing industrial needs and social habits and other relevant considerations."

Was this desire to hand the toxic issue over to someone else the cause of the divisive split? We may never know. It seems some members of the Committee were unwilling to endorse the option of wide-scale closures being pressed upon them by the Ministry of Transport. All the other Stedeford Committee proposals, released to Marples and the BTC in September 1960, but locked away under the 30-year rule for the rest of us, were perfectly fair, and a number might even have pleased the rail lobby, had they only known. It suggested that the Commission's finances be restructured along more favourable lines; that the archaic fares and charges legislation be repealed; and that there should be proper scrutiny of railway capital expenditure, plus a proper system of regional accounting to clarify the complex financial picture.

The Commission had an excessive number of staff, said the Stedeford Committee, and fares and charges should be increased on marginal services:

"Insofar as such services cannot be eliminated (and that will very often be the case), we think that higher fares can and should make a substantial contribution to eliminating the current loss."

But on the subject of railway closures, the Committee had little to say, besides recommending that, "a dated programme of further proposals be prepared."

As its deliberations came to a close, the Committee even began to waver on the Euston to Liverpool and Manchester electrification, agreeing that modernisation should go ahead. Although far from convinced that the project would yield an adequate return on capital, it very sensibly noted that cancellation would waste £20 million that had already been spent, destroy railway morale and damage Britain's standing abroad.

In the final analysis, Mr Marple's committee of industrial experts, "could not give firm guidance" even on this issue that had seemed so clear-cut to the Ministry of Transport. Its terms of reference had been doctored, and some of its members had clearly refused to play along. It's not surprising that Marples refused to reveal that sections of his hard-hitting committee had gone native, but he didn't need to. The silence and gritted teeth implied that the Committee had reached conclusions too awful to contemplate. It was all a bluff.

The British Transport Commission

The effects of the Stedeford Committee's deliberations were felt almost immediately. Marples took the opportunity to tighten his control over the railway system, subjecting the modernisation plans to microscopic scrutiny and cutting investment. Many schemes – particularly those intended for branch and secondary lines – were abandoned altogether.

The Committee had been unsure whether to endorse the Ministry line on the beleaguered Euston to Manchester and Liverpool electrification scheme, but Marples took the opportunity to halt further construction and cancel future contracts. Although the scheme was eventually allowed to proceed, his actions demonstrated that the real value of the Stedeford Committee (or 'Marples' Gestapo' as it became known amongst disaffected railwaymen) was to emasculate the Transport Commission.

In December 1960, Marples committed the inevitable *coup de grace*, announcing that the BTC was to be abolished, and its constituent parts placed under the control of separate boards of management. Not long before, General Sir Brian Robertson, Chairman of the Commission, had warned the Government to stand aside and allow the modernisation schemes to run their course. Marples had neither forgotten nor forgiven Sir Brian, and on 15th March 1961, he was ousted in favour of Doctor Richard Beeching, ex-Stedeford Committee, who became Chairman on 1st June. His task was to simplify the organisation, oversee its final days, and implement the Stedeford Committee proposals.

Sir Brian was elevated to the House of Lords for his trouble, but he was greatly saddened by the collapse of the Commission. In May 1961 he undertook a farewell tour of the network and lingered awhile amid the unfinished catenaries of the Euston to Liverpool and Manchester electrification project. To Sir Brian, who had defended the scheme to the bitter end, it must have been a poignant moment. What really stung, leaving aside the political implications, was that Beeching would receive a salary of £24,000 (about £1.4 million today) against the £10,000 paid to his predecessor.

Dr Beeching came to be vilified in the press as a cold and analytical accountant – a ruthless industrialist with a brief to destroy the railways. In reality he was a much more complex character: a shy, intelligent scientist from ICI with a fascinating past, although the details have only been revealed very recently[7]. In the late 1930s, when Beeching was studying for his PhD at Imperial College, ICI did quite a bit of theoretical work on the atomic bomb, concluding even before hostilities were declared that German scientists were some way down the same path and quite capable of developing a super-weapon, given the time and raw materials. Beeching started the war with the rank of Captain, conducting research into shell casings, but his knowledge of metallurgy and physics made him a natural candidate for the nuclear project. It was at this time that he met and became friends with Ivan Stedeford, head of Tube Investments, another company intimately involved in this secret work. It's almost certain that after the war Beeching played a pivotal role in Britain becoming the third country to build and test a nuclear weapon.

Ostensibly, he was a scientist at ICI, and from 1959, its Technical Director. He is remembered as being highly intelligent, and a cool, rational problem-solver, but socially awkward and shy to the point of being introverted. Strangely, after the years of secret work and esoteric backroom research at ICI, he seems to have taken a real delight in his new-found notoriety, although never quite able to understand why the headlines shrieked axe murderer, rather than saviour, of the railways. In some ways Beeching comes across as a rather pitiful character, an unworldly intellectual, thrust into the murky transport politics of the 1960s, with its pressure groups, union-bashing government and road-building Minister of Transport. It was briefly fashionable in the 1960s to assume that if scientists could crack the codes of the universe, they

The Great Railway Conspiracy

could just as easily cure more down to earth issues. Beeching thought they had asked him to run the railways because of his cool intellect and analytical skills, but he was really little more than a fall guy, and for him this would prove a muddled and rather grubby end to a distinguished career.

Beeching was convinced that a detailed analysis of the railway's position would enable the losses of the Transport Commission to be turned into profits. To do this, he would need to throw out the Commission's newly evolved and rather vague ideas about social obligations, which was exactly what the Government had in mind. In fact, from the Government's point of view, he was the ideal man for the job, an intellectual who would subject the railways to rigorous statistical analysis, while ignoring the wider social implications of what he was doing.

The new Chairman rapidly brought in other private sector managers, including Philip Shirley, an Australian accountant from Unilever, and L H Williams from Shell. The new regime set to work on a wide-ranging review of railway operations, producing a four-stage plan:

- *A series of traffic studies to judge which services were viable*
- *Publication of the results*
- *Publication of a report*
- *The Government would be left to 'reach its own conclusion'*

Cutbacks in investment, and a general feeling that the railways had little future, were already causing a knock-on effect throughout the industry. During a heavy fog on 25th October 1960, two loaded oil barges collided with the Severn Bridge at Sharpness, bringing the centre section

Damaged in a collision in October 1960, the Severn Bridge was due to be repaired, but after it was marked for closure in the 'Reshaping' report, the plans were quietly dropped. The rest of the bridge was later demolished. PHOTO: John Thorn

down into the river. It could hardly be blamed on Marples, but such was the mood within the BTC at this critical time, that the bridge (due for upgrade as recently as 1959) was never repaired. It stood, useless and derelict, until 1970, when the last sections were finally demolished. Many other assets, some that had only recently been brought into service, were to share a similar fate.

A more dynamic railway might have made capital from the road accident figures for 1961, which hit 270,000 killed or seriously injured. But in the general upheaval, the railway had lost all ability to lobby. The accident figure continued to climb throughout the early 1960s, reaching a grizzly peak of 398,000 in 1965, about twice the 2012 figure.

The Objectors

There had been a number of obstacles in the path of earlier railway closures. One – although little more than a technical inconvenience – was the issue of protesters dragging up statutes from the Victorian era when, for one reason or another, the railway company of the time had been obliged to provide a service for a period of time, and in the more optimistic cases, in perpetuity.

The other problem involved the TUCC closure inquiry procedure. True, only a handful of inquiries had actually found in favour of the protesters, and in even fewer were lines consequently reprieved by the BTC, but growing public resentment was already generating sophisticated opposition, with expert witnesses able to undermine the official figures and ask awkward questions about diesel railcars. If nothing else, concerted opposition might lead to future inquiries being drawn out for a considerable period, whereas the Government wanted the trains taken off and the track removed as soon as possible. And if an inquiry found against closure, the Minister might find himself in the awkward position of having to overrule its findings. Legislation would be needed, and it arrived with the 1962 Transport Act, which received the Royal Assent on 1st August that year.

The BTC was dissolved, and its transport undertakings split between four boards: the British Waterways Board, the London Transport Board, the Docks Board, and the British Railways Board, which was charged (amongst other things) with the task of eliminating the railway deficit. Generally speaking, the Board would function much as the former Railway Executive had done, although the new legislation was framed with the intention of handing considerable extra powers to the Minister of Transport.

In keeping with the Government's intention of returning the network to profitability, the railway rates and charges legislation was finally to be jettisoned completely, in favour of a free-for-all, allowing the railways to tender for freight traffic on equal terms with the road hauliers.

The various capital liabilities of the BTC, standing by this time at about £2,000 million (£1,400 million as British Transport Stock), would be apportioned to the various Boards, with the majority going to the railways. Of the debts apportioned to the Railways Board, around £400 million (representing half the modernisation capital) would be written off, another £400 million would continue as an interest-bearing loan, and the remaining £705 million (representing pre-modernisation debts) would enter a 'suspense account'. The Treasury hoped the money would remain 'forgotten' only as long as the railways remained in debt, and that it might prove recoverable at some point in the future. It was a convenient skeleton for the Government to bring out of the cupboard and rattle at frequent intervals.

As an opening dowry for a thoroughly demoralised Railways Board, the financial arrangements were hardly generous, and the remains still brought annual charges of almost £100 million.

The Great Railway Conspiracy

The 1962 Act, like others before and since, covered a wide range of topics, but there were several disturbingly undemocratic aspects to the legislation. Various measures were taken to smooth the railway closure process and, predictably enough, all previous legislation that might conceivably hinder closures was repealed. But it was Section 56 of the Act that caused real consternation in railway circles, for this affected the Transport Users' Consultative Committees.

As we have seen, the TUCCs had never been very satisfactory, but the 1962 Act sought to limit their powers still further. Since 1948, the Area Committees had held inquiries into the railway closure proposals put forward by the BTC. Where a Committee had come down in favour of a proposal, the judgement was usually confirmed by the Central Committee and the closure rapidly implemented. The Area Committees occasionally decided against closure, but they were usually overruled by the central body. In any event, the BTC was entitled to ignore all advice if it so wished, although this never occurred in practise. The system had worked (after a fashion) because the Commission had brought forward relatively few closure proposals, and many of them had been quite justifiable. The Government now intended to close a large proportion of the network, and the new legislation was brought in to tighten the whole 'consultation' procedure.

Crucially, the Committees were no longer to concern themselves with the wider social and strategic implications of a railway closure (not that they had ever done much of this anyway), but merely with the local question of 'hardship' to individuals. The British Railways Board would put forward alternative road bus proposals and it was for the protesters to prove that the new arrangements would be inadequate. The good news was that there was now a proper legal framework governing the advertising and implementation of the closure procedure, but the actual workings of an inquiry were considerably impaired.

There was to be no debate – something that proved hard to enforce in a nominally democratic country – and the Committees had no power to make recommendations, such as economy measures, revised fares and so on. They would report in future, not to the CTCC, but directly to the Minister of Transport. Where the previous arrangements left something to be desired, the new consultation was a sham, and a travesty of democracy, for the TUCCs were empowered to produce a report for the Minister, but ignore most of the available evidence.

The TUCCs were no longer to take account of objections of a political or strategic nature, or those of holidaymakers (even where their patronage might constitute the major part of a line's income, and of course the greater part of its contributory revenue). Even the wider manifestations of hardship, such as the loss of property values to a town, or resultant closure of a local factory, would be unwelcome. The aim was cut the line loose from the greater transport picture, and simply to take submissions from those users who lived in its immediate vicinity. Closure of a railway might well result in seasonal traffic chaos, as many did, but serious issues of this kind were not to be discussed at any inquiry.

Financial figures would no longer be supplied to the TUCCs, unless specifically requested, and they were not to be discussed in public. The Ministry's legal department had clearly worked long and hard to draft legislation which would speed up the closure procedure, because the scale of the proposals was so vast that they could never have been implemented under the previous legislation.

These provisions caused such disquiet that Marples was forced to seek the backing of an outside expert. In August 1963, he invited Sir William Carrington, President of the Institute of Chartered Accountants, to comment on whether accounts should be provided to the TUCCs.

Sir William's general ruling was that the limited financial information was, "appropriate for the purposes of the Consultative Committees," which was of course true, but only because the Committees' terms of reference had been doctored. It would not, he claimed, be wise to furnish TUCC inquiries with a detailed breakdown of income based upon the receipts of individual stations, because such figures might lead to inaccuracies. He recommended instead that the estimate of income for a particular line should be based on an extraordinarily complex procedure.

During a census period of a week, the number of passengers joining and alighting from trains would be recorded at every station, converted into passenger-miles, and multiplied by the average fare. He suggested an additional safeguard for seasonal lines, where traffic would be measured at various times of year and, "appropriately weighted in order to give the most reliable estimate." In the event, seasonal figures were never used to make adjustments of this kind, although they were sometimes provided separately to the TUCCs.

The great advantage to the Railways Board and the Government was that the figures effectively excluded any mention of contributory revenue, even though – as we have seen – it was of fundamental importance. It might be the case that almost all of the passengers boarding a branch line train would continue their journey on the main line but, with no mention of station receipts or contributory revenue, the TUCC would be unaware of this.

Sir William ruled that contributory revenue could only be a matter of, "opinion or judge-ment." Whether he had been deliberately misled by the Minister, or had taken a unilateral decision to assist the Ministry of Transport in its plans, isn't clear, but the contributory revenue from a line was far from being just a 'matter of opinion'.

Nor would it have been difficult to measure. Individual stations kept very accurate records of such things, and market research on a line-by-line basis would not have been difficult to arrange. In fact, the Railways Board already knew in great detail the contributory revenue of particular lines. Before 1962, the BTC had analysed traffic figures on threatened lines, identifying the 'through traffic' component, and estimating the much trickier question of how much would be lost after closure. Beeching himself was later to state that contributory revenue from through traffic varied between 5% and 75% of gross income.

The official view was that contributory revenue – although vital to any realistic appraisal of the financial health and social importance of a given railway line – was outside the limited brief of the TUCC inquiry procedure. It wasn't the Committees' task to consider whether or not a line was commercially viable, as this decision had already been taken by wiser counsel. Why else would the Railways Board have chosen to withdraw a service? The task of the Committees was simply to evaluate the hardship that might result from local travellers transferring from the train to bus, or as increasingly happened, the car.

Thus the TUCCs (and anyone else concerned with the outcome of the inquiries) would have access only to the number of passengers carried in a typical week, and an 'estimate' of the annual income based on those figures. So complicated was the procedure that errors were bound to occur, and protesters were subsequently able to prove, on at least one occasion, that the number of passengers travelling between two stations had emerged at a negative figure! Railway expenditure would be divided into three categories:

Movement expenses - *the cost of actually moving passengers from one point to another, including the cost of providing train crews, fuel, maintenance, and vehicle depreciation.*

Terminal expenses - *the cost of providing stations, including wages and salaries of staff, repairs, heating and lighting.*

Track and signalling - *not necessarily the total cost, but the cost of any additional signalling or track maintenance required solely for the service under review.*

The Great Railway Conspiracy

Above and beyond the 'direct' costs described above, Sir William judged that the TUCCs should be made aware of any additional expenditure which might be required for renewals or maintenance during the five years following the inquiry, in the unlikely event of the line remaining open. This had been standard procedure for some time, but as an accountant, he must have realised that such figures were bound to give a false picture. Most heavy renewals on railway track or fixtures (such as stations, viaducts and tunnels) could be expected to depreciate over several decades... perhaps even 100 years or more. To put these costs on the balance sheet in the 'next five years' category was to imply that such expenditure might be needed every five years. Sir William Carrington's analysis of the figures was in many ways unsatisfactory, but it provided the ammunition that Marples needed to silence his critics.

Fortunately, legislation could do nothing to quell public criticism, and Professor Hondelink, the UN railway expert, continued to battle away at a government that refused to heed his advice. He repeated his earlier message, that railway losses were mostly a result of top-heavy bureaucracy and poor management. Since nationalisation, the network had contracted in size, and the number of productive railwaymen had been reduced accordingly, yet headquarters staff had increased four-fold by 1962. The eradication of the BTC and cutbacks in the modernisation programme did nothing to stem this rising tide of bureaucrats, and by 1965 there were nearly as many senior managers as there had been total headquarters staff three years before. This sort of nonsense pervaded the nationalised industries in the 1960s and 70s, but of course on the railways many of the clerks and managers – rather than looking for new traffic to improve the industry's prospects – were involved solely with line closures. A number of them spent their working days massaging traffic figures to facilitate closure, and a more negative management post is hard to imagine.

According to Professor Hondelink, the losses on the branch lines were very small, and could be virtually eliminated with the application of a few economies. The Government, on the other hand, had put a great deal of effort into proving that railways would have to close, and proving that the remaining elements would return to profitability on their own.

There were no easy answers. Marples, who was later to describe Professor Hondelink as a thorn in his side, responded by instructing government and railway servants to avoid entering into discussion with him. Several attempts were made to discredit the Professor, not on professional or academic grounds, where presumably no fault could be found, but politically. Marples accused Hondelink of 'going over to the Labour camp' through his association with the Labour Peer, Lord Stonham (Chairman of the National Council for Inland Transport), and Labour MP Philip Noel-Baker, but the Professor seems to have remained studiously neutral. Finally, he was ignored altogether. Free speech could not be entirely denied though, and in July 1962, Professor Hondelink rounded upon the Marples-Beeching plans in unequivocal style:

"Branch lines, wayside stations, even main lines and larger stations, have been deliberately starved of proper services to prepare them for closure and abandonment. Slow trains of the wrong composition, running at the wrong hours, with wrong connections and often unclean... the ever increasing rate of closures has now reached the stage where partial and wholesale closures of certain main lines, including partial or total abandonment of some unremunerative passenger services, are planned...

No serious attempt is being made to bring about the elimination of loss by improving operating methods, by meeting customer's needs, not necessarily with new equipment..."
Letter to Philip Noel-Baker MP, 6th July 1962

There was, he said, no evidence that closures had saved, or were likely to save, a penny. So complete was the legislation under the 1962 Act, and so incomplete the financial figures

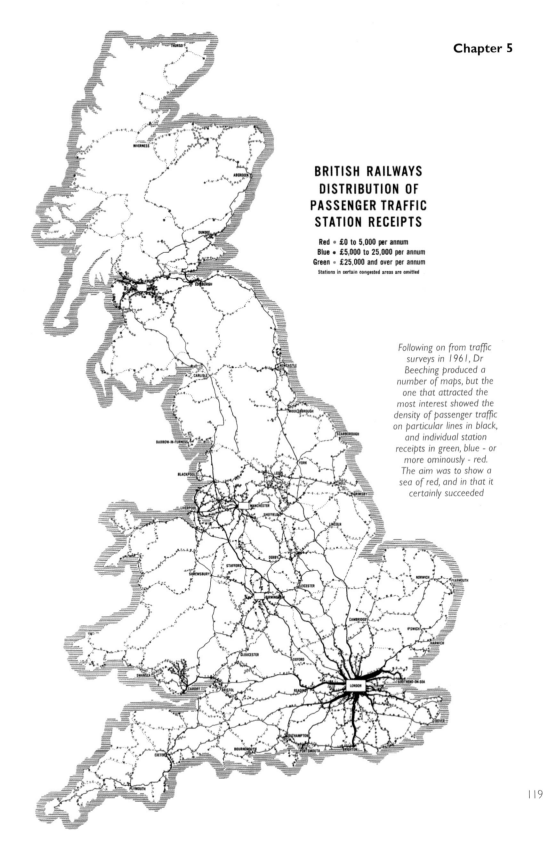

BRITISH RAILWAYS
DISTRIBUTION OF
PASSENGER TRAFFIC
STATION RECEIPTS

Red ● £0 to 5,000 per annum
Blue ● £5,000 to 25,000 per annum
Green ● £25,000 and over per annum
Stations in certain congested areas are omitted

*Following on from traffic
surveys in 1961, Dr
Beeching produced a
number of maps, but the
one that attracted the
most interest showed the
density of passenger traffic
on particular lines in black,
and individual station
receipts in green, blue - or
more ominously - red.
The aim was to show a
sea of red, and in that it
certainly succeeded*

supplied under the Carrington formula, that even that most conservative body, the Central Transport Consultative Committee, felt moved to sound a note of caution:

"...there is an urgent need for the study of overall transport costs, including social costs (such as congestion, accidents and health services) for all forms of transport, and this should be published. The effect of subsidies, open and hidden, may be giving a completely false picture of the costs of various forms of transport...

... the negative policy of closing down uneconomic facilities, while contributing a small financial saving, is not the panacea it has sometimes been made out to be. Each closure diverts some business onto the roads."

Surprisingly modern language for 1963, and meeting the transport issues of the day head-on, but this change of heart by the CTCC, after years of silence and acquiescence, was not published until after the arrival of the Beeching report.

Meanwhile, events began to move with bewildering speed. In the summer of 1962, Dr Beeching completed Stage Two of his plan, by publishing maps indicating traffic density throughout the railway system, based on surveys conducted in April 1961. The full *Reshaping of British Railways* was still some months away, but the traffic surveys produced some very effective soundbites for the media: one-third of the route-miles carried only 1% of the total passenger-miles, and half the route-miles carried only about 4% of the total passenger-miles. These statistics were left to sink in.

The Unions

Many years later, the National Union of Railwaymen would agree that its opposition to the Beeching proposals had been both ineffectual and lacking in direction. That the main railway union mounted no serious opposition either before or after publication of the *Reshaping* report is difficult to understand, for between nationalisation and the Beeching cataclysm, more than 174,000 jobs had been lost. Branch line closures had proceeded without demur from the unions – perhaps they had accepted those BTC promises at face value, that 'pruning' really would promote vigorous growth elsewhere. It was not until events began to take a serious turn in 1959-60 that the NUR belatedly established a Closure of Branch Lines Sub-Committee to deal with the matter, but even then the union took no effective action. Reports from local branch level continued to suggest that there was little point in opposing closures, for the staff on the ground seemed to feel that the early proposals were largely justified.

Whether by accident or design, the much more intensive Beeching plans came to affect the less affluent areas of the country first, with Scotland being particularly hard hit. When the railways had been reorganised in 1923, Scotland had not been given a statutory company of its own. The stated reason was that Scotland – weighed down by the sparsely populated Highlands region – was simply unable to support a viable railway company. As a result, its network was divided up between two comparatively wealthy English concerns, the LNER and the LMSR. Nationalisation in 1947 created a Scottish region, but after the arrival of the free market Conservatives in 1953, this unremunerative region was to bear the brunt of the cutbacks, while the wealthy south remained relatively secure.

One of Dr Beeching's first moves on becoming Chairman of the Commission was to examine the loss-making Scottish lines. A traffic survey was quickly conducted, and within a couple of months, the figures released – of 2,750 daily trains in Scotland, as many as 2,000 appeared to be running at a loss.

In happier circumstances, this might have been the cue for diesel railbuses and better line promotion, but this was 1961, and management drew up plans to withdraw 260 services and close seven branch lines outright from November that same year. In the event, union pressure secured a stay of execution, but the Scottish railwaymen were aware that they had won no more than a temporary reprieve, and delegates from both ASLEF and the NUR decided to lobby Parliament, spreading the word to their brothers in the south along the way. So it was that about 100 railwaymen made the long journey to London, linking up with others from Lancashire, the North East and Wales as they went.

Astoundingly, as the skirl of bagpipes could be heard outside NUR headquarters, only two members of the Executive Committee bothered to greet the delegation, and they were both docked an hour's pay for their trouble! The ASLEF delegation fared even worse, finding their union headquarters locked. Although the men were eventually given a warm welcome at Westminster by Hugh Gaitskell and other MPs, the affair showed only too clearly that a united union campaign was out of the question. Whether Beeching had deliberately instigated cuts in the provinces first was never revealed, but the policy split the union response very effectively.

In the south, where unemployment stood at less than 2% and railway closures were expected to have little overall impact on jobs, the membership and officials of the unions showed little concern. In Scotland, Wales and the less affluent areas of England, the impact was immediate and very serious, but the union leadership in London were unable to decide whether to take action or not. The inevitable result was no action at all, and the unions dithered, throwing away a rare opportunity to mount a concerted campaign. A strike in Scotland would have been distant news, but a strike in London commuter territory might have helped to focus the minds of home county Ministers, civil servants and economists.

By April 1962, details of some of the English railway closures became known and the unions – still prevaricating over how best to react – were caught largely unawares. It was not until June that the publicity machine swung slowly into action, dispatching circulars to branch offices, publishing leaflets and organising meetings up and down the country. Even at this late stage, firm union action might have had the desired effect, but the campaign was lacklustre and ineffective, and pitted against a well-honed Railways Board publicity machine.

Meanwhile, the railway workshops, which had done rather well out of the rush to diesel traction, were feeling the pinch. As many as 11,000 redundancies had been envisaged as early as 1959, but three years later it began to dawn on the unions that Beeching intended to go a good deal further. On 19th September 1962 it was announced that many of the workshops would close, others would lose departments, and the whole programme would be carried through in three years.

The rail unions now thought they were in receipt of the whole picture, but they still failed to organise any effective opposition. The NUR, with assets of more than £6.5 million, had spent only £7,547 campaigning against the closure plans. The only direct action proved to be a one-day national strike over the workshop closure proposals, on 3rd October 1962 – it was the first national stoppage since 1926. It was also an ideal opportunity to rally the public and media to the railway's cause and fight the cuts, but the implications were still not widely understood, and little was done. Only in South Wales did NUR men spend the day canvassing, the result understandably lacking the impact of a national campaign.

Beeching swiftly defused the situation by making concessions over redundancy payments, and the half-hearted campaign rapidly degenerated into local discussions over redundancies and terms.

According to the NUR[9], the Railway Chairman, "leaned over backwards," in his desire to reach a satisfactory compromise. And well he might, for had the unions taken concerted action, and gained the sympathy of a concerned public, the future of the whole closure programme might have been thrown into doubt. As it was, the redundancy terms were unprecedented in their generosity, and the union voice was effectively silenced. So satisfied were the unions with the result of the negotiations, that in December 1962 the NUR Executive Committee voted unanimously to wind up the campaign:

"There can be no doubt whatever that the campaign has been one of the most successful the union has ever undertaken, but we feel that the time has arrived for meetings at Executive Committee level to cease as from 31st December 1962."

It was a disastrous decision. Three months later, Beeching's *Reshaping of British Railways* appeared, and the union was – once again – caught unawares. All the NUR succeeded in doing was reopening the campaign over workshop closures, which proved a waste of effort because the newspapers were engrossed in the details of the widespread line closures in the report. Had the unions spent the previous three years preparing a measured and detailed response to the Railway Board's proposals, and launched them on the media at the right psychological moment, they might have dealt the Beeching regime a devastating blow.

The most poignant side to the affair was that the South Wales NUR branch, which had worked alone to publicise the cutbacks during the strike, had made a unilateral decision to continue the fight. Convinced that a cataclysm was about to wreak havoc on their industry, the branch ignored the platitudes from headquarters and fought on. In February 1963 (just before the report's publication) it canvassed other branches and lobbied MPs at Westminster, with a measure of success. There was a sting in the tale, though, for when General Secretary Sidney Greene heard of the campaign, he reminded the South Wales men that the Executive Committee decision in December meant they would be unable to charge expenses to branch funds. It was a petty, officious and vindictive move that led to a debate at the union's AGM, and

The Beeching cuts were to hid hardest where traffic receipts were low and railways difficult to work. Clydach on the Heads of the Valleys line would shut in 1958 and by 1962 it was clear that many others would follow. Perhaps it's no surprise that the South Wales NUR fought the longest and hardest campaign. PHOTO: I L Wright.

a vote in favour of continuing the campaign. But this was in July 1963, three months after publication of the report... there was little point.

In any event, the union response had already collapsed into farce. The NUR rejected the *Reshaping* report outright, and called for strike action, a move that met with a positive response from ASLEF and the Confederation of Shipbuilding & Engineering Unions. At a meeting between Marples, the TUC and rail unions in April 1963, the Minister of Transport had offered no concessions, leaving the ball in the NUR's court. The Executive met later the same day and voted in favour of a three-day strike in May, but ASLEF was unable to agree, because the strike would have fallen during its Annual Assembly.

Once again, Beeching headed off the strike threat with concessions on redundancy terms. Downgraded staff would no longer be obliged to accept a cut in wages; men between the ages of 60 and 65 would have the option of retirement on almost full pay, and for those asked to relocate, there would be cheaper lodgings and free travel. The Railways Board had split the unions branch by branch, outmanoeuvred them, and finally bought them for a handful of silver.

On 9th May 1963, the unions agreed to lay aside the strike weapon. The NUR continued a low key campaign, however, and a modest sum was put aside for the production of leaflets in 1963, but according to the official history of the union, the campaign lacked conviction:

"The most popular [leaflet]. The Mis-shaping of British Railways... Retort [a pun on Beeching's The Reshaping of British Railways – Report], made clear the vast areas of Britain which would be denuded of railways if the report was implemented. But it was a slim leaflet and not a substantial, closely argued publication detailing a positive alternative... the kind of case likely to inform and educate influential opinion in the Labour Party."

Beeching had achieved an overwhelming victory at the expense of just a single day's strike action. But the cost of the generous redundancy packages and relocation agreements was to be very high in cash terms. As railway assets were scrapped, and income from closed lines disappeared, the former staff were allowed to retire early, or found less productive work for the same money. Consequently, many of the savings forecast under the Beeching plan failed to materialise. The unions had won a few concessions, but Beeching had brought his plan through almost unscathed. The country was about to pay the price.

The Management

The railway management had surprisingly little warning of the impending cuts. Morale during the late 1950s had reached a post-war high, and it was not until the virtual cancellation of the modernisation plans that doubts began to creep in. The real shock came in April 1962 when Beeching chaired the senior managers' conference in York for the first time, and outlined his plans for the industry. As public criticism began to mount, a defensive wall of silence descended around the Railways Board, which would not lift for more than a decade. Few were willing to speak out, and when they did, it was generally in the most guarded of tones:

"There are those who feel that these losses need not have been incurred after 1952, at any rate to the extent they have and, if this is right, to judge all the parts of the service now on the basis of the losses being incurred is open to question."
A J Pearson, Assistant General Manager, London Midland Region, The Railways and the Nation, 1964

Such carefully worded criticism hardly amounted to a forthright condemnation of the Beeching regime, but Pearson, like many others, was bound by loyalty to an industry to which he had devoted his working life. To speak out would only have meant dismissal, and further damage to the already wounded railway.

According to the *Railway Gazette*, the Board was experiencing a 'grand resignation' of experienced managers by July 1962. The result was an influx of outsiders: army officers, civil servants, industrialists and accountants. Pearson stayed to see it through, as did Gerald Fiennes, a maverick, and something of a loose cannon, but one of the ablest administrators in the industry at a time when the quality of management left much to be desired. It has been said that regional managers tended to keep their brightest stars in the provinces to avoid losing them to the BTC – either way, the higher echelons of the railway were starved of experienced railwaymen, but they were desperately needed to counter the views of Beeching and his army of outsiders.

Gerald Fiennes, who displayed a unique blend of common sense, business guile and plain honesty, did more to salvage the position of the railways than almost anyone else in the Beeching era, but his tendency to condemn poor management and quixotic business practices were later to cost him his job when he went public in his 1967 memoir *I tried to Run a Railway*.

British Railways managers, though not necessarily in full agreement with the Beeching philosophy, had enough work on their hands allocating a trickle of investment cash towards the intercity services, without having to worry about the branches and the secondary lines.

According to Fiennes, General Manager of the Western Region at the time, the crucial

In the early 1960s, the best railway managers like Gerard Fiennes had reluctantly conceded that there was little point putting resources into branch lines when the new motorways had shifted the battleground to the trunk lines. Warship D830 'Majestic' thunders through Taunton in March 1961. PHOTO: Revd. John Sutters

challenge facing the railways was to improve the reliability and speed of main line services to compete with road traffic. He was probably right. If the railways had lost the propaganda battle on the trunk lines as well as the branches, they might well have failed to survive the 1960s at all. This view was supported by many railwaymen – the branch lines would have to be sacrificed to satisfy the Ministry, but that would leave the industry free to concentrate resources on the trunk lines, where investment was desperately needed.

The branches were a social and political problem. Some within the industry genuinely agreed with Beeching that the network would only flower if the branches were lopped off, but others saw the closure plans as mistaken, mistimed and misjudged, but a necessary evil, taking pressure off the trunk routes. It was all very painful, but it had become a struggle for survival.

That the railways had a task on their hands can be gleaned from the figures in Fiennes' own region. The fastest scheduled service from Paddington to Bristol before the war had been 105 minutes, and it was not until 1954, nine years after the war, that this pre-war schedule was equalled. But with road traffic accelerating year on year, the Western Region needed to cut minutes off the schedules, and it needed to do it very rapidly.

The early Warship class diesel locomotives, introduced in 1959, cut the journey time to 100 minutes, but the following year it slid back to 105 minutes, and in 1961 it receded even further. It was not until 1971 – the opening year of M4, the London to Bristol motorway – that the headline schedule was cut to 100 minutes on a permanent basis.

Progress might have been slow, but the improved rail services did begin to pay dividends. The number of Western Region passengers had fallen from 112 million in 1948 to a low of 104 million in 1960, but by 1965 had recovered to 110 million.

The plunge into deficit in the late 1950s had been largely due to a loss of freight traffic, but there were more general problems with the performance of the Western and London Midland regions, whose continued losses had been the Government's primary justification for cancelling the modernisation plans. If Fiennes had turned around the traffic figures with little more than hard work, a flair for publicity and some rescheduled services, to what extent might traffic have grown had the BTC investment programme been allowed to run its course?

But by the end of 1962 the writing was on the wall. The BTC had gone, and the new Railways Board was preparing to push through the most savage round of cuts the industry had ever seen. Ironically, the Conservative administration was in difficulties too. The economic boom of the late 1950s had proved short-lived, and after three Tory governments the electorate was restless and ready for a change. In March 1963, the party was hit by the damaging Profumo affair which combined with the Beeching legacy to stifle any lingering hopes of re-election. The decline in the fortunes of the Conservatives were set to mirror the decline they had so carefully engineered for the railways... a wicked irony.

In October 1962, Beeching addressed the Institute of Directors at the Albert Hall and outlined his plans. Even in Parliament, the war of words appeared to have been won, for during a debate in November 1962, there was considerable support for the Beeching philosophy. Perhaps, thought some MPs, the railways really were a relic from the horse-and-cart age, the stopping trains a ludicrous, outmoded form of transport in an era of limit-free motorway travel.

The 1962 deficit had topped £160 million after interest, and Beeching was promising to sweep away the dead wood and balance the books. At the railway headquarters, 222 Marylebone Road, a small team was assembled to oversee the railway closures. This Central Planning Unit of just 'six to eight' officers [10] was to spend the next few years 'reshaping' the network, principally by processing railway closures. All would be revealed in the third stage of Beeching's master plan, *The Reshaping of British Railways*.

6
The Reshaping Report
1963-1964

"Dr Beeching's report has proved to be the most staggering report ever presented to any government...
He has closed the railways. If I stopped a train, I would be fined £5. Dr Beeching stops a third of the
railway system and gets a cheque for £24,000... On the law of averages, as I should be fined £5, the
Minister should be deported."

T W Jones, MP for Meirionnydd, speaking in the House of Commons debate on the 'Reshaping' report, 29th April 1963

PART 1: REPORT

*O*n 27th March 1963, Dr Beeching released the long-awaited report 'The Reshaping of British Railways'. It set out to prove in straightforward terms where the money was going, and went on to furnish a few answers. Freight services would eventually produce a healthy return after substantial investment and reorganisation, but passenger services had little future. They were, Beeching concluded, bound to be squeezed almost to death between road transport for short journeys and the domestic airlines for long distance travel. Considerable emphasis was placed on the inadequacies of stopping and branch line services, and the figures were massaged so as to make individual lines appear quite uneconomic and ripe for closure.

The rail lobby could do little to dispute many of the figures in the report, because there was little alternative evidence to work with. The key to undermining the report's assumptions was Beeching's hypothetical example, laying out the income and expenditure for a typical branch line. As closures were put forward, the expenditure claims were often well in excess of Dr Beeching's hypothetical example, suggesting that economies could have been made. The rail lobby proceeded to dismantle the report's assumptions, with some success.

In the run-up to the 1964 general election, Harold Wilson, leader of the opposition, promised to halt major closures. Within weeks, he had been elected.

The introduction to *The Reshaping of British Railways* made it quite clear that Dr Beeching did not intend (nor indeed did he have the power) to make final judgements. The Chairman of the British Railways Board had investigated and analysed every detail of railway operation, and it was now for the Government to decide whether to take the medicine he prescribed.

"Throughout these investigations and the preparations of this report, the British Railways Board has had it in mind that its duty is to employ the assets vested in it, and develop or modify them, to the best advantage of the nation. Also, because the ultimate choice... must be made by the nation, it is a basic responsibility of the Board to provide, as objectively and comprehensively as possible, information which makes clear the range and nature of choice."

This paragraph, from the Foreword of *Reshaping*, appears to be in contradiction to the following extract which appears not that far away, on page two: "It is, of course, the responsibility of the British Railways Board so to shape and operate the railways as to make them pay..." Beeching was bound by the provisions of the 1962 Transport Act to make the railways pay, or at least break even. But the wording of the Act is somewhat vague on this point: "...the Boards shall so conduct their business as to secure that their revenue is not less than sufficient for making provision for the meeting of charges properly chargeable to revenue..." In other words, the railways were not to lose money overall, but the Chairman had the option to maintain a service or services that lost money individually, yet provided a valuable social function, or substantial contributory revenue to the network as a whole. This option seems not to have been explored, with the subject of contributory revenue very much brushed under the carpet, although the *Reshaping* maps revealed some odd exceptions to the rules, presumably for reasons of political expediency. Otherwise, services were to be considered individually, which was widely taken to mean that Beeching's terms of reference were to eliminate the minor lines for political reasons, rather than, "develop or modify [the network] to the best advantage of the nation."

There was nothing wrong with the objective of returning the network to profitability, and the report made some good points about the past and future patterns of freight traffic, but the passenger section was very obviously written with the aim of eliminating minor services. To this end, it was little more than a collection of figures, shamefully massaged to provide supporting evidence as to the overwhelming size and unprofitability of the network. It was, however, well written and concise, and even Professor Hondelink was moved to concede that point:

"I have now digested the Beeching Report. My comment is as follows: Analysis clear, concise and capable; the accountant's work well done; the conclusions rough and unrealistic; the proposed implementation ruthless to the point of being suicidal..."

Beeching clearly had not been asked to look into the social and economic value of the railway network per se, but merely to find a way of returning the industry to profitability as quickly as possible. He might also have been instructed to err towards closure and retrenchment, because that was the thrust of the report's arguments. It completely ignored various cost-saving measures that had been under consideration both at home and abroad for several decades, which might have turned marginal lines into profitable ones. It had to admit that diesel multiple units (DMUs) were cheaper to run than steam, because this was now common knowledge, but the report rammed home that efficient diesels alone were not enough to ensure profitability.

Reshaping was constructed around a series of passenger and freight surveys that were claimed as the first analysis of costs and income on a line-by-line basis. This was almost certainly the first national survey measuring traffic on the entire network simultaneously, but it certainly wasn't the first line-by-line analysis. In fact, there was nothing new in the report at all, for the handful of positive freight schemes had all been included in the BTC's modernisation plan of 1954. It was only really the clear and concise nature of the report that genuinely broke new ground.

Many of the freight proposals were perfectly reasonable, such as the need to move away from unprofitable wagon-load and freight sundries traffic, and concentrate instead on train-loads, and container traffic... the so-called 'liner train' concept, for which Beeching had developed a particular enthusiasm.

Wagonload traffic – oddly enough, profitable elsewhere in Europe – had been losing money in Britain for years. Wagons were picked up, shunted, carried to the next yard, shunted again, lost in sidings, rediscovered, and finally delivered, after a long and expensive passage through the railway network – up to six weeks for a journey of only 90 miles, according to one Black Country engineering works. It had been estimated that freight locomotives spent half their working lives shunting and the other half hauling an average of just 20 wagons between marshalling yards.

Where passenger services were concerned, the prognosis was relentlessly gloomy, but several sectors were singled out for particular criticism: commuter services, seasonal traffic, stopping trains, and of course the branch lines. There was little future for rail passenger services, said Beeching, because local traffic would continue to be lost to the roads, and long-distance traffic to the airlines.

As expected, the minor passenger services were to bear the brunt of the cuts, but closing branch lines was such a politically explosive issue that the Doctor went to great lengths to justify his belief that they were fundamentally uneconomic, and to counter the arguments that DMUs, railbuses and light railway operating methods might turn things round. But his analysis of the lines the Government had already decided to axe left much to be desired.

Between 1960, when the first data had been collected, and 1963 when the report appeared, many lines had already closed, and it was clear that many others were a long way from viability. The intention of the report was to provide an overwhelming case for closing a much greater mileage. Of 17,800 route-miles of railway, the report concluded that 5,000 miles should be closed to passengers as rapidly as possible, together with 2,363 stations, many on lines that would remain open to through traffic.

This was only the beginning, for Beeching promised a second report at a later date that would make further closures inevitable. Almost a third of the national rail network and its stations would disappear. With a few notable exceptions, almost every branch line was expected to close, leaving much of Devon, Cornwall, Lincolnshire, Cumbria, Wales, and the Highlands of Scotland completely deprived of rail services. A handful of trunk routes were to close as well, notably the Waverley route between Edinburgh and Carlisle, the Great Central linking London and Sheffield, and the Somerset & Dorset between Bournemouth and Bath.

The report represented the most dramatic and far-reaching manipulation of the British transport system since the arrival of the railways more than 100 years before. How then, would it be put into practice, against the will of the unions, the local authorities and the vast majority of the public at large?

Passenger receipts quoted in the report were for individual stations, based on records kept throughout 1960. As such, they represented a fair assessment of income, but of course the drawback was that income was based solely on tickets issued at a particular place. The value of tickets issued at a holiday destination such as Minehead or Newquay would naturally enough represent only a fraction of the total value of the traffic flow through that point. The same was true for any station that tended to receive traffic rather than generate it. As Professor Hondelink pointed out, methodology of this kind would render the summit station on the Snowdon Mountain Railway a substantial loss maker, yet it was the destination that made the whole line viable.

The result, when applied to the whole network, seriously distorted the passenger figures. This should have shown up in the accompanying map and figures indicating the density of passenger traffic on a line-by-line basis. It didn't, because of another distortion built into the passenger density figures. Unlike the station receipts, which covered a whole year, they were collected over the week of 17th-23rd April 1961, two weeks after the Easter holiday weekend. April was hardly mid-winter, but neither was it a significant time for holiday or general leisure travel, being outside school holidays. The weather was unsettled that week, according to Met Office records, and that April was 60% wetter than average, the dullest in England & Wales since 1937.

The Railways Board wasn't to blame for the weather, but for seaside branch lines in particular, the methodology was flawed. Hugely important decisions were hanging on these traffic surveys taken in a miserable week in late April. Branch lines to holiday resorts such as Skegness in Lincolnshire carried a massive volume of traffic in July and August, so intense that closure would cause complete chaos. Yet the line was being put forward for closure based on tickets *issued* at the resort, and traffic figures from a wet week in April. It was a major distortion of the truth.

Innocently or otherwise, the figures had been manipulated to benefit the lines that the British Railways Board intended to retain, and against the lines it wished to close. Far reaching and permanent decisions would be based on these figures, and it was nothing short of a scandal that the evidence should be so flimsy. It was also odd empirical work from a nuclear scientist, who well understood the need to observe and record data with great care in the search for a true picture.

These in-house traffic figures were of the utmost importance, because there was little alternative evidence for the TUCCs to consider when a line came up for closure. But of course the Board had already made up its mind to close a third of the system, and the only way to progress this difficult political and practical task was to show those lines in the worst possible

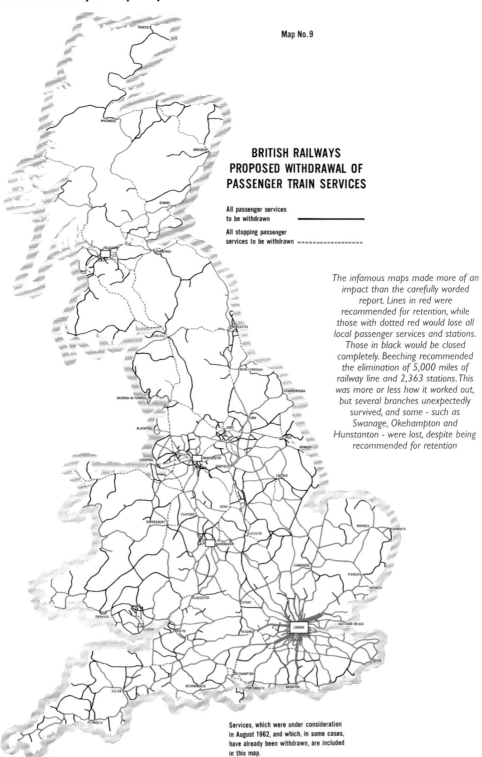

Map No.9

**BRITISH RAILWAYS
PROPOSED WITHDRAWAL OF
PASSENGER TRAIN SERVICES**

All passenger services
to be withdrawn

All stopping passenger
services to be withdrawn

*The infamous maps made more of an
impact than the carefully worded
report. Lines in red were
recommended for retention, while
those with dotted red would lose all
local passenger services and stations.
Those in black would be closed
completely. Beeching recommended
the elimination of 5,000 miles of
railway line and 2,363 stations. This
was more or less how it worked out,
but several branches unexpectedly
survived, and some - such as
Swanage, Okehampton and
Hunstanton - were lost, despite being
recommended for retention*

Services, which were under consideration
in August 1962, and which, in some cases,
have already been withdrawn, are included
in this map.

light. By using these distorted statistics, it was able to demonstrate that a third of its stations contributed less than 1% of the total passenger receipts, and a third of the route mileage carried only 1% of the passengers, a stunning and apparently damning indictment of the branch lines. These figures provided a nice clear message for the press – it was difficult to argue for the retention of 5,000 miles of track and over 2,300 stations that contributed so little to the railway's revenue and cost so much to maintain.

The reality was very different, but in most cases there were no other figures. Besides the traffic distortions already mentioned, the report failed to analyse the cost of maintaining these minor stations. Most of the least remunerative halts were simple unstaffed platforms that cost virtually nothing to maintain. Many others had been left, scandalously, with a full complement of staff since Edwardian days, so costs could have been cut drastically.

Having 'proved' that a third of the network was generating virtually nothing in the way of revenue, the Board needed to show exactly what the losses were on particular lines in hard cash terms. This was a little more difficult, for as well as movement costs, an allowance had to made for track maintenance, station terminal costs and signalling, and the picture became more complicated when these costs were shared with freight, or long-distance passenger services, although for the purposes of comparing branch lines, these components were dismissed.

The *Reshaping* report included vital statistics from a representative selection of real lines, together with the infamous maps to show the big picture, but Beeching also decided to include a theoretical demonstration to prove that such innovations as DMUs would do nothing to help.

The 'Reshaping' report included figures from a selection of real branch lines and a hypothetical example. Beeching was tripped up by the Comrie branch in Perth & Kinross, where the AC Cars railbus was costing less to run than 'Reshaping's' hypothetical railbus, and slightly less than Beeching's 'typical' road bus! The real problem, as suggested by this photo of a rather grand Crieff station in 1961, is that the Scottish Region had done little to reduce staffing and signalling costs, and this ultimately led to complete closure of the line in 1964. As a 'basic' railway, it could, and should, have survived. PHOTO: Frank Spaven

The Great Railway Conspiracy

This was dangerous territory, of course, and the analytical Beeching must have regretted it in quiet contemplative moments for the rest of his life, for certain of the *Reshaping* assumptions were subsequently borrowed by the rail lobby and used to fight real closures.

The report offered the hypothetical example of a single-track branch line, with stations at two-and-a-half mile intervals, and a service of one train an hour in each direction between 7am and 10pm, seven days a week. That was more stations and trains than most rural branches provided at the time, so it sounded pretty uneconomic right from the start.

Costs for this hypothetical branch were broken down as follows: track maintenance and signalling would account for £58 per track-mile per week, and each station (presumably lightly staffed) would account for a further £19, giving a total fixed weekly expenditure in the region of £77 per mile. It is worth recalling that less than a decade before, while giving evidence against the Rural Transport Improvement Bill, the BTC had suggested a figure of £300 per mile per *year*, or just under £6 a week!

As for train movement expenses, steam-hauled trains (at the rate of 15 shillings (75p) per mile) were calculated to cost about £168 per track-mile per week, and a modern DMU (at 4 to 6 shillings (20p-30p) per mile, was £45 to £67 per track-mile.

On these figures, the most economical rail service (assuming no freight or fast passenger services sharing expenses) would cost £122 to £144 (£6,820 to £8,040 today) per track-mile per week to run. With revenue at 2d per passenger-mile (less than 1p), the line would consequently need to carry 15,000 to 17,000 passengers per week to break even. Naturally the Board chose the higher figure when summing up (it became something of a benchmark), but it did make the concession that profitable freight traffic would enable this hypothetical line to break even at lower traffic levels.

By way of comparison, the Board considered the economics of a bus service on the same route, costing only £28 per road-mile per week... less than a quarter of the rail cost. On paper, the evidence was overwhelmingly in favour of road transport, and *Reshaping* suggesting that a bus service might be profitable carrying as few as 3,500 passengers per week.

Here Beeching betrayed a little too much enthusiasm for road transport – again, a strange lapse for a scientist – by suggesting that the bus might be even more economical with a two-hourly schedule, but failing to consider a two-hourly DMU schedule by way of comparison. He didn't, of course, because with a two-hourly schedule, the hypothetical railway would have carried all its inflated costs at a level of only 12,000-13,000 passengers a week. And with the inclusion of some strategic station and signalling economies, the railway might have broken even at as low as 8,000 passengers a week, or even less where freight or through passenger services were able to share the costs.

Indeed, if full maintenance costs were to be borne by other traffic (not unusual on a busy trunk line), the stopping passenger service would prove economically viable carrying just 2,700 passengers a week, and taking into account contributory revenue, even lower passenger figures could well be worthwhile.

But what of the diesel railbus, a vehicle that had been in operational service for some years by this time? Beeching clearly had to dismiss this option as quickly and quietly as possible, and he did this in a single paragraph, claiming that a railbus cost 3 shillings (15p) per mile to operate, and provided no particular advantage over road buses, which cost in the region of 2s 6d (12 1/2p) per mile. However, elsewhere in the report were the actual figures from the Gleneagles to Comrie branch line in the Scottish Highlands, where a railbus had been operating for some time, at a movement cost of 2s 4d (11 1/2p) per mile. This 15-mile line, once part of a network, but now a tenuous lifeline to the towns of Comrie and Crieff, with a combined population of about 7,200, was broadly similar to Beeching's hypothetical line, and a small-scale, but perfectly viable railway operation.

According to *Reshaping*, expenses on the Comrie line amounted to ten times the earnings, but a closer look at the figures reveals a rather different story[11].

Although the railbus was carrying an average of only five passengers per trip, most of them were starting out on much longer journeys to Glasgow or beyond, so the line generated a considerable amount of contributory revenue, effectively boosting income to the point where the railbus easily covered its own movement and terminal expenses, and about half the attributable track and signalling expenses. The railbus cost half as much to run as a DMU, and rather less than a road bus, but it was generating cashflow of £14,180 (£792,000 today) a year.

Dr Beeching had set out to prove that a railway needed to carry 17,000 passengers a week to break even, but he proved nothing of the kind. The reality was closer to 8,000 and often much less. The Comrie branch line was not making a profit, but it was covering most of its attributable costs carrying just a few hundred passengers a week, which demonstrated very well what could be done with a few strategic economies. In the mood of the times, it was still a hopeless case, and the Comrie line was put up for closure in *Reshaping*, and lopped off in 1964.

Of course, such arguments would be academic when a bus service could operate at a profit carrying just a handful of passengers. But could it? Would all the ex-railway passengers transfer to the bus, as Dr Beeching assumed? What allowance had *Reshaping* made for road repairs, environmental damage, accidents and all the other hidden road transport costs?

In fact, no allowance at all. And it was not an oversight, but another example of the selective evidence used in the report. Some months after publication, a private study was conducted into one of its intended victims, the branch from Watford to St Albans, another line similar to Beeching's hypothetical branch, but unlike Comrie, in the heart of commuter country.

Traffic was difficult to predict without access to figures, but 'reliable sources' suggested a total of 7,200 to 9,200 passengers a week. On the Railway Board's own figures, total annual expenditure on the line amounted to £41,236, but the study concluded that a few sensible economies would result in a saving of £14,950 a year, leaving an expenditure of £26,286. If revenue was then based on a more realistic 2¹/₂d per mile (instead of the 2d suggested in *Reshaping*), income would just top expenditure at £26,364. On the evidence of this independent study, the line *could* be made self-supporting (even without contributory revenue, of which there was a great deal, as many passengers commuted into London) and contributions from freight traffic. Whatever the true position, the Watford to St Albans line was one of the lucky few to escape Beeching, and it survives today as a busy commuter route, generating 9,700 passengers a week in 2008 [12], with growth of nearly 10% a year. The line is on target for conversion into a high-frequency tram or light rail service in the near future, bringing considerable growth.

The veritable whirlwind of facts and figures was of crucial importance, because with the Board's stated conclusion that even a single-track branch line needed 17,000 passengers a week to be break even, more than half the system was potentially at risk of closure. In the passenger census ending 23rd April 1961, only the major trunk lines had carried more than 17,000 passengers, with no viable routes from Carmarthen to Bangor (apart, oddly enough, from an isolated section of the Cambrian), and not a single route north or west of Glasgow, Dundee and Aberdeen (in other words, the entire Scottish Highlands). On the Board's own figures, it appeared as though cutting a third of the system was quite a generous compromise.

Reshaping was instigated with the sole intention of eliminating the railway deficit. It was a cold, and ultimately futile, exercise in purely theoretical accountancy.

Had the report been produced as part of a wider evaluation of future transport trends

– as some members of the Stedeford Committee had proposed – the result would have been much kinder to the railways. For instance, there was no evaluation of where traffic forced off the railways would actually go. What damage would be caused to the economic development of hard-hit regions? Most of north Devon, Lincolnshire, Wales, and large areas of the Highlands would be deprived of rail transport. What would be the social and economic costs to these areas? Would people migrate away? Would fewer tourists visit? Clearly this was someone else's headache. But most critically of all, there was very little discussion about the effects of reduced contributory revenue on the rest of the network. Would *Reshaping* permanently damage the viability of the lines left behind?

There was little discussion about the effects of growing road traffic either. In what areas was road traffic likely to reach saturation point? Nowhere in the report was the future growth of private car ownership questioned. On the contrary, there was a clear assumption that the volume of road traffic would continue to rise, presumably indefinitely.

The report did grudgingly accept that commuter rail services were unavoidable in and around London, Glasgow, Edinburgh, Newcastle, Manchester, Liverpool, Leeds, Birmingham and Cardiff. But accepting that commuter services were essential around Britain's nine most important cities was tantamount to accepting that these cities were already saturated with road traffic (as indeed they were). And if *Reshaping* had reached this inevitable conclusion, why was there no discussion on the future for public transport in and around other cities such as

Crucially, Beeching was not asked to look at the wider picture. This example of commuter gridlock is Bristol on a wet winter's evening in 2012, but it could be any British city in any of the last four decades. Bristol's rail commuter network was largely dismantled after the 'Reshaping' report, but the Severn Beach line hung on, and is now being brought together with several others that closed to passengers in the 1960s as part of an urban metro scheme. PHOTO: Robin Whitlock

Bristol, Plymouth, Southampton or Sheffield? All were to lose the majority of their stopping rail services, and all were to suffer problems from traffic congestion. In the fullness of time, chronic congestion would filter down to much smaller cities and towns, in a way the Railways Board of the 1960s could never have conceived, but they failed to even ask the questions.

In other areas of railway business, the report's arguments were sadly lacking. Holiday traffic, particularly during the July and August peak, had long been seen as a lucrative sideline for the railways, keeping commuter rolling stock busy at a time when fewer people were travelling to work. It was traffic for which they were ideally suited – large numbers of people, travelling long distances, and generally moving in the same direction. But there had been a steady decline for a number of years, brought about by changing holiday patterns and the increasing popularity of the private car. The report compared traffic for each of the four summer months of 1961 with the average winter figure:

- **Winter average:**   100%
- **June 1961**   118%
- **July 1961**   147%
- **August 1961**   143%
- **September 1961**   121%

Quiet seaside stations could be extremely in the summer peak, but the Beeching methodology was carefully skewed to omit most of this effect. This is the arrival of the Cornish Riviera Express at the tiny station of St Ives in the late 1940s. This branch line was listed for closure by Beeching, but later reprieved by Barbara Castle. PHOTO: Studio St Ives - the St Ives Museum Collection

The Great Railway Conspiracy

Once again, the way these statistics had been presented was grossly unfair, because they related to traffic on the whole system. The seasonal traffic on some of the branch lines to holiday destinations would have been far greater than these bare statistics revealed, perhaps two or even three times heavier than the winter traffic. Taking figures from the whole network to show the size of peak season fluctuations, yet judging the individual holiday lines on the basis of passenger receipts from a wet week in April, was a sleight of hand, designed to write off the assets the railway wanted to lose. Lines that were profitable for just two months of the year may have deserved to close, but their closure raised serious road traffic issues, and they were never given a fair trial.

As far as the main lines were concerned, *Reshaping* accepted and welcomed the fact that holiday traffic could help fill service trains. But where the traffic required extra capacity it was seen as a liability. There appeared on the face of it to be some justification for this view, because a survey in 1959 had found that out of a total of 30,000 coaches on the network, 18,500 were allocated for fast and semi-fast services, and of these, only 5,500 were utilised on a daily basis. Of the remaining 13,000 coaches, many were assumed to be sitting idle for much of the year, waiting for the holiday season – 2,000 were found to have left the depot on no more than ten occasions in the previous year! It sounded like an accountant's nightmare, and, according to *Reshaping*, it was easily cured.

The seasonal traffic peak would be 'controlled' by pricing holidaymakers off the trains, and introducing compulsory seat reservations. Beeching reckoned that this would enable him to scrap 6,000 coaches, at a saving of £3.4 million a year, against a loss of £500,000 in revenue. But according to at least one authority [13] these figures were quite wrong. Not only was the cost of maintaining 6,000 coaches actually £2.1 million a year (Beeching seemed to have slipped up on the arithmetic), but this was an *average* cost. The true cost of maintaining 6,000 elderly and fully depreciated carriages that left the depot only occasionally for such things as football specials and holiday trains was really minimal. It would have been much more prudent to retain these carriages until they were life expired, and then decide whether seasonal traffic justified replacing them with other well-depreciated stock.

In the event, 15,000 passenger coaches were scrapped between 1961 and 1966, but the railway's total maintenance and depreciation bill *increased* by £13.75 million in the same period. Disposal of 6,000 coaches had lost the railways at least £500,000 a year in seasonal revenue and saved absolutely nothing. And what of the displaced passengers? Naturally the report ignored this point, but if car sales of the time are any guide, most of them went straight out and bought a car.

In 1963, the motor car seemed to herald a new age of personal mobility and, as far as the railway's passenger receipts were concerned, it was clearly the villain. But this was not the time to throw in the towel and hand valuable traffic to the roads. Beeching had concluded that the railways were caught in a pincer movement between road transport and the airlines, as in the United States, where, "the process is almost complete." The assumption was that Britain's domestic airlines would be left with a virtual monopoly over long-distance traffic, as had happened in America:

"On the Scottish routes, air makes quite serious inroads into the loading of day trains, and will continue to do so. Even though trains may be speeded up, they will not match city-to-city transit times by air over such a distance, and erosion of daytime rail traffic between London and Scotland will probably continue to the point where some trains will have to be withdrawn."

Certainly the railways had much to fear from the airlines at the time, but the report made no attempt to examine congestion at airports and flight paths, not to mention road congestion between city centre and airport, something that would inevitably follow a capitulation by the railways. In the event, Beeching's prediction of a takeover by domestic flights didn't happen. British European Airways made a loss of about £1 million on domestic services in 1963-64, and £1.6 million in 1966, thanks in part to the belated completion of the London to Manchester electrification scheme. It was deeply ironic that the modernisation schemes that the authorities had sought to cancel in the early 1960s were to snatch back 30% of the domestic air traffic overnight.

By the early 1970s electric trains were running through to Glasgow, and a few years later the 125mph High Speed Train was stealing back traffic on the Edinburgh route, and domestic business to Cardiff and the West Country too. By the end of 2012, the number of London-Glasgow West Coast trains had reached 15 a day, offering almost 9,000 seats. Beeching got it very wrong.

Although domestic air passenger numbers rose by 14% a year between 1956 and 1966, there followed years of stagnation, largely because the railways had finally introduced competitive technology. Eventually rail would come to completely dominate most of the shorter domestic routes, with research by SNCF and others demonstrating that the modal share of rail was largely dependent on journey times. Where rail could cut journey times below 31/2 hours it would dominate over air traffic, and vice versa. Once rail invest-ment began to bite, the threat from the airlines receded. Domestic traffic was unprofitable for the airlines, and only really useful in providing feeders for more

In the 1950s and '60s the American airlines were expanding rapidly, selling their routes with a mixture of science fiction and (see overleaf) sex. But for all sorts of reasons, the airlines didn't make the same inroads into the UK domestic market

lucrative international routes out of Heathrow. Unlike the Railways Board, they recognised the value of contributory revenue.

Beeching knew well enough that rail modernisation would cut many journey times below that crucial 3 1/2 hour barrier, although whether he had done much research into the mechanisms of air/rail market share, a very new science at the time, is not clear.

For shorter journeys, and journeys of any kind in rural areas, *Reshaping* viewed the road bus as an excellent form of transport:

"With the exception of northern Scotland and parts of central Wales, most areas of the country are already served by a network of bus services more dense than the network of rail services which will be withdrawn, and in the majority of cases these buses already carry the major proportion of local traffic."

The bus network was certainly dense, as outlined on one of the maps thoughtfully enclosed with the report, which indicated an impressive spider's web of bus routes, embracing the country far more thoroughly than the railways had ever done. What the report failed to observe was that many of the bus routes it had so dutifully reproduced saw only a handful of buses a day. Some had just one a week, and there were a few on which services disappeared altogether in the winter months. Not only were country buses irregular, they were also terribly slow, with journey times typically double that of modern diesel trains, in part because of the nature of rural roads, but also because the much vaunted convenience of the bus meant stopping at every hamlet. In urban areas, buses were restricted even more by road congestion, with many routes already losing out to the railways through excessive journey times and the unpredictability of congestion.

Oddly enough, *Reshaping* glossed over this major issue, remarking that, "road congestion is being reduced in many places." And in a magnanimous gesture, the Chairman of the Railways Board even handed the bus companies a little bonus:

"Taken as a whole, they have enough spare capacity to absorb the traffic which will be displaced from the railways... and which will provide a very welcome addition to the revenue of the bus operators."

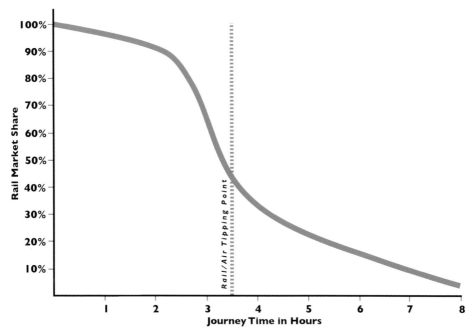

Beeching must have known that the BTC's electrification plans would make rail the dominant transport mode from London to most English cities, and give rail a sizeable chunk of the Anglo-Scottish market too. Unaccountably, he ignored the evidence. Today's High Speed Rail plans suggest a London-Edinburgh journey time of 3¹/2 hours, potentially giving rail almost 50% of the Anglo-Scottish market too. Graph produced from SNCF and Greengauge 21 data

Finally, the report overstretched its brief by advocating a degree of road construction:

"In parts of Scotland, in particular, and to a lesser degree in Wales and the West Country, road improvements or road construction may be necessary before adequate road services can be provided as full alternatives to the rail services which exist at present. Some of these road improvements are required, in any case, for development of the motor tourist trade, on which the future of these areas so greatly depends."

One of the major assumptions of the *Reshaping* report was that rural rail passengers would happily switch to buses for local journeys, and a bus/rail combination for long-distance travel. Trains sometimes had an image problem, but in a time of rapidly growing car ownership, the bus was perceived to be the lowest form of life, and very much a last resort for most people. Rather than switch to a slower, lower status mode of public transport, the majority of displaced rail passengers took the closure of their local line as an excuse to buy a car, and once they had become motorists they tended to desert public transport altogether.

As a statement of transport policy, *Reshaping* was fatally flawed. The idea that losses could be substantially reduced, yet alone eradicated, by disposing of a third of the network was, as discussed, a highly dubious one. And according to A J Pearson, Assistant General Manager of the London Midland Region, the sudden and dramatic implementation of the closure plan would harbour real dangers for the well-being of the remaining network:

"To introduce at this time a dramatic [closure] programme such as the Railway Board's first report contained, has sunk deeply into the consciousness in this country, as it was undoubtedly designed

"...some routes saw only a handful of buses a day. Some had just one a week..."

to do, and it is bound to create and intensify a negative attitude to the lines and services that remain that will be very hard to remove."

As the branches and cross-country lines were lopped off, public confidence began to collapse, and the secondary and trunk lines began to wither. The public perception was of a railway network in terminal decline. If you could afford one, you bought a car, and if you were moving house, choosing a place of work, or establishing a business, you based your decision on access to good roads rather than a railway station. What was the point of backing a network that might disappear? And in 1963, Britain led a Commonwealth of diverse nations that still tended to look to the mother country for help and advice. If Britain closed all its railways, the implication was that this was the modern and forward-looking approach for the whole Commonwealth. Fortunately, most nations made their own decisions, but some did go down the *Reshaping* road, with mixed results.

All the usual suspects lined up to find fault with the conclusions of the report, although no-one was to present a more devastatingly concise reply than Roger Calvert, Honorary Secretary of the National Council on Inland Transport.

The NCIT had been created by a consortium of pro-rail groups in 1962 to counter the growing threat to the railways. Under the Chairmanship of Lord Stonham, a Labour Peer, and with technical guidance from Professor Hondelink and Roger Calvert, it was to achieve a measure of success in fighting the Marples/Beeching proposals.

Mr Calvert was well qualified to oppose the Beeching philosophy, indeed rather more qualified than Dr Beeching was to impose it, having worked for many years for both the New Zealand railway system and British Railways. His technical knowledge of railway operations was to prove invaluable to the rail lobby.

The National Council on Inland Transport was convinced that the losses claimed by the Railways Board were exaggerated, and that the whole *Reshaping* plan was based on false assumptions and dubious figures. It was, however, very difficult to get any alternative arguments across. The only forum for limited public discussion on railway closures was provided by the TUCC inquiries, but since the passing of the 1962 Act, their role had become ineffective. The NCIT was determined to find a legal loophole through which to alter the consultation procedure, and it nearly succeeded.

In October 1963, during the inquiry into the proposed closure of the Southport to Preston line, it put forward a challenge to the local TUCC. If British Railways refused to provide a breakdown of the claimed earnings on the line (in this case put at £52,700), the TUCC would surely be unable to verify the accuracy of the figures. And if the TUCC failed to make every effort to verify the Board's financial statements, it might technically be breaking an obscure Act passed in 1958 to regulate the conduct of tribunals and inquiries.

In the event, the Chairman of the TUCC declined to ask the Railways Board for a breakdown of the figures, citing the wording of the 1962 Act: that the Committee was only concerned with questions of hardship. The NCIT then approached the Council on Tribunals, but the claim against the TUCC disappeared under a welter of legal minutiae, for it was ruled that the TUCCs were independent bodies and their inquiries were not held 'by or on behalf of a Minister' and, therefore they were not bound by the provisions of the 1958 Tribunals & Inquiries Act.

The NCIT decided it might be worth playing for higher legal stakes in order to clarify the position. In November 1963, Roger Calvert and T C Foley, the Council's then Secretary, discussed the inquiry procedure with the Secretary of the Central Transport Consultative Committee and procured a CTCC policy statement, which they passed to Samuel Silkin QC.

Counsel's opinion was that the carefully drafted 1962 Transport Act contained several small, but significant, loopholes. Technically, the TUCCs were not allowed to consider financial matters at all; their task was merely to make a judgement on the degree of 'hardship' that would result from a loss of rail services. Not surprisingly, hardship had proved difficult to define in legal terms and in practice the Committees simply balanced the limited evidence provided by the Railways Board against the weight of opposition.

But the question of hardship was not quite the be-all and end-all of the consultative procedure, for the TUCCs were entitled to view certain financial figures if they so wished. These were often requested by the Committees, because they were sometimes concerned that they might be approving a replacement bus service costing more to run than the railway.

It was a crucial point, because if the Committees were to see the figures, it was reasonable that the protesters should too. And if the Committees were to become embroiled in financial issues by comparing the cost of an existing service with the proposed replacement, it followed that they should also consider possible economies to the existing service. Dealing with these rather arcane arguments was a matter for individual TUCC chairmen or women, who ran inquiries more or less as they chose.

Naturally, even an outright victory at local committee level might be a hollow one, for it could be overruled by the Minister of Transport. All the same, it was felt that a test case might be worth fighting, and the whole affair dragged through the House of Lords if necessary, a procedure that could hold up Beeching's plans for months.

An opportunity arose in May 1964, when the Railways Board put forward proposals to withdraw the Stockport to Buxton service [14].

The Great Railway Conspiracy

It was, in many respects, an excellent choice on which to test the protesters' case. The line carried a considerable volume of commuter traffic beyond Stockport into Manchester, while Buxton – a big spa town, with a population of about 20,000 – attracted plenty of tourists in the opposite direction. High in the Pennines, it suffered badly from winter snowfalls, which often closed the local roads. In short, Buxton exhibited almost every characteristic that made branch lines worthwhile. Most of the two-day inquiry on 27th and 28th May was spent dealing with an overwhelming caseload of hardship claims, but late on the morning of the second day, Sam Silkin was granted leave to speak on behalf of the NCIT. He began by outlining the assumed role of the TUCCs under the 1962 Transport Act:

"The public is being asked to swallow, as it were, this particular Beeching pill, and your committee has been appointed to hear the objections, all the objections; and yet, Sir, as I understand it, you have been told by some other authority, I do not know what, that all you can do is to assume that the pill is going to be swallowed, and advise the powers that be what pain and sickness the patient is likely to suffer as a result, and how you suggest going about relieving that pain and sickness. But when it comes to analysing the pill, or even examining the patient to see if he really needs any medicine at all, you are told this not your job."

Following this inescapably logical introduction, he moved on to the more difficult task of persuading the Chairman to accept a different interpretation of the 1962 Act and take account of the arguments put forward by the expert witnesses from the NCIT. Expecting trouble, the Chairman was determined to scotch such moves right from the start:

"May I interrupt? It is not our intention to report on the economics of the railway proposal, and if there are any questions about that, they are for the Minister and we shall not report on them. Any time devoted to that will be time wasted."

Nevertheless, the Committee allowed the barrister to wade on, first exploring the meaning of the word 'hardship', and then into uncharted territory, with the *piece de resistance* of the

Photographs and sketches of railway closure inquiries are rare. SKETCH: *Margaret Calvert/Diana Powell*

protesters' case – an examination of the accuracy of the Board's financial claims, which had been examined by Roger Calvert.

British Railways had put forward the usual figures: movement costs of £142,600, terminal costs of £70,600, and maintenance of £51,000... a total of £264,000 a year. When projected expenditure in the controversial 'next five years' category was included, the total annual expenses of the line came out at £318,000, against income of £140,000. A loss of £180,000 a year looked pretty clear-cut, but Roger Calvert countered by applying Beeching's own theoretical figures, and thus dismantling the Board's assumptions.

The terminal costs of £70,600 were for ten small stations – *Reshaping* had suggested that an annual cost of £2,500 was reasonable for small stations, giving in this case a total of £25,000. An analysis of the timetable revealed that a movement cost of around 6s 6d (32^1/2p) per mile was being claimed for the usual DMUs, where Beeching had suggested 4s to 6s (20p-30p) in *Reshaping*. And on the basis of information supplied by the Board, the line was carrying 24,000 passengers a week, which equated to 24 million passenger-miles a year. At the 2d per mile rate suggested by Beeching as a reasonable average, the income of the line should have been around £200,000.

Thus, by using Beeching's own figures (which had been formulated to show the inadequacy of branch lines), Calvert had reduced the loss from £180,000 to £42,000, and he was able to go a good deal further. Half the stations could be de-staffed, at an annual saving of £11,500, and rationalisation of the timetable would save a further £12,000 on signalling, and £15,000 on movement costs. The result, excluding income from parcels and goods traffic, would be an annual profit of nearly £6,000, assuming all his assumptions to be accurate. Calvert went on to

At 1,000 feet above sea level in the heart of the Pennines, Buxton's rail link was, and remains, essential, something the TUCC agreed on. In February 1970, six years after the closure inquiry, a dmu from Manchester runs into Buxton station. PHOTO: Pete Hackney

point out the unreasonable nature of the 'next five years' expenditure assumptions, and suggested that the line could be partially reduced to single-track to affect further economies.

Summing up, Mr Silkin rounded triumphantly on the secrecy of the Railways Board:

Silkin: "I think that one would say, Mr Calvert, that despite your own considerable experience, you have been handicapped in making these computations and suggestions by having only the skeleton figures which the railway have supplied?"

Calvert: "That is so. It would be necessary to have many more figures in order to produce a detailed analysis."

Silkin: "Have you done the best you can with these figures, and on that basis are you confident that the line, as modified, could easily run at a profit, taking everything into account?"

Calvert: "I am quite confident that the line could be run at a profit."

There followed a break for lunch, during which the TUCC members ruminated on their invidious position. If they ignored the protesters' evidence there was every possibility the NCIT would take the matter to a higher authority. If they agreed, and informed the Minister that the branch line should remain open along the lines suggested by Roger Calvert, they would be accusing the Railways Board of either incompetence, false accounting, or both. Either way, they had allowed financial matters to be discussed, which was clearly outside their remit under the Transport Act.

When the inquiry reconvened, the Chairman thanked Mr Silkin for his submission, but refused to allow cross-examination of railway staff, who presumably needed time to prepare a response. Mr Silkin, with no other evidence to offer, then entered into a detailed exchange with the Chairman as to whether the Committee was willing to accept, and act upon, Roger Calvert's evidence. The NCIT needed to know, for if the Committee intended to ignore the evidence, the matter would indeed by placed before the High Court.

He was never to receive an answer, nor (as it transpired) was he to need one. The Committee sent an interim report to the Minister, who promptly reprieved the line. The Buxton inquiry resulted in an outright (if local) victory, but in wider terms it proved a total failure. By simply backing down in the face of detailed evidence, and withdrawing the closure proposal, the Government had escaped a High Court action that might have exposed the entire closure procedure for the sham it undoubtedly was. With hindsight, Buxton had presented the NCIT with a case that was just *too* good, and in Roger Calvert's view they had, "let Marples off the hook." During later inquiries, committee chairmen (presumably acting under new directives) simply refused to consider outside evidence.

Today, the Buxton branch carries around 1.7 million passengers a year, with more than 300,000 from Buxton alone. Flexibility is the name of the game today, and the two smallest stations are unstaffed, two are staffed only in the morning peak, and the rest more or less fully staffed. The line plays a key role in the public transport infrastructure of Greater Manchester, and its loss, prevented only by a handful of protesters, would have been a catastrophe.

Lord Stonham of the NCIT and Sam Silkin both turned from poacher to gamekeeper in the railway closure process, becoming leading figures in the next Labour Government, and thereafter strangely quiet on the issue of rail closures.

Roger Calvert's figures had been of real importance, proving that the Railways Board's figures had not only failed to take account of possible economies, but failed to add up against the 'typical' values provided in *Reshaping*. It was, of course, possible to apply the same techniques to any line, provided you had some basic railway figures to work with.

Beeching had suggested that a diesel multiple unit could operate for around 5/- (25p) per mile. If the Railways Board was claiming that a line should close because costs were higher than this, it followed that they were either presenting inflated figures or failing to make reasonable economies. The same was true of the 'terminal expenses' – the cost of operating stations. Beeching had suggested £2,500 for each small country station, yet the Railways Board usually claimed considerably more. Very probably the stations *were* costing more, for the issue wasn't so much that all the railway figures were false, rather that the hapless managers had long since been instructed to prepare the line for closure, and facilitate this by keeping costs up and income down.

The issue as to whether lines destined for closure had been deliberately run down was a contentious one, but there are numerous first-hand accounts from independent railway experts such as Roger Calvert, Professor Hondelink and Owen Prosser to suggest that such practises were exposed again and again. Railwaymen of all grades would occasionally speak out, such as Adrian Vaughan, whose poignant book *Signalman's Twilight* described first-hand the terrible waste associated with the dismemberment of the railways. A few senior managers spoke out too, such as Gerald Fiennes, who was eventually sacked.

Without a doubt, where management had several years advance warning, maintenance schedules were 'rearranged' to fit in some hefty renewals in the years following the proposed closure. This wasn't necessarily a malicious policy, because there was little sense in squandering scarce resources on lines earmarked for closure. The deliberate rescheduling of traffic onto other routes, on the other hand, was intended solely to destroy the viability of a line. After all, if a line was scheduled for closure, the most sensible option would be to make good use of the assets in their last few years, such as transferring heavy and damaging freight traffic onto the track in its last days.

In fact, the lines destined for closure were deliberately and systematically starved of traffic in their final years, and the policy could be seen most clearly on the threatened trunk routes. Even before publication of *Reshaping*, traffic had been steered away from the Great Central, the Somerset & Dorset, and the Waverley route, leaving passengers with no doubt as to the fate that awaited them.

By the end of 1962, all three of these trunk routes were operating without proper maintenance, while through express trains and freight services had been re-routed, leaving ill-timed slow and semi-fast services. Modern technology, such as diesel units or automated crossings, were almost entirely absent. It was easier to kill a railway by starvation than to strangle a healthy concern, and the Railways Board had been preparing the ground for some time. All three were consequently listed for closure in *Reshaping*, but all were to prove remarkably resilient, and their death was to be an agonising and long drawn out affair.

An intriguing piece of evidence for this policy of deliberate neglect came with the testimony of Dennis Taylor, a young clerk working for the independent ABC Rail Guide company. Working year in, year out with the same timetables, Dennis had begun to observe mysterious changes in the pattern of services as early as 1959, but only on particular lines. To an experienced timetable clerk, the missed connections and ill-timed services made no sense, and looked bound to lose customers and add to costs.

Not content with merely observing the changes, he painstakingly 'redesigned' services on some 1,500 route miles along more cost-effective lines, and innocently sent his work to the Ministry of Transport, expecting at the very least a pat on the back. Instead, he was baldly informed that, "the Minister is satisfied with the advice he is being given." "I knew then," he said, "that what was being done to the railways was entirely deliberate."

The Great Railway Conspiracy

Gerald Fiennes, manager of the Western Region, was later to claim that railways were never deliberately run down to pre-empt closure or, in his own words: "A railway manager likes managing railways. The more railways he manages, the higher his salary and the more impressive his status!" Perhaps Mr Fiennes really was innocent, but others certainly did inflict deliberate damage, sometimes by a subtle rescheduling of the timetable, and occasionally in a most blatant manner. Individual managers could of course claim to be merely 'following orders' in best middle-management tradition. What was the point of making waves, and missing out on promotion, or perhaps facing redundancy themselves, for the sake of services that had in many instances been under sentence of death since the mid-1950s? With closure long considered a formality, operating economies would merely have prolonged the agony.

After Buxton, Roger Calvert went on to apply his Beeching inspired basic railway formula to other lines on the closure list, with astonishing results:

Liskeard-Looe	Movement & station costs	Income	Profit/loss (direct costs only)
Railway Board	£12,900	£7,100	-£5,800
Roger Calvert	£6,350	£7,100	**+£950**
Isle of Wight			
Railway Board	£289,000	£147,000	-£142,000
Roger Calvert	£101,500	£250,000	**+£148,500**
Oswestry-Gobowen			
Railway Board	£17,966	£4,800	-£13,166
Roger Calvert	£3,900	£5,100	**+£1,200**
St Erth-St Ives			
Railway Board	£17,934	£9,100	-£8,834
Roger Calvert	£12,320	£12,100	-£220
Hull-Scarborough			
Railway Board	£397,000	£366,400	-£30,600
Roger Calvert	£135,250	£366,400	**+£231,150**

These figures took no account of track and signalling costs (which might or might not have been subsidised by freight or other traffic), neither do they include expenditure under the 'next five years' category under which British Railways often claimed some eye-watering sums to justify closure. On the other hand, nor did they take account of possible operating economies, for which, in many cases, there was considerable scope.

Calvert investigated 95 lines in all [14]. He first made an assumption that British Railway's income figure was correct, but that expenditure could be cut to Beeching's own 'typical' figure. This suggested that 36 lines would be able to cover movement and terminal expenses and ten of these (where the track would be kept in place for other passenger services) were effectively covering their full costs already. A further six would have been profitable provided annual track costs could be kept below £1,000 a mile, a figure which many authorities (including Gerald Fiennes) considered reasonable for a lightly-loaded branch line.

Calvert went on to reassess income on the branch lines at the rate of 2d per passenger-mile. At this fare level, no fewer than 53% of the lines destined for closure appeared capable of covering all relevant expenses.

The balance was to tilt even further in favour of retaining the lines when he considered the benefits of contributory revenue to the rest of the system. As we have seen, British Railways knew the exact level of contributory revenue, although this information wasn't supplied to the TUCC inquiries.

What could not be judged with any certainty was how much of this revenue would be lost after closure, because there were all manner of variables. Former branch line passengers might buy a car and stop using public transport, make the whole journey by bus, or simply stop travelling altogether. Beeching made a rather optimistic assumption that the majority of travellers would take a bus to the nearest railhead. It was to be another 20 years before this rose-tinted view was finally and unequivocally disproved.

Back in the early 1960s, Calvert took advantage of all the available data and reached a final conclusion that closure of exactly two-thirds of his sample of 95 threatened branch lines would leave the railways worse off financially. Not only would their closure cause massive disruption to the travelling public, it would also increase the railway deficit.

There were no new closures between September 1962 and June 1963, in part because implementation of the 1962 Transport Act had taken some time, and the Government probably wished to allow a decent interval for the furore over *Reshaping* to die down before getting on with the job. Unfortunately, there was a general election approaching, and with most marginal constituencies affected in some way, the Government was hoping for a cessation of hostilities in the closure programme. For various reasons, this didn't happen, with the rate of closures actually accelerating in the run-up to the election, and it soon became apparent that the Railways Board had no intention of keeping heat off the politicians.

Paradoxically, while the closure process almost ground to a halt, the working deficit of the railways showed an encouraging improvement, falling sharply from the peak in 1962, thanks mainly to falling costs. Unreliable new diesel locomotives were settling down, the long-established DMUs were earning a healthy return, staffing levels were being reduced and redundant facilities eliminated. What was not clear at the time was that as the line and station closures began to bite, income would fall at a similar rate, putting profitability as far out of reach as ever. [15]

Meanwhile, the Labour Party was busy brushing its radical wing under the carpet and reassuring the electorate that a Labour victory at the forthcoming election would not mean a return to the heady days of the 1945 socialist experiment. During a triumphant

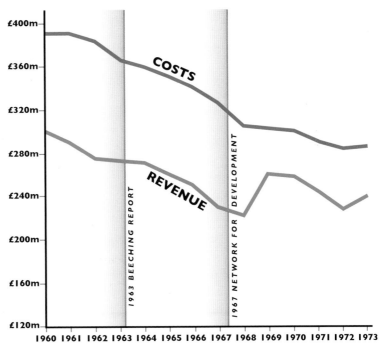

The railway closures of the 1960s did help to drive down costs, but as Roger Calvert pointed out, they were to drive down income just as fast, putting profits firmly out of reach
Source: British Railways, 1948-1973: A Business History

Ignoring the new Hymek diesel, this December 1964 photograph of Dorchester Junction could have been taken 50 years before - the semaphore signals, loose-coupled wagons and guard's van belonged to another era. Some early diesels were notoriously unreliable, and although Beyer-Peacock's Hymek proved to be quite good, it was non-standard, and within eleven years, all 101 examples had been withdrawn. PHOTO: Patrick Henshaw

party conference in October 1963, Harold Wilson put his finger on the national pulse and promised to forge a new Britain:

"We are redefining our socialism in terms of the new scientific revolution...The Britain that is going to be forged in the white heat of this scientific revolution will be no place for restrictive practises or outdated methods on either side of industry."

He had words of encouragement for those who objected to the closure of their local railway too. Should Labour form the next administration, Wilson would call a halt to all 'major' rail closures pending a wide-ranging and thorough review of the nation's transport requirements. Presumably railways would be reprieved in the places where the technological heat was due to burn with a particular intensity, or perhaps vice versa? There were no specific commitments, but it wasn't the tired old Tory propaganda, and it didn't appear to involve the 'axe man' of the popular press, Dr Richard Beeching. The soothing words on rail closures appealed strongly to the electorate and went a long way towards swinging the national mood away from the Conservatives.

    The Railways Board did nothing to help, or perhaps there was an element of revenge involved, but just prior to the election it launched full tilt into the closure programme, bringing the largest and perhaps most controversial proposal into public view at a critical time. So wide ranging were the proposals affecting the former Great Central trunk line between Sheffield and London, that no fewer than five TUCCs became involved, and the standard consultative procedures proved quite inadequate for such a major inquiry. The line was so long, and the arguments for retention and closure so technical, that the very idea of TUCCs trying to quantify evidence of local hardship was completely farcical.

The Great Central ran down the spine of the country, from Sheffield, via Nottingham, Leicester, Rugby and Aylesbury to its own small London terminus at Marylebone. It had been subjected to a war of attrition for some years, even before Beeching arrived on the scene, for the line had been upgraded in the 1950s, but a later change of heart resulted in plans for partial or complete closure.

This unhappy line held the dubious distinction of being the least useful duplicate trunk route of all, passing through a mixed bag of Midlands towns and cities that were all served by at least one other main line to London. And further south, between Rugby and Aylesbury, it ran for almost 60 miles through open country that looked unable to generate any sort of local traffic.

Closure would appear to make perfect sense, were it not for a couple of unique strategic assets in the line's favour. The Great Central's London Extension was the last trunk line to be built, completed as late as 1899, and also one of the finest. It had been built to new Board of Trade dimensional standards that approximated the larger European loading gauge, and involving larger tunnels, bridges and earthworks. But the extra expense was actually a shrewd gamble by Sir Edward Watkin, founding father of the Great Central, who had a substantial shareholding in the Channel tunnel then under construction. If the scheme had come off, the Great Central would probably have become the most important (and profitable) line in the country, carrying through trains to and from the Continent. But British xenophobia, and the vagaries of European politics, put paid to the Channel tunnel for almost a century. When the tunnel project was revived in the late 1960s, this ready-made high speed, Continental gauge link from London to Nottingham had only just closed, though of course the 'Chunnel' would not open for another 25 years.

The other unique quality of the Great Central was its ability to carry through passenger

Victorian engineers were skillful tunnellers, and they had a good understanding of the geology of the English Channel, but a tunnel to France really was pushing the boundaries. After a trial heading was bored in Abbot's Cliff, Folkestone in 1880-81, politics brought the project to a premature end, leaving the Great Central's London extension somewhat under-utilised.
PHOTO: Kenneth Adams

and freight services from the northeast to the south and southwest via a short but crucial connecting link between Woodford Halse on the Great Central and Banbury on the former Great Western. This strategic link was of real importance, avoiding a circuitous and congested detour via Birmingham to the west, or London to the south.

Much political capital had been made of the Great Central's failure to make a profit during its relatively short and chequered career, and as a trunk line between London and Sheffield, it was certainly surplus to requirements by the 1960s. But if services had been modernised and rescheduled to make sense of the Great Central's superb alignment (it was potentially faster than the rival Midland route) it might have had a bright future. Then there was the prospect of faster express trains to the south coast, and the tantalising, if remote possibility of high speed services to France and beyond. The Railways Board did not agree.

Since January 1960, through express trains from London had been rerouted elsewhere, leaving a languid 'semi-fast' service terminating at Nottingham. Then the northeast to southwest traffic was cut to a single daytime express between York and Bournemouth. For the next six years, traffic was gradually removed, with the aim of precipitating outright closure.

In 1961, the Railways Board advertised the withdrawal of all local passenger services between Aylesbury and Sheffield. It took three separate TUCC inquiries at Nottingham, Leicester and Aylesbury to hear all the objections, and for once the local TUCCs – aware of the Railways Board's intention to close the line outright – were extremely reluctant. In the end, most of the closures were approved, but the TUCCs left the strange parting shot that they, "would have preferred," to recommend a new local DMU service between Aylesbury and Nottingham. Reluctantly, they agreed, "that this would not be immediately possible under present circumstances."

This 1911 Railway Clearing House map shows the significance of the Woodford to Banbury link, which provided a through route for express trains and freight from the Great Western lines in the south and west to the East Midlands and beyond. By closing the Great Central in segments, the Railways Board was able to keep the TUCCs unaware of the wider strategic implications.

With local passenger services and express trains withdrawn, the Great Central had few trains left, other than this semi-fast weekday service from Nottingham Victoria to London Marylebone. This 1966 view near Culworth in Northamptonshire gives an indication of the superb engineering on the London Extension. The embankment of the Banbury link can just be seen running in on the far left in the background. Very soon, all these lines would be gone. PHOTO: Peter Green - Copyright RCTS

Most of the closures were rapidly implemented, leaving the trunk route with little through traffic and a few token and isolated local services. In the spring of 1963, the Railways Board tightened the ratchet a little further by withdrawing all Sunday trains between Nottingham and London. There weren't many trains left. The semi-fast services had been skilfully scheduled to avoid connecting with local trains still traversing the short link between Banbury and Woodford Halse, and without connections, the link carried very little local traffic. In December, the Board applied for closure, and the area TUCC, concerned only with the convenience of a few country folk in this quiet corner of Northamptonshire, reluctantly acquiesced to the loss of these local services, without any understanding, or opportunity to debate the wider strategic implications of closing this crucial link.

By focusing attention on the peripheral local services, the Railways Board was able to dismantle the *raison d'etre* of the central section of the Great Central, making eventual closure inevitable. Then despite (or more likely because of) the admission that the Board intended to close the Great Central outright, nothing else happened. The derisory service remained, the line lost money, and the closure debate moved temporarily elsewhere.

In January 1964, Lord Stonham of the NCIT wrote to the Prime Minister, Sir Alec Douglas Home, outlining the state of the nation's railways. Home had succeeded to the premiership in October 1963, being chosen as the least divisive of the available candidates. Sir Alec was far from being every Conservative's choice as Prime Minister – not even his own, in fact. Most of the wise money had gone on 'Rab' Butler, an able politician who might have better handled Harold Wilson. Wilson had promised a scientific revolution, but Home appears to have been confused by the whole process of modern government, having once reputedly remarked: "There are two problems in my life. The political ones are insoluble and the economic ones are incomprehensible..."

Sir Alex was, however, a kindly soul, and during his short stay in office, he found the time to reply to Lord Stonham, expressing incredulity that anything underhand might have occurred:

"It is difficult to resist the impression that you are seeking to imply that the Board are proposing closures of services and stations which can be made to pay."

This most certainly was the case, and as the election approached, the closure process began to accelerate. In March 1964, Marples announced the first major round of closures, approving no fewer than 21 candidates, including most of the railways in Lincolnshire: Peterborough-Boston-Grimsby, and the branches to Skegness and Mablethorpe. Interestingly, the far less remunerative (but shorter) line to Cleethorpes had not found its way onto the *Reshaping* maps and was to be reprieved. For all the talk of scientific methodology, it was often a very random process.

Coming just before the summer season, the Skegness proposal generated even more public concern than the Great Central had done. The various lines through the Lincolnshire Wolds serviced a fixed population of more than 180,000, passing through no fewer than 14 local authority areas and five parliamentary constituencies, all Conservative, and generally safe seats. This was sleepy rural countryside, but the seaside resorts of Skegness and Mablethorpe received almost 500,000 visitors each year by rail, mostly in the top six weeks of the summer season. According to the local MP Herbert Butcher, dealing with those numbers by road would necessitate 27,000 bus journeys. This wasn't a practical proposition at the time, as the police were already turning visitors away from Skegness on summer Saturdays because the roads simply couldn't cope.

The Lincolnshire closures may have been brought forward because of the lack of marginal constituencies, but even so the proposals caused public uproar, and even the East Midlands TUCC voiced objections.

Fotherby Halt near Louth during the diesel multiple unit trials of the late 1950s. The station mistress is Mrs Hobden, who must have been delighted that the BTC had chosen to invest in rural Lincolnshire. It was not to last. The station was closed in 1961, as a precursor to closure of the whole trunk line, which finally came in 1970 - one of the last big closures. PHOTO: Anna Finch

Marples hurriedly instructed the Board to come up with some revised closure proposals, but the result was almost identical: Peterborough to Boston would close, as would Firsby to Grimsby, Willoughby to Mablethorpe and Lincoln to Firsby via Midville. In other words, a reprieve for Skegness, but everything else would go.

In the event, the railways of Lincolnshire proved remarkably hard to dislodge, and the network didn't close until 1970, surviving almost into the modern era. According to author Robin Jones, closure of the Firsby-Louth-Grimsby line was a major error, brought about by Beeching's fixation with axing 'duplicate' routes. It is very much missed today [16].

While major closures made the headlines, the branches involved in the railbus experiments of the 1950s were quietly fading away. In April 1964, after a protracted battle, the lines to Tetbury and Cirencester in Wiltshire were finally closed.

One of the new halts constructed to serve the railbuses in 1959 had been sited within spitting distance of a remote pub and very little else. Fittingly, it was from the aptly-named Trouble House Halt that the now obligatory coffin loaded with empty whisky bottles was put aboard the last Tetbury train and sent up to Dr Beeching in London. The railbus experiments were being wound up, not because they lost a lot of money, but because the Railways Board was now investigating the secondary lines and trunk routes they fed into.

At least the Tetbury and Cirencester branches had seen an attempt to cut costs — many services had never even seen a DMU, let alone a railbus. At the TUCC inquiry into the Taunton to Barnstaple closure, the Railways Board stated that dieselisation had, "been examined," and would not make the service remunerative, "even under the cheapest working methods." It was a common response to questions from knowledgable passengers expounding the benefits of diesel railcars, and an identical reply was given during the nearby Taunton to Yeovil inquiry.

Taunton-Yeovil was a classic example of the sort of rural branch the Railways Board was falling over itself to axe, a 25-mile line linking two country towns and a scattering of villages, with trunk routes at either end. One might have assumed that it was short of passenger traffic, but most trains carried 30 to 40 passengers, rising to 60 or more at peak times. On Saturdays, 100-150 passengers per train were typical throughout the morning, carrying them all home again in the afternoon. Hardly intercity standards, but this was one of the sleepier branches on the closure programme, one that had never seen the benefits of modern traction.

Some routes couldn't even approach these traffic figures. The short branch from Tiverton Junction (on the main line between Taunton and Exeter) and Tiverton, just four miles away, was allegedly carrying only 100 passengers a day. Annual income was put at £3,500, against movement costs claimed to be no less than £21,600, or around 10 shillings (50p) per mile. Yet in *Reshaping*, Beeching had suggested that a three-car DMU could operate for half that amount, and the figures from Comrie suggested that a railbus could have served Tiverton Junction for 2s 4d (11 1/2p), reducing annual movement costs to £4,968. It was easy for campaigners to use the *Reshaping* data, and just as easy for the TUCCs to ignore it, which they generally did.

Whereas the lines involved in the railbus experiments were minor, those involved in the early DMU trials were mostly bigger in scale. The Silloth branch in Cumberland was an exception, serving just 3,000 residents. It had been one of the first to experience a DMU in 1955, during the Cumberland trials, which caused great excitement in the local press, and a sadly misplaced confidence from the 3,000 residents of Silloth, who had flocked to the new service. Now the whole experiment was swept away, and the line abandoned — the result was a riot.

On the evening of 6th September 1964, the last train prepared to leave Silloth for the distant lights of Carlisle. By popular request, the modern railcar had been put aside in favour of steam traction, and as dusk gathered, the engine stood ready for departure bedecked with a wreath on the smokebox door.

The anger and frustration generated by the closure process in these far-flung corners of the network was intense. Distant authorities had seen fit to modernise their branch line, but nine years later the railway was being eradicated altogether. To the ordinary residents of a small town on the Solway Firth, the whole affair must have made little sense.

With the General Election only a month away, the authorities were expecting trouble, and they weren't disappointed. An ominous crowd of 9,000 or more had gathered to witness the last train, watched over by eight police officers and an Alsatian dog. But this wasn't the usual passive send-off. Detonators were placed on the line, missiles hurled at the police, and finally, members of the local Labour Party sat in front of the locomotive, refusing to move. The objectors fought to place a placard on the engine: 'If you don't catch this, there'll be another one if you vote Labour at the next election...' In the battle for the smokebox door, a locomotive inspector finally triumphed, and the placard was unceremoniously removed and the protesters driven off with hot steam.

It was not until 8.30pm that the 7.58 from Silloth finally slipped into the night. As the tail-light of the last train dimmed and disappeared from view, the citizens of Silloth returned quietly to their homes through the cobbled streets of a smaller and sadder town.

Like many rural areas, Silloth was part of a safe Tory constituency, but the loss of the branch line may well have tipped the result Labour's way in the railway town of Carlisle at the other end of the branch, where former railwayman Ronald Lewis campaigned hard against the threat of rail closures. He took the seat from the Tories, and held it until his retirement in 1987. In fact the Beeching effect may well have played a decisive role in the 1964 General Election, squeezing the Tories out in several marginal constituencies, such as Hull North, where the Hornsea and Withernsea branch lines were due to close the following week, and Labour slipped in with a 1,181 vote majority [17].

The Labour Party was set to form the next administration, but there would be no more trains to Silloth, Hornsea or Withernsea. The new Government did not bring the promised reversal of closure policy. In the modern history of political sell-outs, the duplicitous behaviour of Harold Wilson over rail closures must count as one of the most shameful ever documented.

The Carlisle to Silloth branch had seen passenger figures rise by 66% after the introduction of the new diesel services in the late 1950s, something that must have made the line's closure in September 1964 hard to understand. PHOTO: Neville Stead

7
The Axe Falls
1964-1969

"It was a mild wet night with a strong wind making the three gas lights that were alight on each platform flicker. No staff were on duty at the station, and except for the gas light in the passengers' section of the booking office, the station rooms were in darkness.

And the last passenger stood on the deserted platform and thought of all the many journeys that had started and ended there... and of the friends he had travelled with. And realising that a point had been reached where it was more pleasant to look back than forward, he left the still lighted station, and as he walked down the drive, the flickering lamps over the station entrance grew fainter...

Although the last train had gone, the last passenger left, the station lights were still on, flickering in the wind and the rain."

Stanley Keyse of the Railway Development Association, on the closure of Sutton Park station, Birmingham in 1965

The Great Railway Conspiracy

In the General Election of 16th October 1964, Harold Wilson led the Labour Party to a less than decisive victory, winning an overall majority of just four seats. During the campaign, the Labour leader had pledged to halt all major rail closures pending a national transport survey, but with the election safely (if marginally) in the bag, the pledge was soon forgotten and the closure process (overseen by the new Minister of Transport) continued to accelerate.

It was not until the arrival of Barbara Castle in 1966 that an attempt was made to do some cost/benefit analysis of minor railways. Her initial attempts to stabilise the system - the Network Development Plan - met with derision from the road lobby and protest from the pro-rail groups, who felt the financial bar had been set much too high. Mrs Castle went on to mastermind the 1968 Transport Act, that promised grant aid for unremunerative but socially necessary services and increased taxation and restrictions on heavy lorries.

But the 1968 Act proved a serious disappointment. The Government lost its nerve in the face of concerted opposition from the road lobby and eased the lorry taxation proposals. And the unremunerative railway grants system actually precipitated a fresh round of closures, because there was a cap on the total grant aid, and the level of grant for individual lines proved too generous, leading the Government to refuse aid in many cases. By 1970, the implementation of Dr Beeching's Reshaping report was more or less complete, but with railway income falling, overall financial viability remained as far out of reach as ever.

After 14 years of Tory rule, the arrival of a Labour Government was hailed as a generally positive and populist victory. The outcome of the election had been greatly influenced by transport policy, and Labour had gained many votes – perhaps enough to tip the balance – by claiming that major railway closures would be halted, pending some sort of review. It was classic political stuff, carefully worded to mean very little. What was a *major* railway closure? Would there be any retrospective reopenings? Would any lines under stay of execution actually be spared?

Harold Wilson had, for example, given a personal pledge that the Whitby-Scarborough line, one of the most scenic lines in the north of England (if not the most remunerative) would stay open. "I confirm," he said, "that an obviously major decision such as the proposed Whitby closure would be covered by that statement in the Labour manifesto." The citizens of Whitby saw no reason to doubt his word. After all, Wilson had condemned the entire closure procedure in forthright terms during a debate on *Reshaping* the year before:

"Over the last ten years, 3,600 miles of track have been closed. That is 19% of the mileage previously in operation.

Presumably this 19%, roughly one-fifth of our track mileage, must have been the least remunerative of the lot. Presumably that is why it was first selected for closure. Yet its closure saved only 7% of the working deficit of British Railways in 1960, and this takes no account of the additional cost to the nation of the closures, or the loss of main line traffic caused by the closures of feeder services...

If the closing of one-fifth of the track mileage makes so little difference to the operating deficit of British Railways, what will the next one-third do?"
Debate on the Railways, House of Commons 30th April 1963

These were clearly the words of a well-briefed and sympathetic politician, who understood the issues and couldn't wait to reverse this vacuous and counter-productive policy. At the time of the election, the fate of 38 railway lines stood in abeyance, the outgoing Minister of Transport having consented to closure, but the services remaining in operation. Two were large-scale proposals by any standards, and one – the 100-mile line from Dumfries to the ferry port of

Harold Wilson's pledge to reprieve the Whitby to Scarborough line proved worthless after the election. This picture shows a Middlesbrough to Scarborough train at Staithes on the spectacular Yorkshire coast in 1955. This stretch closed in 1958, leaving the remaining Whitby to Scarborough line easier to pick off. It finally closed in 1965. PHOTO: Neville Stead

Stranraer — had provoked considerable opposition from a strategic point of view. It provided a direct link from England to the ferries for Northern Ireland, and closing it would leave a more tenuous rail link north to Glasgow. Not exactly a gift to the Irish Republicans, but sending a less than helpful message nonetheless.

But immediately after the election, Wilson back-tracked, arguing that under the 1962 Transport Act, it was impossible for a Minister to overturn a previous decision and that the closure procedure would have to run its course for the 38 lines under threat. The new Prime Minister did, however, make vague promises to keep track in place pending that all-important transport review, and the voices of dissent were largely silenced.

A positive sign that the new administration had some faith in the railway network came in January 1965, when Anthony Wedgewood Benn, the Postmaster General, formalised an agreement with Dr Beeching under which the railways would contract to carry the bulk of Royal Mail parcels traffic for the next ten years.

A few weeks later, faced with a 9% pay claim, British Rail announced that large pay increases would threaten the success already achieved through the *Reshaping* plans. The report did, of course cover a lot of ground, particularly with regard to freight, some of it very worthwhile, and there really was a brief financial improvement, but it had little or nothing to do with branch line closures. On the Board's own figures, the closure of 148 lines had yielded a saving of only £6 million, against an overall deficit (including interest and charges) of around £125 million in 1964. There were hidden costs behind the closure policy too, including a subsidy to the operators of replacement buses of about £100,000 a year. By

The Great Railway Conspiracy

1966 that would swell to £500,000.

Dr Beeching had promised a second report on the railways, and on 16th February 1965, it arrived. In keeping with an agreement to inform the unions in advance on questions of policy, the Board gave them a whole 24 hours notice, providing a union briefing on the 15th!

The report, *The Development of the Major Railway Trunk Routes*, argued that, of the 7,500 miles of lines advocated for retention in the first report, only 3,000 miles should be actively developed. It was the result of an internal study to gauge the size of network that would suit conditions 20 years hence, assuming that the commercial constraints of the 1962 Transport Act remained in force.

Compared to the light, confident style of *Reshaping*, the *Trunk Route* report was decidedly defensive in tone:

"It is regrettable, though perhaps not surprising, that public attention has concentrated upon the proposed abandonment of the unsound parts of our railway system. Of much greater importance, however, were constructive proposals for the development of a new railway out of the old one which were made in the Reshaping Report... The publication of this report is not a prelude to precipitate action on a broad front."

That establishment stalwart *The Times* generally backed this second report, noting that Beeching had carefully avoided the word 'closure', which appeared only three times, against 43 instances in the first report! He advocated instead that more favoured routes should be 'selected for retention', which was a neat way of saying exactly the same thing. The *Times* leader summed up the report in hawkish mood:

"Dr Beeching has provided, invaluably, a solid foundation on which to build a transport policy... there is no reason at all why, at a current cost of around £70 million a year, and a great deal of unproductive activity by a great many people, the railways should be excused the prudent house-keeping demanded in other branches of national life."

The report made some interesting assumptions about future demand for transport, overestimating population growth up to 1984 (15% against 5% in reality), and economic growth (a rather optimistic 4% a year), concluding that there would be considerable growth in demand for transport overall, and rail freight traffic might double in volume, but passenger traffic would gradually fall in a fast growing market:

"Although it is difficult to assess the total volume of inter-city passenger traffic [presumably bus, rail and air] likely to develop by 1984 with any great precision, it seems reasonable to assume that it will be at least twice as great as it is at present. At the same time, however, it has to be recognised that the railways' share of the total is likely to decline substantially... the total volume of demand for inter-city travel on rail will fall slightly from its present level of 5,000 million passenger-miles by 1984, but this total seems likely to be concentrated even more heavily into a few main flows."

The report envisaged a 3,000-mile core railway network carrying extraordinarily heavy freight traffic, interspersed with occasional passenger trains between the major centres – it was, by and large, a vision of 1960s America writ very small. It was a concise and methodical document, but riddled with basic errors about track capacity and traffic speed, though realistic about the growth of block freight services. Unfortunately, it was also hopelessly pessimistic about passenger traffic, assuming that the railways would abandon everything but a shrinking slice of the intercity passenger market to airlines, buses and private cars. Passenger traffic, it declared, would fall to 4,500 million passenger-miles a year by 1984, and continue to dwindle thereafter.

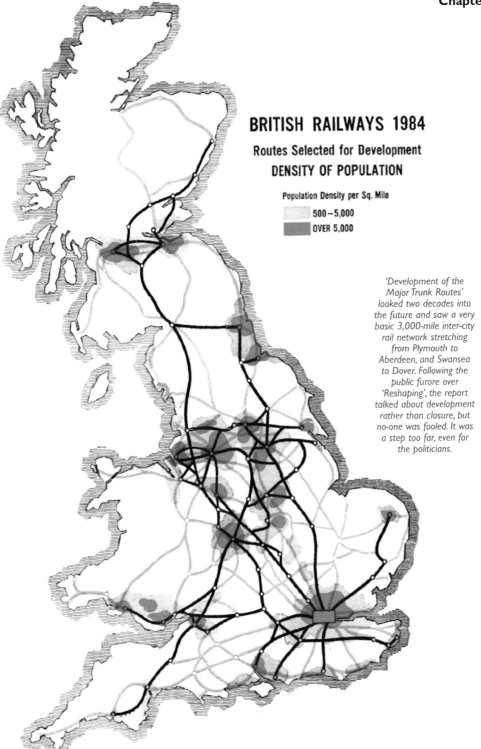

BRITISH RAILWAYS 1984
Routes Selected for Development
DENSITY OF POPULATION

Population Density per Sq. Mile

500–5,000

OVER 5,000

'Development of the
Major Trunk Routes'
looked two decades into
the future and saw a very
basic 3,000-mile inter-city
rail network stretching
from Plymouth to
Aberdeen, and Swansea
to Dover. Following the
public furore over
'Reshaping', the report
talked about development
rather than closure, but
no-one was fooled. It was
a step too far, even for
the politicians.

The Great Railway Conspiracy

What would Beeching have made of today's passenger traffic in excess of 35 billion passenger-miles a year?

Few commentators took *The Development of the Major Trunk Routes* seriously, although it did at least indicate that Dr Beeching had stared into the abyss, and found that further contraction might well lead to the end of the passenger railway altogether. It was the first official admission that line and station closures could guarantee a smaller network, but not a profitable one.

A fortnight later, the TUC had prepared a response. The report was not, it said, "sufficiently well argued to make constructive comment possible." Like everyone else, the TUC had concluded that the 'non-selected' routes were destined for closure, as there would be no real saving in concentrating traffic on the 'selected routes' if they were not. In any event, said the TUC, the report was fundamentally flawed, because the future prospects of British Rail could not possibly be determined without a detailed analysis of transport needs and policy as a whole.

Where *Reshaping* had been acclaimed (in some quarters at least) as a lucid and concise analysis of the railway's position, the *Trunk Route* report, produced while the painful closure procedure was still headline news, failed to catch the public mood – the Beeching philosophy had run out of steam.

Just to reinforce the idea that further rail cuts might not be a panacea, provincial bus drivers flexed their negotiating muscles in the wake of Beeching's first round of closures, and chose March 1965 to demand a pay increase of no less than 16%, together with a reduction of two hours in the working week. When the employers offered 11%, the drivers threatened to strike. The management replied that strike action might lead to the permanent closure of certain rural bus routes. Many of these had been introduced or adapted following the closure of rail services.

There were relatively few closures in 1963 and early '64, but the pace was to quicken dramatically. One early casualty was Somerset's 'Strawberry Line', from Witham to Yatton via Wells, which closed in 1963, leaving Wells as the only English city without a railway station, although it would later be joined by Ripon. This is Shepton Mallet High Street station in 1973. PHOTO: David Henshaw

Yet another example of inefficient operating practices. A local stopping train at Castle Douglas, between Dumfries and Stranraer, in 1960. This was one of the closures put in abeyance by the 1964 election, but despite its strategic importance and relatively busy intermediate stations, Harold Wilson refused to save it, and the line closed in 1965. PHOTO: N Stead Collection

Public transport appeared to be falling apart at the seams, something that was beginning to cause real disquiet with the public at large. One result was an unprecedented demand for driving tests: later in March, the Ministry of Transport took on 150 new examiners to try and clear a backlog of 430,000 test appointments. There had been a record two million tests in 1964, 250,000 more than the previous peak.

As usual there were plenty of suggestions from the road lobby as to what the Minister could do with his railways... A certain Brigadier T I Lloyd advocated using closed trunk lines as road coach super-highways. The coaches would have nine-foot diameter wheels, and stop at railway stations, "razed to ground level... reconstituted as combined stopping places for coaches and access points for other traffic." How the recently launched Austin Mini would cope with nine-foot diameter wheels on a single-track motorway was a problem that the Brigadier had yet to address. The scheme was typical of many, more or less lunatic, proposals at the time, such as the suggestion from the Country Landowners' Association to build 'four or five' dual-carriageways across Wales.

Meanwhile, the Railways Board continued to plod doggedly through the closure proposals and, amid mounting concern, the Labour administration did nothing to stop the process. It had taken some time to force a statement out of Harold Wilson, but when it eventually came, at the end of March 1965, the pro-rail movement and those who had voted Labour in to halt the cuts, were devastated. The Prime Minister had changed his mind. There would be no moratorium on closures, no reprieves, and no wide-ranging report into transport.

In a statement laced with ambiguity, Harold Wilson claimed never to have had any intention of seeking powers to reverse closure decisions on lines that, "had already ceased to exist" (sic). And true to post-election government form, he claimed not to have been aware of the grave financial crisis his party had inherited. Of the 38 closure proposals in the new Minister's in-tray, 25 had already been implemented. Two months later, only six of the lines remained open, and the Government had added another 13 to the list, with 144 in the pipeline.

On 1st June 1965, after a little under five years in the service, Dr Beeching retired as Chairman of the Railways Board when Harold Wilson decided against renewing his contract.

Perhaps Beeching had reached the conclusion that his policies would never achieve the elusive goal of profitability... or perhaps the Government had reached the same conclusion on his behalf. He certainly seems to have gone gently off the rails in his last days as Chairman. In his diaries, Tony Benn describes Beeching launching a tirade against 'overblown democracy' during a House of Commons lunch in January 1965, recalling, "I think Beeching imagined himself as a new de Gaulle, emerging from industry to save the nation."

By this time, Beeching must have known the game was up. Even if his plans were working – and he may have been having private doubts by this stage – he probably already knew that Wilson would not give him the time he needed to finish the job.

Another interesting theory, put forward by Richard Cottrell in *Dr Who?* – a wryly entertaining and somewhat revisionist biography of the railway axeman – is that Beeching displayed all the traits of autism. Awkward and uncomfortable in social situations, an inability to take account of the wider picture while he fiddled with the minutiae of profit and loss on branch lines, and complete bemusement with the furore his carefully laid plans had aroused. This certainly seems to ring true with some of the conclusions of the *Trunk Route* report, which was dominated by Beeching's enthusiasm for containerised rail-freight, the so-called 'liner-train',

A controversial early closure was the line from Brockenhurst to Poole via Ringwood and Wimborne. On 2nd May 1964, the last day of operation, the final train arrives at West Moors from Southampton. The line eastwards from here was lifted soon afterwards, but the route has remained essentially intact, and ATOC has suggested restoration from Brockenhurst as far as Ringwood. There are no serious impediments to reinstatement beyond Ringwood to the outskirts of West Moors. PHOTO: Patrick Henshaw

From West Moors through Wimborne to Poole, the line remained open for freight until the early 1980s, although in this 1973 view, Wimborne's once bustling station is already a picture of dereliction. Once the track was taken up in the 1980s, the station site was rapidly built over, making reinstatement to this fast-growing town impossible. PHOTO: David Henshaw

while the little matter of the railway's public transport role was dismissed in a few paragraphs.

Paradoxically, Beeching had fought hard for modern rail freight facilities and container trains, upsetting the road lobby in the process. In 1964 he had given evidence to the Geddes Committee that allowing heavy goods vehicles on motorways was adding about 70% to construction costs – as Beeching rightly observed, it made a lot more sense to use lorries to pick up and dispatch containers locally, with rail for the long haul in between. He had subsequently been asked to chair an investigation into road/rail track costs, but the new Prime Minister Harold Wilson backed down in the face of intense pressure from the Ministry of Transport and road lobby, and failed to confirm the appointment. There would be no independent review of track costs, and Dr Beeching reluctantly accepted his life peerage and returned to ICI.

After a few promising years, railway losses began to rise again in 1965. Five years of savage cuts had yielded virtually nothing, while the waste associated with the programme, coming so soon after the BTC's substantial investments, continued to make headlines. The problem, as so often with monolithic organisations, was that change could take decades. Some parts of the network were still expanding, while others were contracting, and occasionally the two forces of change bumped into each other with tragi-comic results. In May 1965, the *Daily Mail* reported that a dozen new locomotive boilers were rusting away at Derby, their usefulness overtaken by the dieselisation programme. Around the country, thousands of carriages had been broken up, while new wheelsets were still being turned out at Swindon... and in November, three steam

SPECIAL NOTICE,
CLOSURE OF BRANCH LINE
LYME REGIS TO AXMINSTER.
THE LAST PASSENGER TRAIN
FROM LYME REGIS TO AXMINSTER
WILL LEAVE AT 19:10 ON
SATURDAY NOVEMBER 27th
TO ALL OUR REGULAR
PASSENGER,S THE STAFF
SAY THANK YOU & TRUST
THAT THE WINTER WILL
BE MILD

The Lyme Regis branch was a much loved railway, offering superb views, sinuous curves and testing gradients. It closed in 1965 - an insignificant six miles out of 1,071 miles axed by Tom Fraser that year. ABOVE: Cannington Viaduct seen from the trackbed of the line in 2012. BELOW: Lyme Regis station lingered on for some years, but was later dismantled and re-erected at Alresford on the 'Watercress' heritage line. PHOTOS: David Henshaw

locomotives were treated to a major overhaul, and scrapped immediately afterwards. Even uniforms were being wasted. Three redundant porters received smart new uniforms at Newmarket, as did 61-year-old William Botterill, redundant for three months from nearby Aldeburgh. He decided to send it back.

The vast freight marshalling yards, authorised under the 1955 Modernisation Plan to replace a plethora of smaller yards, were proving largely redundant, for the railways were now concentrating on 'train-load' goods traffic that needed little or no trans-shipment. A classic example was the Thornton New Yard in Fife, constructed in 1955 at a cost of £1.35 million. Those planning the yard had provided coaling, watering and stabling facilities for steam locomotives, and 15 miles of sidings, in a yard designed for the archaic loose-coupled wagons. There were many other monuments to the follies of the Transport Commission, such as the impressive Kingmoor yard near Carlisle, which was never fully utilised. These facilities had been designed when the railways still felt obliged to carry sundry traffic that could have been carried more profitably by road. Ten years later, with the accent on diesel-hauled train-load freight, steam locomotives were being withdrawn and loose-coupled wagons scrapped by the thousand, leaving these yards as ghostly white elephants. Wagon-load freight traffic worked well elsewhere in Europe, but Britain's stop-go transport policies had effectively wiped it out.

Beeching might have gone, but his legacy remained, and the Prime Minister agreed to intensify the closure programme. Ernest Marples had authorised the closure of 991 miles of line for 1964. His Labour successor as Minister of Transport, Tom Fraser, was to give the green light to 1,071 miles before the end of 1965.

Not only was Fraser agreeing to closures suggested in *Reshaping*, he was also signing the death warrant for lines that Beeching had considered worthy of retention. The Board's next candidate for closure was another big one, and a surprising choice in many ways. Beeching had spared the Oxford to Cambridge 'Varsity Line', and with good reason, for it provided a ready-made 'London bypass,' a direct link between the south coast and the north-east, avoiding the capital. It was of particular strategic significance now that the Great Central and its crucial link at Woodford Halse had been dismembered, because this was the only alternative route. With the traffic levels of the time, the Board could get away with

As Professor Hondelink had pointed out, investment followed by disinvestment was bound to result in some staggering examples of waste. The massive Kingmoor marshalling yard near Carlisle was never fully utilised, but it remains in use today in truncated form, primarily handling trainload coal traffic.

Yeovil in Somerset had three stations, of which Yeovil Town was undeniably the grandest and the most convenient. Unfortunately, it was also sited on the weakest of the three railway lines through the town, and it consequently closed to passengers in 1966, although the sheds and locomotive depot remained partially open for a few more years. From 1964, the three Yeovil stations had been linked by one of the AC Cars railbuses displaced from Tetbury and Cirencester.

ABOVE: A seemingly timeless shed scene in March 1965, but it was all about to be swept away.
PHOTO: Patrick Henshaw

RIGHT: By 1972 the station was starting to look a bit tattered around the edges. Soon afterwards, the site was completely levelled.
PHOTO: David Henshaw

Most abandoned railway structures were demolished, but Filleigh Viaduct on the Taunton to Barnstaple line proved to be an exception. The deck was removed after closure in 1966, but 22 years later the A361 North Devon Link Road was built on the railway formation and crossed the valley on a viaduct, reusing the old piers. *PHOTO: David Henshaw*

Stations didn't get much lonelier than Watergate Halt in North Devon on the Torrington to Halwill Junction line. Surprisingly, passenger services survived on this former narrow gauge railway until 1965. This stretch remained open for clay traffic until 1982 and is now a cycle path. The Barnstaple to Bideford section remains a very strong reopening candidate. *PHOTO: David Henshaw*

ABOVE: 'Rationalising' trunk lines could have some odd consequences. By pure good fortune, the Bedford to Bletchley section of the Varsity line survived because adequate bus services couldn't be arranged. A diesel multiple unit is about to depart for Bletchley from a very rationalised Bedford St Johns station in 1982. Services could also depart along the right line leading to Bedford Midland, and have since been diverted direct to the Midland station, leaving St Johns derelict. PHOTO: Gary Thornton

BELOW: The Bletchley to Oxford section continued to carry a little freight into the 1990s before being mothballed. This is Winslow in 1990. By 2017 this view should be completely transformed when the railway is rebuilt with double track and overhead electrification. Bedford St Johns will have to wait until the route eastwards has been clarified. PHOTO: David Henshaw

closing either the Great Central or the Varsity Line, but not both. Without these links, all cross-country traffic had to go north to Birmingham, or south to London, both routes being longer and more congested.

Under a Government that claimed to have put a degree of strategic planning into transport, this was an extraordinary choice. Not only did the line keep rail passengers and freight out of congested London, it conveniently linked the rapidly expanding new city of Milton Keynes with other areas of growth, such as Bedford and Cambridge. This was quite by chance, because Milton Keynes had been designed around the car, but the railway was there, just waiting for a government with a bit of strategic vision to make good use of it.

In July 1965, the hapless Fraser – poorly briefed and seemingly disinterested – consented to closure. During this unhappy period, with lines being put forward and processed at a rate of ten a month, this crucial link fell with hardly any national debate, as did others that were soon regretted. Implementation proved difficult, because there was trouble arranging bus services on a local basis, but the greater part of the line closed to passengers in November 1967, with the western end remaining open for freight, and a short section between Bedford and Bletchley for local passenger trains. These remaining tenuous threads were to be of priceless value 30 years later, when action was finally taken to begin the long and complex task of reinstating the line.

By the end of 1965, with the greater part of the *Reshaping* proposals now processed, there were few realistic candidates left for closure. Why then, did the Labour Government continue the process? According to Roger Calvert of the National Council for Inland Transport, the new and inexperienced administration had been bullied into submission by the powerful anti-rail civil servants at the Ministry of Transport, who were in turn being harassed by the Treasury over the railway's growing deficit. Labour had, technically, arrived in power with a brief to integrate transport, but the railways were making big losses and Tom Fraser was getting top level advice that further closures were the way forward. In the end, there was no other game in town. He certainly seems to have had little interest in the transport job, and was understandably considered by the rail lobby to be openly road-biased.

Whatever the views of individual politicians and civil servants, the real pressure for an accelerated closure programme was coming from the increasingly powerful road lobby. In 1965 it commissioned Victor Morgan, an economics professor at University College, Cardiff, to produce a road study. Inevitably, he came down in favour of a massive increase in road spending, and the report was used to tighten the screw on the Government for a further 1,700 miles of motorway, as part of a £7 billion road programme, worth in excess of £300 billion today.

But the trend wasn't all one way, and in August 1965, a railway closure was successfully challenged. The Board had suggested closure of the 49-mile East Suffolk line from Lowestoft to Ipswich, a once important secondary line, but now being put up for closure. The proposed bus replacement was to pick up passengers en route and connect with London-bound trains at Ipswich. Knowing the local roads, the prospective Liberal candidate for Eye, Donald Newby, rounded up a posse of press hacks, local worthies, and a couple of Suffolk mayors, and put them aboard three buses to challenge the timetable. After 50 miles of hard driving, they reached Ipswich 23 minutes behind schedule, and long after departure of the London train. Despite this embarrassing PR stunt, the newly abbreviated 'British Rail' insisted that the line should close, informing the TUCC that losses were running at around £250,000 a year.

That might have been the end of the story, but as luck would have it, Gerard Fiennes had recently been appointed General Manager of the Eastern Region, and his timely intervention turned the East Suffolk line into a *cause celebre* for the protest movement.

Fiennes' case, initially sketched on the back of the proverbial envelope, was very simple.

The Great Railway Conspiracy

A package of economy measures, together with a frequent DMU service, would form the nucleus of a 'basic railway'... a line operated as economically as the constraints of safety and expediency would allow, while retaining as much of the former traffic as possible. This would not be a low speed 'light railway', but a proper heavy rail line, with trains running at reasonable speeds (a vital component of the

Fiennes saved the East Suffolk line by rationalising services and infrastructure to the bone. It wasn't very pretty, but it kept track on the ground, allowing infrastructure to be restored as traffic recovered. Beccles, pictured here, had a passing loop and second platform replaced in 2012, allowing the service frequency to be doubled. Fiennes' 'basic railway' approach could have saved many other railways from closure in the 1960s. A terrible tragedy. PHOTO: www.myrailwaystation.com

package), albeit with simpler track and signalling and reduced staff. Similar 'basic railway' proposals had been put forward by the Railway Development Association and other groups for more than a decade, but Fiennes was the first highly placed railway official to go native and develop an enthusiasm for such techniques. A basic railway was a lowly form of life, but immeasurably better than nothing, and easy to upgrade should traffic improve, as was later to happen.

A quick calculation suggested that maintenance and renewals could be cut to as little as £30,000 a year for the whole 49-mile line, and total expenses reduced from a claimed figure of several hundred thousand pounds a year to just £84,000. Even after allowance was made for a drop in income from £120,000 to £90,000, the 'basic railway' formula could, at least on paper, turn a £250,000 annual loss into a modest £6,000 surplus.

Such calculations made a nonsense of the entire closure policy, and generally vindicated the views of Hondelink, Calvert and other members of the protest movement. Fiennes caused a storm at the Railways Board for daring to challenge the official line, and he rubbed salt into the wounds a year or two later by pouring scorn on the whole railway closure programme:

"In 1962, the Marples/Beeching axis began to define their territorial ambitions about rural railways. They laid it down in general that rural railways did not pay, which was true; and could never pay, which was false. They did not, therefore, require more than the most elementary arithmetic on the losses either in general or particular. They took no account of the new techniques; either coming into operation, like diesel traction, or just round the corner, like automatic level crossings, mechanised track maintenance, token-less block signalling, and 'bus stop' operation, which could cut the cost of rural railways by more than half."
From I Tried to Run a Railway, Gerard Fiennes

Gerard Fiennes was unceremoniously removed from his post for going public, but the East Suffolk line survived, a rare victory during a period of utter despair. As hoped, traffic steadied and revived, and in 2012 the line was upgraded, with new signalling and a passing loop at Beccles to allow an hourly service and increased line speed. If there had been more managers with the same guts and vision as Fiennes, dozens of other routes might have been saved in the same way.

One such route – or micro-network in this case – was the remaining lines on the Isle of Wight. The Ryde-Newport-Cowes and Shanklin-Ventnor lines had been closed in 1965, despite a previous undertaking to give five and seven years notice of closure respectively. Some reports suggested the short line to Ventnor was carrying 250,000 holiday visitors a year, and according to Professor Hondelink, the entire island network could have been returned to profitability had the Railways Board made a surcharge of 3d (1p) for the short journey along Ryde Pier!

Roger Calvert applied the theoretical *Reshaping* formula to the threatened lines, turning a claimed £142,000 loss into a potential surplus, but such arguments fell on deaf ears at the Ministry, and the TUCC inquiry in 1964 was followed by ministerial consent to closure. So great was the income from the island network that a society was set up with the intention of operating a public service between Ryde, Newport and Cowes in co-operation with the County Council. Like many other schemes, this one ran into difficulties over funding and other practicalities, and while negotiations were ongoing, the Railways Board tore up the track, scuppering any hope of survival.

Tom Fraser had refused to allow closure of the only railway left on the Isle of Wight, the 'main line' from Ryde Pier to Shanklin, leaving the Railways Board, which had long wanted to rid itself of the Isle of Wight altogether, with an obligation to replace the historic steam engines and carriages with rolling stock suitable for the island's restricted loading gauge. With a bit of lateral thinking, this was achieved using ex-London Transport tube stock, a neat solution that could just as easily have been applied to the rest of the island network.

This decidedly grudging electrification scheme was costed at £680,000, and completed in 1967, although according to an internal memo, the Board intended to put the line up for closure again in 1975. Fortunately, this didn't happen, and today this eight-mile line carries around four million passengers a year, the majority using just the short link from Ryde Pier Head to the town, but around 700,000 travelling on to the twin resorts of Sandown and Shanklin.

In October 1965, a month that saw a number of major closures, including the once-busy line between York and Hull, the Railways Board at last announced its intention to discontinue passenger services on the Great Central, with the exception of a few Nottingham to Rugby local trains. The final Ministerial decision was to be long delayed though, for another general election was in the offing.

Another large-scale closure proposal was that of the Somerset & Dorset, no less than 72 miles of line from Bournemouth West to Bath Green Park. This was one of the biggest, but the ground had been prepared in the usual way, with through expresses withdrawn in late 1962, staffing levels kept untouched, and the remaining steam-hauled local trains retimed and given poor connections to reduce traffic prior to the TUCC inquiries.

Bournemouth West had already succumbed to an electrification scheme on the nearby main line, but the line westwards to Bath was to experience an extraordinary, if brief, reprieve. On 31st December 1965, Wakes Bus Company withdrew its application to operate a Blandford Forum-Glastonbury-Midsomer Norton service along the approximate route of the Somerset & Dorset. According to contemporary reports, a number of reasons were put forward for the company's withdrawal, including staffing problems, logistical difficulties, and a quite justifiable belief that this long bus route would be unprofitable. The problem, as in many of the areas

The Great Railway Conspiracy

ABOVE: In September 1966 steam had only a few months to live on the Isle of Wight. No.28 'Ashey' arrives at Shanklin, now the terminus on the island's only remaining line, since closure of Ventnor, Newport and Cowes in April 1966. PHOTO: Patrick Henshaw

BELOW: In 1967 this remaining line was converted to electric traction, using former Underground trains, seen here departing for Ryde Pier from the same spot in 1998. One suspects the Germans would have made a better job of modernising the railways on a holiday island - certainly a bigger network, and perhaps an electric tram and heritage steam solution? PHOTO: David Henshaw

where the closures struck, was that the roads were just not up to the job, and realistically in this rural area, would never be brought up to a standard that allowed buses to approach rail journey times.

British Rail, running scared that the consequent reprieve might turn into something more permanent, scrapped the schedule of 20 trains a day, and introduced a derisory skeleton service supplemented by buses. For more than two months, while surplus track and fixtures were scrapped, this ghostly service was maintained, and it really did look as though the Somerset & Dorset – once counted amongst the most evocative of all British railways – would refuse to die. But it was heading for a lingering, untidy death.

Only two years before, as winter storms cut communications in the area, the Somerset & Dorset train crews had fought to maintain services over the Mendip hills. Many men had given a lifetime of service to this well-patronised and much-loved line, but these same men were now under obligation to act out the last rites.

It was something Tom Fraser, far away in Whitehall, could hardly be expected to understand. Many of the rural lines had become ingrained into the communities they served, integral and indispensible threads binding the rich tapestry of rural life. To Dr Beeching, the Somerset & Dorset was just another duplicate trunk route, but it also served a scattering of rural towns. The population along the line was actually a sizeable one, and it was set to grow very rapidly indeed in the following decades.

The key stations at Blandford, Wincanton, Shepton Mallet, Midsomer Norton and Radstock served a combined population of well over 50,000, and all would be left remote from the rail system, or any sort of transport network for that matter, as there were no significant road schemes for the area. To a greater or lesser extent, such communities were to die a little with the loss of rail services, and it was a blow from which many would never recover.

The Somerset & Dorset was magnificently steam-hauled to the bitter end. The Pines Express in the early 1960s before through services were routed away from the line. PHOTO: Mike Esau

The Somerset & Dorset was one of the biggest closures. It had everything - scenery, thriving market towns and long distance traffic, its only real weakness being a lack of connectivity at the northern end. For various reasons it saw very little investment over the years, and diesel locomotives and multiple units were extremely rare right to the end. Could it have survived? There was a very good case for retention of the eastern Cole-Bournemouth section, including Blandford Forum, shown here in 1972, six years after the loss of passenger services. This site has now completely disappeared under housing. PHOTO: David Henshaw

The counter argument from the British Railways Board was that such lines cost a fortune to run, out of all proportion to the social benefit, but as we have seen, their cost figures were at best dubious, and at worst downright false. The Somerset & Dorset carried a considerable traffic, but it had hardly seen a single DMU in the decade since these had been introduced. With no investment in new technology, it was not surprising that the line lost money.

As early as 1962, the clumsily named Branch Line Re-invigoration Society (later the Railway Invigoration Society) had put forward some interesting proposals aimed at restoring the line to health. Like many others, the Somerset & Dorset had been starved of investment since before the war, and had seen precious few changes since Edwardian days. In 1913 the fastest services had traversed the line in a little under two hours; by 1962 – in an age of jet airliners and E-type Jaguars – the fastest trains took two hours and 13 minutes. Most trains meandered from Bournemouth to Bath at an average of around 20mph, giving a journey time of almost four hours. The Society recommended that certain minor stations be closed, others de-staffed, and a faster, more frequent DMU service be introduced, in place of the picturesque but expensive steam trains that still dominated the timetable. It was an imaginative plan, and with a few signalling and operating economies, it might have saved the line, but the report was ignored, and the Somerset & Dorset simply wasted away.

A handful of lines *had* benefited from new technology of course. As the Somerset & Dorset closure proposal was being implemented, the Ballater branch in Aberdeenshire was also put up for closure. It was here that the BTC had introduced the unique battery-electric multiple unit which slashed movement costs, but the Scottish Region had done nothing to cut

Pictured in 1973, Cole station had lost none of its charm, eight years after closure. Protesters had suggested building a short link to the adjacent West of England line, as a means of saving the eastern section of the S&D, but it was not to be. PHOTO: David Henshaw

other costs, leaving the rural branch supporting an army of staff: four stationmasters, 37 station staff, 16 signalmen, four crossing-keepers and 24 men engaged in track maintenance. Although the electric train almost covered its movement costs, even on the British Rail figures, it came nowhere near supporting the 85 staff employed on the line.

Interestingly, Ballater was a royal branch, serving Balmoral Castle, one of the Queen's private residences. Whether the opinion of the royal household was sought with regard to railway closures will no doubt be revealed in the fullness of time. Windsor was pretty safe, being in commuter territory, but Beeching had made the slightly mysterious decision to reprieve the Hunstanton branch, serving Sandringham Castle, while allowing Ballater to close! In any event, the frenzy of decommissioning had now gone so far that a reprieve in the *Reshaping* report meant nothing, and several branch lines, including Hunstanton, were soon to go the same way as the others.

These 'permanent' ways were being obliterated, but there were no new roads to take their place. The highways of southwest England and northeast Scotland were quite unsuitable for through traffic, and remain so to this day. A popular Ministry line in the 1960s was to sway troublesome local authorities by implying that their area might be eligible for costly road improvements just as soon as the loss-making railways had been swept aside. Many objectors were taken in by this ploy, including the little Bruton Labour Party, which implored the Minister to grant a stay of execution on the Somerset & Dorset pending road improvements:

"British Railways has made a big mistake in hurrying this closure proposal and your consent to it was in error until the road programme for this area was complete... this programme cannot be completed for at least ten years. The retention of this line is the only way to relieve the chaotic congestion of the overcrowded roads in the area...

There is public outcry from end to end of this line."

There was no reprieve, and once what the Ministry deemed an acceptable bus service had been arranged, British Rail withdrew the remaining trains and set about scrapping the remnants of the Somerset & Dorset. Cost had once again triumphed over all other considerations, for the reduced operating expenses of a rural bus service proved a persuasive argument.

But had the S&D and other lines really lost money? Evidence was coming to light that rail closures might be proving very expensive in wider terms. The question of cost versus social benefit had raged back and forth for years, but late in 1965 the protesters tried a radical new approach, with considerable success.

Motorways had always been costed by the 'Social Surplus' cost/benefit analysis technique. The estimated 'income' of a new motorway was assumed to be the saving in motorists' working time, vehicle time (in terms of fuel, depreciation etc), and sundry other benefits to the rest of the road system, should the new road be constructed. When the 'saved' passenger-hours had been calculated, they were multiplied by a prearranged figure (16 shillings (80p) in the 1960s) to give a gross 'income'. As a rule of thumb, a motorway was considered viable if the social benefit exceeded the extra mileage costs incurred by motorists accessing the road, the ongoing maintenance cost, and a return of about 10% on the initial expenditure. With the M1, for instance, construction costs had been put at about £23 million and annual mainte-nance at £200,000. At 1955 traffic levels it was estimated that the proposed motorway would show a rather limited return of 3-4%, but traffic growth by 1960 was expected to push that as high as 10-15%, making the project firmly viable. It was all slightly Alice in Wonderland, of course. How could you assume that everyone using the road would otherwise be doing something productive to the value of 16 shillings an hour? And if the motorway simply generated traffic, which it did, that extra traffic might have no value at all, such as people idly driving to a pub further from home just because they could. And that new traffic might well be causing expensive accident, pollution or congestion issues elsewhere on the network, so growth might actually be a disbenefit. But new roads had to be costed somehow, and many independent experts believed the same techniques should be applied to rail closures. If the loss of a service

produced longer journeys, the wasted passenger-hours could be calculated, and the resulting figure offset against losses.

When the lines from Oxted and Tunbridge Wells to Lewes came before the South Eastern TUCC inquiry in April 1967, the protesters applied the technique. The two lines were of some importance, providing a link between Tunbridge Wells and Brighton, and a secondary main line from Brighton to London, as well as producing consid-erable London commuter traffic in their own right.

Construction of Broughton Interchange on the Preston Bypass, now Junction 36 on the M6. The viability of motorways was determined by putting a value on the time saved by drivers. Protesters argued that the same system should be used to pay for railways too.

But in an area where most lines where electrified with the third-rail system, they were still steam operated. Beeching had proposed closure in *Reshaping*, and the final nail in the coffin came in 1964, when Transport Minister Ernest Marples had approved the first stage of the Lewes Relief Road. To bridge the line would have cost an extra £135,000, and although the Railways Board applied to divert the line at a relatively trifling £95,000, the expenditure was refused in 1966, leading the Board to put the whole line south of Oxted up for closure.

Using the Ministry's own motorway costing formula, the protesters were able to show that closure would result in 712,000 wasted travelling hours at a cost of around £570,000 a year, against the claimed annual loss of only £276,000. Even if the railway figures were accurate, which was very unlikely, the disbenefit to the nation of closing the railway would be £294,000 a year.

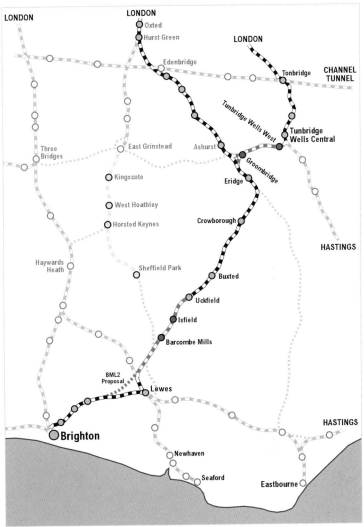

Closure of the Uckfield to Lewes line in 1969 brought about the eventual downfall of the Eridge to Tunbridge Wells line in 1985. Reinstatement of these relatively short links (shown in green) would reconnect Brighton and Lewes to Tunbridge Wells and provide two alternative routes from the south coast to London. Because of these wider benefits, it is one of the strongest reopening campaigns.

This all made sense to the TUCC, because here at last was a means of quantifying the somewhat slippery concept of 'hardship'. The Committee was so impressed that it came down firmly in favour of saving the line:

"...these hardships could not be alleviated other than by retaining the lines proposed to be closed... This arises not from lack of alternative bus services, existing or proposed, but from the inherent advantages of the railway to those using it..."

The Great Railway Conspiracy

Barbara Castle approved the closure, but her successor subsequently reprieved both lines north of Uckfield on the basis of their commuter value, though the final eight miles into Lewes would close. Losing a priceless diversionary route through the loss of just eight miles of track was a nonsense, and the Railways Board knew it, but with structures on the line in need of urgent repair, no funding available for the diversion and

Uckfield has inhabited a strange twilight world since closure of the short stretch to Lewes. Even in 1990 it looks as though trains might still run that way, but the double track ends in a head shunt. Soon afterwards, most of the line was singled, and Uckfield station was replaced with a rather mean platform behind the photographer and the level crossing. PHOTO: David Henshaw

contractors waiting in the wings to breech the line to construct the Lewes Relief Road, the stretch between Uckfield and Lewes was doomed, and it finally closed in February 1969.

Nevertheless, most of the line had been saved, thanks in part to the sophisticated techniques used to oppose outright closure. The Tunbridge Wells inquiry was to prove a watershed moment, for by using the Ministry of Transport's own formula, the protesters had proved that the benefit greatly outweighed the cost of providing the service. And if the Ministry wanted to argue, they would have to justify costing motorways by the same formula. A similar study on the rather tenuous Central Wales line revealed that hidden benefits were worth about 60% of the income from fares, resulting in a true 'value' markedly higher than the figure claimed at TUCC inquiries.

Roger Calvert of the NCIT (who had already applied lateral thinking to the railway authority's figures) went a step further and applied the same criteria to all the closures implemented between 1963 and 1966. The result was an effective annual loss of £36 million in passengers' time, against the £17 million that the Board claimed to have saved by axing the services.

Stanley Raymond, the new Chairman of the Railways Board, was thinking along the same lines. In January 1966 he proposed a 'Transport Highway Authority' to determine priorities for investment and raise money to fund the infrastructure of rail, road, air and water transport. The cost of maintaining the railway 'highway' (ie the entire network) would have been £130 million after interest the previous year... more or less equal to the entire railway deficit.

He went on to ask awkward questions about cost. How were the railways to carry the cost of the uneconomic services the Government had decided to maintain? It was a good point, because such issues as passenger time savings and environmental benefits were external to the railway, so the railway would need some sort of subsidy to keep those lines running.

True, most of the closures had been approved by the Government, but some had been refused, leaving the railway with an obligation to keep the trains running, something not wholly reconcilable with their duty under the 1962 Transport Act to break even.

Stanley Raymond was rapidly becoming unpopular with some elements at the Ministry of Transport, and the Minister Tom Fraser not only refused to allow the application Social Surplus techniques to railways, but also ignored the innovative proposal to establish a Transport Highway Authority. But Fraser's time was up – Harold Wilson was beginning to lose patience with his lacklustre Minister of Transport, who was proving something of a liability with the public and the railway unions. Late in 1965, an imminent election gave him the opportunity to reshuffle the cabinet, and in December, Fraser was ousted in favour of Barbara Castle.

Castle has had a mixed press over the years. After the cheerfully road-biased Marples, and ineffective Fraser, she entered the Ministry like a breath of fresh air, standing up to the powerful civil servants and making a serious attempt to find a fair solution to the railway issue. On the other hand, she oversaw some disastrous closures that should never have been allowed. Unlike previous incumbents, her transport politics were hard to place. She rarely used railways, but needed a chauffeur because she couldn't drive, and apparently had no desire to.

Barbara Castle found the motorway construction programme on auto-pilot under the control of her Permanent Secretary, the cultured and intelligent career civil servant Sir Thomas Padmore. Castle had met her match in Padmore, who didn't share her enthusiasm for transport integration, or indeed any sort of interference with road policy. Castle failed to have him removed, and there seems to have been an uneasy truce along the lines of the TV series 'Yes Minister'. Padmore claims to have become bored with transport, but on retirement he was active in the Institute of Road Transport Engineers, and sat on the Public Policy Committee of the RAC... not something you do without an interest in roads.

Opened in 1925, the branch line to Fawley in Hampshire was one of the last to be built. Just 41 years later, in 1966, it had been closed to passengers. Fortunately it remained busy with freight - principally to the adjacent oil refinery - and is now considered to be a prime candidate for reopening, to ease road congestion into Southampton. ATOC has suggested partial reopening to Marchwood, because Fawley station has been swallowed up by the oil refinery. PHOTO: David Henshaw

The Great Railway Conspiracy

On 1st April 1966, Labour scored a decisive victory in the General Election, and Barbara Castle set about a thorough investigation of the country's transport needs. By 22nd April she seemed to have turned the tide against railway closures by refusing six, most of them (to be cynical) in and around urban Labour constituencies. Traffic congestion, said the new Minister, was reaching critical levels:

"We are already faced with growing traffic congestion in our large city centres, and in my view it would be commercialism gone mad to take decisions which can only add to these problems."

Stanley Raymond was, of course, still waiting to hear who was going to pay, and estimated loudly in public that the six lines would require an annual subsidy of almost £250,000...

The answer came in a Government White Paper later in the year. In a flurry of gripping new phrases, such as 'infrastructure' and 'social and economic criteria', the White Paper, *Transport Policy* outlined the Labour Government's transport objectives. At last there was a realisation that the railways were unlikely ever to comply with the commercial criteria of the 1962 Transport Act, and *Transport Policy* brought the first mention of the 'socially necessary' railway. Commercial viability was described as, "important, but secondary," a phrase that must have made Sir Thomas Padmore wince.

By and large, the Paper said all the right things, and tackled the road problem head on:

"The nation has not yet begun to face up to the implications of the motor age. Each of us still believes he can find his own individual means of escape from the accompanying unpleasantness; for example by finding a house further afield and buying a car... or cars... to enable him and his family to get to it."

According to *Transport Policy*, the nation's transport infrastructure would be modernised, investment carefully planned, and future judgements based upon social need. Once again, although much further down the priorities than in 1945, a Labour government announced its intention to integrate public road and rail transport. Past railway closures wouldn't be reversed though, and in the words of the White Paper, "there is still some pruning to be done," but there was every indication that the wholesale closure programme was almost at an end.

To study the thorny question of finance, the Government introduced a whole new vocabulary of jargon, including 'Joint Machinery' involving the Ministry of Transport and the Railways Board. Aptly, the Joint Machinery would be controlled by a 'Steering Group' under John Morris, the Joint Parliamentary Secretary to the Ministry of Transport. The terms of reference sounded perfectly reasonable, and were surprisingly free of incomprehensible jargon:

"To establish an acceptable basis for costing, and to identify those categories of services... which are not covering costs... and to cost in detail the annual loss on each passenger service which is unlikely ever to be viable."

It was by no means the end of the closure process though, for after deliberating for nine months, the Government announced its intentions with regard to the sad remains of the Great Central. While it had been considering the problem, the Railways Board had done its utmost to move things along, by introducing a timetable so derisory, so ill-considered and poorly planned, that it was surprising any passengers continued to use the line at all. The fastest service averaged just 38mph, and there were gaps of up to five hours between trains.

The suggestion that British Rail never intentionally ran down services prior to closure is an outrageous one, for the schedule in those last days of the Great Central was astonishingly poor. It was also astonishingly expensive, for the Board had done nothing to economise on staff,

LEFT: In April 1969, two weeks before closure, the bay platforms are already being dismantled at Leicester Central. This photograph is taken from one of the ghostly Nottingham to Rugby DMU shuttles.
PHOTO: Nigel Tout

RIGHT: With the last trains out of the way, the Great Central was gradually dismembered, but this was no country branch. Demolition proved to be a massive undertaking that continued for many years. This is the north viaduct, close to Northgate Street, Leicester in 1982.
PHOTO: Nigel Tout

and the handful of local trains that remained were almost exclusively steam-hauled. So lethargic was the schedule in those last gloomy days, that when a DMU occasionally deputised for a missing or failed steam locomotive, it caused embarrassment by arriving early.

The reason this travesty of a service had been allowed to drag on for so long was a political one, because the official announcement was held over during the election. There was thus little doubt what the Minister's verdict would be, for if Barbara Castle had settled on a reprieve, she would have been unlikely to wait until three weeks after the election to announce it...

The Great Central was to close in its entirety, apart from the isolated shuttle service between Nottingham and Rugby, at an estimated annual saving of £900,000. It was the largest and ultimately, one of the most hotly contested savings yet announced. At the TUCC hearings the previous year, gross *expenses* had been put at only £977,000, against income of about £438,000. Against no system of accountancy did the loss equate to £900,000.

It later emerged that the cost of the planning process itself, in terms of investigation, planning, and the deliberate imposition of loss-making services, had been hugely expensive. And little if any money was saved in the years after closure, because most of the staff were moved elsewhere to placate union objections.

Despite all the talk of social need and subsidy, Labour continued to implement the *Reshaping* proposals. Tom Fraser had approved more than a thousand miles for closure in 1965, and Barbara Castle went on to agree to a smaller number of *proposals* in 1966, but they were larger, more controversial candidates, and the mileage lost that year actually amounted to almost 1,200.

For an aging Professor Hondelink it was the final straw. As a consultant to the Great Central Association, he had fought long and hard to save the line, and it now lay in ruins. At almost 80 years of age, and suffering from advancing ill-health, he wrote one of his last campaigning letters to his political friend, Philip Noel-Baker MP:

"I am glad to know that you will continue the battle for a saner transport policy; you are still in a position of responsibility and authority to do so. I have largely given up the struggle. My rewarding work for the World Bank and United Nations has until now mostly balanced the disappointment in my endeavours to help stem the deteriorating transport policy at home.

Since we started nearly 20 years ago, and renewed our efforts about eight years ago to attack the Marples-Beeching planning, all I said and wrote has come true and was completely justified. I have been called a 'major thorn in their side' and instructions have gone out not to attempt arguing with me, an outside expert."

It was all about to get worse. The Waverley route from Edinburgh to Carlisle had endured a ghostly existence since being listed for closure in *Reshaping* back in 1963. As the years passed, the clamour died down, and local people relaxed. Surely, closure of such a major line was just political posturing, and the fact that nothing *had* happened while other trunk lines were being rubbed off the map gave the people of the Borders a sense of security. Closure of the long branches to Fraserburgh and Peterhead, plus the cross-country line from Dumfries to Stranraer in 1965, caused some disquiet, but the Waverley was much bigger and more important. Even after closure was announced in 1966, nothing much happened and the Borders relaxed again. But the plans were quite serious, and they were to affect the entire 100-mile trunk route. Behind the scenes, a desperate battle had been going on to salvage at least some of the Waverley. The Ministry of Transport was obliged to consult the Scottish Economic Planning Council on closure proposals, and in November 1965, the SEPC had asked Minister Tom Fraser to, "oppose publication," of the Waverley proposal, "at this time," in view of, "the nature, size and importance of the area served by the line..."

The SEPC was being guided by regional planning specialist Frank Spaven, an extremely knowledgeable civil servant, who was also a member of the Scottish Railway Development Society. Spaven had the knowledge, the contacts, and the negotiating ability to save the Waverley route, or at least the greater part of it, but in 1966 he moved to the new Highlands & Islands Development Board, where he became a key player in the successful campaign to save the Highland railway network.

Beeching had detested 'duplicate' trunk routes, and the Waverley looked a classic candidate. It was one of four trunk lines north of the border, of which Beeching had suggested keeping three in *Reshaping*, and only one in the more hard line *Development of the Major Trunk Routes*.

Barbara Castle's team would also come down in favour of three routes, and like Beeching, they settled on Waverley as the one to go, being the least suitable for through passenger and freight services. It did, however, have some unique selling points, principally the large and growing towns of Galashiels and Hawick, which would be left a considerable distance from a railhead, and vast swathes of timber further south around the new Kielder Water, which would later become a major tourist attraction.

Throughout 1965, Spaven argued the case for a commuter railway from Hawick north to Edinburgh, and a 45-mile single-track 'basic railway' south of Hawick. The Ministry of Transport replied that the loss of rail transport was not an issue, because the population of around 70,000 within 25 miles of the railway made little use of it, and useage was declining rapidly as car ownership increased. It was the same old story: ill-timed trains, poor connections, and (until 1966) a predomination of slow, all-stations steam services. According to the Ministry, ticket sales in the period 1960 to 1964 had fallen by 37% to 123,000, and season ticket sales had fallen by 62% to 3,000. But as was often the case, the figures were in dispute. Spaven responded that the line was carrying 9,400 passengers a week in the winter, and 12,000 in summer, of which 66% were travelling northwards to Edinburgh. Interestingly, the strongest traffic figures were on Saturdays, the only day that saw regular DMU workings. Taking into account new housing planned for the Borders towns, he estimated that rail traffic, "would increase to between one and a half and three times its present level."

Thereafter Spaven moved on to fight equally desperate battles in the Highlands, and the Waverley's fortunes were left in the hands of the Railways Board. As elsewhere, there were a few railway managers with the drive and ability to save the line, but others had adopted a bunker mentality, unable to make useful decisions, other than the very easy one of letting the Waverley go. Leaving it overstaffed and under-utilised was the easiest decision of all. Staff numbers were to gradually fall, from 439 in 1963, to 274 in 1968, on the eve of closure, but in 1966 the line still had 26 signalboxes and 24 stations, some carrying as many staff as they had in the 1920s.

The objections by the SEPC and political worries during the 1966 election had kept the closure proposal under wraps, with Willie Ross, the Secretary of State for Scotland calling for more time, and Barbara Castle determined to press ahead. With the election out of the way, she made her views very clear:

"I am afraid I cannot ask the Railways Board to postpone the publication of Edinburgh-Hawick-Carlisle as I don't think your proposed timetable is realistic... I do not consider therefore that I should be justified in asking the Board to stay their hand any longer on this very costly service; every week that passes may be costing the Board, and hence the taxpayer, £12,000."
Memo from Barbara Castle to Willie Ross, 27th April 1966

With the benefit of hindsight, the sensible option would have been to retain – at the very least – a basic commuter railway from Hawick to Edinburgh, with the rest of the route dismantled, but safeguarded from development. The problem was that schemes of this kind needed a forceful persuasive advocate, and with Frank Spaven gone, the only option on the table was complete closure, which was finally posted on 17th August 1966, causing the usual panic, petitions and general uproar. But once again, an air of complacency soon returned to the Borders, and only 508 individuals and organisations lodged official objections with the TUCC inquiry in Edinburgh – a very small number for such a major proposal.

During the hearing, the Railways Board made good use of figures, showing a remarkably rapid decline in passenger useage of about 10% a year, and a correspondingly rapid increase in

Diesel multiple units were rare on the Waverley, as they were on most of the doomed lines. In the last days there was one regular working south of Hawick, known locally as 'The Scud', which left Carlisle at about 18.30 in the evening, stabled overnight at Hawick, and worked back to Carlisle as the 06.13 the following morning. In a rather fitting twilight, the evening Scud pauses at lonely Riccarton Junction en route to Hawick. PHOTO: Bruce McCartney

car ownership. The TUCC report (15 pages, plus nine appendices) was one of the longest produced, one of the last, and also one of the most grudging, raising serious concerns about potential hardship and unrealistic bus services. But it was done. The Waverley route was already under sentence of death, waiting in a state of limbo for the Minister in London to wield the pen, though – for the time being at least – no word came.

In May 1967, the newly electrified Ryde to Shanklin service reopened on the Isle of Wight, further closures were refused, and figures from the Euston to Liverpool and Manchester electrification scheme (completed in April 1966) indicated a remarkable 45% increase in passenger journeys. It looked as though Barbara Castle really had turned the Beeching tide, but events were to rapidly overtake such an optimistic view.

Behind the scenes, the Railways Board was developing a highly confidential set of maps. Officially known as 'British Railways System Maps', these were colloquially known as the 'Blue Book' within the organisation, but completely unknown outside until many years later.

The maps had been prepared by Beeching's Central Planning Unit. After his departure, the team seems to have been set the task of redrawing the railway map using data supplied by the nationalised industries and other sources. Where would railways be needed in the future? Where could growth be predicted? More importantly, where was further retraction and closure inevitable? Inevitably, as a 'son of Beeching' enterprise, the Blue Book maps were strong on freight, but weak on passenger traffic. The team knew – sometimes with uncanny accuracy – how

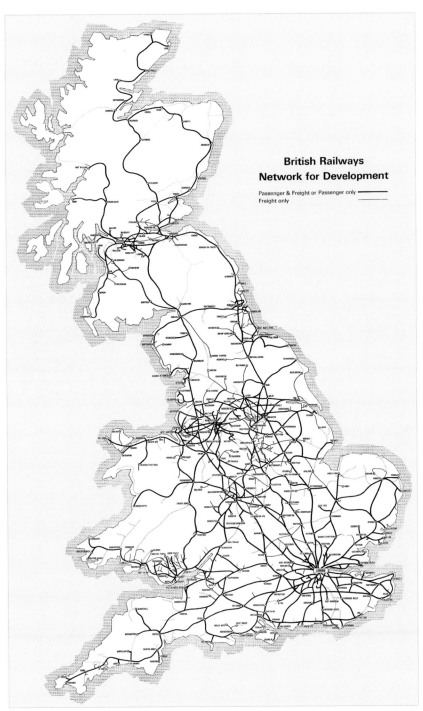

**British Railways
Network for Development**

Passenger & Freight or Passenger only ─────
Freight only

Network for Development was a strange affair, generally kind to urban networks, but putting two big trunk lines - the Waverley and Settle & Carlisle - under sentence of death. It also brought about the demise of numerous rural and seaside branches that were carrying a great deal of traffic. In broad terms, almost every line on this map, including those that were not selected for 'development' (shown in grey), should have survived. Some did, but most didn't.

long coal seams would survive under South Yorkshire, but had no really clear idea of where passenger traffic would develop. Rather chillingly, lines that were expected to close were neatly annotated with the proposed date of closure on the maps. The obvious weakness of this approach was that it rather pre-empted closure, even if new passenger traffic was staring the team in the face. Several lines earmarked in the Blue Book did close, but others survived, thanks to powerful local campaigns or political intervention, and by 2013 were running at full capacity.

Clearly, any whiff of these maps by the public or the unions would have been political dynamite, because they not only listed the proposed closure dates of railways, but of individual coal mines and other industries. Interestingly, the accent was very much on old heavy industries, and the team seem to have taken little interest in the prospect of new lines to serve new industries or even adapting old lines to develop new traffic. At this time, the future of the Waverley route was hanging on a thread, but the Central Planning Unit appears to have taken little interest in transporting the millions of tons of timber that would soon be ready for processing in the Borders.

The public face of the Blue Book was the so-called *Network for Development* plan, unveiled by Barbara Castle in May 1967. This was billed as an effort to 'stabilise' the network around the best estimates of future prospects, based on the work of the Central Planning Unit and Ministry of Transport studies. In practice, of course, it had little to do with stability. Being based on internal studies that continued to suggest a future railway based around expanding bulk freight services and declining passenger traffic, it would inevitably mean further closures, the aim being to 'stabilise' the existing network of 13,200 miles at *11,000* miles, of which just 8,000 miles would be open to passengers. There was a vague promise that the stabilised network would be in place for the long haul, but as we now know, the basis for this new round of closures was

Barbara Castle swept away a whole group of rural lines, from Wadebridge in Cornwall to Peterhead in Scotland. Wadebridge, photographed in 1973, closed to passengers in January 1967, but remained open for freight until 1978. There have been repeated calls to reopen the Bodmin to Wadebridge line for heritage services. It has since become a popular cycle path, making reinstatement controversial, but by no means impossible. PHOTO: David Henshaw

already out of date and – for passenger traffic at least – would prove woefully inaccurate.

At the remunerative end of the scale, most of the remaining trunk routes and a few secondary lines would be developed. At the other extreme, certain commuter lines and a handful of loss-making rural routes (which failed to meet financial criteria, but served a 'social' function), were to be retained and subsidised.

The real shock came with the lines that fitted neither category, and consequently were not to be included in the 'basic' network. These lines, neither profitable, nor (in the Government's view) socially necessary, were left in the hands of the British Railways Board. None, it was claimed, were immediately threatened with closure, but the Government made it clear that none had an assured future either. Thus, many apparently safe secondary lines were likely to be swept away, as were the majority of the remaining branches.

Had the Government agreed to adopt cost/benefit analysis for rail closures, the picture would have been very different, for under such criteria, only a handful of lines produced a negative benefit. Barbara Castle accepted that commuter lines would be needed, but she had failed to be swayed by the argument that seasonal holiday lines or cross-country routes serving a large, but thinly spread population, were essential to the nation's well-being. This abandonment of the middle ground resulted in some absurd anomalies. In Wales, the weak Blaenau Ffestiniog branch would be subsidised, but the much busier Pembroke branch would not. In Scotland, St

Richmond in North Yorkshire was one of those branch lines that simply shouldn't have closed. The town was a tourist destination, and big - though nowhere near as big as the nearby Catterick army base, which provided a lot of traffic, as did the famous racecourse. Richmond was one of the handful of stations whose income exceeded £25,000 a year in the 'Reshaping' surveys, yet it was marked down for closure by both Beeching and Castle, eventually going down defiantly in 1969. PHOTO: David Hey

The Great Railway Conspiracy

Andrews (recommended for retention by Beeching) was out, but the Far North line was in. The West Country would lose nearly all of its busy holiday branches, but it would keep a few commuter services into Exeter and Plymouth.

The cynical pointed out that the proposals would concentrate resources on urban Labour constituencies, while withdrawing facilities from the Tory shires. On the other hand, Castle was fighting her corner in a Ministry with an overwhelming road bias, and attempting to justify her policies to a cabinet that held similar views. Whatever the true position, a number of lines were needlessly sacrificed to meet the slightly irrational *Network for Development* criteria.

And there was to be no last minute reprieve for the Waverley route. A number of trunk lines had failed to make it onto the *Network* list, principally the Waverley, the Settle & Carlisle, the Oxford to Cambridge line (already under stay of execution), the Central Wales, the Cambrian Coast and most of the former LSWR route between Exeter and Plymouth. Many branch lines would be affected too, including some that had been marked for execution in *Reshaping*, such as Kyle of Lochalsh, Fraserburgh, Peterhead, Minehead, Richmond and Ilfracombe, and others that had not: Mallaig, St Andrews, North Berwick, Newquay, Falmouth, Hunstanton, Sheringham and Swanage.

The Government had no intention of repeating Beeching's cardinal error of glibly listing the lines on the execution list. It went to great pains to point out that it had not actually authorised closure of the non-selected routes, and that their future would be in the hands of the Railways Board. On the other hand, they would receive no subsidy, leaving the Board little choice if it wanted to stay afloat.

The largest closures, in terms of both route mileage and infrastructure, were the 'duplicate'

Once the branches had been removed from the LSWR network in Devon and Cornwall, it was just a matter of time before the Plymouth to Exeter trunk route went too, leaving the major centre of Tavistock some distance from the nearest railhead. Devon County Council has now put its weight behind a reopening campaign to the southern edge of Tavistock. The original station, pictured here in 1972, has been immaculately restored, but the trackbed beyond is blocked by West Devon Borough Council's offices! With no clear national guidance on disused rail corridors, issues like this are all too common. PHOTO: David Henshaw

Okehampton fared rather better. The line remained in place to serve Meldon Quarry, and passenger services had been recommended for retention in both 'Reshaping' and 'Network for Development'. But the line eventually closed in 1972, and although some summer Sunday trains and heritage services have run since, full reopening remains elusive. This is the station in 1973, soon after closure - it has changed very little since. PHOTO: David Henshaw

trunk routes. Most of Devon and North Cornwall had been served by the ex-London & South Western trunk line, which ran deep into Great Western territory via Salisbury, Exeter and Okehampton to Plymouth, with branches throughout the West Country. Following the railway grouping of 1923, the network fell into the hands of the Southern, which enthusiastically improved services to the general detriment of Great Western. Following nationalisation in 1948, the railways were broken up on a simple geographical basis, because competition would no longer be needed in the age of transport integration. The former LSWR network was handed to the enemy (now the Western Region) and began to languish almost immediately.

Had the GWR and LSWR routes been genuinely duplicate, the case for closure would have been overwhelming, but they were not. Certainly both started in London and ended in the southwest, but apart from the cities of Exeter and Plymouth, the number of towns served by both companies was small, the 'competing' routes generally serving very different areas.

In September 1964, the Railways Board had withdrawn the Atlantic Coast Express from the LSWR route – a cynical move that plunged all the associated branch lines into terminal decline, and one by one they were closed.

It was a fine example of the fallacy of the Beeching doctrine. As a group, the railways of Devon and North Cornwall had been reasonably prosperous, but once the contraction had begun, it was easy to prove that individual branches were uneconomic. And once the branch lines had been removed, the trunk line itself became vulnerable. On Barbara Castle's watch the rot had reached the trunk line between Exeter and Plymouth. Like Beeching, Castle opted to keep the line open from Exeter to Okehampton. But wielding her social criteria, she also added a short commuter line out of Plymouth to Bere Alston, to keep open the little branch line to Gunnislake on the former Callington branch. This neatly fitted the social criteria, as the line carried commuter traffic and it had been impossible to arrange a suitable bus service.

The Great Railway Conspiracy

The problem lay in the geography of the landscape, for the villages of Gunnislake and Calstock lay in hilly terrain within a loop of the river Tamar, not easily served by road transport. It wasn't natural railway territory either, but British Rail had inherited a fine viaduct across the river, so it was obliged to keep trundling trains across to the villages on the other side. Okehampton and Bere Alston would remain as branches, but the trunk route in between would close, leaving the regional centre of Tavistock – larger than Okehampton, Bere Alston and Gunnislake combined – without a station. The railway was left with two more or less uneconomic branch lines, while the biggest town in the area (and a useful diversionary route) had been lost. Surely, only the most dysfunctional political system could contrive such a disaster from such a rich bag of transport assets?

Areas of North Cornwall were now as far from a railhead as the remotest corner of Wales, with a complete cessation of services to Tavistock, Launceston, Bude, Holsworthy, Camelford, Wadebridge and Padstow. The express services had also helped to support the branches to Ilfracombe and Bideford in North Devon, and Sidmouth, Lyme Regis and Seaton to the south. One by one, these also died, endangering the remains of the trunk line from Exeter to Salisbury, which was downgraded to lowly secondary status and put on the doubtful list. Finally, the Exeter to Okehampton branch, bereft of through traffic, was deemed unworthy of subsidy, and lost its passenger service too.

None of these towns justified a rail link in their own right, but together they had sustained a viable network. Within a few years, the whole operation had collapsed, leaving a

The closure process could be deeply irrational. While busy trunk lines were being closed, some very minor branch lines were kept in operation. Alston in Cumbria and Bridport in Dorset survived until 1975 because alternative buses were hard to arrange. This is Bridport in 1973. PHOTO: David Henshaw

Swanage was not chosen for safeguarding in 'Network for Development', but it took a great deal of effort to close it, the last train finally running on 1st January 1972. By early 1974 the weeds were growing high, but the destination board remained. PHOTOS: David Henshaw

permanent population of over 60,000 people – albeit over a very large area – without adequate public transport. And such figures were just the tip of a very large iceberg, for the number of tourists denied use of the railways and forced onto the roads was considerably higher. This was all wonderful news for the Ministry of Transport, because more cars meant a positive cost/benefit analysis under the Social Surplus system, and more money for motorway construction.

A similar situation would arise should the Settle & Carlisle close, for according to *Network for Development*, much of the line from the north would be retained for freight use to serve military sidings at Warcop near Appleby, and from the south to serve quarries in the Ribble valley. Only the centre section would go, and with it would go all the through freight and passenger traffic.

By the end of 1967, just 9,882 miles of railway remained open to passengers, though the rate of closures was slowing, prompting Barbara Castle to announce that she had, "stopped the Beeching butchery!" In reality, the closure programme had almost reached its logical conclusion... the butchery had only lost momentum because there were few candidates left.

But that still left the 'non-selected routes', and after publication of *Network for Development*, all that stood in the way of their closure was the much maligned TUCC inquiry procedure. But public opinion had hardened since the Beeching era, and local authorities and pro-rail pressure groups had learnt a great deal. Even the TUCCs themselves were taking a tougher line.

As expected, British Rail wasted no time in bringing forward closure plans. In late 1967 it made public its intention to close the Swanage branch in southeast Dorset from September the following year. It had, however, underestimated both the level of opposition and the logistical difficulties of providing replacement buses to cope with summer traffic. The Swanage branch failed to close in 1968... and in '69. Indeed, so vociferous was the opposition from pressure groups, local MPs, the County Council and various other local authorities, that a public inquiry was called. After hearing the evidence, the Department of the Environment inspector decided that the line should be reprieved, but his decision was later overturned by the Secretary of State for the Environment, and closure eventually came in January 1972.

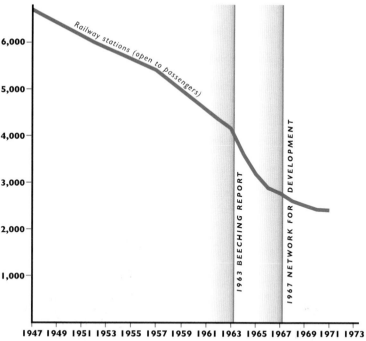

The graph of station closures is quite revealing. Beeching's damaging 'Reshaping' report was *unnecessary, because a measured programme of closures had been underway since nationalisation and was set to continue, although hopefully the network would have stabilised at a higher level. Barbara Castle claimed to have 'stopped the Beeching butchery!' with 'Network for Development', but only because there were few realistic candidates left. These later closures were the most controversial.*

In contrast, some very minor branches were to survive, simply because bus services were difficult to arrange. Bridport in Dorset and Alston in Cumbria had both outlasted much more lucrative branch lines. In Bridport's case the problem was with two very small villages en route, as unusually, the bus to Bridport itself was more direct and faster than the branch line, which wiggled south from Maiden Newton, where a change of trains was required.

Alston was a bit different – a much smaller town, but awkwardly situated high in the Pennines, and suffering from severe weather in the winter and tourist issues in the summer. When the line finally closed after the Department of Transport offered money to create a so-called 'all weather road', Northumberland County Council said it would rather use the money to support the rail service. It was denied the opportunity.

Barbara Castle may have failed to halt the railway closures, but she was emerging as an able transport minister in other areas. After taking advice from the Joint Steering Group, she prepared a formula to head off the railway's financial crisis, while taking a serious look at road problems, particularly where heavy freight vehicles were concerned. In a brave attempt to clarify the road costs debate, she undertook a detailed analysis of the problem, anticipating that major changes would be incorporated into a new Transport Act.

On a simple year-by-year basis, it emerged that road users were paying more in taxes than the Government was spending on road construction and maintenance: in 1965-66, road costs had amounted to £450 million, while tax income stood at £926 million.

If, however, the roads were subject to the same financial scrutiny as the railways and other nationalised industries, the annual costs rose significantly, to £625 million. And after making an allowance for 'community costs', including accidents to non-road users, airborne pollution and noise, it emerged that the road accounts were actually in deficit, and road users were not paying enough. The overall figures were open to debate and interpretation, but it was becoming very clear that heavy road freight was causing a disproportionate amount of environmental damage, just as Beeching had claimed, and provision was made in the forthcoming Transport Act to raise an extra £30 million annually from the road haulage industry. The British Road Federation spent £50,000 fighting the proposals, and it would prove to be money well spent.

The Wilson administration was in difficulties, for the technological revolution had failed to go according to plan, the hottest bits proving not nearly as white-hot as had been expected, while the heavily subsidised car and aircraft manufacturing industries were in need in need of seemingly unending support. The 1968 budget had been harsh, and with the fortunes of the Government teetering on the brink, Wilson moved quickly to placate the road lobby, promoting Barbara Castle to the Ministry of Labour, and bringing in Richard Marsh at Transport. The forthcoming Transport Act was amended to remove the taxation on heavy vehicles in favour of a small extra tax increase on fuel for all road vehicles, effectively a subsidy for lorries paid for by all motorists. Barbara Castle, the only post-war Minister to stand up to the road lobby, had been removed for political reasons.

As expected, railway closures continued to concentrate on the lines that had failed to make it onto the *Network for Development* map, and matters came to a head in July 1968, when the new Transport Minister finally approved closure of the Waverley route, claiming an annual saving of £700,000 (£25.7 million today). Given that the Railways Board had only put forward a loss of £256,000 a year at the 1966 TUCC inquiry, it was an extraordinary figure. The reason for this strange anomaly was shortly to emerge in the provisions of the 1968 Transport Act.

After a record 45 sittings at the committee stage, and no fewer than 2,500 amendments, the most radical transport legislation since 1962 became law in October 1968. The effect on the railways was immediate and profound, because, as in 1962, the intention was to make the railway system financially self-supporting. Once again, various capital liabilities were written off, but it was hoped that the long-term objective of commercial viability would be achieved by the provision of grants, rather than further cutbacks.

The Railways Board had hoped for a 'surplus capacity grant' to cover the cost of maintaining double or quadruple tracks that were not immediately useful, but might, in case of national emergency or severe weather conditions, prove essential. But the Ministry presumably came to the conclusion that surplus capacity would never again be needed, for the Act provided instead for the railways to be paid a grant to scrap surplus equipment, a move that was expected to produce an annual income of around £15 million. The grant arrangements placed great pressure on the Railways Board to remove track and equipment as rapidly as possible – often before they became due for replacement – yet it was an area where careful study of future trends was important, and would have shown up some very expensive errors of judgement.

By the time the 1968 Transport Act had been published, there was already plenty of evidence that over-enthusiastic pruning could be counter-productive. Almost the entire 90-mile route of the former LSWR trunk line from Salisbury to Exeter had been reduced to single-track in the summer of 1967, with gaps of up to 20 miles between passing loops. The effect, far from saving money, was close to disastrous, because the prospect of even a minor breakdown on a long stretch of single-track trunk line was so nerve-shattering that the railway authorities are said to have provided a mechanic on every locomotive, just in case! Gradually, the situation was eased, but putting track back was a lot more expensive than taking it out. A new passing loop was provided near Tisbury in 1986 at a cost of £435,000, and a three-mile stretch of double-track reinstated at Axminster in 2009 cost £20 million.

Integration of road and rail transport remained as elusive as ever, although the 1968 Act made a move in the right direction by establishing Passenger Transport Authorities (initially Conurbation Transport Authorities) in the West Midlands, Merseyside, Greater Manchester and Tyneside, whose job it was to co-ordinate bus and rail services locally. Other PTAs followed in Greater Glasgow (in 1973) and in West and South Yorkshire with local government reorganisation in 1975. The Authorities, managed by Passenger Transport Executives, would make agreements with British Rail and other transport operators as to the level of fares and subsidies in their regions. Finally, the urban branch lines were safe in local hands, and the system went on to be very successful, resulting in many examples of bus/rail integration, renewed investment and fast-growing traffic.

Another attempt at integration, known as 'Quantity Licensing,' was incorporated in to the Act, but it met with such hysterical abuse from the road lobby and the road transport trade unions, that it was never successfully implemented and was repealed shortly afterwards by the incoming Conservative Government. Quantity Licensing was an echo of the freight vehicle mileage restrictions bound up in the 1947 Act. The operators of the largest vehicles would be obliged to offer first refusal to the railways on traffic carried more than 100 miles, or less where the merchandise included coal or minerals. If the railways were unable to match the road operator in terms of price, speed and reliability, the traffic would go by road... but if the railway could offer a better deal it would go by rail. Besides all manner of difficulties in actually implementing the legislation, the whole affair raised one rather obvious question. If the railways were keen to tender at a favourable price, there should have been no need for compulsion, which showed the railway management in a rather bad light, and merely reinforced the widely held view that the railways were just another 'lame duck' nationalised industry.

As expected, the unremunerative or social railways were to be subsidised with the aid of grants. In future, British Rail would put forward grant applications for loss-making services, and the Government would authorise an annual grant (expected to be in the region of £55 million in total) to make good the deficit. Perhaps inevitably, there was a catch. There was no specific guarantee that a particular service would receive grant aid, not even those that had been selected for development the year before. Cash would only be forthcoming for those lines that met vague social and strategic criteria set by the Government, and the grant aid arrangements were to be no more than a temporary measure. None would be authorised for more than three years, and most would be subject to annual renewal. Most critically, with respect to the Waverley route and other big candidates, was that the grants were expected to be capped in the first year. So a £700,000 annual grant for the Waverley route, or even an initial (and inaccurate) estimate of £390,000 for retention of the line north of Hawick, would jeopardise other, possibly worthier, lines.

Of even more significance was the system put in place to calculate the grants. Sir William Carrington's formula, in use since 1962, were thrown out and replaced by a new costing technique known as the Cooper Brothers formula, after the firm of chartered accountants (whose Henry Benson had served on the Stedeford Committee) that produced it.

There were several significant features to this new formula. The Railways Board was to take no account of contributory revenue, true engineering costs would be ignored and replaced by a relatively high 'average' figure, and 12 1/2% would be added to cover administrative expenses, regardless of the actual figure. The formula also took little account of freight and other services that might be sharing certain costs. The new system had the effect of pushing on-paper losses through the ceiling, with the result that insignificant branches suddenly appeared to be responsible for unlikely deficits.

The practical effect of the Cooper Brothers formula became apparent when Corby Urban District Council applied to British Rail for reinstatement of passenger services over the 7½ mile line from Kettering to Corby. As the line carried a good deal of freight traffic, the Railways Board agreed, subject to a token annual grant of £10,000. While negotiations continued, the Cooper Brothers formula was introduced and the Board hastily revised the grant requirement to £45,000, a figure that proved quite unacceptable to the Council. Rail services would not be permanently reinstated to this town of 61,000 people (thought to be the largest town in Europe without a rail service) until 2009. By 2011, the new station was generating 176,000 passengers a year, far more than had been predicted.

The Cooper Brothers formula was responsible for the dramatic jump in subsidy for the Waverley route, and it's worth noting that the figure of £700,000 amounted to about £7,000 per mile, the expenditure Beeching had considered necessary to maintain a railway *with no income at all.*

Willie Ross, the Secretary of State for Scotland, was rightly convinced that the loss of the entire line would be a disaster for the region, and he pushed to the bitter end for retention of the Galashiels to Edinburgh section, at least on a temporary basis. The problem was that the Railways Board was asking £220,000 to £310,000 [18] to keep even this section open, and without Frank Spaven, the Scottish Office had no railway experts to dispute the figures, leaving the Ministry of Transport as the only arbiter, and of course the Ministry wanted the Waverley route closed. Richard Marsh, newly arrived as Minister of Transport, was also looking to his civil servants for guidance, and they were only too willing to oblige. Marsh was never to make a public pronouncement about his pivotal role in the affair, but in 2006, during an off the record conversation with retired railway manager Mike Chorley [19], he volunteered that the biggest mistake of his life had been closing the Waverley route. According to Chorley, after a few drinks, Marsh recalled: "It was not really my fault – I was badly briefed. I should have looked more closely *at what I had been told to say."* [Author's italics]

At 7pm on 21st May 1968, the last rites of this last big railway closure were acted out at a meeting in the House of Commons, attended by Willie Ross, Richard Marsh and five other government ministers. All the usual arguments were raised about railway figures, the lack of investment, loss of confidence in the region, and so on. But crucially, there was no money on the table, as grants under the Cooper Brothers formula were already expected to run £7 million above the £55 million budget.

The meeting decided in favour of closure of the whole line, to be implemented as rapidly as possible. Ross made a final desperate plea to the Prime Minister, making the point that the young Liberal MP for the area, one David Steel, was intending to resign and fight his seat on the Waverley issue, something that would cause great damage to Labour in terms of Scottish public opinion. Richard Marsh had been copied into this memo, and he responded with a telling comment: "If we were to change our minds on this case, then it would be extremely difficult to persuade the country to accept the closure of many other services." On 5th June, the Prime Minister responded, saying he regretted the decision, but giving it his final stamp of approval. On 15th July, Richard Marsh made the announcement to the House of Commons, and it was all over. It can't have been missed by those with nationalist sentiments that the final decision on an essential part of Scotland's infrastructure had been made in London, by an English politician advised by Home Counties civil servants, against the express wishes of the Scottish Office.

The Great Railway Conspiracy

The 1968 Transport Act had set an important principle. The commercial lines and freight operations were to be viewed as self-supporting, and London would receive a single block grant to cover the cost of commuter and social services. All other services were to receive grants, but only where the Government considered the subsidy to be cost-effective.

For British Rail, now very much a minority player on the transport scene, the effect of the over-generous grant formula was quite beneficial, enabling it to make up losses in other areas. According to one member of the Railways Board, the grant-aided lines had become the railway's 'most profitable' services. But for the handful of remaining marginal branch lines, the grant system was to spell disaster.

Whether by accident or design, the Government had come up with an answer to the uneconomic railway problem, by offering grant aid, but inflating theoretical costs to such a degree that the lines were easily written off. It wouldn't have mattered in the slightest (apart from the effect on the morale of provincial rail staff) if all the loss-making services were to remain grant-aided, but it soon emerged that they were not.

The first block of grants, representing estimated losses under the Cooper Brothers formula, amounted to £62 million. So generous was the formula that almost every railway in the country was to receive some degree of financial assistance. The effect on management and union morale of crack expresses receiving subsidy cannot have been very helpful, but the real problems lay in store for the branches.

The Government had decided that a selection would not be eligible for grant aid, including 130 miles that had been declared worthy of retention under the *Network for Development* plans just a year before:

Railway Service	Grant Claims
Bridgend to Treherbert	£150,000
Bangor to Caernarfon	£60,000
Colchester to Sudbury	£90,000
High Wycombe to Bourne End	£60,000
Colne to Skipton	£110,000
Kidderminster to Stourport via Bewdley	£55,000
Cambridge to St Ives	£120,000
Exeter to Okehampton	£150,000
Kirkham to Fleetwood	£120,000

Some of the grant claims for insignificant services were quite astonishing. The Exeter to Okehampton line carried considerable freight traffic, yet the basic passenger service was reckoned to cost £10,200 a mile. Cambridge to St Ives also carried freight, yet it was estimated to be costing £8,100 per mile to maintain the passenger service. For the Railways Board there was every incentive to err on the high side in making grant applications. If the grant was approved, the money could be used elsewhere and if it was refused, it had a perfect excuse to close the line, and a Government-stamped overwhelming financial case to support closure.

All the lines that were refused grant aid, or failed to receive a full grant, were put up for immediate closure by the Board, and all but the Sudbury branch subsequently did, although some lingered for a few years. British Rail subsequently admitted that many

Of all the branch line closures, Caernarfon must rank amongst the most serious errors. Beeching had recommended closing it with the through line to Criccieth in 1964, but it survived as a branch from Bangor, and was given the green light by Barbara Castle in Network for Development, although closure finally came in 1970. The town only has a population of about 10,000, but it's an important regional centre, and a major tourist destination. Reinstatement would be complicated by road developments on the route, and the station site has gone, but there are no insoluble problems. PHOTO: Kevin Lane www.flickr.com/photos/28083135@N06/

decisions taken at this time were in error, particularly the closure of the Caernarfon to Bangor line, where the hidden contributory revenue had been particularly high, and nearly all was lost after closure. Interestingly, of the nine lines that did close, Bridgend to Treherbert partially reopened as far as Maesteg in 1992, and there were very strong campaigns to reopen most of the others (see chapter 10). Even the Caernarfon branch, which was partially obliterated by the Ministry of Transport during trunk road improvements in the early 1970s, was by 2013 being seriously considered for reinstatement.

In addition to the grant package, the 1968 Transport Act wiped out most of the railway's outstanding debts, and the result of these two moves was to produce a modest £15 million surplus the following year, and a rather smaller one of £9.5 million in 1970. It was a totally false situation though, for investment had dropped from a less than satisfactory £121 million in 1965, to a derisory £69 million in 1969.

The new railway system, billed as compact, modern and efficient, was really demoralised, inefficient and chronically short of investment capital. The closure programme was more or less complete, yet even those who had approved of the closure policy admitted that savings had been small. There had been no real administrative savings, and closures had contributed no more than a quarter to the general rise in productivity since the start of the programme, while contributory revenue of at least £11 million a year had been lost for good.

This was the situation on the eve of a new decade, as a smug and self-confident western world floated high on an ocean of cheap and plentiful oil. Just three years later a cataclysmic shock would arrive, changing attitudes to the motor car for ever - the 1973 Arab oil embargo. But in 1970, no-one foresaw that, and the railway crisis was to get a lot worse before it got better.

8
The Energy Crisis
1970-1990

"Our Continental friends just do not understand how we could allow our railways to be butchered as they have been in the last 15 years, and with the impending energy crisis we may very well be frantically trying to restore in ten years time facilities which we gaily abandoned ten years ago..."
J D Wylde, Transport Co-ordinating Officer for Leicestershire County Council, September 1973

Transport policy needs to be prepared for any eventuality - the Yom Kippur War.

*B*y the late 1960s, the burgeoning railway preservation movement appeared to offer hope to those who continued to oppose the railway closures. The first priority was to keep track on the ground then, at a later stage, when the preserved line was up and running, it might be possible to restore a proper service. Wages made up as much as 60-70% of British Rail's operating costs. It followed that a preserved line, staffed almost entirely by volunteers, could realistically maintain a year-round service where the unwieldy national concern had failed.

But after several brave attempts, these 'privatisation' attempts ultimately proved fruitless and the railway system continued to contract. By early 1973 the financial situation had reached crisis point again, but just as the Government was considering whether to instigate another round of closures, the oil crisis arrived, denting the seemingly unassailable position of the road lobby, and permanently altering the balance of transport economics.

In the decade that followed, faith in the private car started to crumble, and railways began to take the initiative. In 1983, the rail lobby scored a decisive parliamentary victory with the introduction of the Speller legislation that eased the path of railway reopenings. By the late 1980s, the long awaited railway renaissance had arrived, and the financial situation was looking relatively secure.

The heritage movement had preserved railways, but none of them had become transport operators in an 'A to B' sense. People usually visited by car, looking for entertainment. This is Horsted Keynes on the Bluebell Railway in 1972, but it could just as easily be 1932 or 1952, which is precisely the aim. The Bluebell finally reconnected to the network in Spring 2013. PHOTO: David Henshaw

From humble beginnings, with the preservation of the little Talyllyn narrow-gauge line in 1951, and the standard-gauge Bluebell line in 1960, the railway mileage in private ownership had steadily increased. It was not, however, until the successful reopening of the Keighley & Worth Valley and Dart Valley lines in the late 1960s that the preservation movement began to be taken seriously.

After a fitful start, the pioneer preservation bodies had proved that railway nostalgia was a marketable commodity. But would they be able to put trains back into service on a year-round basis? There were many sceptics, for although some 50 miles of line had been transferred into private hands by 1969, not a single mile had seen the return of a full service on a permanent basis, and the majority of lines were open to the public for just two to three months a year. The sole exception was the 15-inch gauge Ravenglass & Eskdale in Cumbria, which operated a single daily train... but the Eskdale was a miniature line, and in any event, its 'social' service was withdrawn in 2001.

Many potential operators had grandiose plans, and 1969 saw publication of the longest, most daring and potentially the most prestigious scheme of all. The Waverley route had closed in January 1969, the longest and most hard-fought railway closure in the country, and it seemed fitting that the line should also be the test-bed for a new and radical idea: a privately-owned and fully commercial trunk line.

Many had felt the closure was an act of monumental folly, and even British Rail was later to admit that the line would have been extremely useful, initially as a diversionary route during electrification to Glasgow, then as a feeder route into the fast new electric services after completion of the Glasgow scheme in 1973.

It was exactly as Professor Hondelink had predicted. Paradoxically, the modernised services had improved the viability of former 'duplicate' routes, which found a new role - and many new passengers - feeding traffic onto the main lines. This scenario had never occurred to Beeching, who saw little future for passenger traffic and was completely fixated with the idea of concentrating high volumes of freight onto a small number of trunk lines.

Had the BTC been allowed to electrify the entire West Coast Main Line in the 1960s, the future of the Waverley route would probably have been assured, for when the electric trains finally arrived, they cut the journey time from Carlisle to London to four hours, giving a new potential for a feeder service from Hawick and Galashiels. Today the electric trains do the same journey in 3 hours 20 minutes, so - had the Waverley survived - a Hawick to Euston journey time of a little over four hours would be quite feasible, against five hours 20 minutes by bus to Carlisle and train, and an optimistic six hours 20 minutes by car. In reality, the car and bus options are rather tenuous, and the business traveller from Hawick today would most likely drive to Newcastle and fly south.

All these arguments were being aired in 1969, and it certainly looked as though the 100-mile Waverley route could be operated as a viable and profitable private company. Seasonal steam trains would satisfy the tourists and generate valuable income, while diesel multiple units would handle the day-to-day business and connect with British Rail services at Carlisle and Edinburgh.

A group of individuals formed the Border Union Railway Company in February 1969, and began to seek financial support for the project. Initially, British Rail was by no means unco-operative, offering to negotiate running rights into both stations, and suggesting a sale price of around £750,000 for the line... a reasonable if not over generous figure.

The Border Union scheme was quite out of keeping with any railway heritage project before or since. Most of the line would be reduced to single track, but there was talk of diesel railcars, gas-turbine locomotives, low-loader wagons to

Although the heritage railways prefer to be seen as serious transport undertakings, there is a danger of their become theme park rides. Swanage, pictured here in 2003, is an honourable exception - it already carries visitors to the town from a park-and-ride, and in a couple of years it hopes to have established a 'serious' rail service. The M7 tank engine is the surviving sister to the locomotive on page 49. PHOTO: David Henshaw

pick up containers from an M6 railhead, and other more or less commercial schemes. The line would provide employment for about 100 ex-BR employees and, unlike the majority of heritage lines, the North British Railway (as the operating company was to be known) would not be seeking a light railway order. The promoters were certainly not short of ambition.

Almost immediately, there were financial and legal problems as the company became bogged down in negotiations with the Railways Board purchasing the line and access to the stations and freight yards at Edinburgh and Carlisle:

"...there would appear to be no insuperable difficulty in accommodating your services over the Board's lines into each terminal, [but] your company"s services must at all times take priority behind the Board's services, whether the latter are running late or otherwise... the Board will not be prepared to offer co-operation in respect of through bookings..."
BRB Estates Manager to Border Union Railway Company 12th June 1969 [20]

This sort of thing was bound to give potential investors the jitters, and the Border Union needed £1,500,000 to get things moving, on which they were promising a very optimistic 8-10% return. They received a very flat 'no', when they presented a business case to merchant bank National Commercial & Glyns through the Hawick branch of Royal Bank of Scotland. The end came on 6th October 1969, when the Railways Board lost patience and asked for some serious money: £745,000 to £960,000 for the freehold, track and fixtures (or interest of 10% per annum on the £495,000 of assets the Board was still waiting to recover), £125,000 annually for running powers onto BR tracks, an immediate £10,000 to cover administration costs, and a non-returnable £250,000 deposit to be paid by 1st December. This was a higher purchase price, higher access charges, and all a lot sooner than expected. The Ministry for Transport chipped in, demanding £170,000 to build a bridge over the line for the M6 motorway. The Border Union had a great deal of

The Border Union was an over ambitious private scheme, and once negotiations were at an end, track-lifting recommenced. This is Newcastleton in 1971. PHOTO: Bruce McCartney

enthusiasm, but no real business case, and no backers. Once the company had missed the 1st December deadline, the venture was effectively at an end, and exactly a year to the day after the passing of the last train, British Rail announced that negotiations were at an end, and track-lifting recommenced. By late 1972 it was all over.

Despite all the optimistic forecasts, the Border Union plan had been too ambitious. No private operator had yet succeeded in purchasing such a large railway, and the general feeling from the private companies and enthusiast groups that *had* got heritage schemes off the ground was that there was no particular need for any great rail mileage. Car-borne visitors were generally satisfied with a short ride, and the most successful heritage lines were mostly less than ten miles long, and many were less than five. With the exception of the Keighley & Worth Valley, none had yet secured a proper connection to the rail network, and none had introduced a year-round service. With the collapse of the Border Union, it became clear that 'preserved' railways were to be just that - short stretches of track maintained as working museums and generally preserved in the heady aspic of a rather vague golden era, set somewhere between the 1930s and 1950s.

To those who had become involved with these schemes out of frustration with a Railways Board that seemed bent on self-destruction, the heritage movement was ultimately to prove a disappointment, and there were many heated battles between the preservers and the re-instaters, although the financial case for seasonal heritage services always won through. The heritage groups had neither the resources nor the incentive to operate full commercial

The Ilfracombe branch line was one of many that lingered untidily after closure when a preservation attempt failed. The branch closed in October 1970 and was lucky to have lasted that long, having been recommended for closure by both Beeching and Barbara Castle. By 1973, the platforms were starting to deteriorate, but track wasn't lifted until 1975. PHOTO: David Henshaw

services. The assumption was that volunteer labour would reduce costs sufficiently to make a year-round service pay, but a suitable formula was to prove elusive.

Like the Border Union, several brave schemes were to collapse when faced with the cost of purchasing surplus track and equipment. Sometimes the value placed on a time-expired railway line did seem high, but negotiations with individuals sometimes took years and got nowhere, whereas a quick sale for scrap often raised less, but it raised it straight away. The Government could have instructed the Board to look more favourably on restoration projects, and where schemes were not being discussed, to safeguard the route for possible future reuse, but this was rarely done.

The heritage groups argued that British Rail had a duty to charge sub-market rates for a scheme to preserve railway heritage, but the Board was under pressure to dispose of the assets as quickly and quietly as possible.

The most successful ventures were those backed by enthusiastic local authorities, able to buy the complete railway, or trackbed alone, and lease it back to a heritage group, often for a peppercorn rent. Typical was the Paignton to Kingswear branch, which - typical of many West Country branch lines - carried 20,000 to 40,000 passengers a week in the summer, and less than 6,000 a week in the winter, and was put up for closure in 1968. The prospective purchaser, the Dart Valley Railway Company, was offering to instigate a year-round service, and the overjoyed local authority offered British Rail £3,625 a month to keep things ticking over until the private company was ready to commence operations.

On 30th December 1972, with the line safely transferred into private hands, the private trains took over, but after one gloomy winter and successful summer season, the line closed for the winter in October 1973, Alan Sanders of the Dart Valley Railway explaining that the winter services had proved 'a financial burden'. Something British Rail could have told them at the start.

The loss of winter services to Kingswear marked the end of the privatisation dream, and the County Council, which had expected great things of the arrangement, was left to provide a bus service for school children at short notice. The Paignton & Dartmouth Steam Railway is today a prosperous tourist attraction and most definitely an asset to the local area, but despite having an end-on connection with national rail services, it provides no through fares and no connections. Trains now run for most of the year, but only at times to suit the tourist market. Talk of a diesel multiple unit social service continues to be raised every now and again, but the company - like many others - has little interest or incentive in operating unprofitable trains.

Devon County Council had helped to save the Kingswear line to take pressure off the Paignton to Kingswear road, and the Skegness line had won a full reprieve for similar reasons. Others, including Mablethorpe, Hunstanton, Ilfracombe and Swanage had succumbed, although the case for retaining these branches (during the summer at least) had been very strong.

To the local authorities, the attitude of central government must have been frustrating at the very least. The Government had failed to provide grant aid for branch lines that were a lifeline when the roads were gridlocked, but it had also failed to provide the new roads that might have helped alleviate the worsening traffic situation. Truly, the Cooper Brothers grant formula had worked its wonders in a most peculiar way.

At Swanage, a heritage group circulated a petition in the town and found an encouraging 86% of residents were in favour of a restored service. The line had closed in 1972 after a protracted battle, finally settled by the Minister, and although (or perhaps because) the Swanage Railway Society had offered to purchase the line on the basis of an independent valuation, the Railways Board tore up the track in seven weeks.

Undaunted, the Society grew into a powerful and influential body, and in 1974 it issued

With the threat of a Corfe Castle bypass lifted, the Swanage Railway was able to start relaying into Corfe Castle station in the late 1980s, paving the way for eventual reopening through to the main line. PHOTO: David Henshaw

detailed plans for a proposed year-round 'amenity' service to be subsidised by summer steam operations. Dorset County Council was sufficiently impressed to buy the entire trackbed, a move that prevented the usual piecemeal development (the authority had its own plans for a bypass at Corfe Castle which would have finished the project for good). With the railway gradually being reinstated, the preservation company and local authorities set up the Purbeck Community Rail Partnership in 1997 with a view to furthering the ambition of a genuinely useful amenity service from the main line at Wareham to Swanage. The preserved rails finally met British Rail metals in January 2002 at Motala Sidings near Wareham, and since then many special charter trains have run straight through from the main line to the Isle of Purbeck.

Special trains every few weeks in the summer were a very different thing to an hourly year-round service of course, and there were many obstacles to providing regular amenity trains, not least being the need to fit in with the busy and profitable steam-hauled services, which operated every day for eight months of the year, and used most of the line capacity for the busiest three summer months. The scheme also needed proper signalling arrangements to succeed, and the make or break moment came in 2008, when Network Rail announced that the main line was to be resignalled, giving a one-off opportunity to include bi-directional signalling for branch trains on the short stretch from Worgret Junction to Wareham station, with the new system fully interlocked with the Swanage Railway's own signalbox at Corfe Castle.

Once again, Dorset County Council took the plunge and agreed to underwrite the £3 million cost of the work on the main line and the private branch, with a firm May 2013 deadline for completion. Writing in 2013, it is clear that the resignalling will make charter trains much faster and easier to accommodate, and enable the railway to establish an 'amenity' service connecting with network trains at Wareham. Will a full service ever be restored?

The figures from 1974 show just how much of a financial burden year-round operation can be for a small company. The estimate at the time was that an amenity service for Swanage would earn in the region of £34,000 a year (£645,000 today), but this would have to be offset against costs, including the then insistence that British Rail train crews must pilot trains between Wareham and Worgret, plus signalling and maintenance to main line standards, which would run to around £82,600 (£1.57 million today), the resulting deficit of £48,700 being borne by the summer service, leaving an annual profit of just £3,000.

Today, the figures look more promising, with a consultant's report in 2008 suggesting

More than 30 years after closure, the Swanage Railway may yet become the first heritage line to run a full year-round service. Resignalling work proceeds at Worgret Junction in February 2013. Looking from the Wareham direction, the Swanage branch diverges to the left as a train passes on the Down Weymouth line. PHOTO: David Henshaw

additional revenue of around £1 million a year from a full community service, and on recent form that's bound to be exceeded. But the Swanage Company remains concerned that amenity trains will cause timetabling issues and abstract revenue from premium steam services. On the other hand, the company would earn year-round revenue as a ticket agent, selling tickets to and from network destinations, or even became a main line Train Operating Company. These 'serious' transport activities might eventually prove more valuable than the seasonal heritage services.

In early 2013 the project received a £1.47 million grant from the Coastal Communities Fund to prepare the railway infrastructure for a full service. Through trains will run for 50 days in the summer of 2015, 90 days in 2016, and, hopefully, year-round after that. Exciting times.

One of the longest running closure dramas had been acted out at Minehead. At the closure inquiry in 1968, the local bus company had informed the TUCC that six buses would suffice to operate the winter service, but even 20 vehicles might prove inadequate on a summer Saturday. The bus company didn't have the resources to cope with such an influx and, in any event, the long and rather tortuous road link between Taunton and Minehead would also have trouble coping. British Rail, on the other hand, was determined to close the line and, armed with the Cooper Brothers formula, it announced a loss of £141,000 a year.

The Great Railway Conspiracy

By January 1971 a compromise had been agreed under which the line would close, a move that left Somerset County Council far from satisfied. The County Council agreed to buy the line - in this case largely intact - and lease it back to the West Somerset Railway Company, which would operate a full winter schedule in addition to the usual tourist services in the summer months. In order to get a return on its £245,000 investment, the Council would charge the railway company an annual rent of £14,000, with the inducement that most of it would be returnable should the company instigate a year-round service.

Through no fault of its own, the railway company never fully succeeded. The bus drivers (who were, ironically, mostly NUR men) adopted an intransigent attitude to the scheme, and British Rail found a variety of reasons to refuse running rights into Taunton station. The sight of Sidney Weighell, the then General Secretary of the NUR, arguing *against* a rail reopening scheme did not do a lot of good for the credibility of the union at the time.

As the years passed, the affair was gradually forgotten. The bus company never did require 20 buses, as most of the former rail traffic either evaporated or took to private transport, the local residents came to accept seasonal traffic congestion as a way of life, and the West Somerset Railway - after a very rocky start - began to turn in a small profit on its summer services. It looked as though Minehead had left the national network for good in 1971, but in 2007, Victa Westlink ran summer Saturday timetabled services from Bristol to Minehead, primarily for visitors to Butlins holiday camp. Although a success in terms of passenger numbers, this single unique service left Minehead on Saturday mornings, and returned in the afternoon, making a day trip to the resort impossible. To date it has not been repeated, and despite a more 'can do' attitude from National Rail, even through running into Taunton remains as far off as ever.

Some heritage railways near big cities, such as the Watercress Line, Severn Valley and Keighley & Worth Valley, have found an end-on connection with the national network extremely useful, and others - such as the isolated Bluebell Railway - are going to great lengths to reinstate a link, but these are primarily for charter trains and stock movements. Ironically, the net effect of preserving railways had been to increase road traffic rather than reduce it, because although the tourist potential of the lines had exceeded all expectations, most visitors arrive by car.

Local authorities seeking to

After an all too brief experiment in 2007, the special Butlins trains to Minehead ceased, and for various reasons the trial has not been repeated, despite proven demand. PHOTO: Michael Wadman

maintain or enhance rail services were having more success negotiating with British Rail, as the Railway Development Association and Railway Invigoration Society (which had been working quietly behind the scenes) had long argued that they should. In June 1971 the line between Peterborough and Spalding reopened with local authority grant aid, after being closed to passengers for eight months. It was a unique arrangement that was to provide a template for many similar schemes where track had remained in place for freight services. Unfortunately, proving that lack of foresight was alive and well in the railway mindset, the success of the Peterborough to Spalding link encouraged British Rail to withdraw all services on the March to Spalding line, which was subsequently lifted. Within 20 years, this decision was already being regretted, and in 2013 options were being tentatively explored to reopen this link, principally to keep freight clear of the East Coast Main Line, but potentially for passenger services too. In this case, as in many others, the trackbed has been partially blocked by housing and road construction... a common issue, caused by *laissez faire* planning guidance. Railways were seen as having little value, and former railway corridors even less.

But where track remained in place - especially for other passenger services - it was easier to put a station or local rail service back, and from very tentative beginnings, the tide began to turn, when Gipping Rural District Council finally won a protracted legal battle to have Needham Market station reopened in December 1971. Such small victories heralded a trickle of reopenings in the 1970s.

However, the national picture remained bleak in the first half of the decade. April 1970 saw the demise of the Cambridge to St Ives line, which carried a considerable amount of freight, and had been listed for development by Barbara Castle, but had lost its grant nonetheless, making rather a nonsense of Castle's claim to have 'stabilised' the network. Later in the month, the Ashford to Hastings line, which had *not* been listed for development, won an 11th hour reprieve, when a bus licence was temporarily refused pending road improvements. In October, the Railways Board mopped up in Lincolnshire with what would amount to the last major railway closure, finally killing off the lines between Lincoln, Firsby, Louth and Grimsby. The only remaining link in the south of the county was the line to Skegness via Boston, which had only survived because the approach roads to the town were saturated with traffic in the summer season. In May 1970 the Railways Board began to run down the Settle & Carlisle trunk route, which had also been listed as unworthy of development in 1967, presumably on the advice of the Central Planning Unit. If so, it was an odd choice, as freight was, and would remain, its *raison d'etre*. Following a now familiar pattern, the Board closed all the local stations just in time for the summer season, presumably in the hope of provoking a collapse along Waverley lines.

In June 1970, Ted Heath won a surprise election victory, bringing the Tories back to power, and the road lobby back to a position of influence. The Heath government tried to combine the doctrines of the welfare state with the economics of the market place, and succeeded in doing neither. Indeed, the main effect of this 'soft' capitalism (later gleefully condemned by Prime Minister Margaret Thatcher as 'wet' politics), was an uprising of industrial militancy culminating in the three-day week and strict power rationing, which damaged industry, and of course the railways.

Transport policy stagnated during the Heath years. The new Minister for Transport Industries, John Peyton, made it clear that he had little time for loss-making nationalised industries, and the railways in particular. But his appointment seemed to please the road lobby and, in April 1971, the British Road Federation, the AA, the RAC, the Road Haulage Association and the Freight Transport Association came together to set a target of 3,000 miles of new

The Central Wales line survived on a thread of political expediency. It had been recommended for closure by both Beeching and Barbara Castle, but somehow pulled through. Marketed today as the 'Heart of Wales' line, it is being promoted very positively, both for local and tourist transport. PHOTO: Courtesy of Heart of Wales Line Forum, Colin Baglow

motorway. Two months later, the Government announced a programme that included 2,000 miles of motorway and 1,500 miles of dual-carriageway. It was close enough.

Beyond the commuter lines in and around London and a few major cities, little remained of the 'social' rail services, the majority of the survivors being concentrated in thoroughly unremunerative regions, such as central Wales and the Highlands of Scotland. In these remote regions, poor roads made the railways an essential lifeline, and to city commuters (where the motor car had made travel just as difficult), the railway was grudgingly accepted as the only practical means of transport.

By 1973, the closure process was virtually complete: a system that had once run to more than 20,000 miles had been cut to 11,300 miles, but in terms of passenger services, the picture was far bleaker than the figures suggest, for a proportion of the remaining network carried only freight, and of the remaining passenger lines, many had lost all stopping trains.

Some remote services had survived on a thread of political expediency. The Central Wales, from Swansea to Shrewsbury, had been listed for closure by Beeching and Barbara Castle, but it was said to pass through so many marginal constituencies no-one had dared to do the deed. British Rail, which had begun the familiar winding down process in the early 1960s, was told to make a few economies and keep the trains running. Thanks to better timetabling and promotion, receipts had more than doubled by 1972, but thanks to the odd logic of the Cooper Brothers grant formula, expenses were reported to be a staggering £464,000, against income of only £45,000.

The nearby Cambrian Coast line proved similarly charmed, surviving all manner of vicissitudes, and a pilot cost/benefit analysis study by the Ministry of Transport's new Economic Unit aimed at establishing benchmark figures on the true worth of rural railways. Released in early 1969, the report *A Cost/benefit Analysis of the Retention of Railway Services on the Cambrian Line* caused so much disquiet in scholarly transport circles that several learned papers subsequently disputed the figures. The Ministry had put the net cost of running this basic railway for the next ten years at £1,768,000, less £534,000 for wages paid to employees who would otherwise be unemployed and thus a drain on the public purse, giving a global cost of £1,234,000, against social benefits of £538,500, putting the net cost of retention at £695,500.

The Cambrian Coast line was very lucky to pull through, but it's a thriving operation today, providing local transport for school children, shoppers and commuters, and a vital long-distance link to Birmingham and beyond. In October 2012, a Class 158 pulls into Fairbourne with a train for Pwllheli. The Class 158, introduced in the 1990s, was quiet, fast and efficient, and did wonders for rural train services. PHOTO: David Henshaw

The argument that the railway could be treated as a transport network *and* a job creation scheme in an area with few employment opportunities was an interesting one, but as the economists both for and against rural railways set to work, it all became a lot more esoteric. The Ministry had argued that fare revenue was irrelevant to cost-benefit analysis, which would be fine if the revenue had been included elsewhere in the computations, but it had not. According to a paper by R D Evans [21], this omission was as surreal as anything dreamed up by Lewis Carroll. Evans applied the Ministry figures to a hypothetical railway, providing consumer benefits of £2, fare revenue of £6, and operating costs of £5. On the Ministry's analysis, with fare revenue omitted, the line would clearly be a big loss-maker. But he went on to argue that if the same Ministerial logic was taken to its conclusion, reducing fares to zero would increase consumer benefit to £8, making the line soundly viable!

The Great Railway Conspiracy

A detailed study in 1972 by Keith Richards of the University of Bath [22] took the same data, and turned the Ministry's disbenefit of £695,500 into a net *benefit* over ten years of between £374,000 and £1,011,000. This was in part through the assumption that there would be an increase in road accidents should the railway close, and that within three years of the Ministry's 1967 census, passenger numbers on the line had increased by 64% (actually an 80% rise in summer and a 30% fall in winter). The greater usage naturally increased the social benefits of keeping the line in operation.

In December 1970, while the Railways Board was still scratching its head over the sharp increase in patronage (due in part to a new Sunday service), the Minister announced that the line's Cooper Brothers grant would be withdrawn, and it was subsequently put up for closure. Politicians were getting wise to the public mood by this time, however, and the actual deed was postponed over the 1970 election, and subsequently rescinded altogether, possibly because the politicians couldn't understand a word the economists were telling them. Nevertheless, the Cambrian was to have a bumpy ride in the next few years, including a survey by Professor Graham Rees of the University of Wales, Cardiff, in June 1974, which suggested that only 1.9% of Meirionnydd residents used the line, and just 3% of tourists arrived by it, with another 7.2% coming by coach and the rest by car.

Today, in common with most other rural lines, the Cambrian is seeing a dramatic increase in passenger numbers, running at around 6% a year between 2002 and 2010. But in the 1970s - with railway finances still in a poor state - it had survived by the narrowest of margins. Despite the generous grant provisions of the 1968 Transport Act, the railways had been unable to service investment from revenue, and by 1972, finances were once again on the critical list. Closure proposals had been prepared for most of the Welsh and Scottish lines, and the Government was looking hard at the value of the whole network.

Fortunately, the road system was creating problems of its own. In 1971, annual expenditure on British roads had reached £812 million, while tax subsidies for company cars were said to be costing the nation somewhere in the region of £1,000 million a year. Against such huge figures, a railway line that served most of central Wales for rather less than £70,000 a year looked something of a bargain. Despite the gloom, the British railway system continued to provide excellent value for money when measured against its overseas rivals. In 1971, the German system received a subsidy of £700 million, the French £400 million, while the much vaunted Japanese railways had been subsidised to the tune of £300 million, and received an additional £500 million to cover capital expenditure. British Railways made small losses on top of a grant of around £60 million and wound up £150 million in the red after interest.

In comparative terms, the cost of the railway network was fairly modest, and there was a growing feeling that the roads might not after all be the panacea that had been promised in those heady days of the early 1960s. Railway closures had helped throw such a volume of traffic onto the roads, that local and national authorities were finding themselves forced into a vicious spiral of road spending that promised to far exceed railway losses.

The pendulum had swung so far in favour of road transport that the Government was now obliged to subsidise the road system. If a road improvement scheme was refused, industry would reply with the quite justifiable objection that output would be affected, and with no alternative means of distribution, it might have to move elsewhere. In the early days, the threat was generally to move elsewhere in the UK, but increasingly it came to mean elsewhere in Europe, and eventually to the Far East. Also, if a new bypass was rejected, the local community could legitimately point out that their lives were blighted by the high level of through traffic.

The true cost of pouring investment into a single mode of transport had been high.

Congestion alone was calculated to be costing around £700 million, although like the financial value of railway branch lines, there continues to be considerable debate about the true cost of road congestion to the economy. More recently, estimates have varied from £7 billion a year (Sir Rod Eddington, 2006) to £30 billion a year (Goodwin, 2004) [23]. The role of road building in reducing, or even increasing, congestion has become an equally divisive and complicated subject, although even in the 1970s there was a growing body of evidence that the long-held dogma of judging the railways by financial performance was too restrictive, and that external factors, such as pollution and road congestion, need to be considered when looking at rail subsidies.

In 1972, these arguments were brought sharply into focus with publication of a report by the Organisation for Economic Co-operation & Development, entitled *The Motor Car & Natural Resources*.

In Europe, congestion was still localised, and pollution of little consequence. But North American experience was telling a different story. The brave new super-highways of the 1960s, that had received such praise in the British Parliamentary debates of the Beeching era, were now clogged with traffic, and the Los Angeles skyline wreathed in poisonous smog.

The immediate concern of the OECD was whether the world would actually be able to accommodate the growing volume of road vehicles. By the year 2000, the report predicted, there would be more than 28 million in the UK, and 500 million throughout the world (estimates which proved uncannily accurate). The assumption was that the cities of the world would succumb one by one to the nightmare of airborne pollution and oil (suddenly deemed a finite resource) would run short from the turn of the century, and become a rare commodity by 2075. Car ownership was reaching saturation point, particularly in the USA, and there didn't seem to be any easy solutions:

"...there is now in the USA a great awareness that the growth of the private car must be curbed; that its price is enormous in terms of congestion, pollution, accidents, the destruction of cities by roadworks and many other social costs; and that future growth should be prevented as far as possible, by both restricting the private car and forcing the development of alternative means of transport."

According to the OECD, similar measures would be necessary in Europe within 20 to 30 years. If not the end, it was certainly the beginning of the end for the road-based economy. By 1972, road transport in the USA was guzzling almost 30% of the country's total energy consumption, and almost everyone had grasped that the situation would need to be held in check. Unfortunately, the British had blindly followed the American lead and were still chugging towards the unattainable goal of complete freedom for the private car. The road had led, literally, nowhere.

Although road congestion in the States was a serious issue, it was mostly confined to the big cities, but overall, Britain had the most congested roads in the world. Ignoring the small city-states, Britain ranked high in the world congestion league table, on a vehicle per mile basis, lying in third place behind Korea and Jordan, which had far fewer cars, and even fewer roads. Japan (with a large and viable rail network) supported 24 vehicles per mile, the vast highway network of the United States carried 28 vehicles, and Germany 55, but the little British Isles supported a total of 15 million vehicles... more than 62 for every mile of road. In 2012, it still dominated the tables, but there were now 123 cars per mile in the UK. [24]

Despite clear evidence for Britain being somewhat over-dependent on the car, the OECD report had little impact in the UK. In June 1972, the Minister for Transport Industries called for a review of the railway's current position and future prospects. The Railways Board

The Great Railway Conspiracy

replied in June 1973 by answering the three questions posed by the Minister:

- **What has gone wrong in the past?**
- **Is there a viable rail network?**
- **Is there a 'necessary' rail network?**

It was a crisis examination of the most fundamental kind, but under the decisive leadership of former Labour Transport Minister Richard Marsh, who had gone native, and was now Chairman of the Railways Board, the industry fought back. 'Within the present financial terms of reference,' said the Board, 'no railway network would be viable.' According to Richard Marsh:

"We then told the Government they must accept the fact that there were no benefits from cutting the system and that it must be accepted that the social benefit to the community as a whole by keeping it intact was far greater than the book-keeping loss."

The Board now openly accepted that many of the closures made during the Beeching, Castle (and of course, Marsh) era had damaged the viability of the lines that remained open, and it followed that a smaller network would never be financially viable. Growth, on the other hand, could be achieved, but it would need £1,787 million of investment over a ten-year period. The Board was unable to define 'necessary', as it considered this was something only Government could ascertain as part of its overall transport strategy. The Government, however, was still unable to choose a clear option, and faced with a demand for almost £2,000 million from a loss-making nationalised industry, it stalled.

One option would be to continue investing in roads, in the vain hope that the increase in road mileage would eventually outpace the growth in the vehicle population. The

In the end, it depended what sort of world we wanted. Even Los Angeles, which had become the archetypal car-centric city by the 1970s, would later put back some commuter rail services. PHOTO: Private Los Angeles Tours

One of the last closures was Alton to Winchester, a country line that could have continued to be a useful diversionary route had it been electrified, but it ended up as an island of diesel operation in an electric region. The line had failed to make it onto the 'Network for Development' map, finally closing in February 1973, a week after this photograph was taken. Had it lasted another eight months, the fuel crisis would probably have saved it. PHOTO: David Henshaw

Government, still undecided about whether to impose further surgery on the railways, began to think seriously about such a policy. Construction of Ringway One, an inner orbital motorway for London (first advocated by Marples) was given serious thought as well, although the road would cost £600-£2,000 million and cut a swathe through residential London.

Meanwhile, the public were calling for freight to be guided back to the railways, and the Minister responded by reconstituting the figures that had been trotted out during the Beeching era. Carrying 50% more traffic by rail, it was claimed, would reduce road traffic by only 2%. What this statistic conveniently ignored was that the reduction would be in the heaviest and most damaging long-distance traffic. Increasing the level of rail freight by 50% might well reduce the number of vehicle movements by only 2%, but in terms of ton-miles transferred from the roads, the figures would look very different. In 1972 the roads carried ten times as much freight as the railways, but in terms of ton-miles the ratio was reduced to less than 4:1. Pro-rail campaigners suggested that the railways could easily handle a 100% increase in freight ton-miles, thus reducing road carriage by a third. There were similar arguments, both for and against, with respect to passenger statistics.

Perhaps the arguments served only to prove that statistics could be made to prove anything. There was no disputing the accident figures though. During the two-year period 1971-72, there had been just five deaths amongst rail travellers, and more than 15,000 on the roads. In any event, the various arguments for and against road transport were about to be taken out of the Government's hands by factors far beyond its control.

The Great Railway Conspiracy

In October 1973 - in retaliation for supposed Western backing of Israeli forces during the Yom Kippur war - the Arab oil-exporting countries increased oil prices by 70% and imposed sharp cuts in output. The results were immediate and far-reaching. Fuel prices doubled, then quadrupled, leaving the long-standing complacency of Western governments largely shattered. Despite a gradual realisation that oil would eventually run out, no-one had seriously thought that the oil producers might hold the world to ransom in the meantime...

Suddenly fuel of any kind, but oil in particular, became a valuable commodity, and the private car (as the least efficient consumer of fossil fuels) was to bear the brunt of the crisis. In November 1973, petrol ration books were issued to British motorists (although rationing was never actually implemented) and on 5th December a blanket 50mph speed limit was imposed on all British roads. By the end of the month, the country was in the grip of a full-blown crisis: industrial strife brought a return of the three-day week, and high oil prices caused the balance of trade to lurch disastrously into the red.

The search began for fuel-efficient, and preferably multi-fuel, transport... something like the railways perhaps. Within six weeks, the Government had dusted off its railway files and offered the industry some hard cash... not quite as much as the Railways Board had wanted, but £891 million would finance a five-year investment programme, and there would be grants to keep operations afloat on a day-to-day basis.

There had never been any doubt that rail was the most efficient mover of people and freight (over long distances at least), but it was really only in Britain that the advantages of a

The Isle of Skye is the romantic backdrop as the evening train from Kyle passes Erbusaig Bay on its journey to Inverness in the early 1980s. With little local traffic, the Kyle line had been under threat of closure for 30 years, but it was extremely popular with tourists travelling on 'Rover' tickets - a hidden and very lucrative source of income. PHOTO: N E Stead

broadly-based transport policy had been ignored. Consequently, of all the European industrialized economies, it was Britain that received the sharpest shock. Ironically, we were close to being a major oil exporter ourselves, but although oil had been discovered in the British sector of the North Sea as early as June 1969, the full extent of the reserves had yet to be established, nor was it known for sure that the oil would be economically recoverable. Road transport still relied on large quantities of imported oil.

Independent transport observers had seen the risks of such a policy for years. All of Britain's major competitors - Germany, France, Italy and Japan - had invested heavily in rail electrification and freight facilities, and all had made fewer cuts to passenger services.

The immediate oil crisis soon passed, to be replaced by a global recession, causing the plans of the Arab oil exporters to backfire somewhat. The recession, coupled to increasingly frugal oil consumption, and new reserves (notably in the North Sea) had caused the global price to drop, but transport economics would never be quite the same again.

Unfortunately, the demoralised and crisis-ridden railways were not in a position to capitalise on the motor car's temporary demise, and such was the inertia behind the retrenchment process that closure plans continued to hit the headlines. In Scotland, it was announced that the Dingwall to Kyle of Lochalsh line would close on 1st January 1974, and the Fort William to Mallaig branch later in the year.

In the event, neither plan came to anything. In the case of the Kyle line, Edinburgh-based consultants PEIDA - who subsequently were contracted by the local authorities fighting the Settle-Carlisle closure - carried out a broadly based study which showed, amongst other things,

Sometimes the pruning went too far. The former LSWR trunk line to Exeter was largely singled in 1967. Here at Seaton Junction, just one line remains, where once there were two loops for stopping trains, and two through lines. The line has since been expensively redoubled just to the west, and redoubling is quite possible here too. The station - which depended on traffic from the Seaton branch line - is unlikely to reopen, but it's worth pointing out that the Seaton tramway (built on much of the old branch) terminates just a mile and a half away. It could be extended! PHOTO: David Henshaw

that British Rail had failed to consider the income that would be lost from the sale of 'Rover' tickets, the line receiving much of its income from this source.

Although the railway system wasn't yet ready to grasp the nettle and fight back, the aftershocks from the oil crisis continued to reverberate, leaving even the most sceptical Minister of Transport keen to keep the remaining network intact. The railways were an alternative transport network that could move a lot of people and commodities with relatively little oil, and an electrified railway could bypass the oil sheiks altogether. Gradually, as the reality of the situation began to sink in, the mood swung in favour of rail transport.

In February 1974, the Heath Government finally succumbed to the overwhelming might of the unions. In response to an increasing militancy on the part of the mineworkers that had begun to threaten the very fabric of Britain's parliamentary democracy, the Tories called an election, lost, and returned (possibly with a sigh of relief) to the opposition benches. Harold Wilson returned to power as leader of a minority government, although a second election in October was to give him a distinctly marginal majority of three.

In April 1974, John Peyton, the outgoing Minister of Transport Industries announced a moratorium on railway closures until the end of the year, and the railway press, which had remained oddly acquiesent to the closure programmes of the preceeding 20 years, started once again to lobby on behalf of the industry. Gradually, journalists began to put their heads above the barricades. According to *The Railway Magazine*, some of the economy measures taken by the Railways Board had been counterproductive: removal of points at Windermere at the terminus of the one remaining branch into the Lake District, had made it impossible for locomotive-hauled trains to visit the line, and the last remaining section of the Oxford to Cambridge line (still carrying a few desultory local services between Bedford and Bletchley), was uneconomic and bound to remain so without the traffic from the through route. The Bedford-Bletchley conclusion wasn't surprising. At the east end (see page 168), the trains had continued to run into a near derelict Bedford St Johns station, a long walk from possible connections at Bedford Midland, and at the west end, they terminated at Bletchley, rather than the big regional centre of Milton Keynes. The schedule was 42 minutes - 16 minutes slower than the fastest times a quarter of a century before.

As the smoke cleared from the blood-letting of the 1960s, it became clear that there had been some serious errors in the closure programme - the Cambrian Coast line would have been much more successful had it remained open through to Caernarfon and Bangor rather than terminating at Pwllheli, and there were other gaping holes in a network that suddenly felt very ragged. It looked like poor planning, but the truth was that few people in the Railways Board had expected these disjoined, run-down fragments to survive at all.

Transport 2000, formed in 1973 as one of a new breed of radical pressure groups, unearthed some interesting fuel efficiency statistics, many gleaned from the Department of the Environment's own files. An urban traffic study in 1971, before the fuel crisis, had found that the average car travelled around 30 miles on a gallon of fuel, whereas a two-car diesel multiple unit travelled around four miles on every gallon. These statistics were not new of course, but what had not been studied was that the average car carried just 1.3 occupants, while the average diesel unit carried 35... The fuel consumption per passenger was thus 39 miles per gallon by car, and 140 by train. And had all seats been filled (four in the car, and 140 in the train), the differential would be even more striking - 120 miles per gallon by car and 600 by train. Taking speed into account, the two-car multiple unit was as much as six times more efficient than a car. In fact, the humble diesel units, designed in haste in the early 1950s, appeared to be amongst the most economical of *all* transport vehicles. This had been the case since 1954, but while oil was a burn-and-forget commodity, no-one had given fuel efficiency any thought.

Clearly, in a world of finite resources, it made sense to encourage passengers to use the railways, because the more passengers they carried, the more fuel efficient they were. These new 'environmental' arguments added a new dimension to the fiscal debates that had ranged back and forth since the Beeching era. In global *environmental* terms (something that Beeching had never been asked to consider) a diesel unit bearing a mere 35 passengers was more efficient than a fleet of cars, and far more efficient (with every seat occupied) than a bus, a car, a moped, or any other road vehicle. The environmental case for keeping the railway network was suddenly very compelling, while the short-term and somewhat arbitrary guideline that each service should be profitable (whatever that meant) receded into the background - the fuel crisis had made the railways essential. British Rail announced that most of the diesel multiple units (some of them 20 years old) would be refurbished to provide another ten years of active life... many of them were to remain in service a good deal longer.

The new Government bowed to the inevitable and granted the railway network a total of £2,130 million, including up to £1,500 million to support the less economic services for five years, and a rather more modest sum to cover capital investment. The same Parliamentary Bill introduced incentives to industrial concerns wishing to build (or reinstate) private sidings for rail traffic.

Commercial objectives were thrown out of the window, and for the next five years, the railways were cushioned with a blanket of state finance. Public expenditure cuts and the ongoing energy crisis had brought about a change of policy - the road-building programme would be reined in and the surviving railway network retained. Most of the remaining branches and secondary services were safe, including six that had come perilously close to closure: the Cambrian Coast, Kyle of Lochalsh to Dingwall, Ashford to Hastings, Bedford to Bletchley, Wimbledon to West Croydon and Stockport to Stalybridge. Only the Alston and Bridport branches were to close and, although both provided an essential service in remote rural areas, these closures did at least affect a relatively small number of regular travellers. There were plenty of other closure scares in the mid to late-1970s, but few were successfully implemented.

The downside of the new financial arrangements was an increased burden of state inter-ference, for all policy objectives would, in future, need to be approved by central Government.

Meanwhile further studies confirmed that this new pro-rail policy made sense. In 1975, the Central London Polytechnic initiated a Survey & Review of the Exeter to Barnstaple rail service, the only passenger line remaining in North Devon. British Rail was claiming a loss of £98,000 a year on the service, but the survey estimated that contributory revenue might be as high as £700,000, making closure proposals a nonsense.

Further studies dismantled other Beeching assumptions. Experience had shown that railway subsidies were far more cost-effective than ostensibly smaller bus subsidies, because the rail replacement bus services were losing most of the traffic built up by the much-maligned railways over a century or so, and in many cases simply faded away. Few bus services had kept more than 20% of the former rail traffic.

The cost of subsidising 'rail replacement' bus services had been transferred from the railways to the National Bus Company under the provisions of the 1968 Transport Act. The assumption in the early 1960s had been that most services would be self-supporting, but because of the hemorrhage of traffic, the viable ones were few and far between. As early as 1965, the bus operators had suggested that buses were losing former rail traffic to the private car, but at the time the loss had been dismissed as part of a general move away from public transport. A decade later, according to David Glassborrow of the National Bus

The Great Railway Conspiracy

Company, the writing was on the wall for the buses that had replaced the branch lines:

"Very often these special bus services are very lightly loaded. The fact that any passengers remained on the railway services was almost certainly due to the unsuitability of bus services... in one or two recent cases the average number of passengers was less than one, that is, on some days he got a lift by car one way..."

The failure of the so-called 'bustitution' policy had many causes. In some cases, the railways didn't follow a suitable route. This applied particularly to the Alston and Bridport branches, both of which ran the 'wrong' way to reach the mainline and had only survived because viable bus services had been hard to implement. The high speed and guaranteed connections of the branch line had worked well, while a bus could easily take twice as long to cover the same ground in a rural area. When the Bridport branch closed, the disappointed bus operator found that traffic had slumped to a quarter of its former level in a few weeks, and the service was soon withdrawn. For both Bridport and Alston, the real traffic was east-west rather than north, and a bus that pottered off in the general direction of the railway junction couldn't hope to compete.

Buses were perceived as being low status, and they were certainly slow. This meant they appealed only to those unable to drive, whereas local rail services with modern diesel trains had been holding their own - particularly on services from rural areas into large towns and cities. This was a common scenario where buses lost time on rural roads, then got stuck in traffic entering the urban area. In Bournemouth, where the average speed of the buses had dropped to 11mph, the cost of congestion had been calculated as 5% on gross expenses for every 1mph lost from the schedule. The Greater London Council had reached a similar conclusion - that a 1.5mph drop on speed (from 11.5mph to 10mph), added about 11% to costs.

Bustitution had seemed natural and logical in the 1950s, but with the gradual spread of traffic congestion, and worries over fuel security, the remaining secondary and branch railways began to look much more valuable. This is the 408 Carshalton to Guildford service in 1980. Even with a change at Epsom, this journey would have been quicker by train! PHOTO: John Parkin Collection

Far from reinforcing marginal bus routes, the railway closures had forced many people to buy their own transport (usually a car), precipitating the near collapse of rural public transport. By the mid-1970s, the buses were losing business at the rate of about 2% a year. Cars suffered from poor rural roads and urban congestion too, but motorists were willing to put up with a lot of inconvenience to keep their private space around them.

According to the South Western TUCC, more than half the replacement buses introduced since 1962 had been quietly withdrawn a decade later. Such evidence was to have a profound effect on the attitudes of the Consultative Committees which finally realised they had been seriously misled:

"Had it been known between 1962 and 1969 the replacement buses could by government order be taken off after two years without ministerial approval... it is likely that the committees would not have been so ready to suggest alternative means of transport, but rather to have informed the Minister that no reliable alternative could be suggested."
South Western TUCC, 1977

The various committees began to see themselves as consumer watchdogs, and as bustitution had clearly failed, they shifted their focus towards maintaining and improving rail services. In March 1978, the Central Transport Consultative Committee agreed to publish all future reports into prospective rail closures. It was a milestone in public consultation.

But if the oil crisis had lasted such a short time, why had the public mood continued to swing in favour of the railways? To a great extent, the 1973 oil crisis had provoked an awakening: a crystallisation of public opinion in favour of environmentally 'clean' public transport, and away from destructive road projects. Environmental views that had seemed 'cranky' or even anti-social a few years before had become acceptable, even fashionable.

As the decade progressed, the forecasts of the OECD began to take shape more or less as predicted - car ownership really was on target to reach saturation level by the year 2000. There was evidence that saturation point had already been reached in the major cities, where the growth in car registrations was starting to slow. Few people had predicted that the process would eventually spread to provincial cities, and even to Britain's larger towns, but as time passed the reality began to dawn. And the open road wasn't what it had once been either. In the wake of the fuel crisis, the 70mph national speed limit was restored, but only on motorways and dual carriageways.

Transport planners began to notice that saturation traffic levels produced some strange effects. Paradoxically, new road construction tended to attract traffic away from public transport, increasing, rather than reducing the level of congestion, while the loss of traffic from public transport tended to increase fares and reduce the level of service. The overall effect tended to leave both private and public transport slower and less convenient.

There were problems in store for the motorway network too. Not only had stricter speed limits and urban congestion negated many of the high speed benefits, but maintenance costs were rising far above predictions. Roadworks, and slow, dangerous contraflow diversions had become commonplace, primarily because bigger, heavier freight vehicles were causing more damage than had been expected. To make matters worse, there was pressure from the European Community for Britain to harmonise traffic regulations and allow Continental juggernauts of up to 38 tonnes onto British roads.

After two decades of prevarication, the Department of Transport grudgingly accepted that the tests carried out by the American Association of State Highway Officials in the late 1950s might be of value. After studying the damage caused by heavy vehicles in some detail, the

The Great Railway Conspiracy

AASHO had concluded that the damage to the road surface by a given vehicle axle was proportional to the weight carried by the axle to the power of four.

In other words, where it might be assumed that the wheels of an axle carrying ten tons would cause ten times as much damage as a lighter axle carrying a ton, the figure was actually 1,000 times greater. Heavy freight vehicles had wrought havoc on the motorway network, the figures suggesting that a poorly-designed 12-ton lorry with two axles might be causing as much damage as 160,000 cars.

The true cost of carrying freight by road in terms of congestion, pollution, damage to property and so on, would continue to tax engineers and economists in the years to come, but the 'fourth power' rule was found to be broadly correct. Today's bigger, heavier, but more scientifically designed 44-tonne juggernauts are thought to cause as much damage as 140,000 to 170,000 cars [25].

In the 1970s, the motorways were proving slower, more dangerous, and more expensive to build and maintain than had been predicted, whereas the railways were just finding their feet in an age of rapidly advancing technology. In 1976, a new type of long distance train achieved a permanent advantage over road transport, and put rail schedules within reach of the airlines, against every prediction in Beeching's two reports.

The High Speed Train was arguably the best train ever made, and by any standards a classic example of world-class engineering development that would turn around long-distance passenger services in the UK, and set standards for others to follow. A team of engineers and boffins had been fumbling forward with the Advanced Passenger Train for some years, but this was an over-complex and ill-conceived machine that would ultimately prove to be an expensive failure. While the APT was causing development headaches, a small team under British Rail's Chief Traction & Rolling Stock Engineer Terry Miller were quietly producing the train that would change the public perception of rail travel for good.

A former LNER apprentice who had learnt his craft under the great Sir Nigel Gresley, Miller developed a light, powerful two-engined diesel train that could cruise at 125mph, stop from that speed in the same distance as a conventional train from 100mph, and because of its modest axle loadings (the AASHO formula applied to railways too) had almost universal route availability. Development was authorised in March 1970, initially as insurance against the APT project running late, and the first prototype was ready in 1972. Series production followed, and despite long delays caused by union intransigence, the HST125 entered service on Brunel's superbly engineered Great Western Railway from May 1975, and on most King's Cross to Edinburgh services three years later. British Rail had introduced the 'Inter-City' brand a few years before, but clever branding was not enough on its own - it needed an iconic train too. Suddenly small boys were gathering at railway stations to write down numbers, and British Rail was fighting its corner in the passenger market from a position of real strength.

The High Speed Trains slashed schedules, and were responsible for Britain's first start-to-stop schedule of over 100mph in 1977. They also took a series of diesel train world records: 143mph in 1973, 144mph in 1987 (this time carrying passengers), and finally to 148mph in 1987, fittingly while descending Stoke Bank near Grantham, where the LNER's Mallard had set the steam traction record at 126mph in 1938, almost half a century before. The stream of records and growing InterCity passenger numbers were just what the industry needed after decades of gloom and retraction. The railways were back, with a vengeance.

The turn-round had been painfully slow, but under the energetic and enthusiastic leadership of new chairman Peter Parker, British Rail took the initiative, with the 'Age of the Train' advertisements, fronted by the chirpy, but with hindsight, decidedly odd, Jimmy Savile. The message was not so much that British Rail had turned the corner and limped into the 1970s, but that an entirely new age of rail transport had arrived. It was arguably one of the most successful British ad campaigns ever produced, and fixed the InterCity brand and the fresh, modern lines of the High Speed Train into the public imagination. For the first time in 40 years, the car looked the weaker of the two transport modes: slower, more dangerous and vulnerable to congestion. The headlines were about trunk routes and InterCity transport, but the magic came to touch every railway line from Penzance to Thurso.

In January 1978, the 'Beeching' process was put into reverse, and railway stations began to reopen - 13 reopened that year, lifting the number of stations from an all-time low of 2,358. In co-operation with local authorities, British Rail began to show a bit of imagination, stealing back traffic where the impact of the car had been particularly serious. In June 1978, an experimental park-and-ride facility was introduced to carry tourists into St Ives in Cornwall aboard branch line trains that had been threatened with closure less than a decade before. Ironically, the station had been shifted a few hundred metres out of town in 1971, and the original site turned into a car park for a few hundred cars. Seven years later, the railway was bringing in thousands of motorists, who now had to walk a little further to reach the town, because of the car-centric policies of the 1960s! Nothing could better have epitomised the changes that had taken place in a short time.

In Birmingham, the National Exhibition Centre was constructed adjacent to Birmingham International station, opened in 1976. Paradoxically, when the first motor show was held there two years later, 40% of visitors arrived by rail. Another success story came with the 'Parkway'

In 2012, a High Speed Train arrives at Bristol Temple Meads, the station that had seen the first high speed services 37 years before. In the tradition of the Gresley streamliners, the HST was one of the finest trains ever made. By revitalising InterCity services it helped to turn round feeder branches and secondary lines too. PHOTO: David Henshaw

station concept designed to attract motorists to rail for at least part of their journey. Sited near motorway or trunk road interchanges, the Parkway stations were on occasion used as an excuse for a lack of proper central facilities, as at Mansfield, where a rather optimistic Mansfield Parkway was constructed nine miles from the town centre. Some, like Tiverton Parkway, were expected to draw motorists from a very wide area (most of north Devon in this case), but as local rail made a comeback, the Parkway concept began to look counterproductive and dated. Nevertheless, some, like Bristol Parkway, and Southampton Parkway (adjacent to Southampton Airport) drew in new business, and helped British Rail to capitalise on the success of the High Speed Trains.

In urban areas, the Passenger Transport Authorities established under the 1968 Transport Act, were gradually finding their feet, and there were a number of constructive developments, including new stations and track refurbishment in Birmingham, Liverpool and Manchester. Tyneside went a step further and developed the Tyne & Wear Metro, built largely on the Newcastle suburban rail network, which had been electrified at the turn of the 20th Century, but had reverted to diesel traction under Beeching. Opening in 1980, the Metro was a clever and cost-effective rethink of urban rail transport that deserved to spread to other areas, but for various political reasons this never happened. The Metro continued to grow and expand, accounting for some 60 million passenger-journeys annually by 1983.

By the late 1970s, the Railway Board's attitude towards the heritage railway companies was beginning to change too, following the gradual realisation that a once-and-for-all scrap price was nothing compared to the contributory value of reopened branches, if only as tourist attractions. It became more accommodating.

In 1979 British Rail ran a series of special trains between Birmingham and Bewdley, where visitors were transferred to the Severn Valley Railway, and in 1981 it applied the same thinking to the Nene Valley line near Peterborough. In a more favourable climate, the heritage sector continued to grow rapidly, reaching 200 miles by 1981, and 500 miles 30 years later.

With the influence of the road lobby curtailed, and the railway industry growing again, the pro-rail lobby groups began to assume a more influential role. In 1978, the Railway Development Association merged with the Railway Invigoration Society to create a larger and more streamlined organisation, the Railway Development Society. In 1977, Transport 2000 took on its first full-time member of staff. Against a road lobby whose annual budget ran to hundreds of thousands of pounds, it was all very minor stuff, but sophisticated lobbying techniques began to yield results.

During 1979, British Rail carried almost a billion passengers and clocked up 19,900 million passenger-miles, more than in any year since the publication of the *Reshaping* report, and one of the highest peace-time figures ever recorded. The following year proved difficult financially, thanks to an economic downturn, but things improved in 1981, and at long last the railways scored a parliamentary success.

The pro-rail MPs in Parliament had achieved very little in the lean years, but in May 1981, an apparently insignificant piece of legislation reached its Third Reading in the House of Commons, paving the way for a minor renaissance on the railways. Like all the best legislation, the Transport Act 1962 (Amendment) Bill, put forward by Tony Speller, MP for North Devon, was almost impossible to argue against. It allowed British Rail to reopen railway lines and stations on an 'experimental' basis outside the provisions of the 1962 Act. The TUCC closure procedure had created a positive disincentive to reopen stations, because the Board was loath to reopen anything where subsequent closure might involve lengthy and expensive investigations, particularly now that the TUCCs were adopting a more assertive stance. Having opened a station, and found that traffic did not measure up to expectations, closure might be refused, leaving the Board stuck with a facility it didn't want in perpetuity. Under the Speller amendment, a station could be reopened on an experimental basis, and British Rail would require only six weeks notice to close it again. It was ironic that the impetus to reopen branch lines should come from legislation designed to *reduce* public consultation, but the Bill was to have the desired effect.

Tony Speller was on a mission to restore passenger services to all or part of the Barnstaple to Torrington freight line which ran past his home. Torrington was not a big town, but Bideford, two-thirds of the way along the branch, was.

On the *Reshaping* maps, Bideford was listed as one of only 12 stations in Devon earning more than £25,000 a year, and one of only two (Tavistock was the other) which had closed. By chance, the line had remained open to serve a china clay quarry, and since passenger services were withdrawn in 1965, there had been repeated calls for reinstatement. These had all failed, not because traffic forecasts were particularly pessimistic, but because the Railways Board, steeped in the surreal world of the Cooper Brothers formula, had demanded £175,000 to reopen the line to passengers, and an ongoing subsidy of £90,000 a year from the County Council. The Speller legislation was intended to ease such reopenings by allowing a limited experiment.

Once the Bill became law in August 1981, British Rail adopted a more conciliatory attitude to the North Devon line. The capital cost of reopening was now, apparently, just £36,000, giving an all-in cost for a one-year experiment of £120,000. But by this time the Council had lost interest - the North Devon Link Road was close to becoming a reality, and under tight financial strictures, the Council felt it had more worthy schemes to support. Reopening the line would have cost a third of the total annual subsidy paid to rural buses in the county.

Passenger services never did return to Bideford. Later in the decade the line closed to freight, and the track was lifted. It marked an end to the efforts of Tony Speller and the campaign groups who had fought long and hard for this most practical of reinstatements. In 2007 a new road was constructed across the trackbed, at a high enough level for underbridges to be included in the design, but of course they weren't, leaving the trackbed of the Bideford line blocked. Nevertheless, the reinstatement campaign remains as vociferous as ever.

For almost two years after coming into law, the Speller legislation had no tangible effects, but in June 1983 Pinhoe station on the former LSWR trunk route to Exeter, reopened on an experimental basis, and in October that year, another reopening on the same line brought real success. Templecombe station, formerly an interchange with the Somerset & Dorset railway, had closed in 1966, but a concerted local campaign brought a three-year experimental reopening and a steady flow of passengers. By 2012, a now secure Templecombe was generating over 100,000 passenger-journeys a year, drawn from a large, but sparsely populated hinterland. Within six years of Templecombe, another 48 stations had reopened.

The Conservatives had returned to power in May 1979, led by Margaret Thatcher, a right-wing politician who attacked public spending with an almost religious zeal. The cost of subsidising the railways had risen steadily and there were real fears that the Thatcher Government might attempt to reduce the burden on the taxpayer by drastic means. Thatcher was no enthusiast for railways, and she had an instinctive distaste for nationalised industries, but she was a pragmatic politician. The answer, in time-honoured fashion, was to put someone else's head over the barricade, by commissioning an expert to produce a report with suitably doctored terms of reference. In May 1982, the Government set up an inquiry chaired by Sir David Serpell (formerly Ernest Marple's Deputy Permanent Secretary at the Ministry of

ABOVE: *Bideford station in 2006. Don't be misled by the rolling stock, which sits on a very short stretch of line.*

BELOW: *The only serious obstacle to reinstatement from Bideford to Barnstaple is this major road intersection, built partially across the formation near Barnstaple station. In this 2006 view, the route of the former railway ran just to the left of this road underbridge and straight across the site to the line of trees on the horizon. With the usual lack of foresight, bridges or abutments were not incorporated into the design, although they could be retrofitted at a price.* PHOTO: *David Henshaw*

Transport, and a member of the Stedeford Committee) '... to secure improved financial results in an efficiently run railway in Great Britain over the next 20 years.'

The inquiry is said to have been the idea of railway chairman Sir Peter Parker, who was gambling it would endorse the case for rail investment, and bring an end to what he famously described as 'the crumbling edge of quality'. If so, it was a high risk strategy, because many in the Government were hoping to instigate a Beeching-style hatchet job. In the event, the Serpell Committee recommended neither course of action. Asked by the Secretary of State to 'open the doors' and engage in some blue sky thinking, the Committee put forward a number of more or less unpalatable options.

The most daring was Option A - a vestigial 1,600-mile network, linking London with Bournemouth, Cardiff, Liverpool, Manchester, Glasgow, Edinburgh, Newcastle, Leeds, Norwich, Dover, Folkestone, Eastbourne, Brighton and Portsmouth. This minimalist passenger network was expected to lose some £32 million, but make a £34 million surplus after freight profits were taken into account. Option B was for the identical InterCity network, plus some London

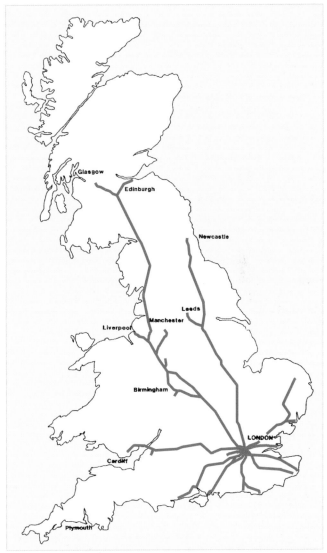

The media and unions concentrated their firepower on Serpell's most extreme 'Option A' scenario, but the committee wasn't recommending this, or anything else come to that. After the Beeching debacle, it would take a brave man to recommend axing almost 90% of the railway network

commuter lines, the Northampton loop, and part of the Berks & Hants line as a commuter branch to Bedwyn, making 2,200 miles in all. It was estimated this option would lose £72 million a year, or £19 million after freight profits. Option C1 lopped off just 80 miles, and some minor stations, leaving the network substantially intact with an annual deficit of around £800 million, and C2 was a tougher version, leaving a deficit of some £700 million after closure of 1,760 miles, mainly in Scotland, Wales and the West Country. C3 was tougher still, leaving only about half the network intact. Option D was similar to C2, but with communities bigger than 25,000 population added on, and Option H, interestingly, was a high investment option, with money put into new rolling stock and continuous welded rail, plus some modest network reductions.

It was all very neatly tabulated, but the conclusions were vague in the extreme. The Committee's preferred option was never stated very clearly, but it seems generally to have concluded that the network could be maintained at about its existing size with a similar or slightly lower subsidy for the foreseeable future.

One member, Alfred Goldstein, was unable to support this 'steady as she goes' conclusion, breaking away to implore the Government to go straight for Option A, cutting the railway back to the core 1,600-mile network, although like Beeching, he was somewhat cautious about guaranteeing a profitable network: '…even a railway service which appears viable is possible…'

In the end, the majority report listed options, but recommended nothing, and the rabid minority report guaranteed nothing but civil disobedience and humiliation at the polls. The Serpell Report consequently appeared, then disappeared under an onslaught of opposition from all quarters, some predictable - like the 25,000 name petition from the Railway Development Society - and others less so. According to the formerly very establishment Central Transport Consultative Committee, which Thatcher needed on side to carry out the dirty work:

"…there is a strong case for restoring rail links to some substantial communities now isolated from the rail network… bus replacement after Beeching was a total failure. If buses are to replace rail services in future, the conditions must be carefully worked out and monitored."

The CTCC, having made its views clear on the policy of bustitution, went on to advocate light rail techniques such as radio signalling, lightweight trains, and simplified level-crossings and stations. The consultative committees were still smarting from their involvement in the Beeching closures. They had been seriously misled, and put in the invidious position of recommending closures that denied much of the country access to public transport. They would not be caught out twice.

As the South Western TUCC succinctly observed, the previous round of closures had not only left people bereft of public transport, they had yielded virtually nothing in the way of financial savings:

"The involvement of this committee in the Beeching closure programme revealed to us that closures such as those envisaged in the Serpell Report do not in the end reduce BR's deficit by a great deal… when a local service is withdrawn, people tend to look for a through service either by coach or private car."

The conclusions of the Serpell Report fell on stony ground, in part because the financial position of the railways was about to improve beyond all expectations. In 1982, Chairman Peter Parker reorganised rail services into five quasi-independent sectors, three of which dealt with passenger services. InterCity would operate the prestige express services, Network Southeast (initially, and less inspiringly known as London & Southeast), the commuter trains in and around the capital, and Provincial the remainder, including the heavily supported rural lines.

If nothing else, the reorganisation allowed a detailed appraisal of the financial value of each freight and passenger service - particularly those that crossed one or more regional boundaries - and for the first time in years, the railways were given a proper financial strategy to follow. There are suggestions that 'sectorisation' was encouraged by the Thatcher Government as a means of preparing the InterCity lines for privatisation, but the effect of devolved decision making, renewed investment, greater manpower efficiency and improved morale was beneficial. More controversially, the railways began to improve the yield management of passenger services, by raising fares where the market could stand it, at peak times and on busy routes. To many people both within and outside the industry, sectorisation was the most successful railway reorganisation since the creation of the Big Four statutory companies in the 1920s.

In 1983, total external finance was running at around £900 million (£4.48 billion today), InterCity receiving £159 million in grant aid, Network Southeast £282 million, and Provincial £502 million, while Freight made a £27 million loss, and Parcels a £10 million profit. The miners' strike of 1984 slightly distorted the figures, but thereafter the financial picture steadily improved. By 1986, passenger volumes had returned to the 1979/80 figure of around 19 billion passenger-miles, with annual growth of about 4% in each sector.

As traffic grew, and the risk of politically-inspired closures began to recede, the decision was finally taken to replace the first generation diesel multiple units from the 1950s, although the last would remain in traffic well into the new Millennium. The new machines were a mixed bunch - faster and more fuel efficient, but in some cases cheaply made and poorly furnished, and crammed with seats to give the greatest possible space efficiency. A few four-wheeled light-weight designs were based on Leyland bus technology, but these 'Pacers' were mostly two-car machines, bigger and heavier than the railbuses of the 1950s. They were well suited to busy urban routes, and their introduction from the mid-80s helped the railway to deal with a rapid growth in local traffic, although passengers preferred more comfortable units...

Some Provincial services had seen traffic increase by 50% or more, and there had been some real success on lines reopened under the Speller legislation. The Bathgate branch in Scotland (closed to passengers in 1956, well before publication of the *Reshaping* report), was reopened in March 1986, with a prediction that passenger journeys might hit 278,000 per annum initially, rising to 335,000. In the first ten months, the line carried 500,000, with annual usage hitting a million by 1989. By 2010, Bathgate alone was generating 600,000 passengers a year, and the whole branch carrying nearly 1.4 million. The branch was later extended west to create a through line, of which more below.

The Bathgate affair raised two important points: early closure meant nothing where new housing and changing commuter patterns were likely to generate new traffic, and the consultant's predictions had been far off the mark. This was to be a recurring issue with line reopenings, and meant that reinstated facilities were often inadequate, requiring expensive upgrading later on. More importantly, if the lines that reopened were exceeding their passenger targets by a hefty margin, it could reasonably be supposed that others were failing to get the green light through pessimistic projections.

While lines were reopening, there were still a few closure dramas to be played out. The most serious, which highlighted once again the lack of strategic thinking behind the TUCC closure procedure, was the short link from Eridge to Tunbridge Wells, put up for closure in 1982. As was so often the case, this had once been an important strategic route, but earlier closures - principally of the short Uckfield to Lewes link in 1969 - had stripped away most of the useful traffic, leaving a loss-making branch.

Eridge to Tunbridge Wells had the potential to carry a great deal of traffic should the short missing link between Uckfield and Lewes reopen, and there had been a strong campaign for reinstatement since closure. But in true 1960s style, the TUCC inquiry in the summer of 1983 heard 300 objections on the grounds of hardship, and numerous other objections from local councils and campaign groups, but it was not allowed to debate the wider strategic implications of closure. In the event, the TUCC did all it could, rejecting closure on the grounds of hardship, but the Secretary of State Nicholas Ridley over-ruled the Committee, and consented to closure in 1985. The decision - one of the last of its kind - was a major strategic blunder, and development on the disused trackbed has since made reinstatement more difficult, though by no

Some of the 'second generation' multiple units were based on bus technology of the 1980s, with lightweight bodywork and a simple two-axle underframe. They were cheap to build and run, but the ride could be rough, particularly on the jointed track of minor branch lines. PHOTO: David Edge

means impossible. The loss of Eridge to Tunbridge Wells, and successful reopening of Bathgate, brought increased pressure for railway trackbeds to be protected from development, but for the time being, the Government refused to be swayed.

Within four years of the Eridge to Tunbridge Wells closure, Network Southeast announced that it was willing to put up a quarter of the then £6 million cost of reinstating the Uckfield to Lewes link. The original route into Lewes had long been obliterated by developments, but the alternative proposed in the late 1960s was still available. Sadly, Kent County Council and East Sussex County Council were unwilling to co-operate, and the moment was lost. It was, however, by no means the end of the story.

Elsewhere, British Rail itself was to look briefly at the viability of converting under-utilised lines into toll-roads. According to *New Scientist* magazine [26], chairman Sir Peter Parker had commissioned a 'Rails into Roads' report, after meeting Premier Thatcher's economic adviser Professor Sir Alan Walters and free market guru Sir Alfred Sherman at a dinner on 23rd June 1983. The whole thing had the stamp of crackpot economics about it, and it's hard to believe that Sir Peter was serious about running his own road coaches, or collecting tolls from other traffic. That might be why he insisted the study include some thoroughly unsuitable candidates, such as the London to Brighton main line and 'some or all' of the routes into Victoria, both of which would have been quite impractical for conversion. More manageable was a proposal to tarmac the long derelict Great Central route from Leicester to London, and close and convert the remaining run-down commuter routes into the Marylebone terminus, a network that was, at least, relatively self-contained. However realistic or otherwise the road coach proposals, British Rail was already planning to close Marylebone by diverting some rail services into Paddington, and extending the Bakerloo Tube line from Amersham to Aylesbury.

Groombridge, between Eridge and Tunbridge Wells, had been a major junction, but after closure in 1985, most of the station site was built over, leaving just the down loop line, which is used by the Spa Valley Railway. The line may yet reopen fully as part of the Brighton Main Line 2 scheme (see below and page 177), but Groombridge will remain a bottleneck. PHOTO: David Henshaw

Brighton Main Line 2 (BML2) is an ambitious scheme launched by the Wealden Line Campaign, which had fought since 1986 without success for the reinstatement of the Uckfield to Lewes line. BML2 proposes reopening Uckfield to Lewes and the associated Eridge to Tunbridge Wells line as part of a much bigger plan to provide double track, electrified secondary routes to London from both Brighton and Tunbridge Wells. Rather than reverse trains at Lewes to reach Brighton, BML2 suggests a new tunnel under the South Downs. This is all a great deal more expensive than a conventional railway reopening scheme, but the benefits are equally impressive. BML2 is an example of a new style of railway lobbying - slick, business-minded and making a well argued and defendable case.

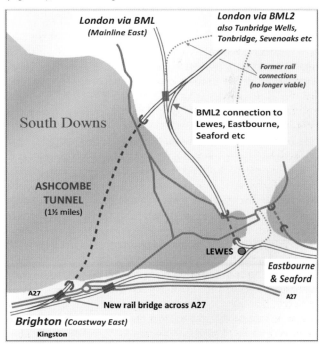

The Great Railway Conspiracy

On 15th March 1984, the same day that British Rail received the Coopers & Lybrand 'Rails into Roads' report, it, proposed closure of the Marylebone terminus, approach lines and minor stations. Fortunately, *Rails into Roads* had concluded - perhaps inevitably - that conversion simply didn't warrant the costs involved. The major lines were out of the question, the small ones uneconomic, and the mid-range Great Central scheme was riddled with glaring flaws. The trackbed to Leicester had long since been sold off, and the final approach to Marylebone involved a long, double-track tunnel that would have been hard to operate with conventional road coaches. There was also the thorny question of dealing with the uproar amongst (largely Tory-voting) Aylesbury commuters.

The Department of Transport already had two negative reports on road conversion on its desk, involving a major scheme to convert the four-mile Woodhead tunnel between Manchester and Sheffield that had failed because of poor ventilation, and a much smaller one involving a disused link near Croydon that simply wasn't viable.

Despite the enthusiasm of Premier Thatcher and her free-market gurus, the collapse of the Marylebone scheme really marked the end of the rail-road conversion debate that had raged since the 1960s. Marylebone was ultimately reprieved, although for the time being, a hostile and stymied government had no intention of allowing any rail investment.

Strategic blunders and road conversion aside, the big picture was looking brighter. By 1986, the railway's burden on the taxpayer had been reduced by a quarter, the Freight division was profitable and InterCity was on target to create a surplus as well. The British Rail Chairman, Robert Reid, proudly announced to his workforce:

"In the last three years we have together transformed the railway. Today we need £260 million a year less from the taxpayer. We have restored passenger volume to its highest level since the start of the decade. We have opened new routes and new stations, and each year new electric services begin operating."

It had been a dramatic turn-round, and the process was set to continue. By 1988, InterCity services had achieved profitability, and the more cohesive nature of the Network SouthEast commuter network had helped to increase passenger levels by 15% in three years. Efficiency had improved to such an extent that, while the number of train-miles had increased by 18%, unit costs had dropped by almost a third.

It all sounded too good to be true, and perhaps it was. When every last drop of efficiency had been squeezed out of the organisation, the Government pushed its financial demands further still. Subsidy had declined by half from 1983 to 1989, but now even the commuter services in the South East would be expected to run at a profit, and the eventual aim was for the whole network to cover costs. For the Thatcher regime, the sectorisation of British Rail would be used as a tool to split away the profitable parts of the organisation, and leave the branch and secondary lines isolated, loss-making and much easier to close... that, at least was the theory.

With little room for further savings through efficiency alone, the railways began to pare costs to the bone by running fewer carriages, and raising fares at above the rate of inflation for five consecutive years. The 1980s was to go down as the era of track singling. Simplifying facilities could save money in the short-term, but most of the economy measures instigated at this time would end up costing far more than they had saved, through delays, and the cost of later reinstating double track.

Sectorisation was further refined in 1990, with the 'Organisation for Quality' initiative, which devolved control further still, to the level of regional profit centres, which began to function more like independent businesses, albeit under central control from the British Railways Board. British Rail - still generally seen as yet another loss-making nationalised behemoth by the public at large, had been transformed into one of the most efficiently-run railway networks in the world.

The railways were to become victims of their own success, squeezed between Government demands for profitability and the demands of an ever increasing volume of passengers. By the end of the 1980s, train services had become overpriced and overcrowded. So high was the demand for certain express services, that aircraft-style boarding cards were introduced. It was all a very long way from the demoralised network of the Beeching era. After 30 years in the wilderness, the age of the train really had arrived, but not all the passengers were enjoying the experience.

In the Provincial sector, losses continued, although tight financial control, renewed investment and close tailoring of supply and demand yielded firm results. In 1983, the Government had given the go-ahead for a £1.7 million investment on the East Suffolk line, most of the money going into technologies that would further reduce manpower, such as radio signalling and automatic level-crossings. According to Gordon Clarke, the Divisional Manager:

"We wanted to show how cheaply we could run a railway... so we put all our forward thinking onto one line..."

It was 30 years since the Railway Development Association had advocated such initiatives, and nearly 20 years since Gerard Fiennes had first applied 'basic railway' thinking to the East Suffolk line. Radio signalling was introduced on the Kyle of Lochalsh line in the same year, and later, on the Mallaig branch and the Cambrian Coast, while the Central Wales line became a test-bed for a variety of light railway techniques.

Slowly but surely, stations continued to reopen, and by 1989 the total had risen to 2,440, growing at the rate of about 15 a year. Some were over-zealous Beeching-era closures on surviving passenger lines, but there were numerous reopenings of freight lines under the Speller legislation too, such as Oxford to Bicester Town (the western end of the Oxford to Cambridge 'Varsity' line), Coventry to Nuneaton and Heysham Harbour to Morecambe, which all reopened in May 1987. The following year saw passenger trains return to Aberdare in the Welsh Valleys, and in 1989 services resumed between Walsall and Hednesford in the Birmingham commuter belt.

The most exciting, and in many ways, reassuring development had involved the Settle & Carlisle, a trunk route that had survived being marked for closure in every railway report since 1963: *Reshaping*, *Development of the Trunk Routes* and *Network for Development*, the iniquitous Cooper Brothers formula, and a variety of bizarre closure proposals during the 1980s that would, at best, have seen the line converted into a sort of linear theme park. In the new era, even under the stewardship of a Prime Minister who would have loved to have signed the death warrant of the line, the authorities finally bowed to the inevitable: the Settle & Carlisle was too important as a freight route, and a diversionary passenger route, and it was fully reprieved in April 1989.

In 1990, the minor stations along the line were reopened and a proper timetable restored on what was, arguably, the most scenic railway in England. Almost overnight British Rail discovered that the Ribblehead Viaduct, far being in a state of imminent collapse, could be repaired economically, and a process of rebuilding and reinvestment commenced that has continued to this day. In 2012, the Settle & Carlisle was dealing with local passenger trains, long distance excursion traffic, diversions from the over-stretched West and East Coast lines, and a considerable amount of coal, although the latter was expected to reduce as coal-fired power

ABOVE: Bicester London Road closed in 1968, along with most of the 'Varsity' line, but this western end remained open for freight, and in 1987 a basic service to Oxford was reinstated from a single platform renamed Bicester Town, pictured here in 1992. From 2014, this whole area will be transformed, with double track and a new chord swinging away to the right beyond the crossing, to link up with the Chiltern line. Overhead electrification will follow, with through services to Milton Keynes and beyond
PHOTO: Ben Brooksbank

Heysham Harbour station reopened to passenger trains in 1987. Like many others, it was reopened under the Speller legislation that simplified closure procedures for reopened services which failed to meet expectations. Very few did. PHOTO: Community Rail Lancashire

stations were run down. Passenger traffic is more reliable, and the line is regarded as one of the best passenger earners in the Northern franchise area [27]. A valuable asset today, yet it came very close to closure more than once.

The Thatcher Government remained doggedly pro-road in its approach to transport policy. In the years 1989-90 rail investment reached an all-time high, with a promise of £3.7 billion in the following three years, but not a penny of that was forthcoming from central government, the whole investment plan being self-financing. Meanwhile, the financial noose continued to tighten around the grant-aided Provincial lines, with a target grant of £345 million (£807 million today) being set for 1993, a remarkably low figure. The funding picture was, however, becoming increasingly complex, with Passenger Transport Executive grants increasing rapidly, as the big urban conurbations looked for ways to ease chronic traffic congestion. In round figures, the total cost of state support to the railway industry was running at about £1.4 billion a year (£3.3 billion today) and on a generally rising trend, the subsidy accounting for 30-40% of railway income. These figures would come to mean a great deal in the years ahead, and would be spun back and forth across the political divide, because the Government was already preparing the railways for partial privatisation in the biggest shake-up in the industry's history.

Meanwhile, Mrs Thatcher's Great Car Economy was forging ahead. Following 'predict and provide' forecasts, suggesting a growth in road traffic of between 83% and 142% by 2025, the Government announced a £12 billion road programme. In a new decade that promised increases in pollution, congestion... and even the unhealthy prospect of global warming, it looked like a remarkably short-sighted decision.

The Welsh Valley line to Maesteg reopened in 1992, after 22 years. It was one of the most ambitious schemes up to that time, bringing back stopping trains to the main line from Cardiff to Bridgend and six new stations on a nine-mile freight branch. The total grant was £3.3 million, which would hardly buy one station today. PHOTO: David Henshaw

9
Privatisation & Renaissance
1991-2013

"The Department of Transport has this theory that there is a profitable core railway in there somewhere, and if you prune and chop enough you'll find it, and then won't the world be wonderful? We think that no so-called rural line is safe any longer."

Laurie Harris, Press Officer of the Rail, Maritime & Transport Union (RMT) talking to the 'Observer'

"Today's railway is a quasi-privatised dog's breakfast overseen by clueless 'here today – gone tomorrow' politicians and civil servants who ineptly micro-manage the shambles... Today's privatised railway has troughed its way through public money that BR could only dream of... Today's railway has come up with nothing that BR wouldn't have – the same BR that produced railcards, Apex tickets, cross-country trains with seven or eight carriages, electrification schemes, new and reopened stations..."

Railwayman Simon Stoddart, in a letter to 'Rail' magazine, 12th December 2012

The
man who...
only wanted a return to
Basingstoke
Tim Pestridge

As the 1980s drew to a close, the worst excesses of the 1960s were made good, and the railway network continued to expand, as a steady stream of new lines, stations and services came on stream. But a vicious recession was soon to cut deeply into railway finances, and the Government compounded the downturn by announcing that the railways were to be transferred into private ownership, throwing a newly confident industry back into a state of introspective confusion.

The lead-up to privatisation saw the eclipse of many 'unprofitable' railway freight hauls, and the closure of freight lines that had been short-listed for reopening to passengers. In some places, rail campaigners, local authorities and sympathetic railway managers found themselves fighting against time to get passenger services on the ground before track was removed and land sold off.

More positively, new planning guidance arrived that would help to safeguard disused rail and canal corridors from unsuitable development, and far-sighted local authorities were already purchasing former *railway land to keep long-term rail reinstatement projects viable while the industry was reorganized.*

Meanwhile, the rapidly weakening Conservative government – now into its second decade in power – was cutting rail subsidies, forcing a 'maintenance holiday' on railway track and structures to skew the books and secure a good price for the infrastructure side of the business.

Late in 1993, the Railways Bill became law. In many places the branch lines were trapped in an extraordinarily complex system, in separate franchises from the main lines they depended on, left to sink or swim on their own. The DfT's plan was to allow them to die quietly, and – most importantly of all - independently of the state machine, but so many concessions had been made to get the legislation through Parliament that passenger services were now almost impossible to close.

'Privatisation' turned out to be nothing of the kind: it was neither market sensitive nor efficient. It ultimately grew into an expensive, unwieldy monster, too complex and irrational in its functions to either develop new services or close minor ones. The ensuing fragmentation and chaos would cost billions of pounds, and – directly or indirectly – many livelihoods, and lives too.

But as travellers fought to escape the nightmare of car-saturated roads, rail traffic began to grow at an unprecedented rate, and some of the most breathtaking growth was to take place on the secondary lines and branches that had survived 50 years of retrenchment and turmoil. Whatever the Tory and succeeding 'New Labour' governments had expected to see, they were to witness the renaissance of the rail industry.

In 1991, it was becoming increasingly clear that Premier Margaret Thatcher's avowed, and very public, preference for road transport had failed to turn the tide against the railways. Despite a deepening financial slump (felt most strongly in the southeast, where railways played a crucial transport role), finances remained healthy, and investment continued to run at a reasonable level.

Among a number of schemes being discussed with increasing confidence was an upgrading of the West Coast Main Line to 150mph standards – the creation, in effect, of Britain's first high speed line. Much smaller schemes were under investigation on the fringes of the network too, either to improve schedules (a shorter route to Newquay in Cornwall), or connectivity (a chord linking Yeovil Junction with the Bristol to Weymouth line in Somerset).

In May 1991, a brand new three-and-a-half mile railway was opened to Stansted Airport. Many freight lines had reopened to passengers in the previous decade, but apart from the Selby deviation in 1983 (funded primarily to avoid mining subsidence rather than to upgrade infra-structure), this was the first wholly new railway construction on any scale since the 1930s. As local authorities and passenger transport authorities cast covetous glances at the success of the newly reinstated rail services to Aberdare, Bathgate, Hednesford and Bicester Town, there was a scramble to get new projects off the ground: new stations on existing passenger lines, more daring schemes to reopen freight lines, and a few authorities thinking the unthinkable – the complete reinstatement of long-abandoned rail corridors.

In 1991, the Provincial sector of British Rail became Regional Railways. Since its inception it had been something of a cinderella within the British Rail hierarchy, but it was the only sector to increase passenger revenue in the last years of the 1980s, with passenger volumes growing from 180 million in 1986 to 198 million in 1991, while the Government grant fell over the same period, from £561 million to £428 million.

In 1988, the Government finally agreed to invest in the Great Central's Marylebone terminus and commuter network. This concept – involving new trains, depots, signalling and track – became known as 'Complete Route Modernisation', and was developed by dynamic Network SouthEast boss Chris Green. Doing everything in one hit caused a lot of inconvenience in the short-term, but it was a cost-effective way of building what was in effect a new railway.

By May 1991, the rebuilt 'Chiltern' lines out of Marylebone had changed out of all recognition, from the run-down stump of a trunk line closed in the 1960s into a modern, well-equipped commuter network. Thoroughly modern, and relatively self-contained, Chiltern would later prove to be an easy and successful privatisation, and the only one to renew with a 20-year franchise. In the hands of career railwayman Adrian Shooter, the network gradually expanded, and by 2012 had its own inter-city trains running into a reopened Birmingham Snow Hill terminus. It was also leading the reconstruction of the east-west Oxford to Cambridge 'Varsity' line, which would give Chiltern access to Oxford and Milton Keynes, and provide a second route from Oxford to London.

In the longer term – if politics allow – the aim was to rebuild a stretch of the Great Central trunk line north of Aylesbury as part of High Speed 2, and Chiltern also made no secret of its ambition to rebuild northwards along the Great Central to a park-and-ride near Leicester. Fifty years earlier, the line had been condemned by Beeching and others as a worthless, duplicate trunk route.

There was no escaping the demand for new rail links. Heathrow was one of the busiest airports in the world, but it was almost an hour from central London by congested motorway or Underground – the only major European airport without a proper rail link. By the 1980s, Heathrow's chronic road congestion was throttling west London.

After years of prevarication from a Government ideologically opposed to new railway infrastructure, the Heathrow Express Railway Bill was eventually given the green light in 1990. It

After the abandonment of the rather surreal scheme to convert Marylebone into a road coach terminal, the station was completely rebuilt in the first example of 'Complete Route Modernisation'. PHOTO: David Henshaw

was predicted that by 1995, the line would carry six million passengers a year, and remove 3,000 car movements a day from the congested M4. But the seeds of the process that were to delay the Heathrow line were sown just two weeks after the Bill began its long journey into law, in a series of initiatives announced by new Transport Secretary Malcolm Rifkind.

Margaret Thatcher had gone down in flames in spectacular fashion in November 1990, when a bloody coup orchestrated by Michael Heseltine had failed in its primary aim of bringing the former Environment Secretary to power. As a result, Mrs Thatcher's sycophantic Transport Secretary Cecil Parkinson (who slavishly followed the PM's pro-road policy) was gone too, replaced by the more thoughtful Malcolm Rifkind.

Mild-mannered John Major had succeeded to the premiership more by accident than design, being considered the least divisive of the available candidates, like Sir Alec Douglas Home in 1963.

Major's Britain, in stark contrast to Mrs Thatcher's dynamic, if deeply divisive vision, was a place of cricket greens, afternoon tea, and handsome trains of chocolate and cream carriages steaming gently through unspoilt pastures – a rose-tinted view of the early 1950s, without the socialism. The Rifkind transport proposals – long on rhetoric, but rather lacking in substance – envisaged road pricing, a 'carefully targeted' road construction programme, and private sector cash to control burgeoning traffic chaos, with a revitalised rail network picking up the pieces. Said rail-minded Tory MP Robert Adley: 'It looks as though we might have the glimmerings of a transport policy.'

There was, inevitably, a catch. To the dismay of many, the Conservative government, having rolled back state ownership from most of the public utilities, was now determined to extend the process to the railways. Beneath the veneer of road pricing, Rifkind's real agenda was to 'liberalise' railway freight and passenger services, enabling private operators to gain access to the network.

Privatisation of the railways had been a long-term goal for the Conservatives since Mrs Thatcher's election victory in 1979, but the Prime Minister – whose political instinct had only really deserted her over the poll-tax fiasco – had steered a cautious path, allegedly telling Secretary of State Nicholas Ridley, who was keen on the idea: 'Railway privatisation will be the Waterloo of this government. Please never mention the railways to me again.' [28] The enterprise was considered so fraught with political pitfalls that a procession of Tory ministers had gratefully nodded in agreement and moved on. Malcolm Rifkind might have done the same, but as was becoming the norm in British politics, matters European were to bring the unwelcome debate to a head.

In late 1990, the European Commission had produced a report on European rail policy, containing four key proposals:

● *Railway infrastructure should be owned by a separate authority, with any European operators allowed equal access on payment of common charges.*

● *International passenger and freight trains within the Community should be operated by trans-national commercial undertakings.*

● *Financial support for unremunerative services should be extended to take account of environmental considerations.*

● *A trans-European high speed network should be established by the year 2010.*

The Great Railway Conspiracy

By 1991, the substance of the report had become European Directive 91/440, which did *not* instruct member states to privatise their railways, as the Tories were later to claim. For a start, it did not apply to urban, suburban or regional services, and with long-distance and inter-city services, it merely instructed that management and accounts be independent of government, something that could be done in a variety of ways. The same was true of the infrastructure/operations split – the two functions merely had be to given separate management and balance sheets. The Directive also instructed member states to allow trains from other states access to their rail networks, but interoperability issues made this more or less unenforceable, and the countries that wanted to ignore this rule (primarily France) did so with alacrity.

Later Directives sought to liberalise the European rail market with respect to freight services, private or otherwise, and harmonise interoperability and safety standards, but there was never any real pressure from the Commission to sell off the family silver.

As usual, different European governments interpreted the Directives in different ways. Most saw a blueprint for international high-speed services and cross-European funding, paying

no more than lip-service to the free market proposals, but in Britain, John Major's enthusiastic new Conservative government saw things differently. A separate infrastructure company could be inter-preted as meaning full-blown privatisation, and an oppor-tunity for the state to rid itself of any involvement, with the useful bonus that any ensuing untidiness could be blamed on the European Commission.

The Commission's proposals had arisen from a desire to emulate the Swedish privatisation exper-iment put into practise from 1985. While British Rail was being reorganized into efficient business units, the Swedish state railway operator Statens Järnvägar, had entered the 1980s heavily dependent on grant aid, and was considered to be an inefficient and unimaginative concern. The Swedes decided to tackle the problem from

Until very recently, Swedish state operator SJ retained a complete monopoly of inter-city services, such as the iconic X2000 tilting train. PHOTO: Bombadier

The local rail, ferry and bus authority in the county of Västra Götaland is Västtrafik, owned by the regional council. Operations are currently contracted out to DSBFirst Väst, a joint venture between Danish State Railways (70%) and UK company FirstGroup (30%). When the contract was let in 2010, four companies tendered, but not the incumbent SJ. PHOTO: Västtrafik

several angles, starting by writing off historic debts for infrastructure improvements, leaving a clean financial slate on which a new funding formula could be written. Then extra financial support was pumped in, so that trains could be 'licensed' and taxed at relatively modest rates in a similar manner to road vehicles, whose license rates were also adjusted, the aim being to put road and rail funding on as equal a basis as possible.

In 1988, Statens Järnvägar was split into two divisions – an operating company, SJ, running the trains, and Banverket, an infrastructure company charged with maintaining and improving the network, the operating arm paying the infrastructure company for access to the rail 'road' network. The measures certainly levelled the playing field between road and rail, but did little to improve the *efficiency* of the state operator.

While SJ retained control over freight and long-distance trains, the second, more controversial, innovation obliged county transport authorities to put unremunerative services out to tender, forcing SJ to bid in competition with the private sector. At first, private bus companies, such as BK Tåg, did rather well as rail operators, but as the state company became leaner and more cost-effective it began to win back franchises, and costs were reduced by up to a third.

In 1995, the market was further deregulated, allowing private freight operators to bid for new traffic, and private passenger operators to run regional county-wide trains on main lines. But the former state operator continued to play a dominant role, allegedly bidding low to keep private operators at bay, while Banverket remained as inefficient as before. The Swedish market was far from perfect, and when SJ began to lose money on both passenger and freight in 1996, it became clear that this was a far from ideal blueprint. Right-wing politicians said the reforms hadn't gone far enough, while the left-wing said they had gone too far, but SJ remained state-owned and was to keep its monopoly of long-distance services (until 2010 at least). Thanks to modest track charges, SJ now operates profitably, with all profit going back to the state, while local subsidised services remain open to tender, with some long-distance competition too.

Imperfect though they might have been, the Swedish reforms involved proper funding, a real determination to equalise road and rail infrastructure costs, and an element of competition to keep the state operator on its toes. Many argued that a similar model could be effective in the UK, but the Government, and more particularly the civil servants at the Department of Transport and the Treasury, had very different ideas. In the Swedish model, the train operator (whether publicly or privately owned) paid only a third of the track costs, the remainder being topped up by government in recognition of rail's positive environmental and social role. The British Government had no intention of emulating the Swedes in that respect, and it was this determination to remove all subsidy from the infrastructure side that would shape events over the coming years.

Other European countries had done no more than tinker with rail privatisation. Some eventually separated operations from infrastructure, but generally kept both in the state sector. Others allowed limited access to private operators, but none had any intention of going as far as the British.

Excluding the status quo – which was by far the favourite with the public and a sizable minority of MPs – there were thought to be five options:

● *Privatisation of British Rail as a single company* – *the option favoured and lobbied for by the British Railways Board*

● *Privatisation as a single holding company with a range of private subsidiaries*

● *Establishment of a private or state-owned infrastructure company like Banverket, with separate private companies running the services*

● *Privatisation along regional lines, to produce four or five big regional businesses similar to the pre-war statutory companies* – *the option that appealed most to Prime Minister Major*

● *Piecemeal privatisation of the recently introduced and generally successful 'internal' businesses* – *InterCity, freight, parcels, Network SouthEast and Regional Railways*

Another option was to keep privatisation quite a low-key affair, with private operators being invited to tender against British Rail to run subsidised services, on a 'minimum subsidy' basis. But under the enthusiastic guidance of free-market zealots in the Treasury and Department of Transport, looking for a market-orientated solution, option three looked strongest. And so the dreadful notion of 'franchising' services to private operators began to take on a momentum of its own, and 'privatisation' – billed as clean, simple and efficient – grew into a creature of frightful complexity and breathtaking cost. It later emerged that Richard Branson's Virgin Group, which the Government assumed would be a key bidder for franchises, had been thinking more along Swedish lines. 'We didn't need privatisation,' said a Virgin spokesman, 'We were prepared to run in co-operation with British Rail.'

The various options threw up more questions than they answered. Unless subsidies were hidden elsewhere in the system, like the low Swedish track charges, the passenger railway would continue to require funding for the foreseeable future, and transferring assets into private hands was unlikely to alter that simple equation. Cutting the network back would be political suicide, but in any event, the lesson of history was that replacement bus services would probably fade away, and no amount of railway closures could be *guaranteed* to deliver a profitable railway.

If subsidies remained, the whole edifice would be entirely artificial. Profitable lines were relatively straightforward as privately-run operations, with a few safeguards over fares and service levels, but the loss-makers were trickier, because without profit there could be no proper competition and no free market. If companies were to be paid to run trains, they would have to sign up to provide minimum standards and service levels. Who would set and monitor those requirements? If the timing and the number of trains were not to be regulated by market forces, who would decide what the public wanted or needed? Would train operators buy into services indefinitely, or would they be required to rebid for a 'franchise' once in a while? If the franchises were too short, the cost of bidding would be disproportionately high, and the company would have no time to invest and reap the rewards. If they were too long, a tired, lethargic operator could keep lazily drawing its subsidy while innovators waited frustrated in the wings.

If a private operator asked for insufficient subsidy, what safeguards were there to stop it walking away mid-franchise? If the potential operators were asked to put up a financial bond in lieu of default, they would ask for a higher subsidy to cover the cost of borrowing and the risk involved. If they got their sums right and creamed off a fat subsidised profit on an unprofitable franchise, would the public accept funding the dividends of private companies? To what purpose? And of course, there would have to be a fair and equitable system for dividing up income from long-distance cross-company or cross-franchise tickets.

The legal and administrative bill promised to surpass anything seen before, because a competitive framework would require countless safeguards, mountains of red tape, and an army of administrators. The Byzantine complexity of it all boggled the mind. Privatisation could only make sense if the private operators were much, much more efficient than British Rail, and by the early 1990s British Rail had become quite a slim and efficient machine. Clearly — and this raised the most objections — British Rail could not be allowed to bid, or it would use its experience and economies of scale to keep most of the franchises in-house. Some argued that it should be allowed to do exactly that — all British Rail needed was a gentle run-in with the likes of Richard Branson, and costs would be cut in no time. Others argued that the whole expensive exercise would turn into a farce if any franchises remained with the state operator.

The infrastructure side was a problem too. If it was run by a publicly owned engineer-led company, remote from any involvement with passenger or freight customers, it might become lazy and inefficient. If it was fully privatised, it could become a dangerous monopoly. Another option was to vest the entire railway infrastructure — the track, signals and earthworks — in a private company jointly owned by the train operators, rather as electricity's National Grid had been brought into the private sector. But how would costs be apportioned? Who would regulate to allow fair access? And who would decide when or where to invest, or disinvest?

Many on the left-wing of the Conservative Party had their doubts that the thing could be made to work in any form, while those on the right argued that the proposals were too cumbersome, leaving little provision for free market endeavour and were thus hardly worth pursuing. To the right wing, each railway service needed to stand on its own and fight for death or glory against bus, coach, airline, and private car.

The popular entrepreneur Richard Branson had already announced his intention of leasing InterCity 125 trains from British Rail to operate peak-hour Virgin services on a number of plum routes — not running the routes themselves, or committing to provide trains at unprofitable times of day — simply creaming off some of the more lucrative business.

This was just the sort of entrepreneurial zest the Government wanted to encourage, but it wouldn't fit with a regional break-up, or a rigid franchising system, so a formula was needed that would give access rights to small, nimble operators too. This raised a whole series of new questions. British Rail could be told to sit and watch Richard Branson taking all the profitable train paths, but a private operator who had paid good money for an exclusive franchise would not. And if the minnows were not allowed to share the pot of long-distance income, they would only accept passengers who had bought their branded tickets. Different trains accepting different tickets on the same platform was a recipe for chaos.

If small operators *were* to be offered a share in the pot for that route, on what basis would the income be apportioned? If it was simply based on the number of trains provided, where was the free-market incentive to cut prices and improve service levels? And what exactly was a 'route'? British Rail generally allowed passengers to travel by any route, provided it was 'reasonable,' they were going in the right direction, and didn't break local ticket conditions. On a market-based railway network, that sort of freedom might leave operator B carrying most of operator A's cut-price ticket-holders. One of the many hidden costs of privatisation involved working out 'Permitted Routes' for every ticket and every potential journey. For the public, it was just another baffling complication.

A genuinely free market, similar to the regime imposed on the bus industry, would prove a free enterprise nightmare on rails. It simply wouldn't be practical to run competing trains along the same tracks, with separate fare structures, booking offices and staff. Despite the obvious difficulties, there was quite strong support for this scenario on the loony right-wing fringe. Even when applied to the much simpler bus industry, complete deregulation had proved a dismal failure, with competing buses fighting for customers on a few lucrative urban routes, while other services were reduced or discontinued. Staff wages had fallen, working hours had risen, as had bus fares (by an average of 12% in real terms), and passenger numbers – surely the *raison d'etre* of public transport – had fallen sharply. There had been a downward trend in the early 1980s in any event, but following deregulation in 1986, the decline became much more marked. Outside London, where the market had remained largely unregulated, passenger numbers were to fall by 37% from 1981 to 2001, with bus mileage rising by 21% in the same period [29].

Bus stations had been sold off for development, buses were getting older, and even the initial surge of competition had been eroded after a few years. Inefficient operators were easily dispatched by more efficient ones, but if a small, but efficient operator controlled a bus route, the only way it could be winkled out was by dirty tricks – such as selling tickets below cost – take-over or merger. Inevitably, after a series of mergers and acquisitions, most of the profitable routes were left in the hands of two or three big operators, and as these had no interest in fighting each other, they carved out private fiefdoms every bit as monopolistic as the regulated, mostly local authority-run operations they had replaced. The only real difference was that minor routes no longer received a cross-subsidy, and if fares rose, the surplus evaporated from the local economy as shareholder profit. The good news was that annual bus subsidies fell from £1.7 billion to £700 million in ten years, but thereafter it climbed steeply, exceeding £1 billion by 2001 and £2.4 billion in 2010-11. In short, the bus subsidy, after 25 years of deregulation, was almost unchanged in real terms.

Faced with a series of almost irreconcilable challenges, the Department of Transport set to work with renewed vigour, aided by a growing army of outside consultants and lawyers, to find a railway scheme that might just satisfy all parties. Only three small networks were felt to be sufficiently self-contained to be sold into the private sector en bloc, complete with infra-structure, stations and other facilities. These were the newly modernised Chiltern line out of Marylebone, the London, Tilbury & Southend (the so-called 'misery line' between Fenchurch

Street and Shoeburyness) and the vestigial branch from Ryde to Shanklin on the Isle of Wight. Elsewhere the access rights situation was considered too complex for such a 'vertical' franchise to work, and in the end vertical franchising – which would have provided some useful figures by which to judge other systems – was dropped.

As half-baked privatisation proposals began to clog up the arteries of communication at the Department of Transport, British Rail was 'encouraged' to divest itself of freight traffic that couldn't produce an 8% return on capital, an ambitious target, and far beyond the sort of margins the road hauliers were achieving. The result was that marginal and even profitable freight flows were simply handed to road transport operators. The Speedlink 'wagon load' service was discontinued in 1991, barring smaller freight customers from the system overnight, and putting an estimated 150,000 extra lorry movements onto the roads in the first year. Many new railway sidings – built or rebuilt with Government assistance – were suddenly redundant, as were 17 out of 38 military complexes, the tanks, explosives and other military hardware being transferred onto Britain's congested roads. Within a couple of years, Transport Secretary Rifkind's revitalised railway network had voluntarily shed all but its core heavy freight activities, primarily coal, steel, aggregates and bulk petrochemicals.

As the recession of the early 1990s deepened, railway passenger and freight revenue began to fall, and the short-term windfall from property sales, that had been underway for a few years, began to dry up, leaving railway finances at crisis point yet again. In the Network SouthEast commuter belt, daily commuter traffic fell from a peak of 473,000 in 1989/90 to less than 380,000 in 1992.

In an effort to stem the financial losses nationally, services were pared back and staff thinned down, particularly in the regions, leaving many busy stations virtually unstaffed. Hapless travellers on the Cumbrian Coast and Whitby lines found the number of trains cut almost by half, making straightforward commuter journeys hard to achieve by rail.

In October 1991, fare increases of nearly twice the rate of inflation did little to improve the financial situation and allied to the service cuts, served merely to damage the public perception of the railways. But to a Government that wished to discredit British Rail, this was no bad thing, and with hindsight may even have been orchestrated from behind the scenes. According to the *Daily Mail*, the cost of a single 10km (six-mile) rail journey into central London was already the most expensive in Europe, at £1.40, against 32p in Paris, and 30p in Athens. In most other European capitals, the equivalent cost was less than £1, and only Copenhagen came close, at £1.18. *The Daily Telegraph* unearthed a similar differential on longer journeys, a 100-mile single fare in the UK costing £24.50, against £13.75 in Germany, and only £9.60 in France.

As the 1992 General Election approached, the public debate intensified, and the media began to focus on the branch and secondary lines that were bound to suffer under a fragmented, free-market system. For a major line relying on a branch for perhaps 10% of its traffic, loss of a physical or branded connection with the branch might not be all that serious. Managers could make operational savings, or perhaps build a Parkway station and encourage former branch users to come by car. For the branch, of course, the loss of connections and through ticketing would be catastrophic, and probably terminal. The intention was that only major stations would be allowed to sell cross-franchise tickets, so a traveller from, say, Looe in Cornwall – long able to buying a through ticket to Exeter from the guard on the branch train – would now be obliged to buy a Wales & West ticket to Liskeard, and queue at the Great Western ticket office there for the Exeter ticket. More troublesome, more expensive, and designed to encourage the user to miss out the branch and drive to Liskeard, it obscured the contributory revenue paper trail at a stroke. Thus the process of breaking up the system looked bound to gnaw away at the weakest elements – the small branch lines that carried comparatively little traffic themselves, but contributed to the success of the whole, and made a unified system a reality.

Shortly before the election, the Rail, Maritime & Transport Union published crudely rendered maps that were claimed to have originated in the British Rail strategy unit. According to these leaked documents, 12 InterCity lines would probably be demoted to 'regional' status, and 27 branch lines in England and Wales were likely to close, leaving only a handful in existence.

In addition, problems were already becoming apparent on the ground. A steady cut in the Public Service Obligation grant had left the branch lines woefully underfunded, as the drive intensified to balance the books. Among the losers were the Welsh valley branch lines, the Uckfield branch in Sussex, the Pembroke branch, and others on the Celtic fringe. Elsewhere, in a complicated picture, late evening services were cut back across the board, and a number of minor stations virtually closed, but some branches saw *more* trains, as Regional Railways fought to utilise staff and scarce resources as effectively as possible. How far could the process go? The Government was demanding a further 50% cut in the PSO grant over the following two years, and the figures just didn't seem to add up.

The only way out was a short-term cessation of investment, described rather obliquely as a 'maintenance holiday'. Initially this affected the branch lines, but it came to include the West Coast Main Line, where investment plans were cancelled in a depressing re-enactment of 1960/61, and even the Forth Bridge, where regular painting came to a halt after 103 years of continuous brushwork. Painting the Forth Bridge cost £600,000 a year, but if its future really was assured, how would reduced maintenance improve the long-term financial prospects?

The Major Government had no intention of clearing the backlog. If privatisation brought

If local stations and guards were unable to sell through tickets, a traveller from - for example - the Looe branch line would have to rebook here at Liskeard if making a longer journey, making it impossible to clarify how much contributory revenue the branch was supplying. Fortunately sanity prevailed and, although the two lines were franchised to different companies, the privatised guard on the Looe branch continued to sell tickets to any station in the country, just as his predecessor had done. Today, as in many places, the local and InterCity franchises in the West Country have been recombined to produce a regional operation. A First Great Western HST leaves Liskeard for Penzance in August 2012
PHOTO: David Edge

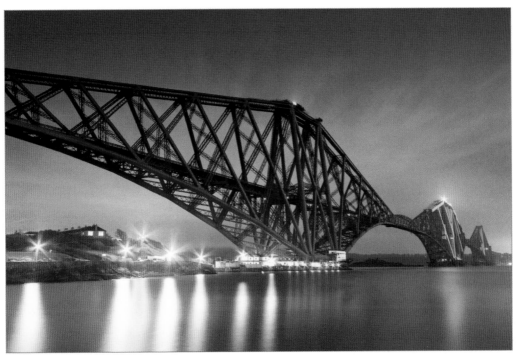

Cuts in grants prior to railway privatisation resulted in a so-called 'maintenance holiday', that is even said to have affected the maintenance schedules of the Forth Bridge. Luckily this didn't last long, and for a decade from 2002 the bridge was stripped back to bare metal one section at a time and repainted. PHOTO: Open Buildings

enough private capital into the industry, the maintenance would be brought up to date, or so went the dogma. If the reforms failed to revitalise the railways, the backlog of maintenance would make lines easier to close.

As the propaganda battle entered its final phase in the last weeks before the 1992 election, the Government fought back against its many critics, citing the success of other privatised companies, such as British Airways, which had been transformed from a nondescript state concern into one of the world's most admired, most profitable (and according to Virgin Airlines, dishonest) airlines. But British Airways was competing against other airlines playing a similar game by broadly similar rules. Ministers always followed the line that British Rail was cushioned by Government cash – which was arguable at the very least – and that it was inefficient because it had no competition, which was laughable. The railways had fought for half a century against road competition – lorries, buses, coaches and private cars – and they were now fighting the airlines as well.

If the aim had been to adjust road/rail track costs, or even simultaneously privatise the road network, all would be well, and in May 1992, the rail unions and other campaign groups found an unlikely ally in the right-wing Adam Smith Institute. In a report entitled *Tomorrow's Way*, the Institute argued for private ownership of the roads, funded by pay-as-you-drive fees of £1 to £5 a day. This sort of scheme would have removed hidden subsidies and levelled the transport playing field, but it inevitably fell foul of the well-entrenched road lobby groups.

Perhaps wisely, the Conservatives chose not to feature railway privatisation too prominently in their 1992 election manifesto, which stated only that the party would 'break the

The Great Railway Conspiracy

BR monopoly', by means of franchising and the sale of the freight operators. It was all quite carefully worded, and the implication was that it would all be done and dusted within the next Parliament. Secretary of State Malcolm Rifkind went so far as to announce: 'The Conservatives have no proposals to privatise British Rail's passenger services.'

The Conservatives won the election of April 1992 by their smallest margin for 40 years, and the earnest Malcolm Rifkind was replaced at Transport by John MacGregor, a comparative unknown, who began to push enthusiastically for (state funded) road construction and railway privatisation. With what might loosely be termed a mandate from the electorate, the pace began to pick up.

Within a month, the Government had instructed British Rail to attach seated coaches to the Aberdeen sleeper, enabling Stagecoach – a Scottish bus company that had done rather well out of bus deregulation – to launch a headline-grabbing 'private enterprise' service. From 12th May 1992, this embryonic private service enabled up to 116 Stagecoach passengers a day to travel to London for a £38 single fare. The scheme was intended to demonstrate the viability of private rail services, but by November – in an atmosphere of high farce that helped to relieve the general gloom in the industry – Stagecoach had pulled out, citing lack of demand. One of the key issues had been a lack of inter-availability between Stagecoach and BR services, with BR staff struggling to interpret a nine-page booklet when issuing private tickets.

For the next few months, nothing appeared to change, but behind the scenes the infrastructure crisis was blossoming, and less remunerative rail freight services continued to be off-loaded onto the roads, with all freight services to Oban and Mallaig being withdrawn, putting the remaining passenger services at risk.

The lack of continuity, in an industry where investment needs are considered in terms of decades, was causing a major upheaval. For County Councils and Passenger Transport Authorities hoping to fund new services, the uncertainty was, at best, a distraction, and at worst, a threat to the very survival of their railway reopening schemes.

Many lines on target to reopen in the early 1990s were put on hold, or abandoned altogether. Rugeley to Hednesford, Stirling to Alloa, Huddersfield to Halifax, Burton-on-Trent to Leicester, Nottingham-Mansfield-Worksop, Cambridge to St Ives, and many others, were either delayed by years or scaled back, as railway rebuilding ground to a halt. Other schemes that required relatively high expenditure, such as the reopening between Uckfield and Lewes, and Bere Alston to Tavistock, were abandoned altogether.

In the last months of 1992 the railway equipment manufacturers could see trouble ahead too, as investment was cut back and orders cancelled. No new track and signalling equipment was on order beyond 1994, and no new trains after 1995, putting 15,000 jobs at risk.

It was not until the publication of the proposed Railways Bill in January 1993 that a clearer picture began to emerge of the shape and form privatisation would take, and even then, the future remained cloudy, with a number of key questions still unanswered.

All, or virtually all, of the railway infrastructure would be transferred to a state-owned company, while passenger services would be franchised along broadly regional lines, usually in two tiers, with former Regional services expected to compete against former InterCity trains. The successful franchisees would pay access charges to Railtrack, the new infrastructure company, which was originally intended to be state-owned, but was later sold off.

There would be no national timetable, no compulsion for franchisees to allow through ticketing, no InterCity branding unless the franchisees wanted to keep it, and no national discount railcards for the young, the old and the disabled. It wasn't even clear how much of a railway network there would be in the long-term, John MacGregor admitting during a Labour sponsored debate in the House of Commons: 'We expect most, or a very high proportion of the national rail network to survive.' As political answers go, it was tantamount to an admission that a great many services would fall by the wayside.

On 2nd February 1993, further details were released. Initially, seven 'model' franchises would be created and run by British Rail on commercial lines. Once sufficient information had been gathered to produce a prospectus for potential franchisees, the companies would be transferred into the private sector as rapidly as possible. As expected, the InterCity network was to be dismantled from Day One, with the Great Western Main Line, East Coast Main Line and Gatwick Express services joining the first round of these 'shadow' franchises. Incorporating the East Coast might have explained the 'maintenance holiday' on the West Coast – traffic was being channelled onto the line due for early privatisation.

The other four franchises were to be the South West Division of Network SouthEast (broadly speaking, the remains of the old LSWR); the Isle of Wight line (uniquely as a 'vertical' franchise, maintaining the infrastructure too); ScotRail; and the London, Tilbury & Southend. It was an interesting and varied selection, chosen to entrap a third of British Rail's passenger revenue.

Perhaps the inclusion of the Great Western and East Coast echoed Mr Major's rather naive desire for a return to the pre-war statutory companies, but of course without the branch lines – which were to be franchised separately, or left in a rump BR organisation – while the track, signals and most of the stations, would be owned by Railtrack. The Scotrail and South West Division franchises included most of the lines in their respective regions, but here again, the infrastructure would not belong to, or be the responsibility of, the franchisee. The Isle of Wight and London, Tilbury & Southend were both geographical oddities that could easily be operated as self-contained units, but would offer no real lessons for franchising the rest of the network. The rest of British Rail would be divided into 18 Train Operating Units, based loosely on existing railway cost centres. They would remain in British Rail for the time being, but were scheduled for franchising at a later date.

These rigid franchises didn't leave much room for competition, a major flaw noted by the first Rail Regulator John Swift QC, whose ostensible role was to see fair play and promote competition, which didn't exactly fit with the notion of companies bidding for exclusive franchises. After a great deal of horsetrading, Swift came up with the rather clever notion that Railtrack would not be allowed to sell train paths already claimed by the franchised operator. This solved the problem, but largely killed the competitive element, because there were few paths available on the busiest lines, and these were the only routes on which competition was likely to flourish.

On 4th February 1993, the Government published details of its *Roads to Prosperity* programme, involving a 6% increase in road spending in the next financial year, to almost £2.1 billion (£4.9 billion today). The investment programme – the highest in real terms for 20 years – would include 41 trunk road and motorway schemes and, in Mr MacGregor's own words would, 'clearly demonstrate the extent of the Government's commitment,' to road infrastructure improvements. The Government's commitment had never really been in doubt.

Although the Railways Bill received a relatively comfortable majority of 33 at its second reading in February 1993, there was vociferous opposition to the proposals from all quarters – even from Tory backbenchers, who could see their majorities dwindling by the day. To the fury of the free-marketeers, the concessions were many and varied, from strengthened closure procedures, making it almost impossible to close services, to guarantees on through ticketing,

The Great Railway Conspiracy

which further watered down the free market nature of the enterprise.

According to Robert Adley, Chairman of the Commons Transport Committee, the decision to separate responsibility for infrastructure and train services was 'fundamentally flawed'. The Bill, said Mr Adley, was, 'a laboratory experiment conducted by civil servants in Marsham Street [the Department of Transport headquarters] on a vital piece of transport architecture', and the culmination of a, 'total lack of any coherent transport policy over the past 14 years'. It was during this debate that Adley described rail privatisation as 'a Poll Tax on wheels', a phrase that struck home very successfully with Tory backbenchers.

The trade union reaction to the shadow franchising was predictable enough, and Jimmy Knapp, the ebullient General Secretary of the RMT union, voiced the fears of many:

"This confirms all we have been saying about cherry picking the best routes. If you take the best lines, there is no way the rest can survive... [Privatisation] is the biggest threat since Beeching in the 1960s."

In April, Roger Freeman, Minister responsible for Public Transport, met with a delegation from the Railway Development Society, and reiterated the Government mantra – that the railways needed competition, and, 'Our reforms will not lead to closures.' Freeman travelled widely at this time, reassuring the public that there would be no service reductions, a promise he couldn't possibly expect to keep, and didn't even believe. In a private meeting with railway managers, he warned that he couldn't guarantee there would be no closures...

The Government certainly had no intention of funding local railway reopenings when framing the legislation, and even vital strategic projects like the Channel Tunnel high speed line, and the more modest Heathrow rail link, were already close to collapse for lack of capital.

By May 1993, the Railways Bill squeezed through its third reading, passing by a majority of just 15, after Tory rebels had been placated with a growing list of concessions over railcards, fares and interavailability of tickets. On 13th May, Robert Adley MP died from a heart attack, at the age of only 58. Adley was essentially the last hope for injecting some common sense into the Railways Bill. He was one of very few MPs able to rally the troops against the more crackpot provisions, and he had even succeeded in swinging the Tory-dominated Transport Select Committee against privatisation. His death came just a few days before his Committee was due to release a report damning the muddled thinking behind the process.

Two months later, a defeat in the House of Lords did little to stem the Bill's inexorable progress into law. Peers had voted by 150 to 112 to back an amendment tabled by Lord Peyton of Yeovil, who had briefly held the office of Transport Minister under Edward Heath in 1970. Peyton's amendment would have allowed British Rail to bid for franchises, as in the Swedish model. It was a simple proposal that would have made privatisation a very different animal, but the Government responded by twice throwing out the Lords' demands. In an atmosphere of high political drama verging on constitutional crisis, their Lordships backed down, and opposition was effectively at an end. An ironic side-effect of privatisation was that, whereas the British state operator was barred from bidding for franchises, many were later won by state operators from elsewhere in Europe.

Away from Parliament, the propaganda war reached a climax when it was revealed that Conservative Central Office had been briefing against British Rail's alleged failings. It also emerged that the Department of Transport had looked into the franchising model for the bus industry back in 1985, but concluded, damningly, that it was not a viable system: 'Franchising,' said a leaked report, 'appears to offer the benefits of competition without the effort of its actual practise. However, experience has shown that much of this promise is illusory.' But such bombshells had come too late – by October 1993 the battle was already lost.

While the sterile privatisation debate ground on, railways continued to reopen. The biggest project was the Robin Hood line north of Nottingham, which reached Newstead in 1993. Further along the route, this tunnel at Annesley - which had been buried beneath mountain of spoil - was re-excavated, and a new line carved through to Kirby-in-Ashfield and Mansfield, which reopened in 1995, followed by a through route to Worksop in 1998. Privatisation would halt new projects for a decade. PHOTO: David Henshaw

With the timetable for implementation ticking away, City analysts Coopers & Lybrand (successors to the firm behind the infamous rail subsidy formula of 1968) were unable to produce a figure for the all-important track access charges on which the franchise bids would be based, and the very future of rail services would depend. When the Gatwick Express was launched as the first shadow franchise in October 1993, the vital figures had still to be fixed.

On 5th November, the Railways Bill received Royal Assent and passed into law... Robert Adley's 'Poll Tax on Wheels' was rolling, although it would take several years to be fully implemented.

The average free enterprise-minded Conservative MP, probably genuinely believed (or had been persuaded by the Whip's Office) that privatisation would result in greater efficiency: better marketing, improved manpower and rolling stock utilisation, reduced subsidy, and for the passengers, a service more closely tailored to demand, and (rather optimistically) lower fares. He or she would have been reassuring their constituents for some time now, that railway lines and services were safe.

To right-wing elements, the privatisation had been weakened so as to be almost meaningless, but powerful figures within the Department of Transport were convinced that nothing had changed since the closure debates of the 1960. According to this view, Intercity services were, or could become, profitable at the right track access price, and urban commuter lines would probably need support indefinitely, but the majority of rural lines could be closed without serious damage to the nation's fabric.

The Great Railway Conspiracy

The framework of privatisation had been tailored to enhance the position of the stronger lines, and allow the weaker ones to fade away with as few political repercussions as possible. But it was all going to be a lot more difficult than it had been in the 1960s because, to the fury of the right, the parliamentary concessions had taken away most of the competitive elements. And the theory and practise of contributory revenue and cost/benefit analysis were now well understood by increasingly sophisticated pro-rail and environmental groups. Local authorities, and even the Transport Users Consultative Committees (renamed Rail Users Consultative Committees in the 1993 Act) were now unwilling to acquiesce quietly to service cuts, let alone line closures.

Nevertheless, under the new regime, local services would be harder to defend, because costs were about to escalate through the roof. Someone had to pay for the army of accountants and consultants now making a living from the railways, and as the fog cleared, it was revealed that the cost of subsidising the rail network had effectively more than doubled overnight, the 1993 subsidy of £900 million expected to top £2 billion in 1994, without the loss of a penny in revenue, or the introduction of a single new service.

The railway infrastructure was to be controlled by Railtrack from April 1994, and the company would charge access fees to operators set at a level designed to give a healthy 8% return on its assets, the highest of any monopoly utilities, to allow for the underlying risks and uncertainties of the proposed rail market. Meanwhile, rolling stock was to be placed in the hands of three leasing companies, initially hewn out of British Rail, to lease existing trains back to operators and hopefully purchase new ones.

Like Railtrack, these 'shadow' companies were expected not just to cover expenses and the cost of investment, but to generate a surplus. The public face of this pyramid would be the private Train Operating Companies, which would bid for enough subsidy to provide a healthy return after making allowance for the risks involved, and generating surpluses for Railtrack and the rolling stock leasing companies. Once all the different levels were generating stable surpluses, Railtrack and the leasing companies would be sold off.

It all sounded like capitalism, but the pyramid was entirely artificial, and dependent on the Government injecting enough public money to pay for the army of administrators, and the various surpluses. These substantial sums could be seen as a temporary subsidy to kickstart the enterprise, which would ultimately soar away, producing 'real' profits. But to believe that private expertise and investment really was going to make enough difference to absorb the extra £1 billion in costs, you needed to be either very, very optimistic or somewhat delusional. A more likely scenario was that money would continue to be injected into this strange public-private conglomerate, which would continually threaten to deflate like a holed bicycle inner-tube. And, of course, once everything was privatised, that £2 billion subsidy would effectively be propping up the dividends of private companies.

The Government had pushed the Bill through by strengthening the legislation surrounding closure procedures, but protesters would now have to make a case against seemingly overwhelming financial losses, without recourse to the time-honoured claim that the railways were running the service inefficiently. Why would a skillfully managed, competitive private company, that had risked a lot of capital on the franchise, run it inefficiently? If private enterprise couldn't make a go of it, a line must be fundamentally flawed, and with money the only criteria by which to gauge success or failure, it would be swept away.

There were a number of issues with the leasing arrangements too. There appeared to be nothing to stop the three leasing companies from swapping rolling stock until each had a monopoly in a particular market. They might also refurbish the world-beating, but elderly,

InterCity 125 fleet, and lease the units back to the operators at inflated prices, rather than investing in new state-of-the-art equipment. In the event, that was more or less the way things unfolded. Despite dismissive comments from the likes of Richard Branson of Virgin, the InterCity 125 was to remain the backbone of the privatised railway, undergoing refurbishment after refurbishment. This success served in part, to demonstrate the soundness of the underlying design, but its survival was also to highlight how ill-equipped the privatised railway was to specify and invest in the next generation of long-distance passenger trains.

As so often in this story, the future of the railway network was about to be decided by events elsewhere. As the sterile privatisation debate raged back and forth, road transport had been largely ignored. But the financial and environmental cost of the Government's road programme was causing disquiet, and in the summer of 1993, a popular uprising had called for a halt to road building and renewed investment in public transport. The turning point came with an ill-timed and generally unfortunate speech by the corpulent Roads Minister Robert Key in July 1993. The speech, at an awards ceremony laid on by *Auto Express* magazine, had disturbing echoes of John Hay's speech at the Road Haulage Association annual dinner 33 years before. (see page 109).

Like Mr Toad, Robert Key had a deep affection for the motorcar – an excellent qualification for the job, one might think – but like Mr Toad, he couldn't resist taking it all too far:

"I love cars... I loved my father's cars and my mother's cars... I even loved my first car... I love cars of all shapes and sizes. Cars are a good thing... I also love roads. I have always loved roads... The car is going to be with us for a very long time... If ever there was an environmentally unfriendly form of transport it was railways."

Railways, continued the Minister, warming to his theme, carved up the countryside and spewed out polluting gases. Although he was later to claim that he had been speaking tongue in cheek, the damage was done. The Minister of State was using the language of the early 1960s, when steam trains really did spew out polluting gases, and cars were relatively thin on the ground. But in the summer of 1993, with public transport facing an uncertain future, and road congestion and pollution rising fast, the public reaction was one of outrage.

Protest spread rapidly, as strange alliances were forged between anarchists and conservation groups, direct action volunteers and respectable middle class matrons from the Home Counties. Few road schemes were actually halted, but many were delayed, and some of the more damaging schemes reappraised. A road programme that had looked a vote-winner a few years before, was suddenly a liability.

Matters came to a head at Twyford Down near Winchester, where the Department of Transport was pushing ahead with an extension to the M3 motorway, against widespread public opposition.

For 40 years the Department had glibly assumed that the public would welcome any new road scheme, particularly this long-awaited missing link between two finished sections of motorway. But in 1993, the public mood was beginning to turn. People still wanted roads, but not at any price, and they wanted quality public transport too. Above all else, they wanted the right to choose how they travelled.

By the 1990s, road transport accounted for more than a quarter of all CO_2 emissions in Britain; traffic pollution had been implicated as a contributory factor in an epidemic of asthma and other respiratory diseases, and as at Twyford, road schemes were damaging Sites of Special Scientific Interest and Areas of Outstanding Natural Beauty. People were starting to voice the unthinkable – that on a small and overcrowded island, further road construction might not be acceptable.

To the Government's surprise, opposition spread to organisations close to the very heart of the Establishment – the National Trust, Tory shire councils, the Council for the Protection of Rural England, and even the Women's Institute (John Major had been steered away from the WI garden at the Chelsea Flower Show after the organisation voiced opposition to rail privatisation!) To the Department of Transport's anger, even the Department of the Environment began to cause waves, urging officials to rethink a number of road schemes.

There were financial issues with the road programme too. Most of the much-trumpeted private enterprise schemes had collapsed, leaving road construction largely dependent on the public purse. Research by Professor Phil Goodwin of Oxford University had suggested that most road building was actually a bad investment, because traffic would always grow to restore the level of congestion, removing the perceived benefits. With the nation's finances back on the critical list, the Treasury began to question the long held assumption that road construction should be funded entirely by the state, and the state-funded road programme was quietly brought back under control. A few private roads were built, but the only one of any size was to be the M6 Toll road north of Birmingham, and that wouldn't be completed until 2000.

The arguments over taxation came back with a vengeance, with the release of new statistics. The road lobby groups maintained that tax revenue from road vehicles was around £20 billion a year, and the cost of road construction and maintenance was running at around £7 billion a year, leaving the motorist and haulier overtaxed by some £13 billion. But Transport 2000, now better funded and better organised than ever before, put the annual hidden cost of road transport at £15 billion for congestion, £10.16 billion for accidents (the Department of Transport's own figures), £1.5 billion in company car subsidies, £2.5 billion in pollution, £2.1 billion for noise, and £657 million to cover road transport's contribution to global warming.

And with Railtrack now obliged to find an 8% return on the capital value of railway assets, it seemed reasonable that the road network should produce a similar return, amounting to some £25 billion a year, making a total of more than £50 billion in hidden subsidies [30].

This was a conservative estimate. Other independent analysts, such as Norman Bradbury

The M3 protests at Twyford Down failed to stop the road, but the involvement of academics, historians and politicians alongside the usual 'green' suspects left the Government looking for an excuse to scale back the 'Roads for Prosperity' programme. In the end the road-building programme was curtailed by Treasury angst that the whole process was not cost-effective.

and Graham Nalty were to go even further, by attempting to apply the same financial logic to the roads as had been applied to the railways, arriving at a subsidy figure of £67 billion a year, of which only 21% was paid at point of use, against 67% in the case of rail transport.

For one of the most unpopular Governments in modern British history, transport had become dangerous ground, and Robert Key's ill-timed speech tested any sympathy the public might have been harbouring. Even the most ardent motorists, it seemed, wanted greater investment in the railways, if only to keep the roads clear for themselves...

Early in 1994, the Government began a massive U-turn that struck at the very foundations of Mrs Thatcher's 'great car economy'. Road building was scaled back, out of town developments opposed, and local authorities encouraged to look again at public transport and cycleway schemes.

This new direction was summed up in Planning Policy Guidance 13, better known as PPG13 – government transport guidance to local authorities. When PPG13 was upgraded in 1994, it had become a lot greener, steering planning authorities towards projects that reduced car use and encouraged alternative means of transport, but much more importantly for the railway closure story, it gave tentative advice on safeguarding former railway land:

"Authorities should ensure that disused transport routes, such as old canals and railways, are not unnecessarily severed by new buildings and non-transport land uses, especially where there is a reasonable chance that such routes may be put to use in the future. As well as their original uses, such routes may serve as cycle routes, pedestrian paths or bridleways.'
PPG13, paragraph 5.8, 1994

Seven Meadows Road in Stratford-on-Avon was built on the Stratford to Cheltenham trackbed, the northern section of which is now expected to reopen. Consultants' reports all suggest that the railway can be squeezed in, the recommendation being a single track to the west side (left in the photo) of a slightly realigned road, dropping at a gradient of 1:40 to pass under the roundabout in the background. If the route had been protected, this could have been avoided. PHOTO: David P Howard/Geograph.org.uk

The Great Railway Conspiracy

PPG13 was riddled with caveats, and it wasn't binding, but for the first time a government had recognised that railway corridors were worth safeguarding. There was no statutory duty to safeguard railway land, but planning authorities were expected to take it into account. And whatever the Government was saying in PPG13, it was still encouraging the British Rail Property Board, and later BRB (Residuary) Ltd, to sell off non-operational land, even where local authorities and campaigners were actively seeking to reopen a line. Very often, the safeguarding of strategic railway land was left to a handful of activists liaising with helpful local authority contacts. It was no way to build a railway fit for a new Millennium.

The wheels of local government turn very slowly, and there were to be many more needless and expensive infringements onto railway corridors, as at Stow in the Scottish Borders, where planning permission was given for a bungalow to be constructed right across the railway formation in 1993. Less than 20 years later – and very much against the owner's wishes – it was demolished to make way for the reconstruction of the northern section of the Waverley route. Similarly, a third of a mile of the route from Stratford-upon-Avon southwards to Honeybourne was obliterated by the Stratford Inner Relief Road. In 2013, reinstatement of the railway is now being taken very seriously, but the cost and complexity could be as much as ten times higher because the railway corridor wasn't safeguarded.

Some routes had survived intact by pure chance, often because the land was unsuitable for redevelopment. Many others had been damaged beyond economic repair through careless – often pointless – redevelopment, and the damage was to go on through the 1990s. The PPG guidance would later be strengthened, but without a coherent national plan for strategic rail corridors, safeguarding remains in the hands of local authorities, whose officers were – reasonably enough – more concerned with local issues than national infrastructure.

The privatised railway arrived, in shadow form at least, on April Fool's Day 1994. British Rail would remain in existence in the short-term, while the former passenger business sectors – InterCity, Network Southeast and Regional Railways – were broken up into 25 Train Operating Units that would be taken over by Train Operating Companies when the market was ready. Rolling stock passed nominally into the hands of the three 'ROSCO's', or train leasing companies – Eversholt, Porterbrook and Angel Contracts – all part of British Rail for the time being, but also scheduled for sale. The track, signals, stations and other infrastructure passed to Railtrack, and the new Chairman Bob Horton set about squeezing the assets, looking for the 5.6% return demanded by the Treasury, the optimistic 8% return having been postponed for a few years.

The lynchpin of the whole operation was Franchise Director Roger Salmon, who would function as the Government's man at the Office of Passenger Rail Franchising, overseeing the sale of franchises and the distribution of financial support, a role that would sometimes bring him into conflict with John Swift, the Rail Regulator.

In keeping with the free market ambitions of the experiment, but absurdly for passengers, it was initially announced that only 294 'core' stations would be obliged to sell cross-franchise tickets and, even then, only for full-price standard fare journeys, but this nonsense was laughed out of court by the media, and soon abandoned. Thankfully, the Disabled, Young Person's and Senior railcards would be protected by law thanks to parliamentary pressure (but not necessarily on pre-privatisation terms), leaving the Network Southeast and Family cards at the mercy of any new operator's commercial judgement.

The Isle of Wight line had been mysteriously dropped from the first round of shadow franchises, but the other six duly came into being as quasi-private concerns. The operators – still British Rail managers in reality – began paying track charges of £7-£15 per train-mile, and adapting to the bizarre commercial realities of the new situation. As expected, the Railways Act had left every British Rail service, with the exception of Gatwick Express, requiring a subsidy – a total that was expected to exceed £2 billion in 1994-95.

The Government had no option other than to pay up, but for Passenger Transport Authorities, many of which had invested heavily in rail through the 1980s, the increased costs caused real problems. Particularly hard hit was Greater Manchester, whose bill for local rail services rose by £22.3 million – an increase of 147%.

The Department of Transport had already agreed to underwrite the extra cost in 1994-95, and to head off a revolt (Strathclyde had refused to pay a penny since April), the Metropolitan Railway Grant was extended for a further year. Extra grants would at least keep the urban wheels turning, but there was no help for the rural branches.

The Government was still hoping that privatisation would be a pain-free avenue for closing loss-making rural services, but when Franchising Director Roger Salmon flexed his muscles for the first time, and announced in December 1994 that the Fort William sleeper service would not be included in the ScotRail franchise – tantamount to announcing its withdrawal – the battle lines were drawn for the first (and possibly the last) big battle over retrenchment. British Rail subsequently initiated the familiar winding down procedure, but the closure was fought so vociferously by campaigners – from rail enthusiast groups to the Highlands & Islands Regional Council – that the Government had backed down by June 2005.

Roger Salmon had seen it as part of his remit to improve profitability by withdrawing loss-making services, but to the fury of the right wing, it wasn't going to be that easy. The easy closure of lines and services had been a key plank in the privatisation edifice, and for many it was the primary reason for going down this infuriatingly complex and expensive road.

In the early months of 1994, it was hard to find a single independent commentator who thought that privatisation could make the railways function more efficiently than British Rail, as even the potential franchisees began to melt away. But the Department of Transport was confident (or, at least, determined), announcing in March that the privatisation programme, which had begun to slip badly, would be accelerated, to bring more than half the franchises into the private sector by April 1996.

Railtrack was floated on the stock exchange in May 1996, but it got off to a bad start. In June, routine wage negotiations with signalmen were virtually complete, with a management offer of 5.7% on the table, when Minister John MacGregor allegedly intervened and the offer was withdrawn. After 'discussions' with the Department of Transport, Railtrack returned offering a derisory 2.5%. The outraged union negotiators insisted on their original 11% and negotiations broke down, resulting in a series of 24- and 48-hour strikes during the summer.

For potential franchisees the risks were all too clear – namely total reliance on an ineptly managed, publicly-owned company whose strings were being pulled by the DfT. Privatisation had been billed as freedom from political interference, but Railtrack had demonstrated all too clearly that this single, positive objective had not been achieved.

South West Trains, the first franchise, was sold in February 1996, just before Railtrack was itself floated and sold to the private sector, and the last (ScotRail) was let in April 1997, weeks before Tony Blair's 'New Labour' Government won a landslide victory at the polls. Labour had made its opposition to privatisation very clear, but like Harold Wilson and the Beeching report, Tony Blair changed his mind once in power, and did little but tinker with the ramshackle edifice.

The Government's failure to kill the Fort William portion of the Caledonian sleeper was a turning point. Whatever else happened, privatisation wasn't going to be a 'Beeching-style' hatchet job. On 7th June 2006, a year after the reprieve, a Class 37 hauls the sleeper through Westerton, Glasgow. A week later the sleeper went over to modern Class 67 haulage. PHOTO: David Black, Eastbank MRC

Competition had been largely absent for the early rail franchises, but as the process continued and bidders became more confident, it became increasingly fierce, with Save Our Railways predicting that five of the 25 had bid too high, and would run into difficulties during the 7- to 15-year life of the franchises. In most cases, the winning bids were for a high initial subsidy, falling rapidly as efficient operating methods improved returns, so that the total subsidy bill to the franchisees would fall from £1.8 billion in 1997-98 to £0.7 billion in 2003-04.

In reality, after falling much as predicted in the first few years, the subsidies paid to TOCs was to grow rapidly after 2000, reaching some £2.5 billion by 2003-04 [31]. The reasons for the commercial failure of railway privatisation have been covered in great detail elsewhere, but in the briefest terms, the new train operators (primarily the big three bus operators) had expected to cut staffing levels and wages as they had done in the bus industry, but for various reasons these policies simply didn't work in the much more complex and safety-orientated railway industry. Over-optimistic bidding by franchisees was, however, a mere pin-prick against the failure of Railtrack, which more or less single-handedly destroyed the viability of the whole structure.

Problems began with two major rail crashes in West London: Southall in 1997, and Ladbroke Grove in 1999. Both were caused by drivers running through red lights, but in both cases the fragmentation of the industry was shown to have played a role. Railtrack was held partially responsible, and consequently harangued by the New Labour administration into adopting a 'safety at any cost' mentality.

Compared to the relatively engineer-led British Rail, Railtrack was a management organisation, nearly all of whose engineering and research & development functions had been outsourced to contractors. Confident that British Rail had expensively over-engineered maintenance and renewals, Railtrack had cut back investment, which did wonders for the bottom line for a while, but on top of the years of cheese paring as British Rail was fattened up for market, it led to a backlog of renewals.

If there had been a strong engineering presence on the Railtrack board, the deterioration of the assets would have been properly understood and made safe. But the Government had deliberately brought in senior managers and board members from outside the industry, and because of the tangled nature of the subcontracting process, almost non-existent contract management, mistakes by poorly trained staff, and a general lack of coherency, a series of blunders inevitably led to a calamity, when a rail shattered under a Great North Eastern express at Hatfield in October 2000, resulting in four deaths.

With no understanding of the breadth or seriousness of the problems, and dependent on outside consultants, few of whom properly understood railway operations, Railtrack panicked, introducing 20mph emergency speed restrictions at 81 suspect sites, then gradually bringing the network to a near standstill by extending the speed limits to 1,286 sites by May 2001. Replacing worn rails – many of which did not warrant immediate replacement, let alone draconian speed restrictions – cost Railtrack well over a billion pounds and took well over a year. The disaster was compounded by maintenance engineers seizing the opportunity to get long-standing repairs completed. And once temporary restrictions were in place, they could only be removed with the sanction of the Railway Inspectorate, whose officers were understandably cautious. A few weeks after Hatfield, a Virgin express was derailed at low speed near Glasgow, due to the condition of the track, although thankfully no-one was hurt.

Although Southall, Ladbroke Grove and Hatfield had been tragic, they were not disastrous in themselves, but they served to destroy all confidence in Railtrack's ability to maintain the infrastructure on which the train operators depended. Not only were the operators subsequently compensated for loss of income during the chaos of 2000-2002, they were to claim that the financial predictions on which they had based their falling subsidy bids were now in ruins, and they would thus need long-term compensation. The total cost would run into billions.

A more farcical episode that at least didn't kill anyone, was Railtrack's confident guarantee that the West Coast Main Line would be rebuilt as a 140mph high speed line using moving block signalling technology, at a cost of £2.1 billion. Virgin subsequently based its highly optimistic franchise bid on the availability of a 140mph

Not all franchises are overpriced and under-performing. South West Trains, run by Stagecoach since 1996, had a difficult start, but has proved one of the most stable. PHOTO: David Henshaw

railway, contracting to pay a surplus of nearly £1.4 billion to the Government in the later years.

Absurd though it may sound, Railtrack, a company with little engineering or train operating knowledge – and, it seems, even less business acumen – confidently signed a deal with Virgin to share the windfall profits, or pay a £250 million penalty if the upgrade couldn't be delivered. The cost and complexity of the West Coast upgrade subsequently rose through the roof, to £5.8 billion in 1999, and an estimated £7 billion in 2001. The cost would ultimately rise even higher, but the 140mph railway never materialised, because those involved simply didn't understand the technology they were promising.

The only winner was Virgin, which was to receive a great deal of public money for its gamble: £189 million in the year to March 2003, when it had contracted to pay a £4 million surplus, and £332 million the following year, when it should have paid out £59 million. These payments were made to the private operator of one of the busiest and most profitable railways in the country – an appalling waste of public money, when other lines were desperate for investment, and there was a backlog of stalled reopening schemes.

The whole thing had turned into a financial and legal morass. In the words of the Transport Select Committee, now chaired by the formidable Gwyneth Dunwoody:

"… it is clear that the vast majority [of franchises] have not been able to produce the efficiency gains that were confidently anticipated at the time of privatisation. The network is now being run by a patchwork of companies, which operate with a variety of incentives…

In our view, the essence of private sector involvement is that the private sector pays if it gets its sums wrong. It is outrageous that such astonishingly large sums of taxpayers' money have been used to prop up palpably failing businesses…"

By this time, Railtrack had long since gone bust. It had asked for extra funding to cover this series of largely self-inflicted disasters, and in October 2001 New Labour Secretary of State Stephen Byers responded by putting the company into administration. It was replaced by the state-owned Network Rail, but in May 2002, as this new organisation was still trying to get things back under control and restore a semblance of normality, a West Anglia Great Northern express derailed at speed while passing over points at Potter's Bar station, resulting in seven deaths and 76 injuries. The points were the responsibility of outside contractor Jarvis, and this incident more or less marked the end of the outsourcing of infrastructure works, which were progressively taken in-house by Network Rail after 2003.

Network Rail was set up as a company limited by guarantee, and would remain a strange beast, neither state owned in the post-1947 mould, nor fully commercial. The company had no shareholders as such, but was nominally accountable to an executive of 120 members, including representatives of train operators, passengers and employees. Network Rail is generally thought to be 'not for profit', although it can and indeed does, make profits, but not in the form of dividends to shareholders, or in this case, members.

Network Rail would take years to settle down, but it was at least engineer-led, and ultimately proved a stable bed on which to reconstitute a failing industry. By 2001, some of the Train Operating Companies were in a serious financial position, and most were looking weak. The Government could have progressively taken franchises back in-house, but it took what it considered to be the 'least worst' option of shoring them up with extra cash payments. Some have argued that the franchise bidders had got into this tangle because they had deliberately put in unrealistic bids, gambling that the Government would not allow them to fail.

Railtrack wasn't the only organisation to disappear during the tangled evolution of the privatised railway. In 2001, the New Labour Government had replaced the Office of Passenger

Virgin ordered the 140mph Pendolino on the basis that Railtrack would supply a 140mph railway. Railtrack would pay a heavy price for its failure to deliver the infrastructure. A Pendolino passes Wolverton near Milton Keynes in 2012. PHOTO: David Edge

Rail Franchising with the Strategic Rail Authority. It sounded a perfect organisation to inject a bit of forward planning into the industry, particularly with regard to new lines and stations, and protection of disused rail corridors, but it had neither the powers nor the funding to find a satisfactory role, and was abolished in 2006.

In its brief career the SRA did at least provide a glimpse of what full public ownership might look like, when in June 2003, it took control of the failing Connex South Eastern franchise. State-owned South Eastern Trains ran the franchise until 2006, when it was again relet, but the genie was out of the bottle – it was obvious that state-run companies could run franchises, and run them well. In November 2009, when National Express walked away from the East Coast franchise, losing £79 million worth of bonds in the process, the Department for Transport took control, and was still running the franchise successfully three years later, trading as East Coast Main Line Ltd, a subsidiary of Directly Operated Railways, a DfT vehicle purpose-made to run franchises in an emergency.

East Coast went on to do rather well, generating profits of £53 million in its first nine months, and £183 million in 2010-11, a little more, incidentally, than National Express had contracted to pay the Government in the same period. In other words, the performance of East Coast was much like that of any private franchisee. Long-distance franchises are amongst the toughest to run reliably, so it was no surprise that East Coast received the second highest level of complaints of all the franchises, but its privately-owned competitor, the Virgin-run West Coast, received the highest number. In terms of train punctuality, East Coast did rather worse than Virgin but much the same as Hull Trains and Grand Central, the two open access operators sharing the same route, which suggested that the passenger grumbles are more about congestion and infrastructure issues than franchisee performance.

The Great Railway Conspiracy

      The franchise system reached its nadir in August 2012, when it was announced that the West Coast franchise would be taken away from Virgin Trains and awarded to rival FirstGroup. Richard Branson started a loud and successful rearguard action, arguing that the FirstGroup bid of £13.3 billion over 15 years was too high to be sustainable. As Virgin instigated a judicial review, the Government announced it would hold firm, but in October, the DfT announced that following the discovery of significant technical flaws in the bidding process, the decision to award the franchise to FirstGroup would be scrapped, and the whole process repeated, at a cost of £40 million.

      In the end, the system had proved unworkable. Short franchises left no room for innovative private investment, but 15-year franchises were impossible to price accurately, leading to default or excessive profits. With the whole system in disarray, other franchise renewals were put on hold.

      Despite the fact that Directly Operated Trains was waiting in the wings for just such an emergency, it was later announced that the West Coast would remain with Virgin in the interim. A once in a decade opportunity to take the process back in-house appeared to have been lost, but in early 2013, with four major franchise renewals in limbo, there was everything to play for.

Minor railways proved almost impossible to shut after privatisation, primarily because the mechanism for providing services was so unwieldy, and set in contractual stone for so long, that changing *anything* was complex, and withdrawing public funding for a whole service would presumably result in a compensation claim from the franchisee contracted to run it. Another reason, paradoxically, was that the privatised railway saw a period of spectacular and

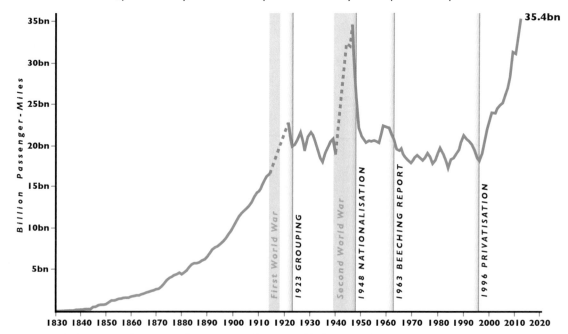

A graph of passenger-miles over time demonstrates just how susceptible the railways have been to upheaval and reorganisation. It's also interesting that the strongest growth has taken place during periods of relative commercial freedom.

sustained growth, far beyond anything experienced under private or national ownership in the past. Even in the monopolistic heyday of the railways before the First World War, passenger growth was nothing like as fast as it was in the early 21st Century, and by 2012 annual passenger-mileage stood higher than it had *ever* done, either in war or peacetime.

With the franchising system so dysfunctional, and service levels – and even some timetabling – now micromanaged by the Department for Transport, it simply isn't credible that privatisation itself could have fuelled this boom, as supporters argue. True, in the early days, liberalisation had allowed operators to exploit latent demand on busy routes, primarily by increasing service frequency. But overall, fares had risen sharply, trains were becoming over-crowded, and marketing – on a national level at least – had been almost non-existent.

No doubt there were many reasons for the rise in rail traffic, including congested and unpleasant road conditions, but the primary issue seemed to be stability. Historically, whenever the future of services was left in the unpredictable hands of 'here today, gone tomorrow' politicians, confidence in the railways tended to fall. When the railways have been left to get on with the job, traffic rises. A glance at the diagram on page 260 shows clearly how traffic has fallen in the lead up to every period of reorganisation, generally rising sharply afterwards, except in the ongoing turmoil that followed the *Reshaping* report.

Post-privatisation, the Department of Transport (renamed the Department *for* Transport after 2002) may have been interfering over timetables and rolling stock purchases on the modern railway, but for the first time in half a century, the Department was no longer plotting to destroy it, and that brought a certain confidence back to the industry.

By 2013, many branch and secondary services were bulging at the seams. This is Bristol Temple Meads at lunchtime on a Friday afternoon in October - a busy travel day, but not exactly rush-hour. The 14.22 to Portsmouth Harbour has arrived full and standing, with some 50 passengers trying to board. One of the problems is that privatisation has failed to provide enough new rolling stock - this 20-year-old BR-built two-car Class 158 is normally strengthened with a third coach. PHOTO: David Henshaw

The Great Railway Conspiracy

Proximity to a railway station was once again a key selling point for housing, something unknown since the 1960s except in the London commuter belt, while shops and businesses increasingly saw a convenient station as an asset instead of an irrelevance.

This renewed confidence had a marked effect on the branch lines, some of which had lived with the threat of closure for 50 years, and would now see some of the strongest growth. Since 2005, many have benefited from being given Community Rail status, with input from local Community Rail Partnerships, usually comprising the operator, local rail user groups and local authorities. The most successful of these have funded full- or part-time officers, who in some cases have been credited with greatly increasing passenger numbers. The most successful, the Devon & Cornwall Rail Partnership, has been based at the University of Plymouth since 1991, well before privatisation, and has had a considerable effect on the growth of the six branch lines in its care.

Sadly, with the franchising system so inflexible, the privatised railway has been singularly ineffective at opening and reopening railways, because new services now necessitated a whole raft of new paperwork, agreement by numerous parties, and a new contract price, unless outside revenue support could be found, or the train operator agreed to take the financial risk.

British Rail had often been intransigent about building new stations, but it did at least generally have one eye on the lucrative new traffic flow. Network Rail had no such incentive, other than the indirect promise of increased track charges. There was no mechanism for funding and instigating experimental services from central government, or for using profits made elsewhere on the railway network. Even if agreement could be reached amongst all the players, there was often no rolling stock available. Bringing new services on stream had become a long, slow, bureaucratic business.

Back in the mid to late-90s, there was a brief flurry of activity as local authorities and other stakeholders rushed to get new services on board before the franchises were finalised. The biggest, and arguably the most successful reopening in this era was the 'Robin Hood' line, bringing passenger trains back to the industrial area north of Nottingham that had once been congested with competing lines (see map page 12), but had been completely denuded of services by the 1960s, leaving the very large towns of Mansfield and Sutton-in-Ashfield without stations. This 'Beeching too far' couldn't remain for long, and services finally reached Mansfield in 1995, and further through this depressed former coal-mining area to Worksop in 1998, just as line reopenings elsewhere were drawing to a halt. At 29 miles in length, the Robin Hood line is – to date – one of the biggest reopenings, and integration with Nottingham's successful tram system helped passenger numbers to climb rapidly to over a million a year.

Other reopenings in the early years of privatisation included the strategically useful Middlesbrough to Northallerton line in 1996, and the outer suburban Walsall to Rugeley Town in the West Midlands. This freight line had reopened to passengers on an experimental basis as far as Hednesford in 1989, and like so many others, far exceeded its passenger estimates. In 1997 the services were extended northwards to Rugeley Town, although the final mile to the Trent Valley junction – which would restore through trains to Birmingham New Street for the first time in 40 years – had to wait a little longer. The Walsall to Rugeley line went on to be included in a round of electrification proposals in July 2012, and electric trains were planned to be running by 2019, giving faster commuter services, a diversionary route for InterCity trains, and perhaps even semi-fast long-distance services too.

Success on this scale was bittersweet: the line from Walsall to Rugeley had only survived intact from the 1960s to the 1980s because it had been useful for freight, and the same was true for much of the Robin Hood line. By the turn of the Millennium, freight lines to collieries, steelworks and other heavy industries were fast disappearing, while the demand for passenger services was growing fast. Where track remained, reinstatement was easy, but where it had gone – especially where developments had occurred – it was much harder.

Bizarrely, the reinstatement of track, even where it had existed for a hundred years, now required a Transport & Works Act order, which could be drawn out into a long and involved procedure if there were objections. Sometimes, reinstatement was held up even where all parties were in agreement. The Oxford to Bicester section of the East-West line already carried trains, but the need for a short new chord at Bicester triggered the Transport & Works procedure, and the project was subsequently delayed because of fears that bats in Wolvercote Tunnel would be upset by an *increase* in the number of trains, a problem expected to be solved by lighting the tunnel as trains approach.

As Railtrack sped on its way to collapse, and the various contractors and franchisees in the railway privatisation morass became constipated with writs and contracts, railway reopenings ground to a halt. Apart from a short link from Halifax to Huddersfield in 2000, the only railways to open between 1998 and 2005 were new-build projects, such as the short Heathrow Express line and phases one and two of the Channel Tunnel Rail Link. These were vital international infrastructure projects, but they had nothing to do with righting the wrongs of the 1960s.

But the demand for reinstatement was growing rapidly, and no amount of contractual complications could hold back the log-jam for long. Even the serious downturn of 2008 onwards had little effect on railway passenger growth. Contrary to the expectations of the

Under privatisation, regional rail reopenings almost ground to a halt, but some big schemes were completed, such as phases 1 and 2 of the Channel Tunnel Rail Link, now generally known as HS1. As with previous main line improvements, the high speed Javelin commuter trains have helped the viability of connecting branch lines, such as Ashford to Hastings, which was very lucky to survive the 1960s, and like many similar lines, is now thriving. Rye, for example, is just over an hour from London, against an hour and 50 minutes in 2005. PHOTO: Brian Stephenson

Chatelherault on the Larkhall line in 2009. Trains returned here exactly 50 year after closure during the 'Reshaping' era. The line has been very successful and may be extended. PHOTO: Gordon Thomson

politicians and civil servants who had designed a privatised railway to deal with managed decline of local and regional services, demand was growing rapidly, with traffic growth in excess of 10% a year in unlikely places, such as the once threatened line to Barnstaple in north Devon, which had been expected to fade away after construction of the North Devon Link Road to the M5 and Tiverton Parkway station. Between 2001 and 2011, traffic here increased by 157%. On the Truro to Falmouth branch in Cornwall, traffic increased by 212% in the same period, helped by reinstatement of a passing loop at Penrhyn in 2009.

Since 2000, most railway reconstruction has been in London, Scotland and Wales, largely because devolved government has taken responsibility for transport away from the dead hand of the Department for Transport. The first big reopening of the modern era was the Vale of Glamorgan freight route in South Wales. Closed in 1964 at the height of the Beeching cuts, the 19-mile line reopened in June 2005, complete with new stations at Llantwit Major and Rhoose, which was linked by shuttle bus to the nearby Cardiff International Airport.

Later in 2005 the Glasgow northern suburban line, which had reopened as far as Maryhill in 1993, was extended to an interchange with existing services at Anniesland. To the south of the city, a 2.9-mile line was relaid to put Larkhall (population 15,000) back on the railway map. By 2008, the service was carrying 40% more passengers than had been predicted, encouraging Strathclyde Partnership for Transport to investigate extending the line another four

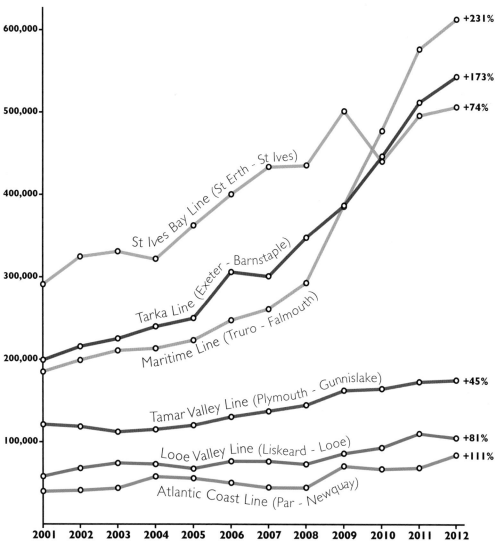

Some of the most spectacular growth has taken place on the branch lines in Devon and Cornwall, all of which were under threat at some point in the 1960s. Well targeted investment has helped, such as the passing loop on the Maritime line, and more will produce further big gains. Reopening of the Bere Alston to Tavistock line will greatly boost the Tamar Valley figures, and the proposed St Austell to Newquay link will have a similar affect on the Atlantic Coast line (if it goes ahead). Overall growth in 11 years is 127%. NOTE: The graph only shows local traffic to Newquay, and both the Looe Valley and Tarka lines were badly affected by flooding in late 2012. The Avocet line from Exeter to Exmouth - which like the Looe and St Ives branches was recommended for closure by Dr Beeching - carried 1.4 million passengers in 2012, an increase of 9.7% in a single year.

FIGURES: Wessex Trains/First Great Western/Devon & Cornwall Rail Partnership

miles to Stonehouse, or seven miles to Strathaven. These two towns have smaller populations and reinstatement would involve the reconstruction of a viaduct, but it was a measure of how much the transport picture had changed that such a major scheme has even been considered.

The next successful project was in Wales, with the long-awaited reopening of the Ebbw Vale line. This had remained open for freight to a steelworks, but with the complete closure of the Ebbw Vale industrial complex in 2001, reinstatement of passenger services became a priority before the line could be torn up and the land sold off. After October 2002 the line was mothballed, but it would be almost six years before passenger services were re-established. Unusually the £30 million, 18-mile line was commissioned and built by local authorities, with funding coming from a variety of sources.

Once again, traffic far exceeded the forecasts, the Ebbw Vale line carrying a quarter of a

million passengers in the first six months, and stabilising at around 44,000 passengers a month, double the original forecast, and 25% higher than the target for 2012. In 2011 Ebbw Vale Parkway alone (there are six stations in all) generated 247,000 passenger movements. But once again, there was frustration that the line had been designed and built using forecasts that were badly wrong, resulting in penny-pinching construction of a largely single-track railway, making extra services to Cardiff, and the proposed reinstatement to Newport, difficult and expensive.

In early 2013, a second phase was being planned, involving a long section of double-track to boost capacity, and extension into Ebbw Vale town centre, the Parkway station being more than a mile from the town... a strange omission in a relatively poor area where one of the key aims was to revitalise the town itself. It looked like the Newport

Despite being done 'on the cheap' - mostly single track, and terminating well short of the town centre - the Ebbw Vale line has been a huge success. The terminus, Ebbw Vale Parkway, generated a quarter of a million passengers in 2011. PHOTO: Wikipedia

link, double-track and town centre station could end up costing more than the original reopening, and would have been much cheaper and easier to implement if completed in 2008.

After Ebbw Vale, the focus returned to Scotland with the Stirling-Alloa-Kincardine reopening. In this case, only the seven miles from Stirling to Alloa were reopened to regular passenger trains, the rest of the 13-mile line being used principally for coal traffic, although full passenger reopening was expected to follow, with trains running through to Dunfermline and Edinburgh. Repeating a now familiar pattern, the first year passenger usage figure of 400,000 far exceeded the pessimistic 155,000 forecast. Less positively, the scheme exceeded its £35 million budget by £50 million, with much of the expenditure going on a new link road and stabilisation of old mine workings.

A rare failure of a reopened line occurred close to Rugeley, when services were restored over the direct freight line between Walsall and Wolverhampton in 1998. Although useful for people in Walsall and Wolverhampton, the reopening was a half-hearted affair, poorly advertised or integrated with other trains, and with no new stations. Trains were withdrawn in 2008 after passenger figures proved disappointing, just as they had been at Corby in 1987, when an equally unsuitable shuttle to Kettering was reinstated, without proper station facilities, and an irregular, unreliable service pattern.

Corby subsequently returned in spectacular fashion early in 2009, with a £10 million station and services to London, traffic growing rapidly to 176,000 passengers in 2011. The core traffic was to Kettering and London, but a few trains later ran northwards from Corby to Melton Mowbray and Derby, with further extensions under consideration. The Walsall to

In May 2008, passenger services were restored from Stirling to Alloa. The line on the left continues to Kincardine and is currently only used by coal trains, although through passenger services are expected to follow. PHOTO: Jeffray Wotherspoon

The Great Railway Conspiracy

Wolverhampton line wasn't been so lucky, but proposals were gradually taking shape to restore passenger trains to the nearby Sutton Park line (closure of which forms the introduction to Chapter 7), and Walsall to Wolverhampton might eventually form part of this wider scheme.

The return of trains to Corby had taken much longer than expected as a direct result of the fragmented nature of the privatised railway network. The local franchised operator Midland Mainline had acknowledged that demand existed from this town of 50,000 people, but on a short-term contract, it inevitably took a short-term view and refused to build a station. With population growing fast (Corby's population would hit 61,000 by 2011), the station was eventually funded by local authorities and development agencies. Services should have begun in late 2008, but further delays were caused by a lack of rolling stock and heavy handed management by the Department for Transport.

The problems at Corby were not unusual. The average cost of building new stations was around £300,000 in the 1980s, but it had risen three-fold within a decade, and would rise a further four times in the decade that followed, partly because of contractual red tape and bureaucracy, but also through factors not directly linked to privatisation, such as the need for wheelchair accessible ramps. When a station reopened at Beauly, north of Inverness in 2002, the cost was a staggering £250,000 for a single-car platform, car park and bus shelter. Usage rose rapidly to 50,000 passengers a year – not bad from a village with a population of 1,164, but it was becoming increasingly difficult to justify expenditure on this level, particularly where consultants were consistently suggesting pessimistic usage figures. Beauly was by far the cheapest station to open since privatisation, and the average cost is now around £4 million.

Alloa, Ebbw Vale and Corby were all minor lines, but in the 1980s tentative moves

After a false start in 1987 with an irregular shuttle service, Corby did it properly in 2009 with a smart new station and an hourly service to London, plus a few trains heading northwest to Derby. On 23rd February 2009, the media await the first train.

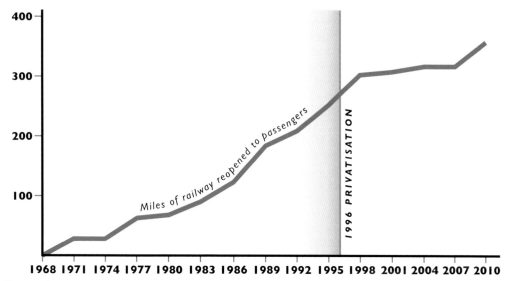

The rate of railway reopenings slowed dramatically after privatisation, but has picked up again since, reaching nearly 400 miles in early 2013 - nearly 10% of the mileage closed during the 1960s, with a lot more to come

began to restore the Oxford to Cambridge 'Varsity' line, and associated services. The first section, between Oxford and Bicester Town, reopened experimentally in 1987 along what was still then a functioning freight railway. Freight was later withdrawn, but a rather basic passenger service survived.

In 1995, when national government was – to put it mildly – disinterested in rail restoration, and the Department of Transport still openly hostile, a group of local authorities formed the East-West Rail Consortium with a view to filling the missing link between Bicester and Bletchley, restoring passenger and freight services over much of the Varsity line. This was a relatively straightforward project, as the entire route was intact, and had been used by occasional freight trains until 1993. The more daring thinkers were willing to suggest restoration of the entire route, bringing passenger trains back between Oxford and Cambridge, and providing a convenient route for freight from the fast growing East Anglian container ports. It was an obvious, and relatively easy scheme, but in the early years of railway privatisation progress was painfully slow, and it was to be more than a decade before some form of reopening began to look politically feasible.

The key proved to be the dynamic Chiltern Trains, which had its sights set on Oxford. Chiltern had looked into restoring the direct Princes Risborough to Oxford railway, but concluded that the route was too badly damaged. A longer, but altogether easier route, would be from Oxford to Bicester on the already reopened line, then via a short new link onto Chiltern's main line, and south to High Wycombe and London Marylebone. This may not have been the most direct option, but it gave Oxford a second route to the capital, a Parkway station to the north of the city, and improved commuter services to Bicester. This promise of private capital would provide the cornerstone of the entire east-west rail project, because Chiltern also had ambitions to reopen the former Great Central line north of Aylesbury (still used by occasional freight trains) as far as the Oxford-Cambridge line, then eastwards to Milton Keynes, by now a fast growing regional centre. The first stage of this scheme was a short 2¹/₂-mile link from

The Great Railway Conspiracy

Aylesbury to a new Parkway station north of the town, which opened in December 2008.

The £130 million Oxford-Bicester-Marylebone project was finally given the go ahead in October 2012, and the line was expected to be completed by 2015. It was designed to be compatible with the East-West Rail Consortium's proposed Oxford-Bicester-Bedford service, which would link the then-isolated Oxford-Bicester and Bletchley to Bedford services. As the Chiltern scheme was being approved, it was announced that the Oxford to Bedford stretch of the Varsity line would be electrified to reinstate the strategic freight and long-distance passenger route lost when the Great Central trunk line and associated links were closed.

The western section of the East-West Varsity line was given a benefit/cost ratio of 6.3, even if the entire project was state-funded, and an even better rate of return if developers along the route could be persuaded to contribute. In 2012, Oxford to Milton Keynes took about 60 minutes by car off-peak (peak-time journeys could take two or three times longer, according to the Consortium) and the express coach schedule was 75 minutes, with no realistic railway option. The East-West line would link the two cities in 35 minutes. This passenger service alone was expected to produce a £4 million surplus after operating costs, and the tracks would also be shared with Chiltern services, and freight and long-distance passenger trains.

Writing in 2013, it looked likely that within a few years a whole swathe of lines in Oxfordshire, Buckinghamshire and Bedfordshire, left almost derelict in the late 1960s, would be restored to main line standards, but only because the majority of the route had remained open for freight into the 1990s.

What of the remaining stretch of Varsity line, eastwards to Cambridge, which had closed throughout in 1968? Even in the early 1990s, the Department of Transport was prepared to argue at a public inquiry into the A421 Bedford Southern Bypass that the handful of railways reopened to date had been dismal failures, and there would thus be no point in bridging the Oxford-Cambridge trackbed east of Bedford. The road was subsequently constructed with insufficient clearance, making reinstatement of the railway much more difficult, but not impossible.

Further east in Sandy, a school and a small housing estate had been constructed across the trackbed. Had any sort of protection existed for such nationally important infrastructure, these developments would never have been allowed, or would have been adapted to make future reinstatement possible.

Between Sandy and Oxford, many small developments had occurred, but at Barton near Cambridge, the trackbed had been appropriated as a base for radio telescopes, one of which, ironically, moves on rails, and on the final run into Cambridge the trackbed had become a guided busway. Just one of these issues would be enough to rule out reinstatement, and the East-West Rail Group was forced to look at a number of alternative routes. Front runner in the medium-term was restoration on a new alignment between Bedford and Sandy, then south on the relatively congested East Coast main line to a new chord north of Hitchin, and finally north-east to Cambridge. This looked like the preferred option to get services running, while work could progress on a direct link in the longer term. But even with the positive benefit/cost ratios, proven demand, and some private sector capital, government remained uneasy about the more 'difficult' parts of the East-West project, and although the reopening of the mothballed sections looked certain, there was no leadership to complete the project.

Even while politicians were tripping over each other to be photographed cutting ribbons at Bicester, other railway routes were being obliterated, because Government policy – in England at least – was to go for the cheapest possible option, with guided buses very much in vogue.

In theory, the guided bus has much to recommend it. Unlike a train or tram, the vehicles can pick up passengers on conventional bus routes before entering the guided section to run fast to a city centre, then returning to the road network to deliver passengers in the conventional way. There were however, many issues. The technology, although claimed to be simple and cheap, was largely unproven, and busways would prove to be very expensive technology. More importantly, conversion would rule out a rail reopening for freight and long-distance traffic in the future, and the buses were significantly slower on the guided section, and just as prone to delays on the city streets as a conventional bus. It was a very expensive way of providing rather limited services. The stage was set for one of the most hotly contested public transport debates since the Beeching era.

The Cambridge to St Ives line in the Fens was the last remnant of a large network that had survived primarily to carry sand and gravel from quarries at St Ives. With infrastructure costs largely paid for by this heavy freight traffic, passenger services had remained until 1970, when the line was refused a grant under the over-generous Cooper Brothers formula. This didn't need to be a serious issue while the line remained open for freight, and as commuter routes into Cambridge became more congested, the general view was that reinstatement of the passenger service would be a mere formality. British Rail had no objections, and the local authorities were very keen to see passenger trains re-established. There were more ambitious proposals too, such as reopening from St Ives eastwards to Huntingdon, giving a through passenger and freight link from Cambridge to the north, relieving the East Coast main line.

Matters came to a head in the 1990s when freight services were withdrawn, and the line mothballed. With privatisation under way, it was a difficult time for rail reopening projects, and despite strong interest from local authorities and the public, the Government was indifferent and the Department of Transport typically hostile. With the arrival of Tony Blair's New Labour Government in 1997, 25 new tram projects were briefly under consideration, but the accent moved towards buses as a cheaper alternative to tram and rail schemes, and as there was little evidence either way with regard to guided buses, it was decided to test the water with a major scheme. There would be no money for the rail option, but generous funding if the local authorities went for the guided bus.

Development of the scheme – which would also convert the extreme east end of the Varsity line – proved a divisive and painful affair, with the Secretary of State allegedly receiving 2,700 objections, with only four residents writing in favour! Nevertheless, the busway had been costed at some £54 million, against £109 million for rail reinstatement, although both figures were hotly contested by Cast Iron, the pressure group established in 2003 to fight for the railway.

With encouragement from central government, Cambridgeshire County Council voted in favour of the project in 2006 and work began on the world's longest guided busway. Building a concrete trackway through boggy Fenland was never going to be easy, and costs and delays rapidly escalated, the busway finally opening in 2011 at a cost (again, the true figure was argued over) of £181 million, a bill that could rise to £230 million if the County Council lost a legal battle with contractor B A M Nuttall.

As with modern railway reopenings, the busway proved a considerable success with the public, stabilising at around 200,000 passengers a month, and a total of 2.5 million passengers in the first year, 40% above the target figure of 1.75 million. Many of the passengers had previously travelled by bus, but a quarter were car drivers, drawn principally to the larger bus halts, designed to look and function more like railway stations than bus stops. Clearly the busway has proved very effective for carrying commuters into Cambridge, with early figures suggesting a reduction of about 1,700 vehicles a day on the busy A14 road [32], but whether it represented value for money against rail reinstatement in the longer term was still very much open to debate. Cast Iron continued to campaign, but later moved its focus to the provision of a railway station at Milton Road in the northern suburbs of Cambridge, which would give direct trains to London from the Science Park, and a cross platform interchange with the busway.

Such was the rush to get guided buses up and running, that even as the bills and frustration were mounting in Cambridge – and long before a single passenger had been carried – BAM Nuttall was awarded the contract to build a similar busway between the towns of Luton and Dunstable along the route of a freight line disused since 1989. Once again, the line had come very close to reopening to passenger trains, and there was considerable debate about whether a guided busway was the best solution, either for local journeys, or London-bound commuters heading for Luton railway station. Once again, the railway was part of a longer route, in this case linking the West Coast Main Line at Leighton Buzzard with the Midland Main Line at Luton. Even though reinstatement of this line was actively being considered as one of the options for reconnecting Oxford to Cambridge, no wider strategic thought seems to have gone into the decision to build a four-mile busway on the route.

Although of purely local benefit, the Luton to Dunstable guided busway and associated works had been costed at £89 million, of which no less than £80 million would come from central government, but in 2012, costs began to spiral, and as at St Ives, the opening date was pushed back.

In Hampshire, the County Council and Portsmouth City Council had put together an innovative plan to rebuild the Gosport branch line, closed to passengers in 1953, for light rail operation, with trains running from Fareham town centre, via Fareham station, to Gosport, then diving under Portsmouth Harbour in a new submerged tube tunnel to link up with heavy rail services in Portsmouth. Later stages would link Fareham to Southampton city centre, and Portsmouth to Waterlooville, with the tantalising possibility of extending the tunnel all the way to the Isle of Wight in the future – trams being the ideal solution for the Island's constricted

The Hampshire light rail scheme proposed to reuse the Gosport branch line as the core of a light rail network running under Portsmouth Harbour to the city centre. It was killed off by a cheaper busway concept.

While local authorities in England rushed for the bus, railway reopenings in Scotland were getting increasingly sophisticated. The Airdrie to Bathgate line, which reopened in 2010, was double track and overhead electrified throughout. PHOTO: Balfour Beatty

railway network.

In 2005, after a considerable amount of work had been put into the £190 million scheme, and a Public Inquiry in 1999 had concluded that it was fully justified, the New Labour Transport Secretary Alistair Darling refused to back the project, also vetoing similar schemes in Leeds and Merseyside. With no money on the table for light rail, the authorities were forced to go for buses, not guided in this case, but segregated on the old railway formation, which would be designated as a 'protected street' in the ownership of the County Council. As Hampshire County Council wryly put it, after spending more than £10 million planning the light rail scheme:

"Central Government refused to finance the proposed LRT project, despite significant efforts to promote it by Hampshire County Council. While the BRT does not provide all of the benefits that LRT would have done, it goes a significant way to providing improvements in public transport..."

One got the impression that British transport policy wasn't so much in a mess as completely non-existent.

Fortunately regional government has given strong impetus to growth elsewhere, particularly in London. From 2003, the Silverlink franchise in North London was rebranded as 'London Overground', to match the long-established 'Underground' brand. From 2007 control of these services was transferred from the Department for Transport to Transport for London, which had ambitious plans for new trains, increased service frequencies and new and restored track. By December 2012, the run-down and uncoordinated North London services had been transformed into an 'outer circle' line by rebuilding the disused Broad Street viaduct (fortunately free of development since closure), absorbing the East London Tube line, and adding a few other bits of infrastructure. Helped by the new trains, clear, consistent branding, and easy access from

The Great Railway Conspiracy

The Overground has brought together a mixed bag of inner urban railways and with sensible investment and meticulous branding, created a network London can be proud of. This is Hoxton, a new station on the Broadstreet viaduct, which closed in 1986, but fortunately remained free of development

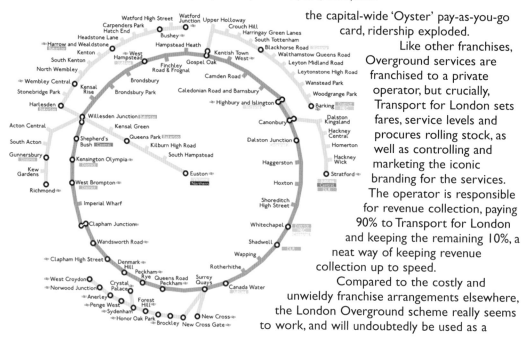

the capital-wide 'Oyster' pay-as-you-go card, ridership exploded.

Like other franchises, Overground services are franchised to a private operator, but crucially, Transport for London sets fares, service levels and procures rolling stock, as well as controlling and marketing the iconic branding for the services. The operator is responsible for revenue collection, paying 90% to Transport for London and keeping the remaining 10%, a neat way of keeping revenue collection up to speed.

Compared to the costly and unwieldy franchise arrangements elsewhere, the London Overground scheme really seems to work, and will undoubtedly be used as a template for local control in other urban – and perhaps rural – areas in the future.

As the privatised railway began to settle down, a few innovative developments were taking place elsewhere too. Some 50 years after the British Transport Commission had first trialled lightweight railbuses, the technology was finally adopted in the UK in 2009. The Parry People Mover (PPM) company had been established in 1992, to develop, and hopefully sell, the concept of a flywheel-assisted ultralight railbus. With the 500kg flywheel able to store energy while decelerating or idling, the machines provided adequate acceleration using a 2.3-litre car engine, making them much more fuel efficient than a normal diesel multiple unit, or even a 1950s railbus.

Despite the fact that the lightly built Pacer units of the 1980s had been mixing with normal traffic for decades, the more risk-averse railway of the new Millennium would not sanction the use of new railbuses running with other traffic, so PPM needed to find a short, isolated branch to conduct trials, with room for stabling and servicing on site. Conveniently, the 3/4-mile long branch between Stourbridge Junction and Stourbridge Town was quite near to the company's West Midlands base, and in 2006, permission was given to test a railbus on Sundays, when the line was closed to all traffic. During this 12-month experiment, the little machine ran 4,000 trips, achieving 99% punctuality, and reducing emissions by 80% compared to the normal diesel unit.

Official acceptance was a long-drawn out affair, but eventually a contractual arrangement was put together, the trains being owned and maintained at Stourbridge by Pre Metro Ltd, a

In 2009, the ultra-light railbus made a welcome return, some half a century after the BTC's experiments, brought to a premature end by the Beeching regime. The Class 139 units run between Stourbridge Junction and Stourbridge Town in the West Midlands. A flywheel energy storage system makes the units very fuel efficient, and although seating capacity is limited, the trains run an intensive service. Unfortunately, they are not cleared for mainline running. PHOTO: David Henshaw

company created specifically for this role. Pre Metro would provide services under contract to the local franchise holder London Midland, which was itself owned by GoVia, while the track and stations would remain the property of Network Rail!

Apart from teething issues caused by flange wear, the Class 139 railbuses built specifically to operate the Stourbridge service from 2009 have proved very successful, carrying 200,000 passengers in their first incomplete year, rising to 557,000 in 2010 and 592,000 in 2011. Not bad for a railbus with 20 seats, and a nominal maximum capacity of 60 passengers. The only inefficient part of the operation is double manning, with a driver and guard being carried on the three-minute journey, the guard playing little role except at busy times.

The railbus concept had finally been vindicated. The Class 139 proved cheap to run and popular with the public, but while they are banned from mixing with conventional rolling stock, their applications will be very limited. In 2012 PPM was developing a bigger twin-bogie design with a 50mph top speed and 120-passenger capacity. Although this would be more like a conventional rail vehicle than the Class 139, the target weight was 20 tons, half the weight of the equivalent single-car Class 153 diesel unit. Ironically, the surviving branch lines are now mostly too busy for units like this to handle all services, but had less remunerative branch lines such as Tetbury and Cirencester survived, these machines would have been ideal, and they may yet find a role as a cost-effective means of getting new services under way, to be replaced by larger units as traffic expands. Interestingly, it was widely assumed that traffic on reopened branch lines would take years to build up, as a whole new generation rediscovered the railway, but the evidence suggests a strong suppressed demand in most cases, with actual passenger

A rare thing: a road scheme in Galashiels has made allowance for the coming railway. Several earlier road schemes, such as the A720 Edinburgh Bypass, simply sliced through the formation and must be expensively bridged or tunnelled beneath. Far more expensive than doing the work when the road was built. PHOTO: Peter Delaney

numbers soon surpassing the pessimistic forecasts.

Railway reopening may have ground to a halt in England, but it has continued to move ahead in Scotland and Wales. The biggest and most controversial closure north of the border had been the Waverley Route from Edinburgh to Carlisle in 1969. It is hard to believe that a basic railway wasn't retained to serve the large towns of Galashiels and Hawick, which were both incidentally, in the select group of stations earning more than £25,000 a year in Beeching's *Reshaping* report, putting them in the same league as Mansfield amongst the stations that have since reopened.

With this proven passenger demand in mind, and soon-to-be-harvested Forestry Commission plantations growing in the wild country further south, the passenger and freight prospects for the Waverley Route just wouldn't go away.

Some building work had obstructed the trackbed, and as usual, trunk roads had been sanctioned and built across the former line at unsuitable elevations and angles, but more or less by chance, this 100-mile railway remained largely intact 30 years after closure. The first mile reopened to Edinburgh Crossrail passenger services in 2002, but an altogether bigger proposal was approved by the Scottish Parliament (by 114 votes to one) in 2006, to completely rebuild another 29 miles to Tweedbank, a couple of miles beyond Galashiels – the biggest project of its kind yet attempted. The line would be partly double-track with seven new stations serving a total of 200,000 people, and was expected to generate 1.4 million passenger journeys a year, although on past evidence it seemed almost certain

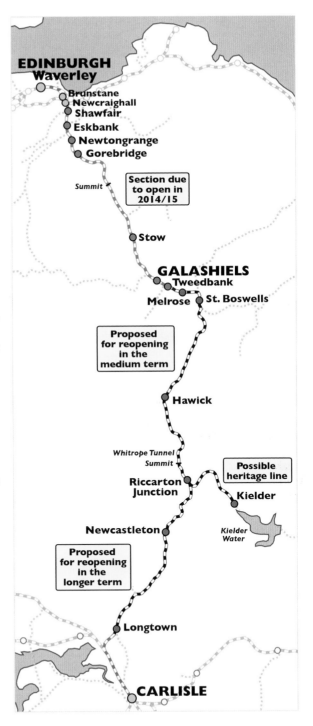

Not so much the end of the line as the beginning of the line. In 2012, Network Rail relaid the first 300 metres of the Waverley line while extending an existing turnback at Millerhill, Edinburgh. Another 30 miles will follow! PHOTO: Waverley Route Heritage Assoc.

that figure would be safely exceeded.

Although it was originally hoped the line would reopen in 2011, construction was long delayed by contractual issues, as bidders were sought to finance, build, maintain and operate the line, but after this scenario fell apart, and it began to look as though the project would fail, a more conventional arrangement was signed in November 2012, with Network Rail co-ordinating the construction phase and taking responsibility for the line.

At that time, the cost of the project was expected to be around £290 million, with completion scheduled for 2015, although as with most reopenings, a great deal of extra cost has been incurred through the unnecessary cost of dealing with the buildings and roads blocking the railway formation.

The Tweedbank line will effectively be 30 miles of new railway, putting it in a completely different league to the reopenings that have come before. Aware of the lessons learned at Ebbw Vale in particular, the authorities went some way to future proofing the project, agreeing at the 11th hour to a long platform at Tweedbank and other changes to allow passenger excursions and possibly freight use. The line will also be built with clearance for overhead electrification – useful for a commuter railway, but essential for a cross-border main line.

Once the northern section had been approved, campaigners moved on to making a case for reinstatement of passenger trains beyond Tweedbank to Melrose and Hawick, with the long-term aim of rebuilding the line in its entirety, all the way south to Carlisle. In many ways, the rebirth of the Waverley route marked a turning point. By 2012, railways were no longer being tentatively restored on an experimental basis, but rebuilt from scratch, like any other modern infrastructure.

What of the future? Fifty years after publication of *Reshaping*, the railway has been transformed, and intriguingly, rural railways are flourishing as never before. Even the doughty band of protesters who fought a rearguard action against the closures all those years, would find it hard to grasp quite how the railways have been transformed. In the 1950s and '60s they fought for *cheaper* railways, just to keep track on the ground. They could never have dreamed that half a century later rural rail would be growing at 5-10% a year, with no apparent end in sight.

Similarly, predicting transport patterns 50 years from today would be a rash undertaking. We know there will be an urgent need for efficient carbon-free transport, and we can hazard a guess that the population of the countryside will continue to grow, and expect greater mobility. Without a doubt the process of railway closure and retraction in the last 50 years was overdone – even for today's world, let alone the world our children will inherit.

There is still a great deal of work to be done to repair that damage, principally by reopening stations and lines, a process that will become increasingly difficult as time passes. Several houses were demolished to make room for the Waverley line, and there will be more on other schemes, thanks to perhaps the greatest scandal of the railway closure story – the refusal of successive governments to safeguard railway corridors.

Nevertheless, reopenings can and will continue, and the following pages look briefly at the top prospects for full or partial reopening. Realistic? The first edition of this book listed 61 lines, some of which seemed unlikely candidates back in 1991, but 22 years later, 12 have wholly or partially reopened, a further two have become guided busways, and nearly all the remainder are under active consideration. The arrival of the first train in Melrose will be a grand day for the Borders, but it will also carry the ghosts of those who spent their lives fighting for sanity in transport. After the pain of that tragic, wasted era, may they at last find rest.

The picture that says it all. Once a busy railway station, now an antique shop beside a trunk road, Melrose station will be just a mile and a half from the advancing Waverley line railhead from 2015, and a relatively simple target for the next stage of reinstatement, as the railway pushes on towards Hawick. The A6091 will not be despatched like the Waverley line before it, but road and rail will find space, as they must, both here, and in British transport planning. PHOTO: David Henshaw

10
The Top Reopening Prospects

"Railway stations that fell victim to the "Beeching Axe" in the 1960s could be rebuilt under plans announced today by Patrick McLoughlin, the Transport Secretary... Norman Baker, the rail minister, believes that many lines should not have been closed and that reopening routes will benefit communities and help the network adapt to significant population shifts over the past 50 years."

The Daily Telegraph, 25th January 2013

A typical new station - Newstead, north of Nottingham, on the Robin Hood line, a few weeks after the reopening in 1993. PHOTO: David Henshaw

This list of potential railway reopenings, and their order of priority, is entirely personal, and is not supposed to be exhaustive. Other potential candidates follow on page 289, and there are many more. Railways reopen for a number of reasons, but principally because the original decision to close the line was poorly thought through, and a clear case for reinstatement has always existed. Twelve stations listed in the top earning category of £25,000 a year on the 1961 *Reshaping* maps were subsequently shut (not all on Dr Beeching's watch, of course), and many of these high-earning stations have found their way into this top 30 list.

In other places, population growth has changed the shape and size of communities to such an extent that reinstatement of a rail link has become viable since closure. Washington New Town, Skelmersdale in Lancashire, and the area north of Bournemouth in Dorset are examples where the population has risen three-fold since closure, making a rail link strongly desirable. Paradoxically, other towns have stagnated since closure of the railway, and the return of decent public transport is seen as a means of kickstarting the local economy.

Useful evidence comes from the Association of Train Operating Company's 2009 report *Connecting Communities*, which looked at English towns with a population in excess of 15,000 and no railway station. Of the 75 towns studied, 20 had seen such degradation of the railway route that reopening was no longer considered viable, and in another 20 cases, existing stations nearby were considered adequate, leaving 35 towns where the case for reinstatement was subjected to preliminary cost/benefit analysis, giving a figure for what is (confusingly) called the benefit to cost ratio, or BCR. Of these 35, nine were found to exceed the Department for Transport's own BCR benchmark of 1.5, and five others had a BCR in excess of 1.0, meaning that reinstatement would still poten-tially give a net benefit after the cost of reconstruction. Nearly all of these appear in this top 30 list.

Of the others, six had a BCR below 1.0, but the ratio exceeded 1.5 in an operational sense (ie omitting the capital expenditure of reconstruction), eight had a BCR of between 1.0 and 1.5 with capital expenditure omitted, and seven were not considered viable by any criteria.

This work by ATOC has proved extremely useful, but much has changed since 2009. Costs have risen dramatically, but so has railway passenger usage, from just over 30 billion passenger-miles in 2007, to a

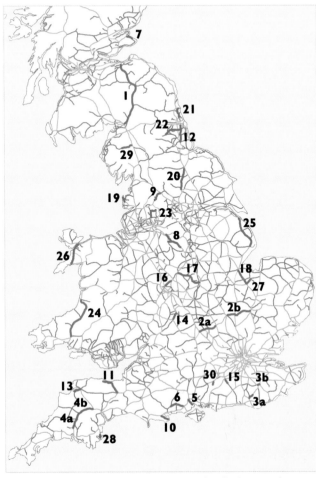

provisional figure of around 37 billion in 2012. With growth running at such a high rate, the potential for railway reopenings needs to be constantly reassessed, and a failure to attain a BCR of 1.5 in 2009 certainly does not prevent a candidate becoming firmly viable in the future.

1. **Edinburgh-Galashiels-Hawick-Carlisle** - 100 miles
Partial reconstruction underway
Cause célèbre of the reopening movement, this trunk line closed very late and very controversially. Thanks in part to local decision-making from the Scottish Parliament, the major project to rebuild the northernmost 30 miles from Edinburgh to Galashiels is already underway, and campaigners have switched their efforts to the middle and southern sections. The good news is that most of the route obstructions were around Edinburgh, so - more by luck than any sort of judgement - the remaining 70 miles

do not pose any serious issues. As Edinburgh to Galashiels is being rebuilt with clearance for overhead electrification, the eventual aim must be for an electrified line throughout, taking freight pressures off the East and West Coast lines, providing a diversionary option for both lines and restored passenger services throughout the Borders region. *www.campaignforbordersrail.org*

2(a). **Bicester-Milton Keynes** - 23 miles
Mothballed, complete reconstruction due to start soon

An essential section of the 'Varsity' route from Oxford to Cambridge. Not much comment is needed here, because the case has been made, and funding allocated. The line will carry local passenger traffic, as well as long-distance freight and passenger services.

2(b). **Bedford-Cambridge** - approx. 40 miles
Route partially obstructed, some new-build required

Having been closed to passengers and freight since 1968, this eastern-most section of the 'Varsity' line is a much more difficult prospect. Bedford to Sandy is obstructed in one or two places by road-building and housing, but it is still considered viable, with some new-build around Sandy itself. Further east, there are the radio telescopes and recently completed guided busway to think about... With no real indigenous traffic on this stretch, most campaigners feel a better option is to head south from Sandy and build a new chord onto an existing line at Hitchin. This might prove to be a more realistic short-term solution, with full reopening kept for the future.

3(a). **Uckfield-Lewes**-*(Brighton)* - 8 miles
Derelict, and some new-build required

For forty years a procession of transport ministers have refused to accept the argument that Uckfield to Lewes is worth reopening for local passenger services and occasional diversions. The Brighton Main Line 2 scheme has successfully widened the debate by putting this essentially local scheme into a regional context. Reopening this eight-mile line will give an alternative route from Brighton and Eastbourne to London, a prize that makes the costs look relatively trivial. The line is largely unobstructed, apart from a short heritage railway and the awkward elevation of the Uckfield bypass, which was, of course, built without any thought as to the railway's future prospects. At the Lewes end, the former rather inconvenient route is now lost for good, but a straightforward alternative exists along the north bank of the River Ouse, a route that BML2 would follow to tunnel directly under the South Downs towards Brighton. *www.bml2.co.uk*

3(b). **Tunbridge Wells-Eridge**-*(Brighton)* - 5 miles
Mostly heritage railway, some derelict

Like Uckfield to Lewes, this line makes little sense until seen in a wider context. The route is largely intact and operated as a heritage line as far as the former Tunbridge Wells West station. Here a supermarket obstructs the route, but this is not considered a serious obstacle, and BML2 considers that a double-track station could be rebuilt with some car parking rearrangements and minor adaptation to the supermarket building. The line would give Tunbridge Wells back what at one time was considered its main line to London, and provide many local travel opportunities, principally Brighton to Tunbridge, taking pressure off local roads. *www.bml2.co.uk*

4(a). **Okehampton-Yeoford**-*(Exeter)* - 16 miles
Heritage railway

Exeter to Okehampton could reopen tomorrow given the political will. After closure to passengers in 1972, a basic single line remained to serve the Meldon granite quarry. Freight has now ceased, but the line remains in place, although in private hands. Devon County Council already sponsors summer Sunday passenger services, taking visitors into the Dartmoor National Park, but there is no serious obstacle to restoring a full passenger service to Exeter.

4(b). **Okehampton-Tavistock-Bere Alston**-*(Plymouth)* - 20 miles
Derelict, limited obstruction

Tavistock to Bere Alston seems to have finally started on the long road to reinstatement as an essential element of a major house building scheme in Tavistock, but the long-term aim must be to restore the whole of the former trunk line from Exeter to Plymouth. This would give an alternative to the Great Western coastal trunk route via Dawlish, which is frequently disrupted by storms, and give Tavistock and Okehampton full access to the rail network east and west, as well as improving access to the Dartmoor National Park. Devon County Council also supports the idea of a Parkway station close to the A30, about four miles west of Okehampton. This would provide a railhead for the vast hinterland of North Devon and Cornwall that is unlikely to ever see rail services restored. The trackbed is essentially intact and in good condition, apart from council offices built across the route in Tavistock. Awkward, but not insoluble.

5. **Fawley-Totton**-*(Southampton)* - 13 miles
Freight

It would be difficult to find a more straightforward reinstatement candidate. The branch line to Fawley closed to passengers in 1966, leaving the towns of Fawley, Hythe and Marchwood (with a combined population well in excess of 40,000) relatively isolated. Fortunately, the line has remained open for freight, largely from the oil refinery at Fawley, and reinstatement is really only a matter of rebuilding the railway stations to modern standards. Fawley station presents a few

problems as it is now part of the refinery site, but reopening to Hythe is strongly supported by the local authorities and ATOC, which puts this simple £3 million project at the top of its priority list, with a BCR of 4.8. Trains would run into Southampton, possibly as an extension of the existing suburban service from Romsey and Southampton Airport.

6. **Brockenhurst-Ringwood-West Moors** - 26 miles
Derelict, limited obstruction

The area to the north of Bournemouth has seen considerable growth since closure of this line in 1964, and had it survived, there is no doubt that it would be thriving today. The eastern end has been largely obstructed, so the prospect of a through route being restored are slim, but the eastern end from Brockenhurst to Ringwood is completely intact, except for a short stretch of road built on the trackbed at Holmsley.

ATOC puts the cost of reinstatement from Brockenhurst to Ringwood (population around 13,000) at £70 million, with a BCR of 1.5, but there is certainly scope for rebuilding further west too. The only major obstacle is the A31 trunk road, which obstructs the trackbed, but at a sufficiently high elevation to be tunnelled under. West Moors itself has a population of only 7,500, but as a Parkway station, it would serve 40,000 people.

7. **St Andrews-Leuchars**-*(Edinburgh)* - 6 miles
Derelict, some new-build required

There's a consensus that St Andrews should never have left the rail network in 1969. The permanent population is not large, at around 17,000, but it's a university town on the outer edge of Edinburgh commuter territory, and home to major golf tournaments, factors that add considerably to the case for reinstatement. A detailed report for Tata Steel in 2012 suggested that much of the original route could be used, with some new-build near Leuchars to avoid development issues at Guardbridge and improve the line speed. The recommendations in this report have been developed and worked up into a full-scale proposal. The future of this link is now in the hands of the Scottish Parliament. *www.starlink-campaign.org.uk*

8. *(Manchester)*-**Buxton-Matlock**-*(Derby)* - 20 miles
Derelict, heritage railway

The former Midland Railway trunk line from Manchester to Derby was actually recommended for development in the *Reshaping* report, but later changes of policy brought about its closure in 1968, while Barbara Castle was at the helm. Apart from Bakewell, the local population is small, but the line would carry a considerable amount of freight, mainly from the quarries at Peak Forest, plus regional passenger services from Manchester to Derby, and local services providing car-free access to the Peak District National Park. The route is largely intact and reopening was a target for heritage operator Peak Rail, but like many similar schemes, it proved too big for a voluntary organisation.

9. **Skipton-Colne**-*(Burnley)* - 11¹/₂ miles
Derelict

Like other serious errors in the railway closure programme, this former trunk line was recom-mended for retention in the *Reshaping* report, but subsequently allowed to close in January 1970. Reinstatement would fill a major gap in the network, providing a useful trans-Pennine link for freight and passengers from Blackpool and Preston to Leeds, plus many local travel oppor-tunities from the sizeable towns along the route, and incidental improvements to the remaining branch line to Colne. SELRAP, the very active and successful campaign group has kept Skipton-Colne in the news, and several consultants' reports have looked favourably on reinstatement. The BCR is put at up to 2.4 for a basic £40 million single-track railway, or 1.5 for complete restoration, including redoubling track and platforms on the Colne branch. *www.selrap.org.uk*

10. **Swanage-Wareham** - 10 miles
Heritage railway, expected 2016

Another line that Dr Beeching thought best to keep! The Swanage Railway expects to reopen to the main line at Wareham on a seasonal basis from summer 2016, but the full benefits will only be realised with full year-round services, something a heritage railway has never succeeded in doing before. A strong case exists for trains to be extended right through to Bournemouth, but this would be a more complex and expensive option, requiring national as well as local funding and support. *www.swanagerailway.co.uk*

11. **Taunton-Minehead** - 25 miles
Heritage railway

Although fully reopened as a heritage railway, services terminate five miles from a main line interchange at Taunton, due to continuing awkwardness by Network Rail, which takes much the same line as Railtrack and British Rail before it. A natural service would be Bristol-Taunton-Minehead, as an extension of the existing stopping service. All that's needed is to knock a few heads together. *www.west-somerset-railway.co.uk*

12. Ferryhill-Washington-Newcastle - 16 miles
Mothballed, dismantled 2013
The strongest candidates have several potential uses, and the Leamside line has it all. Although passenger services faded away in the 1950s, and finally ended in 1964, freight continued until 1991, when the line was quietly mothballed, leaving the infrastructure essentially intact.

Demand for local passenger services is very strong. Washington, the biggest town on the route, was granted 'new town' status the year after passenger services ceased (one wonders if the railway team actually talked to anyone when making these decisions), and the population has risen by 184% since, to somewhere in excess of 54,000, making it almost certainly the biggest British town without a railway station. As well as purely local traffic, the line would make an ideal diversionary route for long-distance passenger trains, and a useful route for freight, avoiding the busy East Coast main line. Ironically, ongoing metal thefts have resulted in much of the remaining track being lifted by Network Rail for reuse on the Edinburgh to Galashiels 'Waverley' line! ATOC puts the Leamside line at number ten on its reopening priority list, giving the £80 million project a BCR of 1.4.

13. Bideford-Barnstaple-*(Exeter)* - 9 miles
Derelict, partially obstructed
A relatively short, and until recently, unobstructed route, but with a 20,000+ population, there is strong demand for services to Barnstaple and Exeter, and an ongoing campaign. Even allowing for tunneling under the roadworks at Barnstaple, boosting the cost to some £80million, ATOC puts this project at number 30, with a BCR of 0.2.

14. Stratford on Avon-Honeybourne-*(Oxford)* - 9 miles
Freight, derelict, partially obstructed
Like Bideford, this was a short and straightforward reopening until the local authority built a road on the trackbed. There have been several consultants reports into rebuilding the line, and all have been positive about the prospects for finding a route alongside the new road and underneath the roundabout at the north end. The line would give new travel opportunities from Stratford-on-Avon to Worcester and the West, and a shorter route to Oxford and London.

15. Cranleigh-Guildford - 8 miles
Derelict
Guildford to Shoreham-on-Sea was one of very few big closures in the Home Counties, and although the route was mostly rural in nature, it included Cranleigh, eight miles from Guildford, and now the only town of any size in the area (population 11,000 and growing fast) without a railway station. The route is largely clear of obstruction and ATOC puts this project at number eight in its league table, with estimated capital expenditure of £63million and a BCR of 1.7.

16. Walsall-Brownhills-Lichfield - 10¹/₂ miles
Derelict, freight
Relatively short, and unobstructed, this link to the north of Birmingham would provide an alternative through route for freight and passenger services, and several local passenger opportunities. ATOC puts this line at number seven, costed at £53million, with a BCR of 1.7.

17. **Burton on Trent-Coalville-Leicester** - 32 miles
Freight, partially obstructed
A long-standing issue, this freight line takes in several towns with a combined population of 94,000. The only serious issue is that the direct chord to Leicester station has been closed and obstructed by industrial buildings, but this is not insurmountable.

18. **March-Spalding** - 20 miles
Derelict, some new-build required
Closed when services were diverted via Peterborough, in a classic bit of 1980s rationalisation, this link is more about freight than passenger services. There is a desperate need for new freight paths bypassing the East Coast main line, and reopening this relatively short stretch clears the way from London, and east coast ports such as Felixstowe, all the way to Doncaster. The route is essentially clear, except for a small diversion around a prison (who made *that* strategic decision?) and some limited new-build at the Spalding end.

19. **Fleetwood-Poulton** - 6 miles
Mothballed
The closure of the Fleetwood line came as late as 1970, but fortunately the route remained open for freight until very recently and is completely unobstructed. Reopening would bring rail services back to a total population of 58,000, and it's not surprising that ATOC puts the Fleetwood line at number four, with a BCR of 1.8.

20. **Northallerton-Ripon-Harrogate**-*(Leeds)* - 22 miles
Derelict, some new-build required
There's no escaping the fact that this is a very major project, but like all the best reopening schemes, it would expect to carry both freight and passenger services. Local passenger services would be centred on the cathedral city of Ripon, with a population of 16,000 and considerable tourist potential, thanks to its proximity to Fountains Abbey and other attractions. The route would also be useful for long-distance north-south and trans-Pennine passenger services, something that would benefit Harrogate as well as Ripon. With electrification, it would provide an effective diversionary route, and bring the wires to Harrogate, something now being considered.

Complete closure came in 1967-68, and the intervening years have seen some development on the route, principally the A61 Ripon bypass which runs alongside the railway formation, but curves onto it to reuse the bridge piers over the River Skell, making through reinstatement complex and expensive. Nevertheless ATOC puts Ripon 17th on its reopening target list, at a cost of £100 million, with a BCR of 0.6 (or 4.3 if the construction costs are taken out of the equation). Yes, a bit of route safeguarding would have made a huge difference.

21. **Ashington-Blyth-Backworth**-*(Newcastle-upon-Tyne)* - 15 miles
Freight
Passenger services on the Ashington, Blyth & Tyne railway ceased in 1964. Fortunately, the route through to Newcastle remained open for freight, and with a combined population of 80,000, there have been repeated calls for passenger services to be restored. This could be done by establishing a heavy rail service into Newcastle, extending the Metro, or a combination of the two. Local campaign group SENRUG suggests reopening as far north as the Woodhorn Experience Museum, or even to Newbiggin-by-the-Sea. The cost is hotly disputed. Railtrack put a figure of £46 million on the scheme, but more recent research by ATOC suggests a price of £34 million, with a BCR of 1.1. ATOC puts the line at number 13 on its priority list. *www.senrug.co.uk*

22. Consett-Stanley-Chester le Street - 12 miles *(or via Washington, 16 miles)*
Derelict
Passenger services to Consett and Stanley ceased as long ago as 1955, but the line remained very busy for freight until the Consett steelworks closed in 1980. A reopened passenger railway would provide improved transport links for more than 40,000 people and rail access to the Beamish Open Air Museum. Services would run to Newcastle, either joining the existing East Coast line near Chester-le-Street, or via Washington on a reopened Leamside line. ATOC puts the cost of the first option at £123 million, and the second at £209 million, with BCRs of 0.1 and 0.4 accordingly, demonstrating just how important a centre Washington has become.

23. Bury-Rawtenstall-Bacup - 13 miles
Heritage, derelict, partially obstructed
Although the line to Bacup closed in 1966, passenger services on the Bury to Rawtenstall line lasted until 1972, with freight until 1980. With time, the once very busy Bacup line has been partially overbuilt, making reinstatement a complex process (but no less desirable for that). Bury to Rawtenstall became the East Lancashire Railway in 1987, and has operated heritage services ever since. Rawtenstall has a population of 22,000, but with feeder bus services from Haslingden and Bacup, the total population with access to a new rail service would be in excess of 60,000.

    ATOC puts Rawtenstall at number five, and suggests that a rail service could be established by negotiation with the heritage railway, at a cost of about £50 million, giving a BCR of 1.8.

24. Aberystwyth-Carmarthen - 40 miles
Mostly derelict, short heritage line, partially obstructed
Wales has no north-south rail links of its own, and since devolution, the country has found a new desire to develop (or redevelop) strategic links, so this route is primarily political, but none the worse for that. This is a long railway, but little affected by development, except in Carmarthen, where the railway formation has been obstructed by the A40 Carmarthen Bypass. Nevertheless, space could be found alongside the road for a basic single-track railway, and there are few other serious issues. It's worth pointing out that this scheme is no more complex than Edinburgh to Galashiels, where construction is already underway!

25. Grimsby-Louth-Firsby-(Boston) - 33 miles
Derelict, seriously obstructed
One of the last big railway closures, the line from Grimsby to Boston served a large, but relatively thinly populated part of Lincolnshire, with Louth - population 17,000 - at its heart. Other towns, such as Mablethorpe (population 11,000) and Sutton-on-Sea (population 4,500), although not directly served, would be close enough to benefit from long-distance rail connections. Grimsby would also benefit from links to the south. A road has used the track bed in Grimsy, and ATOC costs reopening at a hefty £142 million, giving a marginal BCR of 0.1.

26. Bangor-Caernarfon-Criccieth - 26 miles
Derelict, heritage railway, partially obstructed
Put together with the existing Cambrian Coast line from Criccieth to Aberystwyth, and a rebuilt line from Aberystwyth to Carmarthen, reopening of this line would give a 130-mile through route along the west coast of Wales. The six miles from Bangor to Caernarfon is the most important section, and the most difficult with respect to route damage, mainly because of roads crossing the railway formation at awkward levels. Beyond Caernarfon, the route has been used by the Welsh Highland narrow gauge railway as far as Dinas, but this would benefit from being shortened, and the new railway would bring many passengers to the line. Beyond Dinas

to Bryncir, the route was made into a road for quarry traffic after closure, but is now disused and largely clear of development, as is the final derelict stretch. Reopening of the northerly Bangor-Caernarfon section would put Caernarfon back on the railway map, but reopening throughout would halve the current six hour journey from Bangor to Carmarthen by train or bus, and open up numerous travel opportunities between north, mid and South Wales.

27. **Wisbech-March** - 7 miles
Mothballed

Very much a local scheme, Wisbech to March has the great advantage that track is already on the ground, making reinstatement to this town of 20,000 easier than most. Railfuture believes a 35 minute schedule to Cambridge is feasible, and this would help the relatively impoverished 'capital of the fens' to tap into the jobs market and other opportunities in thriving south Cambridgeshire. ATOC places Wisbech 14th in its league table, suggesting a modest capital expenditure of £12 million, giving a BCR of 1.1. www.wisbechrail.org.uk

28. **Paignton-Churston** (for Brixham)-**Kingswear** (for Dartmouth) - 7 miles
Heritage railway

When the seven-mile Paignton to Kingswear railway closed in 1972, it became a heritage line - the South Devon Railway. ATOC believes there is a very strong case for reopening as far as Churston, putting Brixham (population 18,000) within reach of rail services again. The rather optimistic suggestion is that this could be done without capital expenditure, giving the reopening a BCR of 3.0. Reopening the whole line to Kingswear would bring rail services to Dartmouth, adding a population of 7,000.

29. **Keswick-Penrith** - 18 miles
Derelict

When the line from Penrith closed in 1972, the Cumbrian town of Keswick was left without adequate public transport. With a population of about 7,000, Keswick falls well short of ATOC's reopening criteria, but the special ingredient here is tourism. The southern part of the Lake District is quite well served by rail, but the north is not, and a restored link from Penrith on the West Coast Main Line to Keswick, with connecting bus services to outlying districts, would make a huge area accessible. Reinstatement is widely supported, and most structures remain intact, although the local authorities continue to allow piecemeal developments that will make reinstatement both more difficult and more costly. www.keswickrailway.com

30. **Bordon-Bentley**-(London Waterloo) - 6 miles
Derelict, some new-build

The passenger rail service to Bordon ceased in 1957, when the population of this former military town was very small, but today it stands at 16,000, with another 5,000 homes promised as part of the development of Bordon and Whitehill into an 'Eco-town'. Residents have expressed concerns about the lack of infrastructure, roads in particular, and ATOC's response has been to include the town in the 'Connecting Communities' feasibility study, which costed a reinstated line at £50 million, giving a favourable BCR of 1.9. This was followed by a more detailed study by Halcrow, suggesting that both costs and benefits would be higher - £170 million of capital expenditure, producing up to a million trips a year, giving a BCR of 2.14.

Other Prospects

This mixed group is drawn from various sources. All these routes are fairly clear of development, but the table makes no attempt to look at the viability or practicality of reopening - just the size of the population and the rate of change, giving a clue to potential demand

Route *(with existing lines in italics)*	Miles	Pop+/-	Population	Condition	Traffic	ATOC
Skelmersdale-Rainford-*(Kirkby)*	2¹/₂	+515%	38,800	Derelict	Commuter	BCR1.1
Abingdon-Radley-*(Oxford)*	2	+157%	33,000	Derelict	Commuter	
Fraserburgh/Peterhead-Aberdeen	60	+32%	30,413	Derelict	Commuter	
Witney-Yarnton-*(Oxford)*	12	+198%	27,500	Derelict	Commuter	BCR0.5
*(Cambridge)-***Shelford-Haverhill-Sudbury**	40	+397%	27,000	Derelict	Commuter	BCR0.3
Portishead-Bristol	11	+257%	23,000	Freight	Commuter	
Daventry-Weedon Beck-*(Milton Keynes)*	4	+293%	23,000	Derelict	Commuter	BCR0.2
Clevedon-Yatton-*(Bristol)*	4	+110%	22,000	Derelict	Commuter	
Radstock-Frome-*(Westbury)*	8	+67%	22,000	Mothballed	Commuter	
Newport IOW-Cowes	5	+9%	22,000	Derelict	Tourist/Commuter	
Ripley-Little Eaton-*(Derby)*	6	+20%	21,100	Derelict	Commuter	BCR0.2
Wells-Shepton Mallet-Witham-*(Westbury)*	14	+70%	20,700	Derelict/Heritage/Freight	Tourist	
Richmond *(inc Catterick)-***Eryholme-***(Darlington)*	11	+42%	20,200	Derelict	Tourist/Military	
Biddulph-Congleton-*(Manchester)*	3¹/₂	+42%	20,000	Derelict	Commuter	BCR0.4
Hailsham-Polegate	3	+318%	20,000	Derelict	Commuter	
Ilfracombe-Barnstaple	14	+120%	19,100	Derelict	Tourist/Commuter	
Leek-Stoke-on-Trent	12¹/₂	-2%	18,800	Derelict	Commuter	BCR0.3
East Dereham-Wymondham-*(Norwich)*	12	+153%	18,200	Heritage	Heritage Commuter	
Cirencester-Kemble	4	+52%	18,000	Derelict	Tourist/Commuter	
Havant-Hayling Island	4	+142%	17,300	Derelict	Commuter/Tourist	
Ryde-Newport IOW	9	+9%	17,300	Derelict	Tourist/Commuter	
Grangemouth-Falkirk	2¹/₂	-11.7%	17,000	Freight	Commuter	
Poole-Templecombe or Bruton	31/39	+120%	16,000	Derelict	Commuter	
Maldon-Witham	7	+48%	15,500	Derelict	Commuter	
*(Perth)-***Stanley-Forfar-Kinnaber-***(Aberdeen)*	40	+28%	13,200	Derelict	Tourist/Commuter	
Bodmin-Bodmin Parkway	3	+106%	12,800	Heritage	Tourist	
Thornbury-Yate-*(Bristol)*	7	+306%	12,700	Freight/Derelict	Commuter	BCR0.4
*(Bath)-***Holt-Devizes-Patney-***(Reading)*	13	+33%	11,300	Derelict	Commuter/Tourist	
Seaton-Seaton Jct	4	+277%	12,900	Heritage/Derelict	Tourist	
Mablethorpe-Willoughby	9	+117%	11,700	Derelict	Tourist	
Stafford-Newport-Wellington	33	+148%	10,800	Derelict	Tourist/Strategic	
Bewdley-Kidderminster	4	+116%	9,200	Heritage	Commuter/tourist	
Brechin-Montrose-*(Dundee)*	9¹/₂	-3%	6,977	Heritage	Tourist/Commuter	
Ventnor-Shanklin IOW	4	-2.4%	6,250	Derelict	Tourist	
Hunstanton-Kings Lynn	15	+2%	5,000	Derelict	Tourist/Commuter	
Amlwch-Gaerwen-*(Bangor)*	17¹/₂	+18%	3,450	Mothballed	Commuter	

Urban, tourist or diversionary routes, where population is less relevant:

Clitheroe-Hellifield	25		Freight	Seasonal tourist	
Coalbrookdale-Telford	5¹/₂		Freight	Seasonal tourist	
Avonmouth-Filton	6		Freight	Avon Metro	
Yate-Mangotsfield-Bristol	11		Derelict/Freight	Diversionary	
Winchester-Alton	19		Heritage	Commuter/Diversionary	
Walsall-Aldridge-Sutton-*(Birmingham)*	12		Freight	X City North Line	BCR1.7

Appendix 1
Busy stations and railways closed during the 'Beeching' era

A short list of relatively high-earning stations in the 1961 'Reshaping' traffic surveys that subsequently closed. These maps were not very detailed, and were certainly inaccurate. It seems unlikely that Hirwaun or Calne were exceptional high earners, for example, and Tavistock was probably muddled with Lydford, but the whole list is included here as a matter of historical fact:

Alloa	Closed 1968	Subsequently reopened in 2008
Bicester London Road	Closed 1968	Subsequently reopened as Bicester Town in 1987
Bideford	Closed 1965	Ongoing campaign for reinstatement
Calne	Closed 1965	Population growth of 144% to 16,000, but no scheme to reopen
Fleetwood	Closed 1970	Ongoing campaign for reinstatement
Galashiels	Closed 1969	To reopen in 2016
Hawick	Closed 1969	Ongoing campaign for reinstatement
Hirwaun	Closed 1964	Small Welsh valleys town, with existing freight line
Leicester Central	Closed 1969	No longer exists
Louth	Closed 1970	Ongoing campaign for reinstatement
Richmond	Closed 1969	Strong case for reinstatement, but no strong campaign
St. Andrews	Closed 1969	Ongoing campaign for reinstatement
Swanage	Closed 1972	Heritage railway, with seasonal reopening due in 2015/16
Tavistock	Closed 1968	Ongoing campaign for reinstatement

Principal railways shown as carrying 5,000 to 50,000 passengers a week in the 'Reshaping' traffic surveys, that subsequently closed. Again, there seem to be some significant errors, such as the branches from Hull to Withernsea and Hornsea, which were probably no that busy, and have been omitted:

Barmouth-Llangollen-Ruabon	Closed 1964	No campaign for reinstatement
Beverley-Market Weighton-York	Closed 1965	Ongoing campaign for reinstatement
Cheltenham-Stratford-on-Avon	Closed 1960	Support for reinstatement of north end
Stanley Jct-Forfar-Kinnaber Jct	Closed 1967	No campaign for reinstatement
Edinburgh-Hawick	Closed 1969	Ongoing campaign for full reinstatement
Fleetwood-Poulton	Closed 1970	Ongoing campaign for reinstatement
Grimsby-Louth-Firsby	Closed 1970	Ongoing campaign for reinstatement
Harrogate-Ripon-Northallerton	Closed 1969	Ongoing campaign for reinstatement
Huntingdon-St. Ives-Cambridge	Closed 1970	Mostly converted to guided busway
Manchester-Derby *(Midland)*	Closed 1967	Ongoing campaign for reinstatement
Minehead-Taunton	Closed 1968	Ongoing campaign for network services
Nottingham-Melton Mowbray	Closed 1966	Mostly test-track, no campaign for reopening
Nottingham-Rugby *(Great Central)*	Closed 1969	No campaign for reinstatement
Yate-Bath-Templecombe *(S&D)*	Closed 1965	No campaign for reinstatement
Skipton-Colne	Closed 1970	Ongoing campaign for reinstatement
Manchester-Penistone-Sheffield	Closed 1970	Ongoing campaign for reinstatement

Appendix 2
Survey of small European towns July 1991
(population 10,000-15,000)

Country	Sample size	Passenger rail station	Integrated rail/bus service	No proper facilities
Britain	88	52%[1]	2%	46%
France	29[2]	24%	69%	7%
Germany[3]	55	82%	16%	2%

[1] *A further 4% of these had already reopened by 1991*

[2] *Although stopping trains had been withdrawn, nearly all had track in place in place for freight or through passenger services*

[3] *Former Federal Republic only*

Three very different approaches to public transport. Obviously there are many factors that might restrict the validity of such a comparison, but having started with a denser network, Britain might be expected to have retained a relatively large number of railway stations.

In France (and to a lesser extent, in Germany) the towns tend to be more thinly spread, something that might be expected to count against efficient public transport. but thanks to Britain's poor record in such matters, the opposite is true.

In 1991, the German network was close to the ideal, with 82% of small towns having a railway station of their own, the remainder being served by integrated buses connecting with rail services at the nearest station. In France, many local rail services have been abandoned, but almost every town is served by rail, or rail and connecting bus, and the vast majority of towns are on lines used for freight or through passenger services. Few local passenger stations were actually demolished in the 1960s. Indeed, some remain open and staffed for the convenience of bus passengers, and the collection and delivery of goods and parcels.

In Britain, where the integration of bus and rail services is almost unknown, the picture was comparatively bleak in 1991. About half the towns were served by rail, but very few axed rail services had been replaced by comparable bus services - that is, buses that British Rail recognised, and advertised as connecting with trains at the nearest rail-head. Through bus-rail timetabling and ticketing, although technically straightforward, was, and remains, extremely unusual in Britain.

It would be interesting to look again at this issue, a quarter of a century after this appendix was produced. France and Germany have probably lost a few bus and rail links, and reunification of the former East Germany brought a rail network into the West that was essentially unchanged since the 1940s, and some of these lines subsequently closed.

Appendix 3

Random sample of 254 towns and villages throughout England & Wales

Population:	500-1,000	1,500-5,000	5,000-20,000	20,000-60,000
Rail service in 1948:	62%	86%	98%	100%
Rail service in 1984:	16%	32%	59%	84%
Potential for reinstatement:	45%	51%	77%	96%
Sample Size:	58	90	81	25

Another interesting bit of research that could do with updating. Although many stations have reopened since 1984, most towns have grown, some moving up a column, which would make today's figures look relatively depressing, despite the steady stream of reopenings. Without this sharp population growth, there would be few towns left without a railway station in the 20,000-60,000 column, but a glance at the top half of the 'other prospects' table shows that a large number have joined this, and although most are under investigation for rail reinstatement, not all will achieve it. It's hard to imagine the long cross-country line via Haverhill in Suffolk being reinstated, for example. Note too, that some entries in the table - Wells & Shepton Mallet, and Peterhead & Fraserburgh - refer to the population of two smaller towns.

Keswick had a population over just under 5,000 when the 'Reshaping' report was published, and about 7,000 today. This is one of the first appearances of a diesel multiple unit in 1955, during the early Lake District trials. PHOTO: Cumbrian Railways Association

Footnotes

Chapter 2:

[1] Throughout this book I have used economic cost relative to the size of the economy, rather than retail price inflation to produce equivalent modern prices. This gives a much bigger price increase (around 11,500%, against 2,800%, from the 1950s to 2013), but the figures are believable by modern standards. There are many shades of opinion, but Tim Leunig of the London School of Economics agrees that this makes sense as a means of demonstrating the relative 'pain' of capital expenditure

[2] *Transport Disintegrated*, Roger Calvert

Chapter 4:

[3] Archer Baldwin, House of Commons, debate on the Rural Transport Improvement Bill, 9th December 1955

[4] Frost & Sullivan, November 2009

[5] The cost of maintaining the portfolio of useless structures was to be carried for decades, and despite having disposed of most of the assets in the intervening half century, and receiving a considerable income from property rental and land sales, BRB (Residuary) Ltd made a loss of £14.2 million in 2012.

Chapter 5:

[6] Report from the Select Committee on Nationalised Industries (British Railways), 1960

[7] *Doctor Who?* Richard Cottrell (unpublished as of February 2013)

[8] Introduction to the Select Committee on Nationalised Industries Report on British Railways

[9] *The Railwaymen*, The History of the NUR, Philip Bagwell

[10] *Beeching: The Inside Track*, Robin Jones

Chapter 6:

[11] Page 100, *The Reshaping of British Railways*, BRB 1963

[12] The Railway Consultancy report for Hertfordshire County Council, November 2008

[13] Page 30, *Transport Disintegrated*, Roger Calvert

[14] *Transport Disintegrated*, Roger Calvert

[15] *British Railways, 1948-1973: A Business History*, Terence Gourvish

[16] *Beeching: The Inside Track*, Robin Jones

[17] *Government, the Railways and the Modernization of Britain: Beeching's Last Train*, Charles Loft

Chapter 7:

[18] Page 87, *Waverley Route, the life, death and rebirth of the Borders Railway*, Argyll Publishing

[19] Page 71, *Waverley Route, the life, death and rebirth of the Borders Railway*, Argyll Publishing

Chapter 8:

[20] *Waverley Route, the life, death and rebirth of the Borders Railway*, Argyll Publishing

[21] *Fare Revenue & Cost/benefit Analysis*, R D Evans 1971

[22] *The Economics of the Cambrian Coast Line*, K Richards 1972

[23] Gathered by Resource for Urban Design Information 2012

[24] World Bank Data

[25] *Heavy Lorries - Do They Pay for the Damage they Cause?* Metropolitan Research Unit, April 2008

[26] *New Scientist* 4th August 1983

[27] Conservation Area Appraisals in the Yorkshire Dales National Park: Settle-Carlisle Railway, Yorkshire Dales National Park Authority 2010

Chapter 9:

28] *Competition, Regulation and the Privatisation of British Rail*, Jon Shaw, 2000

[29] *The Deregulation and Privatisation of Public Transport in Britain: Twenty Years On*, Dr John Preston, Transport Research Foundation

[30] *Transport Trends and Transport Policies - Myths and Facts*, Transport 2000, 1993

[31] *British Rail Privatisation: Competition Destroyed by Politics*, Professor Steven Glaister

[32] Cambridgeshire Guided Busway, Post-Opening User Research, Cambridgeshire County Council/Atkins 2012

Bibliography

Hansards Various editions
TUCC Annual Reports Various
CTCC Annual Reports Various
Nationalisation Bill HMSO 1947
The Report from the Select Committee on Nationalised Industries (British Railways) HMSO 1963
The Reshaping of British Railways British Railways Board 1963
Review of Dr. Beeching's Report Professor E R Hondelink 1963
The Railwaymen Philip Bagwell, National Union of Railwaymen, Allen & Unwin 1963
The Railways and the Nation A J Pearson, Allen & Unwin 1964
Anatomy of Britain Today Anthony Sampson, Hodder & Stoughton 1965
The Development of the Major Railway Trunk Routes British Railways Board 1965
I tried to Run a Railway Gerard Fiennes, Ian Allan 1967
The Organisation of British Railways Michael Bonavia, Ian Allen 1971
Public Enterprise in Practise Richard Pryke, MacGibbon & Kee 1971
Fare Revenue & Cost/benefit Analysis R D Evans 1971
The Economics of the Cambrian Coast Line K Richards 1972
Transport Disintegrated Roger Calvert, 1973 T Calvert
Rail 150 Editor Jack Simmons, Methuen 1975
Economics & Transport Policy K M Gwilliam & P J Mackie, Allen & Unwin 1975
Transport Policy (vol 2) HMSO 1976
Transport Bill HMSO 1967
Railway Policy HMSO 1967
The Birth of British Railways Michael Bonavia, Allen & Unwin 1979 **ISBN: 0043850715**
The Social Consequences of Railway Closures Mayer Hillman & Anne Whalley 1980
Railway Policy Between the Wars Michael Bonavia, Manchester University Press 1981
BR: The First 25 Years Michael Bonavia, David & Charles 1981 **ISBN: 0715380028**
British Railways, 1948-1973: A Business History
Terence Gourvish, Cambridge University Press 1986 **ISBN: 978-0521188838**
The Tunnel, the Channel & Beyond Editor Bronwen Jones, Ellis Horwood 1987
Rural Transport: What Future Now? Rural District Councils Association
Accounting for Life Henry Benson, Baron, Kogan Page 1989 **ISBN: 978-0749400293**
Beeching - Champion of the Railways? R H N Hardy, Ian Allan 1989 **ISBN: 0711018553**
Wheels within Wheels Mick Hamer, Routledge & Kegan Paul 1987 **ISBN: 0710210078**
Railway Finances: Report of a Committee Chaired by David Serpell HMSO 1983 **ISBN: 0115505903**
Fiennes on Rails: Fifty Years of Railways Gerard Fiennes, David & Charles 1986 **ISBN: 978-0715389263**
BR Diary 1958-1967 John Glover, Ian Allan 1987
BR Diary 1968-1977 Chris Heaps, Ian Allan 1987 **ISBN: 978-0711016118**
To Kill a Railway Stan Abbot & Alan Whitehouse, Leading Edge 1994 **ISBN: 978-0948135019**
Competition, Regulation and the Privatisation of British Rail Jon Shaw, 2000 **ISBN: 978-0754614838**
Government, the Railways and the Modernization of Britain: Beeching's Last Train
Charles Loft, Routledge 2006 **ISBN: 978-0714653389**
Connecting Communities: Expanding Access to the Rail Network ATOC 2009
On the Move: Making Sense of Car & Train Travel in Britain S. Le Vine & P. Jones, RAC Foundation 2012
Beeching: The Inside Track Editor, Robin Jones, Mortons Media Group 2012 **ISBN: 978-1906167844**
Doncaster Archive Owen Prosser papers and records, DD/PROSS: **doncaster.archives@doncaster.gov.uk**

Glossary of terms

Branchline Committee

Formed by the Railway Executive in 1950 to establish which railway lines were suitable candidates for closure. Later replaced by the Unremunerative Railway Services Committee.

Branch Line Re-invigoration Society

Formed as the Society for the Re-invigoration of Unremunerative Branch Lines in the United Kingdom (or SRUBLUK) in 1954, the Society was later renamed the Railway Invigoration Society and merged with the Railway Development Association in 1978 to form the Railway Development Society.

Bogie

A short pivoting truck,usually fitted with twin axles, or occasionally three, fitted beneath each end of a rail vehicle, reducing rail wear, and giving a smoother, quieter ride.

BRF

British Road Federation. A road lobby group formed in the 1930s.

BTC

British Transport Commission - formed under the 1947 Transport Act to co-ordinate and integrate public transport in the British Isles.

Chord

Railway (and mathematical) term for a short length of curved track joining together two separate railway lines.

CTCC

Central Transport Consultative Committee. Formed under the 1947 Transport Act to liaise between the Local Transport Users Consultative Committees and the British Transport Commission.

DMU

Diesel Multiple Unit. A group of diesel rail-cars connected to form a single unit, usually comprising a power car (with driver-s compartment) at either end, and a single unpowered car in between. Such three-car units could be joined together to form multiple units of six, nine, or more vehicles.

Lightweight Trains Committee

Formed by the Railway Executive in 1951 to investigate the suitability of railcars and railbuses for marginal services.

NCIT

National Council on Inland Transport. A railway pressure group formed in 1962.

Push–pull unit

A small steam locomotive coupled to one or more carriages, with facilities for remote operation from a small driver's compartment in the rearmost carriage, to allow the driver to operate the steam engine remotely while travelling in reverse. Pre-dated the DMU on many minor branch lines.

Railbus

Originally a road bus adapted to run on rails (and usually a two-axle unidirectional vehicle), but the term was later applied to more specialised light weight vehicles designed specifically for railway operation, but still usually with a two-axle layout.

Railcar

A single, powered, railway carriage, usually with a driver's compartment at either end, a road bus-type diesel engine beneath the floor, and two bogies, each with two axles. A larger and more powerful cousin of the railbus.

Rail-motor

Originally a small steam locomotive, permanently articulated to a railway carriage, with remote control at the rear, allowing for reverse operation. Later machines were more closely related to railcars, with a small steam power plant inside the carriage, driving one of the bogies.

Railway Executive

Created under the provisions of the 1947 Transport Act, the Railway Executive effectively managed the railways under the guidance of the British Transport Commission. The Railway Executive was abolished under the 1953 Transport Act (together with the Executives empowered to manage other forms of public transport), and control of the railways was passed to the BTC.

RDA

Railway Development Association. A rail lobby group formed in 1951 for the purpose of fighting branch line (and in later years, secondary and trunk line) railway closures. Merged with the Railway Invigoration Society in 1978 to form the Railway Development Society.

Index

297

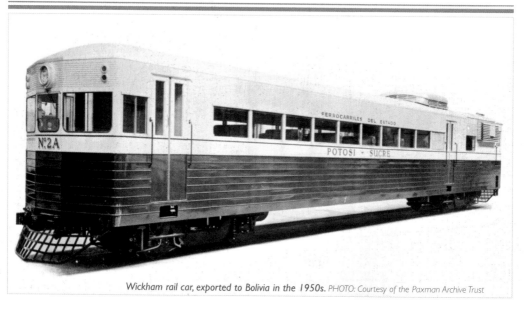

Wickham rail car, exported to Bolivia in the 1950s. PHOTO: Courtesy of the Paxman Archive Trust

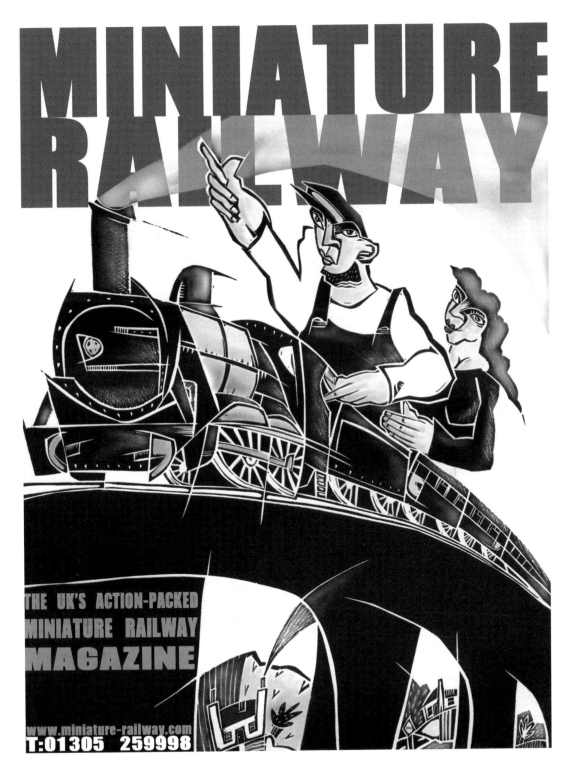

MINIATURE RAILWAY

THE UK'S ACTION-PACKED MINIATURE RAILWAY MAGAZINE

www.miniature-railway.com

T:01305 259998

Contacts

A to B magazine
Green transport magazine, covering rail, trams, electric cars and other low-impact transport
W www.atob.org.uk
M atob@atob.org.uk
T 01305 259998

Campaign for Better Transport
Successor to Transport 2000. Campaigns on public transport issues, including fares, service levels, and rail reinstatement
W www.bettertransport.org.uk
M projectmanager@bml2.co.uk
T 020 7566 6480

Campaign for Borders Rail
Campaigning for full reinstatement of the Waverley line from Edinburgh to Carlisle
W www.campaignforbordersrail.org
M chairman.bordersrail@uwclub.net
T 01890 781698

Brighton Main Line 2
Campaigning for reinstatement of the Uckfield to Lewes and Eridge to Tunbridge Wells rail links, and new links to provide new services throughout the region
W www.bml2.co.uk
M projectmanager@bml2.co.uk

East West Rail
Campaigning for reinstatement of local, regional and long-distance services on the Oxford-Bletchley-Bedford-Cambridge line
W www.eastwestrail.org.uk

Railfuture
Successor to the Railway Development Association. Campaigns for new rail services and railway reinstatement on a national basis
W www.railfuture.org.uk
M info@railfuture.org.uk
T 0117 9272954

Skipton East Lancashire Rail Action Partnership
Campaigns for reinstatement of the Skipton to Colne line
W www.selrap.org.uk
M Derek.jennings01@gmail.com
T 01282 690411

South East Northumberland Rail User Group
Campaigns for restoration of rail services to Ashington and Blyth
W www.senrug.co.uk
T 01670 825 500

StARLink
Campaigns for reinstatement of a rail link from St Andrews to Leuchars
W www.starlink-campaign.org.uk
M starlink@starlink-campaign.org.uk